O9-BTZ-461

1. Adam Smith
2. Christofella.
3.

ESSENTIAL PRICE THEORY

950

ESSENTIAL PRICE THEORY

Albert M. Levenson
and Babette S. Solon

Queens College

HOLT, RINEHART AND WINSTON, INC.

New York   Chicago   San Francisco   Atlanta
Dallas   Montreal   Toronto   London   Sydney

To E, I, and B and TFT.

Copyright © 1964 as *Outline of Price Theory* by Holt, Rinehart and Winston, Inc.

Copyright © 1971 by Holt, Rinehart and Winston, Inc.

All rights reserved

Library of Congress Catalog Card Number: 72-115853

SBN: 03-078250-3

Printed in the United States of America

1   2   3   22   9 8 7 6 5 4 3 2 1

PREFACE TO REVISED EDITION

In this revised and expanded version of *Outline of Price Theory*, we have endeavored to expand and strengthen the characteristics of our book that have made it useful to the many teachers who have communicated with us. In keeping with this intent, we have provided eight new mathematical appendixes and two new chapters in income distribution and welfare economics. Other chapters have been rewritten to improve exposition. Furthermore, so that the student can immediately see the relevance of the mathematics, all mathematical review is now placed where it will first be used.

—A. M. L.
—B. S. S.

New York
November 1970

PREFACE TO THE FIRST EDITION

This text on intermediate price theory the authors hope will fill a lack felt by them in their experience in teaching intermediate price theory courses. Concisely presenting the topics usually covered in a one-semester course, it avoids the encyclopedic approach and thus permits the instructor to introduce relevant readings and empirical material as he sees fit. A companion workbook, *Exercises and Problems in Price Theory*, is composed of sets of exercises designed to foster proficiency in the use of the theoretical tools and sets of problems drawn from empirical investigations to which the theory is applied by the student.

We assume no mathematical knowledge on the part of the student beyond first-year high school algebra, which is reviewed in the first chapter. Anything requiring more advanced mathematics is treated in footnotes or in short appendixes to some of the chapters.

We thank our colleagues in the Queens College Department of Economics for their friendly assistance, especially Professor William Hamovitch, who was kind enough to read some of the chapters. Professor Percia Campbell, chairman of the department, gave particular encouragement to this enterprise. Students in our price theory classes have made valuable suggestions on the earlier drafts.

We gratefully acknowledge our indebtedness to Mrs. Evelyn Nagdimon, Miss Elke Meldau, Mrs. Evelyn Levenson, Miss Lillian Mittleman, Mrs. Lynn Alcosser, Mrs. Rose Kraus, and Miss Gloria Natale for their able typing and clerical assistance in the preparation of the manuscript.

A. M. L.
B. S. S.

New York, March 1964

CONTENTS

1

INTRODUCTION

Microeconomic theory is concerned with the operation of the price mechanism in the allocation of the resources of the economy. Although this book is concerned only with the allocation of resources in a free-market enterprise economy, the price mechanism may play a role in planned economies with decentralized decision making. Free enterprise is taken to mean an economic system in which individuals are substantially free to sell the services of their resources to the highest bidder and to spend their incomes thus obtained by buying from the cheapest source of supply the goods and services that yield the greatest satisfaction; and businessmen are substantially free to combine resources in enterprises and to produce goods and services that are sold on markets to the highest bidders.

In such an economic system, the interaction of consumers and producers in resource and product markets solves the economic problems of the society without any central direction. Economic problems all arise from the fact that resources are scarce relative to the human wants for the goods and services produced with these resources. Therefore, every society is faced with the problem of allocating these scarce resources among their competing alternative uses. First, society must set up priorities concerning what goods and services should be produced, because scarcity of resources prevents all desired goods from being produced. Second, given the fact of scarce resources, society will desire to make the optimum use of these resources; this involves choosing the most efficient techniques of production. Third, once the national output has been produced, it must be distributed to the members of society in some fashion.

Although all societies face these problems, the manner in which they are solved depends on the institutions of the society. In this book, we shall be concerned with market economies, such as that of contemporary America. There is not now, nor has there ever been, a completely free enterprise economy. In contemporary economies, government impinges on producer and consumer free choice to varying degrees. In addition, markets exhibit to varying degrees imperfections attributable to imperfect knowledge, immobility of resources, and monopoly power. Nonetheless, it is impossible to understand the operation of the modern American economy without understanding how a pure free enterprise system works, and this shall be the first task we turn to in subsequent chapters. After that, we shall compare the pure case with the effects of the imperfections just mentioned.

METHODOLOGY IN ECONOMICS

The heading of this section could very well have been simply "Methodology in Science," because we believe that the method of inquiry is substantially the same in all sciences. The objective of all sciences is to understand the workings of a complex reality whether this reality be in the physical universe or the institutions of a society. Facts are important at two stages in the process of achieving an understanding of reality, that is, in the scientific method. Facts suggest crucial variables and the relationships among them that may be fundamental in understanding phenomena of interest. The investigator then formulates a hypothesis that is based on these suggested relationships among the facts. This hypothesis is sometimes called the "assumptions" of the theory. The investigator then draws the relevant implications of this hypothesis. This stage is generally accomplished by the use of deductive logic that may either be informal or of a formal mathematical nature. The combination of the hypothesis and its implications is usually called a model. This model is a caricature of reality because the assumptions on which it is based are necessarily "unrealistic"; that is, the variables considered unimportant have been ignored in drawing up the hypothesis. In an attempt to strip away the unessential complexity and lay bare the fundamental variables and relationships, there is always the danger that we have "thrown out the baby with the bath water"; that is, we have neglected some crucially important variable.

The second point at which facts play a necessary role is in testing the predictions of the model. Of course, the facts used at this stage must be a different set from the one used to suggest the hypothesis. A single confrontation with the facts does not prove a theory; it simply does not disprove it, yet. Repeated successful confrontations are necessary before we can begin to have some confidence in the truth of the model. The necessary number of successful confrontations at which the investigator is willing to declare the theory a law will depend in part on the compatibility of this theory with previously accepted laws.

If the predictions of the theory are of the form "if X is true, then Y must be true," one unsuccessful confrontation with the facts (if the facts are indisputable) is sufficient to disprove the theory.

If the assumptions are indisputably false, then a process of correct reasoning must produce false conclusions. However, it is often impossible to determine the truth or falsity of the assumptions a priori. Hence, the only possible test is a test of the predictions drawn from the model.

Models can be used for two purposes. First, they can be used to predict. Second, models may provide insight into the causal mechanism that connects the dependent to the independent variable. The ideal model would provide both insight and a predictive device. We are often forced to accept provisionally the models that only predict, but our ultimate goal is to achieve models that perform the dual role. The models that at a given time can only be used for predictive purposes can be thought of as being on a lower level of creditability than those that perform the dual function.

Before concluding our discussion of methodology, we should add that those untutored in the methodology of science often claim that models are unrealistic. We must plead guilty to this charge if it is taken to mean that our assumptions are not photographic representations of reality; they are abstractions of reality and, indeed, the model gains its analytic power from this process of abstraction. If the claim of unrealism means that the assumptions of a particular theory are demonstrably false, then no valid predictions can be drawn from them.

A second criticism often takes the form "that's all right in theory but not in fact." It should be clear from our previous discussion that no theory can be all right that does not hold up against the facts. This position has been most persuasively stated by Sir Henry Clay.[1]

> The practical man's objection to "theory" is a valuable protest against hasty generalization on an insufficient basis of fact or on an inadequate survey of available facts. But the opposition of "facts" and "theory" is a false one; their true relation is complementary. We cannot in practice consider a fact without relating it to other facts, and the relation is a theory. Facts by themselves are dumb; before they will tell us anything we have to arrange them, and the arrangement is a theory. Theory is simply the unavoidable arrangement and interpretation of facts, which gives us generalizations on which we can argue and act, in the place of a mass of dis-

[1] Henry Clay, *Economics: An Introduction for the General Reader* (New York: The Macmillan Company, 1918), p. 11.

jointed particulars. What we are seeking in our study of economic problems, whether it is a conscious and systematic study or not, are principles. We want to know what, in the operations we observe, is the rule, what is the exception; why certain arrangements are as they are, and what will happen if we change them. Unrelated facts will not answer our questions; we want chains of facts, regularities, relations of cause and effect. We are seeking principles in order that we may act on them, because the ultimate motive of economic study is not curiosity, but the necessity to act, and rational action must be based on some principle. All arguments are based on principles, facts are of use only as they represent or illustrate principles. Economics, therefore, in order to discover the principles on which the present system is constructed and operates, surveys the facts of the system, arranges them, analyzes them, generalizes on the basis of them. Like every other science it advances by constantly discarding generalizations which newly discovered facts have revealed as unsound or inadequate, and devising new generalizations which will cover and explain the new facts.

A final point needs to be made. Economics is a policy science. Economists are often asked to make recommendations on policy. A policy recommendation is necessarily compounded of two parts: first, a *scientific* judgment as to the possible consequences of alternative policies; and second a *value* judgment as to the desirability of the alternative consequences. Positive economics is concerned with the former, while normative economics deals with both.

This book is concerned with positive economics. Further, it deals primarily with the analytical or deductive process of deriving models concerning the allocation of scarce resources in a free enterprise economy. It should be obvious from our discussion that the empirical testing of these models is a crucial enterprise; our excuse for neglecting it here is that we have learned the lesson of Adam Smith's pin factory.

2

DEMAND, SUPPLY, AND PRICE UNDER PERFECT COMPETITION

We stated in Chapter 1 that prices play a fundamental role in the allocation of resources. Prices in turn are determined by the interaction of the desires of consumers and the offers of sellers; that is, demand and supply are basic concepts in the understanding of the determination of prices in all kinds of markets. In this chapter we will explain these concepts and the determination of price under perfect competition.

DEMAND

An individual's demand for a good is the alternative quantities per time period he would be willing to purchase at all relevant prices. His demand for the good is a function of the following variables: the price of the good, the prices of other goods (especially substitutes and complements), his income, and his tastes (this latter category is a catchall that includes psychological, sociological, and culturally conditioned attitudes). We may wish to isolate the relationship between the quantity demanded and the price of the commodity. To do this, we must regard the other variables as being constant at some given level—the *ceteris paribus* assumption.[1]

[1] In general terms, a dependent variable (y) is considered a function of a group of independent variables $x_1 \ldots x_n$ if for a given set of values of the independent variables, there exists a unique value or set of values of y.

There are occasions when it is desirable to isolate the relationship between one of the independent variables and the dependent one. For example, if it is desired to determine the effect of a change in the value of only x on the value of y and if it can be assumed that the other independent variables remain constant at given levels, then we can write

$$y = y(x) \; cet. \; par.$$

In functional notation, this demand relationship can be written as

$$q_d = D_q(P_x, P_s, P_c, Y, T) \qquad [2.1]$$

which reads: quantity demanded (q_d) is a function of the following:

P_x = price of the good
P_s = prices of substitute goods
P_c = prices of complementary goods
Y = individual's income per time period
T = his tastes

With the *ceteris paribus* assumption, we can write

$$\overbrace{}^{\text{held constant}}$$
$$q_d = D_q(P_x, P_s, P_c, Y, T) \qquad [2.2]$$

which is usually abbreviated as

$$q_d = D_q(P) \; cet. \; par. \qquad [2.3]$$

The individual's demand schedule presents his demand for a good in tabular form. The equation $q_d = 10 - P$ can be presented in tabular form for a relevant range of prices as shown in Table 2.1. This schedule shows an inverse relationship between price and quantity. We discuss the reasons for this inverse relationship in Chapters 4 and 5.

TABLE 2.1 $q_d = 10 - P$

P ($ per unit)	q (units per time period)
10	0
9	1
8	2
7	3
6	4
5	5
4	6
3	7
2	8
1	9
0	10

The individual's demand curve for a good is a graphical representation of his schedule and is plotted from the schedule. This is done in Figure 2.1.[2]

[2] The usual procedure is to plot the independent variable on the horizontal axis and plot the dependent variable on the vertical axis. In economics, price (which is usually

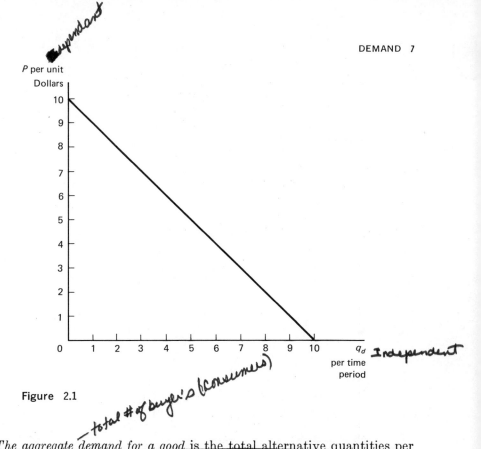

P per unit
Dollars

Dependent

qd *Independent*
per time
period

— total # of buyer's (consumers)

Figure 2.1

The aggregate demand for a good is the total alternative quantities per time period that all individuals in the market would be willing to purchase at all relevant prices. Aggregate demand is a function of the same variables that determine an individual's demand; but in addition it obviously depends on the number of potential buyers in the market.

If we are given the demand schedules of individuals in a market, we can derive the total demand schedule by adding, at each alternative price, the quantities that each of the buyers will be willing to take. We shall demonstrate this for a market that consists of two buyers as shown in Table 2.2.

The aggregate demand curve can be derived in two ways: first, by simply plotting the aggregate demand schedule; second, by a horizontal aggregation of the individual demand curves. The latter method is demonstrated in Figure 2.2.

---

the independent variable) is plotted on the vertical axis. This convention is due to Alfred Marshall.

A demand schedule and the corresponding demand curve derived from it are to be interpreted as a representation of a series of mutually exclusive alternatives; that is, the demand schedule does *not* say if the price were $9, the individual would buy one unit and then if the price were reduced to $8, he would buy an additional two units. The two prices cannot exist within the same time period.

TABLE 2.2

(1) P	(2) q_{d_1}	(3) q_{d_2}	(4) = (2) + (3) Q_d
1	8	4	12
2	6	3	9
3	4	2	6

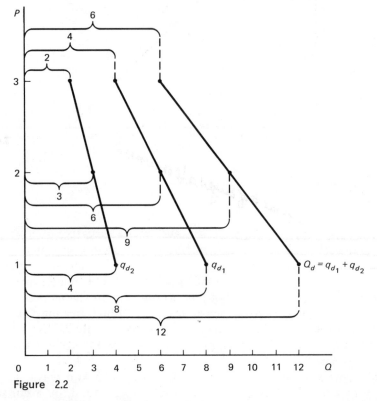

Figure 2.2

Shifts in Demand

$\uparrow$ D up $\rightarrow$ A
$\downarrow$ D down $\rightarrow$ L

When the price of a good changes, resulting in a change in the quantity purchased, this is referred to as a change in quantity demanded. When there is a change in one of the variables impounded in the *ceteris paribus* assumption, a new price-quantity relationship results. This is referred to as a change (or shift) in demand and is represented graphically as an upward-to-right movement for an increase in demand and a downward-to-the-left movement for an increase in demand and a downward-to-the-left movement for a decrease.

In Figure 2.3 we show the original demand curve as DD, and we assume an increase in demand due to, say, an increase in income. The shifted demand curve is $D'D'$. Thus, an increase in demand can be looked at in two different ways: first, at the level P_1,[3] consumers used to be willing to purchase Q_1 units; after the increase they are willing to purchase Q' units; second, before the increase consumers were willing to pay a price of P_1 for Q_1 units; after the increase they are willing to pay a price of P' for Q_1 units.

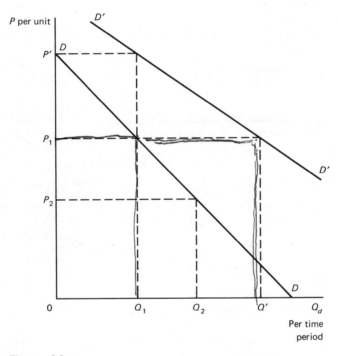

Figure 2.3

We also show in Figure 2.3 a change in quantity demanded. Suppose price changes from P_1 to P_2 when DD is the relevant schedule. (We shall discuss some possible reasons for this later.) This causes the quantity purchased to change from Q_1 to Q_2.

SUPPLY

An individual producer's supply of a good is the alternative quantities per time period he would be willing to put on the market at all relevant prices. His supply of the good is a function of the price of the good and

---

[3] The correct notation on a coordinate system would be OP_1, but because the meaning is clear, for simplicity we use P_1.

Land—Labor—Capital

costs of production.[4] If we wish to isolate the relationship between the quantity supplied and price of the good, we make the *ceteris paribus* assumption; that is, we assume that the other factors are held constant at some given level.

In functional notation, the supply relationship can be written as

$$q_s = S_q(P_x, C) \qquad [2.4]$$

where

q_s = quantity supplied
P_x = price of the good
C = a catchall variable representing all those factors influencing costs of production

With the *ceteris paribus* assumption, we can write

$$q_s = S_q(P) \ cet. \ par. \qquad [2.5]$$

The individual producer's supply schedule presents his supply of the good in tabular form. If the relationship between price and quantity supplied is

$$q_s = -2 + 2P \qquad [2.6]$$

the supply schedule will be the one presented in Table 2.3. Now we show a positive relationship between price and quantity; but once again the reasons for this will not be discussed until Chapters 6 and 7.

TABLE 2.3 $q_s = -2 + 2P$

P ($ per unit)	q_s (units per time period)
10	18
9	16
8	14
7	12
6	10
5	8
4	6
3	4
2	2
1	0
0	0

The supply curve is analogous to the demand curve. It is a graphical representation of the supply schedule and is shown in Figure 2.4.

[4] The relationship between costs of production and supply will be explained in more detail in Chapters 6 and 7.

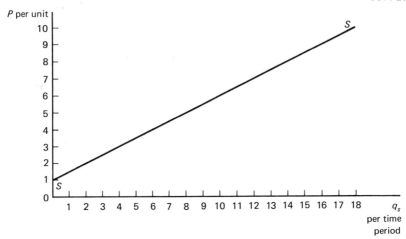

Figure 2.4

The aggregate supply schedule of a good is the total alternative quantities per time period that all producers of this particular good would be willing to put on the market at all relevant prices. It is a function of the same variables as an individual's supply of a good, but in addition is a function of the number of producers. It can be derived by summing the supply schedules of individual firms in the same way as we derived the aggregate demand schedule by summing individual demand schedules.[5]

The aggregate supply curve is simply a graphical representation of the aggregate supply schedule. It can also be derived from the horizontal summation of the supply curves of the individual firms.

A shift in supply occurs when one of the factors held constant by the *ceteris paribus* assumption changes. An increase in supply means that for all relevant prices producers are now willing to supply more to the market; a decrease in supply means the opposite. We demonstrate a decrease in supply in Figure 2.5, where SS represents the original supply and $S'S'$ the new one. At a price of P_1, producers originally were willing to supply Q_1; after the decrease they want to supply only Q'. Looked at in another way, the decrease in supply means that for a quantity of Q_1, producers, before the shift, were willing to accept a minimum price of P_1 and now they must get at least P'. *along supply curve*

A change in quantity supplied (as distinct from a change in supply) is also shown in Figure 2.5. If price changes from P_1 to P_2 and the relevant supply schedule is SS, we have an increase in *quantity* supplied (as distinct from an increase in supply); that is, quantity increases from Q_1 to Q_2 as we move along the supply curve.

[5] Some modifications to this will be discussed in Chapter 8.

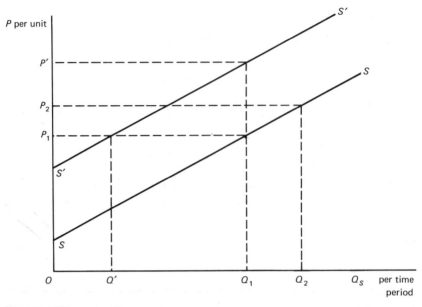

Figure 2.5

DETERMINATION OF PRICE

Perfect Competition

A market is a perfectly competitive one if the following conditions exist:

1. The numbers of buyers and sellers are sufficiently numerous so that no one of them exerts a significant influence on the price of the good.
2. The good is a homogeneous one; that is, consumers are indifferent among the outputs of the firms in the market.
3. There is no interference with the free determination of price or with entry into or exit from the market either through collusion among firms or consumers or by government intervention.
4. Producers and consumers have knowledge of prices and quantities.[6]

---

[6] It is not necessary to assume perfect knowledge in the sense that each producer and each consumer is aware of all prices and quantities in the market. It is sufficient to assume that there are enough buyers who are acquainted with more than one seller so that there is a locking together of the market by the actions of such individuals in buying from the cheapest seller and selling factor services to the highest bidders. For a more detailed discussion of this point, see George Stigler, "Perfect Competition, Historically Contemplated," *Journal of Political Economy*, Vol. LXV, No. 1 (February 1957).

The presence of these conditions implies that over some time span, the price for any product or factor of production will be the same throughout the market.

Perfect competition is one of the "models" used in economic analysis. A model, as used in economics, is a simplified picture of some part of the economy and should capture its most significant features. Like a good caricature, it should emphasize the salient characteristics and omit the less important ones. Therefore, although we recognize that our model of perfect competition is "unrealistic" in the sense that it is not a detailed picture of the workings of actual markets, it serves to point up the crucial elements in the operation of many real markets. The validity of this model, as of any other, is in its ability to predict behavior in the real world. Thus, the degree of reality of the model is in no way a measure of its usefulness; as a matter of fact, the simpler the model—in the sense of requiring less information for its use—the more useful it will be, given its predictive power.

Although our model of perfect competition is not intended to mirror the real world, it may be helpful to bear in mind some examples of actual markets that approach this model. Some of these are organized stock markets, such as the New York and the American Stock Exchanges; organized commodity markets, such as the New York Coffee and Sugar Exchange; and auction markets, such as the kind at which rare paintings are sold.

Equilibrium Price

The word "equilibrium" means such a balance of forces that there is no tendency for the system to change. We can distinguish between stable and unstable equilibriums. A stable equilibrium means that should a disturbance occur to a system in equilibrium, forces will be set up that will tend to return the system to equilibrium. In an unstable equilibrium, a disturbance to equilibrium will set up forces that will cause the system to move still further away from equilibrium.

We illustrate these terms in Figure 2.6, in which we show a ball first balanced on the top of an inverted bowl and then resting at the bottom of the bowl. The first, Figure 2.6a, represents unstable equilibrium: if we push the ball away from equilibrium, it will roll down the side of the bowl and away from the initial position. In Figure 2.6b the ball, if disturbed, will tend to return to equilibrium.

Stable equilibrium in a perfectly competitive market exists when the prevailing market price will tend to be maintained if the underlying supply and demand conditions remain unchanged. We illustrate this with the following example: A market for a product X consists of 1000 consumers, all of whom have demand schedules represented by $q_a = 10 - P$

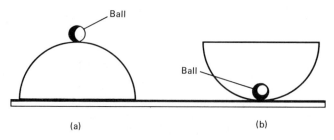

Figure 2.6

(see Table 2.1), and 1000 suppliers, all with supply schedules represented by $q_s = -2 + 2P$ (see Table 2.3). Thus, the aggregate demand schedule can be written as

$$Q_d = 10,000 - 1000P$$

and the aggregate supply schedule as

$$Q_s = -2000 + 2000P$$

These market schedules are presented in tabular form in Table 2.4 and graphically in Figure 2.7.

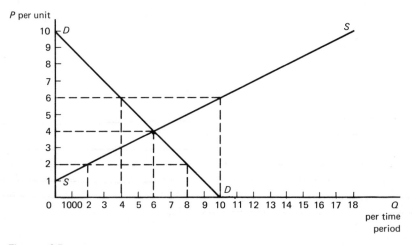

Figure 2.7

The equilibrium price is at the level at which the demand and supply curves cross, that is, when demand and supply are equal. In algebraic terms, this amounts to the simultaneous solution of the demand and supply equations. Since

$$Q_d = 10,000 - 1000P \qquad [2.7]$$

and

$$Q_s = -2000 + 2000P \qquad [2.8]$$

TABLE 2.4

P ($ per unit)	Q_d (units per time period)	Q_s (units per time period)[6]
10	0	18,000
9	1000	16,000
8	2000	14,000
7	3000	12,000
6	4000	10,000
5	5000	8000
4	6000	6000
3	7000	4000
2	8000	2000
1	9000	0
0	10,000	0

$$Q_d = 10,000 - 1000P$$
$$Q_s = -2000 + 2000P$$

at the intersection of the demand and supply curves

$$Q_d = Q_s$$

Therefore,

$$10,000 - 1000P = -2000 + 2000P$$
$$3000P = 12,000$$
$$P = \$4 \text{ per unit}$$

Through substitution in either the Q_d or the Q_s equation, we can determine the corresponding value of Q:

$$Q_d = 10,000 - 1000(4)$$
$$Q_d = 6000 \text{ units per time period}$$

or

$$Q_s = -2000 + 2000(4)$$
$$Q_s = 6000 \text{ units per time period}$$

It is not sufficient merely to state that the equilibrium price is determined by the algebraic or graphical solution of the supply and demand equations. We must specify how, in an actual market, price would be forced to this equilibrium level. We shall describe the mechanism for the attainment of equilibrium by selecting a market as close to perfect competition as is known in the real world—an auction at which potential buyers and sellers are in close contact.

This kind of market can operate in the following fashion: The suppliers make known to the auctioneer the quantities they are willing to supply at a specific price. The auctioneer then relates this information to the demanders. The demanders, in turn, inform the auctioneer of the quantities they are willing to purchase at that price. No sales, we shall see, take place until a price is reached at which the total quantity that suppliers are willing to sell is just equal to the total quantity that demanders wish to buy. By referring to Table 2.4 and Figure 2.7, we can see how this equilibrium price is reached.

Assume that when the auction convenes, the suppliers inform the auctioneer that they are willing to supply 10,000 units at a price of $6 per unit. Consumers, upon receipt of this information, respond to the auctioneer that at $6 per unit they are willing to purchase 4000 units. Thus, there is an excess of supply over demand of 6000 units at $6 per unit. If sales were allocated by the auctioneer on the basis of order of bids of the suppliers or on a prorated basis, it would become obvious to the sellers that not all of them would be able to sell all they want to at $6. Each supplier, acting individually, thinks that by decreasing the price by just a little he will be able to dispose of all he wants to.[7] Thus, a process of competitive price reduction ensues. Each time one supplier reduces the price slightly there are two effects: First, the total quantity consumers are willing to buy increases as some increase the amounts they are willing to buy at the now lower price; in other words, there is a movement down the aggregate demand curve away from the $6 level. Second, after each shading in price, suppliers are willing to offer less to the market, and there is a downward movement along the total supply curve.

Therefore, as the price shading continues, the excess of demand over supply gets smaller. Finally, when the suppliers inform the auctioneer that they are willing to sell 6000 units at $4 per unit, equilibrium will be attained, because there is no motive for further price cutting as the demanders are willing also to buy 6000 units at $4. In order to test his understanding of this market mechanism, the student should be able to describe how the equilibrium price of $4 would be reached if suppliers started their offers at $2 per unit.

Perfect knowledge is an ideal that is rarely approximated in the real world. (The only example that readily comes to mind is the almost instantaneous knowledge provided by a high-speed stock ticker-tape machine.) In the absence of perfect knowledge, the real world competitive markets achieve equilibrium over time by a process of successive approximation.

---

[7] The student is reminded that perfect competition assumes a homogeneous good and that each seller supplies only a small part of the total market—in our case, only $\frac{1}{1000}$. Thus, a very slight price decrease is sufficient to ensure to any individual supplier that he will be able to increase his sales. We shall further explore this point in Chapter 8.

3

REVENUE CONCEPTS AND DEMAND ELASTICITY

There are a set of measures that are fundamental to economic analysis. We illustrate these now with respect to demand.

REVENUE CONCEPTS

q= output.

Total revenue is equal to price times quantity [output]:

$$TR = Pq \qquad\qquad [3.1]$$

Average revenue is equal to total revenue divided by quantity:

average: ÷ 0

$$AR = \frac{TR}{q} = \frac{Pq}{q} = P \qquad\qquad [3.2]$$

Discrete marginal revenue is defined as

$$MR = \frac{\Delta TR}{\Delta q} \qquad\qquad [3.3]$$

Continuous marginal revenue is defined as

$$MR = \frac{dTR}{dq} \qquad\qquad [3.3a]$$

where $\frac{dTR}{dq}$ means the value that $\frac{\Delta TR}{\Delta q}$ approaches as Δq approaches zero.

A DIGRESSION ON SLOPE (THE MARGINAL CONCEPT)

Often in economics as well as in other areas, it is important to determine the effect upon the dependent variable of a change in the independent variable. The concept of slope measures the rate of change of y in relation to changes in x. For example, there is a relationship between distance travelled by an automobile and the time of travel. Assume an individual has travelled 40 miles during a time interval of one hour; we would say that his average rate of speed over the time interval was 40 mph. At the start of this interval, he travelled slowly to observe the scenery and later speeded up to get past the billboards so that 40 mph represents an average *over* the hour. This functional relationship can be shown graphically in Figure 3.1.

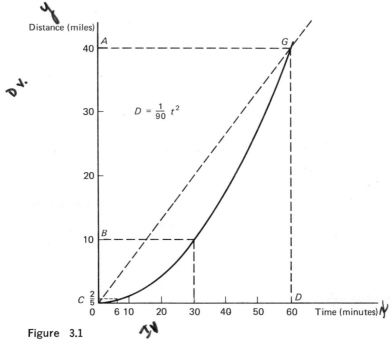

Figure 3.1

In this figure, to measure the rate of speed diagrammatically, we read 40 miles on the vertical axis (OA) and one hour on the horizontal axis (OD); and because we want distance per hour, we take the ratio $\dfrac{OA}{OD}$. This is often written as $\dfrac{\Delta \text{ distance}}{\Delta \text{ time}}$, that is, $\dfrac{\Delta y}{\Delta x}$ and this is the slope of the chord joining points O and G.

Because he was travelling at different rates of speed during the hour, a measurement taken for a shorter time interval would be more representative of the speed during that interval. If he had taken a measurement at the end of 30 minutes, he would have gone 10 miles or at the rate of 20 mph. And if he had taken a measurement at the end of 6 minutes, he would have discovered that his scenery watching had caused him to cover only $\frac{2}{5}$ of a mile or to have travelled at the rate of 4 mph. These last two measurements can also be shown diagrammatically respectively as $\dfrac{OB}{OE}$ and $\dfrac{OC}{OF}$.

Clearly, if the speed had been a constant over the time interval so that the graph was a straight line, the slope would also be a constant; that is, the measurement of the slope over the entire interval or any fraction of it would be the same.

To generalize our procedure, we can say that to find the slope between two points on a curve, we assume a straight line exists between the two points and then measure the slope of that line. This gives us the average slope along the curve between the two points. This measures discrete slope or discrete marginal. Consequently, for the purpose of drawing a continuous marginal revenue curve, the values of discrete marginal revenue are placed at the midpoints of the relevant intervals.

Let us consider another curvilinear function that is shown in Figure 3.2. In this diagram we can measure the average slope of the curve be-

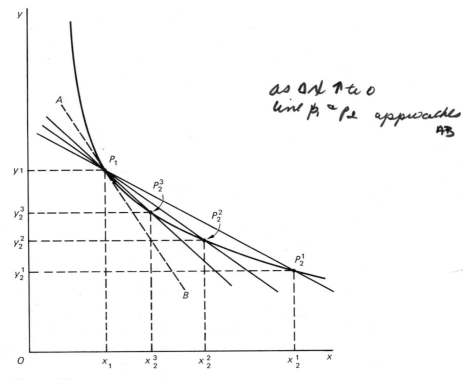

Figure 3.2

tween points P_1 and $P_2{}^1$ by finding the slope of the straight line between those points. Now visualize that P_1 is fixed but that P_2 moves closer to it along the curve. We can determine the slope between P_1 and $P_2{}^2$ and between P_1 and $P_2{}^3$ by computing the appropriate $\Delta y/\Delta x$. Notice that as P_2 gets closer to P_1, Δx gets smaller and smaller. As Δx approaches zero the line between P_1 and P_2 approaches the line AB. Thus, we can consider the slope of a curve in the vicinity of a point, rather than between two points along the curve. And this continuous slope is the value that the discrete slope approaches as P_2 approaches P_1 (or as $\Delta x \rightarrow 0$; this expression is read as "Δx approaches zero"). This continuous slope may be written as

$$\lim_{\Delta x \to 0} \frac{\Delta y}{\Delta x} \quad \text{or} \quad \frac{dy}{dx}$$

The slope of the curve at P_1 is measured by determining the slope of the line AB, which is the tangent to the curve at P_1. Because the slope of a straight line is a constant, to get the slope at P_1, $\Delta y/\Delta x$ can be computed between any two points on this line, and this is the same as computing dy/dx at P_1 on line AB. Thus, the discrete slope of the line tangent at P_1 and the continuous slope of the curve at P_1 are the same.[1]

REVENUE CONCEPTS CONTINUED

Table 3.1 gives TR, AR, and discrete and continuous MR for the demand function

$$P = \frac{600}{q + 6} - 10q \qquad [3.4]$$

Total revenue is shown graphically in Figure 3.3, and average revenue and continuous marginal revenue are shown in Figure 3.4.

AR at 4 units of output can be measured graphically as the slope of the line OA—that is, AB/OB or $\sphericalangle \theta$ in Figure 3.4: \$200/4 units = \$50/unit. Continuous MR at 4 units can be measured as the slope of line AC—that is, AB/BC or $\sphericalangle \phi$: \$200/7.69 units = \$26/unit. Discrete MR between 3 and 4 units is equal to $\dfrac{\$200 - \$170}{1 \text{ unit}} = \$30/\text{unit}$.

We have demonstrated graphically the measurement of average revenue and continuous and discrete marginal revenue from total revenue. Clearly, TR can be derived from AR: In Figure 3.4, at 4 units $AR = 50$. Since $TR = AR \cdot q$, $TR = \$200$ or the area OP_1Eq_1. It is not so clear, however, that TR can be derived from either discrete or continuous MR;

---

[1] Computing $\dfrac{dy}{dx}$ is known as taking the derivative of y with respect to x.

TABLE   3.1

(1)	(2)	(3)	(4) Continuous	(5) Discrete
q	P	TR	MR	MR
0	$90.00	$ 0	$ 90.00	$ 75.71
1	75.71	75.71	63.47	54.29
2	65.00	130.00	40.00	40.00
3	56.67	170.00	34.44	30.00
4	50.00	200.00	26.00	22.73
5	44.54	222.73	19.75	17.27
6	40.00	240.00	15.00	13.08
7	36.15	253.08	11.30	9.78
8	32.86	262.86	8.37	7.14
9	30.00	270.00	6.00	5.00
10	27.50	275.00	4.06	3.24
11	25.29	278.24	2.46	1.76
12	23.33	280.00	1.11	.53
13	21.58	280.53	−.03	−.53
14	20.00	280.00	−1.00	−1.43
15	18.57	278.57	−1.84	−2.21
16	17.27	276.36	−2.56	−2.88
17	16.09	273.48	−3.20	−3.48
18	15.00	270.00	−3.75	−4.00
19	14.00	266.00	−4.24	$−4.46
20	$13.07	$261.54	$−4.68	

The demand function is $P = \dfrac{600}{q+6} - 10$; $TR = \dfrac{600q}{q+6} - 10q$;

and continuous $MR = \dfrac{3600}{q^2 + 12q + 36} - 10$.

these processes we shall now demonstrate with the aid of Table 3.1 and Figure 3.5, which repeats the MR curve of Figure 3.4.

Column 5 of Table 3.1 lists MR for finite changes in output. Because we know that TR is zero at zero level of output, it can be computed for any other level of output in the following manner (which we shall demonstrate with reference to total revenue at 3 units of output): We can get TR for one unit of output by determining the addition to TR (MR) due to selling the first unit of output ($75.71). Analogously, we can get TR for two units of sales by adding to $75.71 the MR of the second unit of output ($75.71 + $54.29 = $130). Finally, we can compute TR for three units by adding the MR of the third unit to the $130 [($75.71 + $54.29) + $40.00 = $170.00]. Note that we are adding MR of every unit of output up to and including the level of output for which we are computing total revenue.

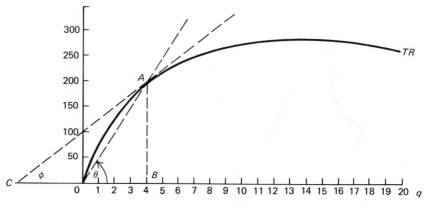

Figure 3.3   Total revenue

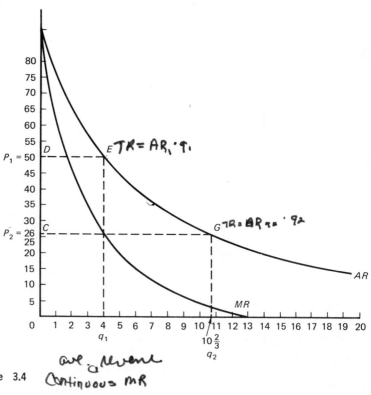

Figure 3.4   average revenue
              Continuous MR

Total revenue can be derived graphically from marginal revenue, and this is done in Figure 3.5 where the vertical bars represent the discrete MR from column 5 in Table 3.1. The stepwise function shows that the average rate of change over the discrete interval is assigned to the entire interval. The procedure of adding the marginal revenue up to and including that for an output of 3 is equivalent to adding the first three vertical bars on the diagram; and one can obtain total revenue for n units of output by simply adding the bars up to and including the nth.

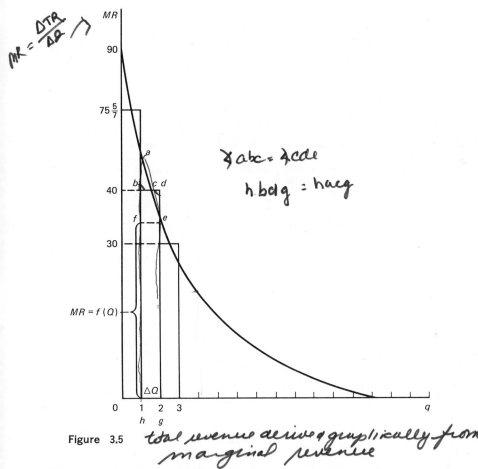

Figure 3.5 total revenue derived graphically from marginal revenue

If we wish to obtain total revenue from continuous MR, we no longer can rely on the tabular technique. The reason for this is that we have the continuous MR at specific points only, but we need it for all possible levels of output. With the use of Figure 3.5, we illustrate the derivation of TR from a continuous MR curve. The continuous marginal curve, jk, goes through the center points of the bars of the discrete marginal function. Now let the bar *hbdg* be representative of any bar on the step function. For small changes in q, the segment of the continuous curve *ae* will approximate a straight line, and, consequently, Δabc and Δcde are congruent. (Two angles and the side between them are equal: $\angle acb = \angle dce$; side bc = side cd by construction; and $\angle abc = \angle cde$.) Thus the area *haeg* is equal to the area *hbdg*, since one of the congruent triangles (of equal area) is excluded by this polygon, but the other is included instead. Further, *haeg* is the sum of the rectangle *hfeg* and the triangle *fae*. Now let Δq diminish and approach zero. The base of the rectangle decreases and its height remains the same. However, both the base and the altitude of the triangle decrease. Consequently, the area of the triangle is decreasing much more rapidly than that of the rectangle. Thus, as Δq approaches zero, $\Delta q[f(q)]$ becomes an increasingly better approximation to the area under the curve for very small increments in q. Thus, at the limit, finding total revenue from continuous MR may be viewed as taking the sum of a series of very narrow rectangles, that is, the sum of $f(q)dq$, where dq denotes an infinitesimal change in q. This is written $\int f(q)dq$ where the sign "$\int$" means continuous summation or integration.[2]

RELATIONSHIP BETWEEN THE MARGINAL AND AVERAGE CONCEPTS

We now desire to show the relationship between marginal and average concepts; this is done with reference to Figure 3.4. We take any two points, E and G, along the AR curve. At point E total revenue may be expressed as $AR_1 \cdot q_1$; at point G total revenue may be expressed as AR_2q_2.

We can determine the discrete MR between outputs q_1 and q_2 as follows: Let

$$\Delta q = q_2 - q_1$$
$$\Delta AR = AR_2 - AR_1$$
$$\Delta TR = AR_2q_2 - AR_1q_1$$

AR_2q_2 can be written as

$$AR_2q_1 + AR_2(q_2 - q_1) = AR_2q_1 + AR_2\Delta q$$

AR_1q_1 can be written as

$$AR_2q_1 + q_1(AR_1 - AR_2) = AR_2q_1 - q_1(AR_2 - AR_1) = AR_2q_1 - q_1\Delta AR$$

Substituting, we get

$$\Delta TR = (AR_2q_1 + AR_2\Delta q) - (AR_2q_1 - q_1\Delta AR)$$
$$= AR_2q_1 + AR_2\Delta q - AR_2q_1 + q_1\Delta AR$$
$$= AR_2\Delta q + q_1\Delta AR$$
$$MR = \frac{\Delta TR}{\Delta q} = AR_2 + \frac{\Delta AR}{\Delta q}q_1 \qquad [3.5]$$

[2] This amounts to taking the definite integral from 0 to 3 units of output as follows:

$$\int_0^3 \left[\frac{3600}{q^2 + 12q + 36} - 10\right] dq = \left[\frac{60q}{q + 6} - 10q\right]_0^3 = 170$$

Note that since AR is falling, its slope $\Delta AR/\Delta q$ is negative, and MR is less than the new average, AR_2.

Let us now suppose that point G is made to approach point E and, therefore, that Δq approaches 0 or q_2 approaches q_1. We may now rewrite our expression as[3]

$$MR = \frac{dTR}{dq} = AR + \frac{dAR}{dq}\,q \qquad [3.6]$$

Although our proof of the relationship between an average and its related marginal was done for revenue concepts, the relationship holds between any average and its related marginal. Thus, in general terms, if the average is rising, so that $\frac{dy}{dx} > 0$, the marginal will be greater than the average. If the average is declining, $\frac{dy}{dx} < 0$ and the marginal is less than the average. Finally, when the average is at either a maximum or minimum, $\frac{dy}{dx} = 0$ and the average and marginal will be equal.

A concrete example of this relationship follows. Four men in a room have the following heights:

Man	Height in Inches
1	68
2	72
3	74
4	66
Total	280

$$\text{Average} = \frac{280}{4} = 70 \text{ inches}$$

An additional man (the marginal man) enters the room. If the average of 70 inches is to fall, his height must be less than 70 inches; if it is to rise, his height must be greater than 70 inches; and if it is to remain the same, his height must be equal to 70 inches. Further, as long as his height is a positive number (as it must be by the nature of the case), the total would rise; it could fall only if the fifth man's height were negative.

---

[3] Note that we have dropped the subscripts because AR_1 and AR_2 and q_1 and q_2 approach each other as ΔAR and Δq approach zero. This result can be obtained directly with calculus by using the rule for obtaining the derivative of a product:

$$TR = AR \cdot q$$

and because MR is defined as the rate of change of TR,

$$MR = \frac{dTR}{dq} = AR + \frac{dMR}{dq}\,q$$

DEMAND ELASTICITY

We are interested in measuring the responsiveness of quantity to changes in price (that is, the responsiveness of the dependent variable to changes in the independent variable). It must occur to the reader that we have discussed such a measure in the concept of slope. The need for another measure will be made clear in the following example. Consider the individual demand function for gasoline: $P = \$1 - \frac{1}{10}q$, shown in Figure 3.6.

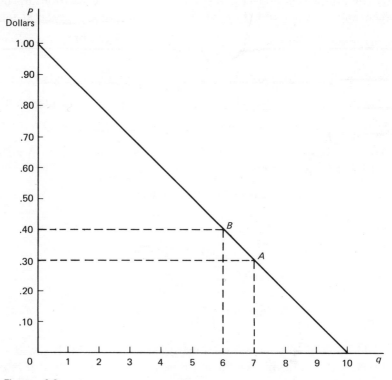

Figure 3.6

Suppose the price changes from $.30 to $.40. The responsiveness of quantity can be measured as $\dfrac{\Delta q}{\Delta P}$ (that is, the reciprocal of the slope of the demand schedule—see p. 6, n. 2), which is equal to $\dfrac{-1 \text{ gallon/week}}{\$.10/\text{gallon}} = \dfrac{10 \text{ gallons/week}}{\$/\text{gallon}}$. We can see, therefore, that slope is a measure that depends on the units in which the variables are expressed.

If a comparison were made between two such measures, we would have to be quite sure that they were expressed in the same units, and often a conversion to comparable units would be quite difficult. For example, suppose that in Britain an individual's demand for petrol is $P = 8.33 - q$. However, in Britain, price is measured in shillings (until 1971) and quantity in imperial gallons. (At the official exchange rate, 8.33 shillings is the equivalent of $1, and an imperial gallon is 120 percent of an American gallon.) Actually, this demand schedule is identical to $P = \$1.00 - .1q$. However, if we compute the reciprocal of the slope of the British demand, we find it to be -1.00. Through the use of the appropriate conversion ratio, we would arrive at the same slope.

In addition to these conversion problems, many times we want to compare quantity responsiveness to changes in price when the units are not capable of conversion to one another; for example, peanuts are measured in cents/weight and Rolls Royces are measured $/units.

Point and Arc Elasticity

The concept of elasticity obviates this difficulty and has certain virtues of its own. To make our measure independent of units, we use a ratio of the percentage change in q to the percentage change in P, instead of taking a ratio of the absolute change in the dependent variable to the absolute change in the independent variable. The elasticity coefficient is computed as

$$E = \frac{\Delta q/q}{\Delta P/P} \qquad [3.7]$$

The elasticity, when price changed from $.30 to $.40 can be computed as

$$E = \frac{\dfrac{-1 \text{ gallon/week}}{7 \text{ gallons/week}}}{\dfrac{\$.10/\text{gallon}}{\$.30/\text{gallon}}} = -\frac{3}{7} \approx -.4 \qquad [3.8]$$

If we compute elasticity for a price change from 2.5s. to 3.3s. (the equivalents of $.30 and $.40), we get[4]

$$E = \frac{\dfrac{-.83 \text{ imperial gallon/week}}{5.83 \text{ imperial gallons/week}}}{\dfrac{.83s./\text{imperial gallon}}{2.5s./\text{imperial gallon}}} \approx -.4 \qquad [3.9]$$

[4] The small difference in the second decimal place of the two numbers is because of rounding.

Notice that the use of a ratio of percentage changes results in the cancellation of units of measurement; or, in other words, the elasticity coefficient is a pure number. Thus we have a measure that is independent of units and that frees us of the necessity of converting our functional relationships into comparable units before we can make comparisons of responsiveness.

The elasticity formula can also be written as

$$E = \frac{\Delta q}{\Delta P} \cdot \frac{P}{q} \qquad [3.10]$$

and we can see that elasticity is the product of (1) the slope between the two points and (2) the ratio of the initial values of P and q, that is, the location on the line of the two points.

Some problems do arise with the elasticity formula just given. If we were to measure the edge of a table, we would expect to get the same measurement whether we placed the ruler from left to right or from right to left. In the same way, we would expect to get the same elasticity coefficient between two points whether we measured from left to right along the graph or from right to left. Let us return to the two points we used before in Figure 3.6, but this time we shall compute elasticity for a change in price from $.40 to $.30, rather than from $.30 to $.40.

$$E = \frac{\dfrac{1 \text{ gallon/week}}{6 \text{ gallons/week}}}{\dfrac{-\$.10/\text{gallon}}{\$.40/\text{gallon}}} = -\frac{2}{3} \qquad [3.11]$$

The answer is $-\frac{2}{3}$, compared with our previous answer of $-\frac{3}{7}$ in equation 3.8. We are thus faced with the anomalous situation that our results differ, depending on the direction in which we decide to measure the change. To see the cause of this result, let us compare our elasticity measures:

$$E_{.30 \to .40} = \frac{-1 \text{ gallon/7 gallons}}{\$.10/\text{gallon}/\$.30/\text{gallon}}$$

and

$$E_{.40 \to .30} = \frac{1 \text{ gallon/6 gallons}}{-\$.10/\text{gallon}/\$.40/\text{gallon}}$$

It is clear that our difficulty exists because the base for computing our percentage changes is different for the two computations.

The way out of this dilemma can be seen if we visualize point B as getting closer and closer to point A in Figure 3.6. As the distance between A and B approaches zero, Δq and ΔP approach zero and the differences between the initial and subsequent values of p and q approach zero. Therefore, the difference between the two elasticity measures will also approach zero. Hence, our elasticity formula should be written as

$$E = \frac{dq}{dP} \cdot \frac{P}{q} \qquad [3.12]$$

which is called point elasticity. It should be remembered that dq/dP represents the rate of change of q with respect to P in which the change in P is infinitesimally small.

Thus, in Figure 3.6, the elasticity at point A is[5]

$$E = -10 \left(\frac{.3}{7} \right) = -\frac{3}{7} \qquad [3.13]$$

Although we now have an exact formula for computing elasticity, we are still faced with a problem. Most of the changes in variables that arise in economics are finite rather than infinitesimal. So we must still devise a method for finding elasticity between two points on a function (called arc elasticity) that will give us the same results no matter in which direction we measure. As we saw before, the reason that we obtained different answers is the fact that different bases were used, depending on the direction in which we measure. We can overcome this problem in the following way: In computing the percentage change in q, instead of using the original q ($\Delta q/$original q), use the average of the initial and the new q values as the base; the same applies to computing the percentage change in P. This amounts to using as a base a point halfway between the initial and final points. Thus

$$E = \frac{\% \text{ change in } q}{\% \text{ change in } P} = \frac{\Delta q/[(q_1 + q_2)/2]}{\Delta P/[(P_1 + P_2)/2]}$$
$$= \frac{\Delta q[(P_1 + P_2)/2]}{\Delta P[(q_1 + q_2)/2]} \qquad [3.14]$$

where the subscripts 1 represent initial values and subscripts 2 represent new values. Because division by 2 appears in both the numerator and the denominator of the ratio, we can cancel out the 2's without changing the value of the fraction. In simplified form, then, the arc elasticity coefficient is

$$E = \frac{\Delta q/(q_1 + q_2)}{\Delta P/(P_1 + P_2)} = \frac{\Delta q}{\Delta P} \cdot \frac{P_1 + P_2}{q_1 + q_2} \qquad [3.15]$$

[5] The reader should note that the following point elasticity is the same as the one obtained in equation 3.8. This is true only for a linear demand curve for which continuous and discrete slopes are identical and constant for the function.

To test this new arc elasticity formula, we shall once again measure elasticity between points A and B on Figure 3.6 in both directions. Going from A to B, we find

$$E = -10 \cdot \frac{.30 + .40}{7 + 6} = -\frac{7}{13} \qquad [3.16]$$

Going from B to A, we find

$$E = -10 \cdot \frac{.40 + .30}{6 + 7} = -\frac{7}{13} \qquad [3.17]$$

The elasticity between various points on the function $q = 10 - 10P$ is presented in Table 3.2. Note that elasticity (arc or point) varies along

TABLE 3.2

P	q	E
0	10	
		$-\frac{1}{19}$
.10	9	
		$-\frac{3}{17}$
.20	8	
		$-\frac{1}{3}$
.30	7	
		$-\frac{7}{13}$
.40	6	
		$-\frac{9}{11}$
.50	5	
		$-1\frac{2}{9}$
.60	4	
		$-1\frac{6}{7}$
.70	3	
		-3
.80	2	
		$-5\frac{2}{3}$
.90	1	
		-19
1.00	0	

a straight line, while the slope is a constant. This is perfectly logical because elasticity depends only partly on slope; its other determinant is the location of the points or point being considered, and this varies along a straight line.

The concept of elasticity is perfectly general and can be used to measure the responsiveness of any dependent variable to a change in the related independent variable.

Determinants of Demand Elasticity

There are five important determinants of elasticity.

1. The availability of substitutes for the good. If a commodity has substitutes, when there is an increase in its price, consumers will shift to the substitutes. The greater the number of substitutes and the closer they are, the more elastic will be the demand.

2. The proportion of income spent on the good. If expenditure on a good represents a large percentage of income, an increase in the price of the good will lower the consumer's real income substantially and cause him to react sharply in readjusting his expenditures.

3. The degree of complementarity. If a commodity is complementary to another considerably more expensive one, then the responsiveness of its demand to a change in price will be less than it would otherwise be. For example, if a tape recorder costing $400 has been purchased in the recent past and now the price of a roll of tape goes from $5 to $6, this represents a 20 percent increase in tape cost. But as a proportion of the combined cost per recording of the machine time and tape, this increase is much less significant.

4. Durability of the commodity. Durable commodities will tend to be more elastic than nondurable commodities for the reason that they are usually replaced before they have completely worn out in the physical sense. A car or a TV set can usually be made to do a bit more service with appropriate maintenance. Further, durable commodities are storable and can be purchased for future use when the price is propitious.

5. The time period. Demand tends to be more elastic over a longer than a shorter time period because consumers have the opportunity to become aware of existing alternatives and to adjust their purchases to a price change. This is particularly true when some complementary product is involved that also needs to be replaced for the adjustment to be made; for example, if electricity were to decline in price relative to gas, in the long run when gas ranges had worn out and people could buy electric ranges, the response to the change in the price of electricity would be much greater than in the short run when gas ranges were not yet depreciated.

Revenue Concepts and Elasticity

To show the *relationship between TR and elasticity,* we start with the definition of total revenue:

$$TR_1 = PQ$$

Assume a change in price, ΔP, and a resulting change in quantity demanded equal to ΔQ.

$$TR_2 = (P + \Delta P)(Q + \Delta Q)$$

Multiplying out, we have

$$TR_2 = PQ + \Delta P \Delta Q + \Delta PQ + \Delta QP$$

The change in TR is

$$\Delta TR = TR_2 - TR_1 = \Delta P \Delta Q + \Delta PQ + \Delta QP$$

Now let ΔP and ΔQ approach zero and we have

$$dTR = dPdQ + QdP + PdQ$$

Now note that dP and dQ are extremely small quantities, say $1/100,000$ and $1/500,000$. If we multiply them, we get a very much smaller quantity. In the example just given it is $1/50,000,000,000,000$, which is close enough to zero so that we can ignore it. We therefore write

$$dTR = QdP + PdQ \qquad [3.18]$$

The point elasticity formula may be written as

$$E_d = \frac{dQ \cdot P}{dP \cdot Q} \qquad [3.19]$$

and the numerator and denominator are always of opposite signs; that is, when $dP > 0$, $dQ < 0$ and when $dP < 0$, $dQ > 0$. Thus, ignoring signs, that is, using absolute values, denoted by $|\ \ |$,

	A	**B**
if $|E| > 1$,	$(dQ \cdot P) > |dP \cdot Q|$	
if $|E| = 1$,	$(dQ \cdot P) = |dP \cdot Q|$	
if $|E| < 1$,	$(dQ \cdot P) < |dP \cdot Q|$	

If we consider a price rise, the algebraic value of the "B" term above is positive and that of the "A" term negative, and since dTR is the sum of the algebraic values of the "A" and "B" terms, TR will fall when $|E| > 1$, remain constant when $|E| = 1$, and rise when $|E| < 1$. If we consider a price fall (continuing to use algebraic values), the "B" term is negative and the "A" term positive. Again, since dTR is equal to the sum of these terms, TR will rise when $|E| > 1$, remain constant when $|E| = 1$, and fall when $|E| < 1$. When demand is inelastic the direction of change of TR is always the same as that of price, and when demand is elastic the direction of change of TR is always opposite to the change in price.

We may return to equation 3.18 and derive an extremely useful relationship among MR, AR, and E.

$$dTR = QdP + PdQ$$

We divide both sides by dQ:

$$\frac{dTR}{dQ} = \frac{dPQ}{dQ} + P$$

Since dTR/dQ is MR, we can rewrite[6]

$$MR = \left(\frac{dP}{dQ}\right) Q + P \qquad [3.20]$$

Since

$$E_d = \frac{dQ \cdot P}{dP \cdot Q} \quad \text{and} \quad \frac{1}{E_d} = \frac{dP \cdot Q}{dQ \cdot P}, \; P\left(\frac{1}{E_d}\right) = \left(\frac{dP}{dQ}\right) Q$$

We may now rewrite equation 3.20 as

$$MR = P\left(\frac{1}{E_d}\right) + P \text{ or } P\left(1 + \frac{1}{E_d}\right) \qquad [3.20a]$$

where it is to be remembered that $E < 0$.

By a rearrangement of terms, we can write

$$E = \frac{P}{MR - P} \qquad [3.21]$$

or in absolute terms:

$$|E| = \frac{P}{P - MR} \qquad [3.22]$$

GEOMETRICAL INTERPRETATION OF POINT ELASTICITY

If a function is presented graphically, there is a time-saving method of obtaining graphically the elasticity at a point on the function. We can demonstrate this technique with the use of Figure 3.7. We know that the formula for point elasticity of demand is

$$E_d = \frac{dQ}{dP} \cdot \frac{P}{Q}$$

If we want to find the elasticity of the curve at point P, we can substitute in this formula as follows:

$$E_d = \frac{CP}{AC} \cdot \frac{OC}{OD}$$

Since $CP = OD$, we can write

$$E_d = \frac{CP}{AC} \cdot \frac{OC}{CP}$$

---

[6] This, it should be noted, is a relationship already obtained in equation 3.6.

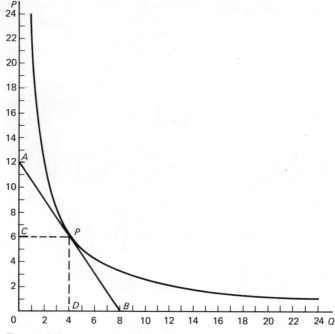

Figure 3.7

The CP's cancel out and we are left with

$$E_d = \frac{OC}{AC}$$

In words, this is the ratio of (1) the price to (2) the difference between the vertical axis intercept of the tangent at P and the price.[7]

Notice that this interpretation does not explicitly take into consideration the sign of the coefficient but gives us the absolute value of elasticity. Thus, it must be kept in mind that if the function is downward sloping, the coefficient will be negative. At point P, then, the elasticity is -1.

The elasticity at a point on a straight-line function can be obtained graphically, too. Assume the demand schedule is the tangent AB in Figure 3.7. The elasticity at P would simply be

$$E_d = \frac{OC}{CA}$$

[7] Elasticity at point P can also be derived as

$$E_d = \left(\frac{dQ}{dP}\right)\left(\frac{P}{Q}\right) = \left(\frac{DB}{DP}\right)\left(\frac{OC}{OD}\right)$$

Because $DP = OC$, $E_d = DB/OD = 4/4 = 1$.

where OC is the price at point P and CA is the price-axis intercept of the function. Therefore, the elasticity of a downward-sloping linear demand function is equal to -1 at the midpoint of the line (as at P); $|E| > 1$ and increases as C moves toward A; and since the numerator increases as the denominator approaches 0, $|E|$ approaches ∞. $|E| < 1$ and decreases as C approaches 0; and since the numerator decreases and approaches zero, as the denominator increases, the measure approaches zero at the horizontal axis-intercept.

Thus, at the quantity corresponding to the midpoint of a linear demand curve, $MR = 0$; for smaller quantities MR is positive and for larger quantities it is negative.

Thus it follows from our graphical measure of elasticity that a perpendicular dropped from the midpoint of the demand curve to the quantity-axis will bisect the distance from the origin to the horizontal axis intercept of the demand schedule. Furthermore, since $|E|$ approaches infinity at the vertical axis, the demand and marginal revenue curves have a common price-axis intercept. This can be seen from the relationship

$$MR = P\left(1 + \frac{1}{E}\right)$$

which is equivalent to

$$MR = P\left(1 - \frac{1}{|E|}\right)$$

with $|E| \to \infty$, $MR \to P$, which establishes the common point.

Thus having established that (1) the MR curve has the same vertical axis intercept as the demand curve and (2) the MR curve cuts the horizontal axis at one half the distance from the origin as does the demand curve, we have established the fact that the absolute slope of a linear MR curve is twice the slope of the corresponding demand curve.[8]

Supply elasticity is defined as the responsiveness of quantity supplied to a change in price and is measured as

$$E_s = \frac{dQ_s/Q_s}{dP/P} = \frac{dQ_s}{dP} \cdot \frac{P}{Q_s} \qquad [3.23]$$

for point elasticity, and

$$E_s = \frac{\Delta Q_s/(Q_{s1} + Q_{s2})}{\Delta P/(P_1 + P_2)} = \frac{\Delta Q_s}{\Delta P} \cdot \frac{P_1 + P_2}{Q_{s1} + Q_{s2}} \qquad [3.24]$$

for arc elasticity.

[8] In terms of calculus, this relationship can be proven as follows. Given the linear demand schedule,

$$P = a + bq$$

$$TR = aq + bq^2 \qquad \text{and} \qquad MR = \frac{dTR}{dq} = a + 2bq$$

In Figures 3.8a and 3.8b we derive a geometrical measure of supply elasticity analogous to the one for demand elasticity. Using Figure 3.8a and substituting in equation 3.23, we have

$$E_s = \frac{OQ}{BP} \cdot \frac{OP}{OQ} = \frac{OP}{BP}$$

Supply elasticity can thus be measured as the ratio of price to the difference between price and the vertical axis intercept of the tangent to the supply curve. However, if the tangent hits the horizontal axis, as in Figure 3.8b, then

$$E_s = \frac{DQ}{OP} \cdot \frac{OP}{OQ} = \frac{DQ}{OQ}$$

and this is the ratio of (1) the difference between quantity and the tangent's horizontal axis intercept to (2) the quantity.

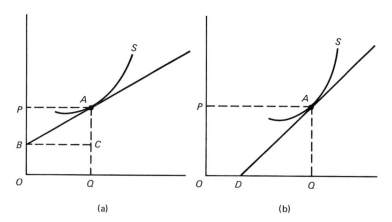

(a)   (b)

Figure 3.8

The student should be able to show that in the special case of a supply curve the tangent to which passes through the origin (or a linear supply curve from the origin), $E_s = 1$.

It should be noted that no unique relationship exists between supply elasticity and total revenue because total revenue is monotonically increasing along the supply curve.

Cross elasticity relates the responsiveness of quantity demanded of commodity A to a change in the price of another commodity B. It is measured as

$$E_{AB} = \frac{dQ_A/Q_A}{dP_B/P_B} = \frac{dQ_A}{dP_B} \cdot \frac{P_B}{Q_A} \qquad [3.25]$$

for point elasticity. For arc elasticity it is measured as

$$E_{AB} = \frac{\Delta Q_A/(Q_{A1} + Q_{A2})}{\Delta P_B/(P_{B1} + P_{B2})} = \frac{\Delta Q_A}{\Delta P_B} \cdot \frac{P_{B1} + P_{B2}}{Q_{A1} + Q_{A2}}$$ [3.26]

The concept of cross elasticity permits us to give an empirical definition to substitutes and complements. (A more detailed discussion of the meaning of substitutes and complements is in Chapter 5.) Goods that are substitutes for one another will have a coefficient of cross elasticity between them that is positive. Analogously, complementary goods will have a negative coefficient.

Income elasticity measures the responsiveness of quantity demanded of a good to a change in income along an Engel curve[9] and can be expressed:

$$E_I = \frac{\Delta Q}{\Delta I} \cdot \frac{I_1 + I_2}{q_1 + q_2}$$ [3.27]

for finite changes and

$$E_I = \frac{dQ}{dI} \cdot \frac{I}{Q}$$ [3.28]

for infinitesimal changes.

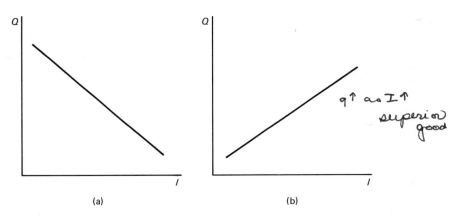

(a)   (b)

Figure 3.9

The Engel curve in Figure 3.9b represents a superior good, that is, a good for which quantity purchased increases as income increases; most goods are of this kind. In Figure 3.9a, we show an inferior good for which there is an inverse relationship between income and quantity purchased.

Notice that while income elasticity refers to a movement along a given income (Engel) curve, in terms of demand curves, it measures a movement

[9] These curves are named after Ernst Engel, a pioneer in the study of the relationship between family income and expenditure.

from one demand curve to another as does cross elasticity—because in both cases one of the *ceteris paribus* assumptions is being changed.

SPECIAL CASES OF ELASTICITY

There are several unique elasticity cases that will be used in later chapters. If a function is of the form $P = a$, where a is a constant, the graphical picture of the function will be a horizontal line, parallel to the quantity-axis, at the level of a. In Figure 3.10 we have drawn the function $P = 7$. The elasticity at any point or between any two points on this function, or any function of the type $P = a$, approaches infinity. Demonstrating this first with the arc formula between points A and B,

$$E = \frac{\Delta Q}{\Delta P} \cdot \frac{P_1 + P_2}{Q_1 + Q_2} = \frac{1}{0} \cdot \frac{7 + 7}{2 + 3} \rightarrow \infty \qquad [3.29]$$

To get the point elasticity at point A, we have

$$E = \frac{dQ}{dP} \cdot \frac{P}{Q} \rightarrow \infty \cdot \frac{2}{7} \rightarrow \infty \qquad [3.30]$$

Whenever the denominator of a quotient approaches zero, the quotient approaches infinity. It is obvious that, since the slope of a horizontal demand or supply curve is zero, the reciprocal of the slope approaches infinity and the elasticity of such a line will approach infinity.[10]

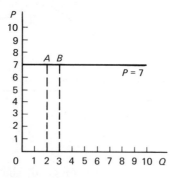

Figure 3.10

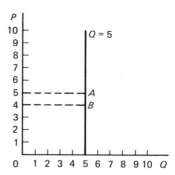

Figure 3.11

A second special case is elasticity along a vertical line that is parallel to the price-axis, that is, a function of the form $Q = a$, where a is a constant. Such a function is pictured in Figure 3.11 where it is assumed

[10] For the sake of brevity, we shall state in the future that the elasticity of such a function is infinity instead of is approaching infinity.

$Q = 5$. If we compute elasticity between points A and B, we get

$$E = \frac{\Delta Q}{\Delta P} \cdot \frac{P_1 + P_2}{Q_1 + Q_2} = \frac{0}{1} \cdot \frac{5 + 4}{5 + 5} = 0 \qquad [3.31]$$

Thus, the elasticity all along a vertical demand or supply curve will be zero.

The last special case we shall consider is the elasticity of a function of the form $PQ = a$, where a is a constant. We have already considered such a case in the function $PQ = 24$, presented in Figure 3.7. If we compute the elasticity between any two points or at any point on this curve, the coefficient is equal to -1, and this would be true for all functions of this type. (The graph of this kind of function is a rectangular hyperbole.)

The reason for the constant elasticity of -1 is quite simple. Remember that the basic purpose of the coefficient of demand or suply elasticity is to compare the percentage change in quantity with the initiating percentage change in price, $\dfrac{\% \text{ change in } Q}{\% \text{ change in } P}$. Since the product of P and Q must stay the same, any percentage change in P must be offset by an equal percentage change in Q in the opposite direction.[11]

PROBLEMS OF EMPIRICAL DEMAND CURVES

The ordinary demand and supply curves of economic theory are schedules of intentions; they tell us what producers and consumers would like to do at various prices. At any one point in time in a market only one point on the supply and demand curve is observable, the equilibrium (P, Q) pair that is consistent with the desires of both producers and consumers.

[11] This is demonstrated rigorously on page 32. The reader familiar with double-log paper will realize that when the function $PQ = 24$ is plotted on such paper, it will be a straight line with a slope of -1. Furthermore, there is a family of constant elastic functions, of which $PQ = a$ is only one member. The basic function for this family of curves is $x^n y = a$ and $E = -n$. Therefore, in our previous example, we have $P^1 Q = 24$ and $E = -1$.

We can prove this as follows:

$$x^n y = a$$
$$y = ax^{-n}$$
$$\frac{dy}{dx} = -nax^{-n-1}$$
$$E = \frac{dy}{dx} \cdot \frac{x}{y} = (-nax^{-n-1}) \frac{x}{y}$$
$$E = \frac{-n(ax^{-n})}{y} = -n\frac{y}{y} = -n$$

Thus, the empirical problem of deriving the demand curve is really a problem of observing equilibrium (P, Q) pairs as the curves shift over time. The first possibility is that demand may be constant and supply shift (Figure 3.12). Here the movement of the supply curve traces out the demand curve.

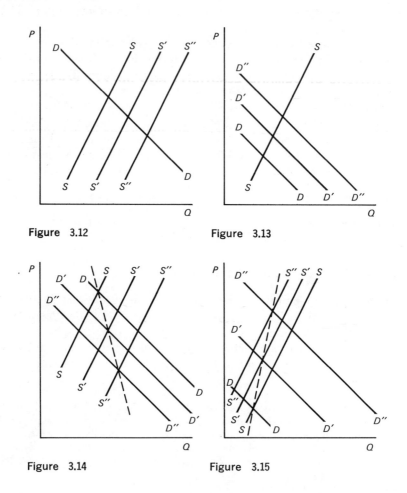

Figure 3.12   Figure 3.13

Figure 3.14   Figure 3.15

This is the ideal case and it is most closely approximated in agricultural markets; it is thus no accident that the most work in estimating empirical demand curves has been done for agriculture commodities.

A second extreme case is where the supply curve is constant and the demand curve shifts. Here it is the supply curve that is traced out by our observed points (Figure 3.13).

A more likely case is one where both supply and demand shift as in Figures 3.14 and 3.15.

If supply shifts more than demand, a negatively sloping curve will be traced out by the observed equilibrium points but its elasticity may differ sharply from that of the true demand curve. If the demand shifts more than supply, a positively sloped curve will result that will differ from the true supply curve.

The problem we have been discussing is called the problem of identification, and it is the most serious faced by the economist who attempts to derive statistical demand curves.

APPLICATIONS OF DEMAND ELASTICITY AND SUPPLY ELASTICITY

Effects of an Excise Tax

Elasticities of demand and supply are important in determining the effects of an excise tax. This is illustrated with reference to Figure 3.16

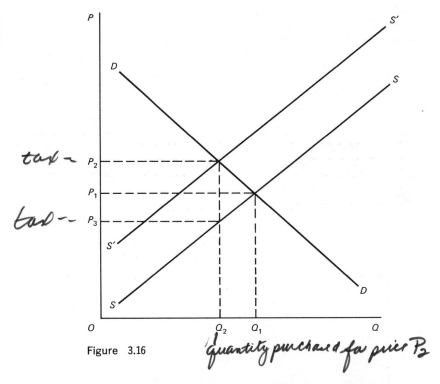

Figure 3.16

quantity purchased for price P₂

where *SS* and *DD* represent the initial supply and demand schedules and P_1 and Q_1 the equilibrium price and quantity. We assume the tax levied to be equal to P_2P_3, and we can show the effects of the tax by shifting the supply curve vertically upward by the amount of the tax. This new supply curve, $S'S'$, shows the prices suppliers must receive for selling various alternative quantities. Thus, after the imposition of the tax, P_2 is the price paid by consumers and Q_2 is the quantity purchased. P_3 is the price kept by producers—P_2 minus the tax of P_2P_3. Whether consumers or producers physically pay the tax makes no difference; this graphical technique—which seems to indicate it is the producers who pay the tax—will show the effect of the tax.[12]

No matter who actually pays the tax, we areed in interest its *incidence*. The concept of incidence simply asks: If a tax of t per unit is imposed upon a commodity, when all adjustments have been made and the market is once again in equilibrium, how will the price paid by the consumer (including the tax if it is imposed on the consumer) compare with the price before the tax was imposed? Analogously, how does the price per unit (after tax if the tax is imposed upon the producer) compare with the price received before the tax was imposed?

The incidence concept does not take into account the loss to consumers who now buy less of the commodity because of its higher price, nor the possible loss in revenue to the producer.

The entire burden of the tax is borne by consumers if the price increases by the amount of the tax; analogously, producers bear the entire burden

[12] There is another graphical technique that will give the same results; in the accompanying diagram, the demand curve is shifted vertically downward by the amount of the tax. Thus, P_2 is the price paid by consumers including the tax; P_3 is the price paid by consumers exclusive of the tax; and Q_2 is the quantity purchased after the tax is levied. This technique indicates that it is the consumer who actually makes the tax payment. The consumer pays P_3 per unit to the producer, but his total cost per unit is P_3 + the tax = $P_3 + P_2P_3 = P_2$. Note that in both cases quantity goes to Q_2. We see, therefore, that the result is identical in the case where we impose the tax on producers or on consumers.

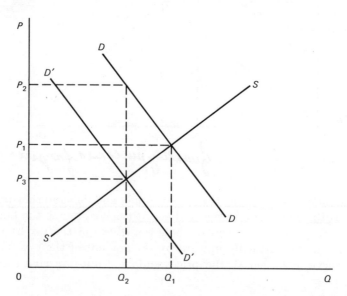

if price, inclusive of the tax, remains the same, for the price then kept by the producers is equal to the original price less the tax.[13] Usually the tax burden is shared in some degree by producers and consumers together; this is the situation in Figure 3.16. We now investigate the determinants of the share of the tax borne by each group. Let

$$T = \text{tax} = P_2 P_3 = \Delta P + \Delta P'$$
$$\Delta P = P_2 - P_1$$
$$\Delta P' = P_1 - P_3$$
$$\Delta Q = Q_2 - Q_1$$
$$a = \text{slope of } DD \text{ (in absolute terms)}$$
$$b = \text{slope of } SS = \text{slope of } S'S' \text{ (in absolute terms)}$$

Therefore,

$$a = \frac{P_2 - P_1}{Q_1 - Q_2} = \frac{\Delta P}{-\Delta Q}$$

$$b = \frac{P_1 - P_3}{Q_1 - Q_2} = \frac{\Delta P'}{-\Delta Q}$$

$$\Delta P = a(-\Delta Q)$$
$$\Delta P' = b(-\Delta Q)$$
$$T = \Delta P + \Delta P' = a(-\Delta Q) + b(-\Delta Q)$$

$$\frac{\Delta P}{\Delta P + \Delta P'} = \text{the proportion of the tax borne by consumers}$$

$$= \frac{a(-\Delta Q)}{a(-\Delta Q) + b(-\Delta Q)} = \frac{a}{a + b} \qquad [3.32]$$

We see the share of the tax borne by consumers is based on the relative slopes of the demand and supply schedules. We now wish to translate this into terms of elasticities of demand and supply[14]:

$$E_d = \frac{1}{a} \cdot \frac{P_1}{Q_1}$$

and

$$E_s = \frac{1}{b} \cdot \frac{P_1}{Q_1}$$

where E_d and E_s are in absolute terms. These can be rewritten as

$$(E_d)a = \frac{P_1}{Q_1}$$

[13] An example will help to clarify this concept. If a $1.00 tax were imposed upon consumers and as a result of the change in their demand the equilibrium price went from $5.00 to $4.50, the price to consumers, including the tax, would now be $5.50. Clearly, 50¢ or 50 percent of the tax is borne by consumers. Also, producers were getting $5.00 per unit and are now getting $4.50; hence, they bear 50¢ or 50 percent of the tax.
[14] This is the point elasticity formula and means we assume a small tax.

and

$$(E_s)b = \frac{P_1}{Q_1}$$

or

$$a = \frac{P_1}{E_d Q_1}$$

and

$$b = \frac{P_1}{E_s Q_1}$$

We can substitute as follows:

$$\frac{a}{a+b} = \text{percentage of tax paid by consumers}$$

$$= \frac{P_1/(E_d Q_1)}{P_1/(E_d Q_1) + P_1/(E_s Q_1)}$$

This expression can be rewritten in simplified form. First we simplify the denominator; then we invert it and multiply it by the numerator:

$$\frac{P_1}{E_d Q_1} + \frac{P_1}{E_s Q_1} = \frac{P_1(E_s Q_1) + P_1(E_d Q_1)}{E_d E_s (Q_1)^2} = \frac{P_1(E_d Q_1 + E_s Q_1)}{E_d E_s (Q_1)^2}$$

$$\frac{a}{a+b} = \frac{P_1}{E_d Q_1} \cdot \frac{E_d E_s (Q_1)^2}{P_1(E_d Q_1 + E_s Q_1)} = \frac{E_s Q_1}{E_d Q_1 + E_s Q_1} = \frac{E_s}{E_d + E_s} \qquad [3.33]$$

Therefore, the share borne by consumers will tend to be greater the higher is E_s or the smaller is E_d.

The student should be able to determine the relationship between the share of the tax paid by producers and the elasticities of supply and demand.

Cobweb Theorem

In our usual supply-demand analysis we assume that suppliers and demanders react to changes in price instantaneously. It is interesting, however, to investigate the process by which equilibrium is achieved in a market in which there is a lag in adjustment of supply to demand. Specifically in markets for agricultural commodities, once the crop has been planted, the supply is, in effect, fixed for the year or some other time period (ignoring weather and other natural phenomena). A change in price of the commodity can be reacted to only after a one-year lag—at the next planting season.

Let us assume an agricultural market in which an equilibrium price and quantity have been established at P_1 and Q_1. (See Figure 3.17a.) Farmers plant an amount Q_1 but during the growing season the demand curve shifts to $D'D'$ and the amount Q_1 sells at a price per unit of P_2. Now, based on a price of P_2, farmers plant Q_2, which fetches a price of P_3; this induces farmers to plant Q_3; and so on.

Notice that price and quantity fluctuate around their new equilibrium values of P_1' and Q_1' and that the fluctuations diminish over time so that equilibrium is finally reached. Figure 3.17b shows a case in which the fluctuations around equilibrium are divergent: They increase in magnitude over time, and so equilibrium is never reached. Figure 3.17c shows a case in which the fluctuations are of constant magnitude, but again equilibrium is not reached.

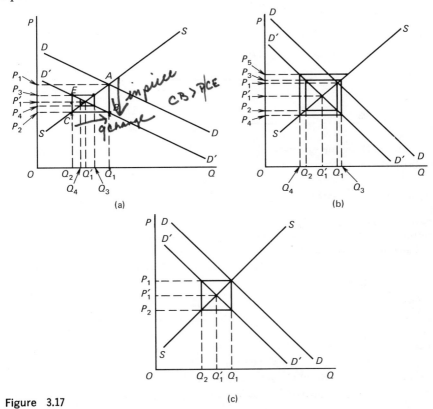

Figure 3.17

It is important to investigate the conditions under which such a lagged system will approach equilibrium—that is, of the type shown in Figure 3.17a. If the movement is to converge, the decrease in price, AB, which gives rise to the quantity change, CB, must be greater than the change in price, CE, that results from the quantity change. In other words, $AB/CB > EC/CB$. Since AB/CB is the slope of the supply curve and EC/CB is the slope (disregarding sign) of the demand curve, we can see that for convergence, the slope of the supply curve must be greater than the slope of the demand curve (disregarding sign).

This condition can be stated in terms of elasticities of demand and supply.[15]

$$|E_d| = \frac{CB}{EC} \cdot \frac{P_1}{Q_1}$$

and[16]

$$|E_s| = \frac{CB}{AB} \cdot \frac{P_1}{Q_1}$$

Therefore,

$$\frac{P_1}{Q_1} = |E_d| \cdot \frac{EC}{CB}$$

and

$$\frac{P_1}{Q_1} = |E_s| \cdot \frac{AB}{CB}$$

Since

$$\frac{P_1}{Q_1} = \frac{P_1}{Q_1}, \qquad |E_d| \cdot \frac{EC}{CB} = |E_s| \cdot \frac{AB}{CB}$$

We know that for convergence, $AB/CD > EC/CB$. Therefore, it must also hold that if there is to be convergence, $|E_d| > |E_s|$.

EMPIRICAL STUDIES

Demand for Subway Service

Table 3.3 gives an estimated demand schedule for subway service in New York City as of 1950: In addition we show the arc elasticity coefficients between each pair of prices.

Although the demand is inelastic for the range of prices shown, the student should note that it becomes less so as price increases. One probable reason for this is that the range of available substitutes increases as price increases; for example, for a short distance, a taxi becomes a fairly good substitute for a \$.30 subway ride. The reader should now be able to predict what happened to the revenue of the subway system in 1950 after the fare was changed from 5 to 10 cents.

Demand for Beef and Pork

The information in Table 3.4 was obtained from a consumer survey in Medford, Massachusetts, during 1952 to 1953.

[15] Note that we are using absolute values of the elasticity coefficients.
[16] See note 14. Further, with straight-line demand and supply curves, the slopes are the same along the curves. This permits us to state our conditions for divergence and convergence at the point of intersection of the curves where the point is the same for both curves and the elasticity measures will have a common term.

TABLE 3.3

Fare	Passengers (millions per year)	Arc Elasticity
$0.00	2248	
		—.07
0.05	1945	
		—.36
0.10	1683	
		—.36
0.15	1458	
		—.50
0.20	1262	
		—.65
0.25	1092	
		—.79
$0.30	945	

[handwritten annotation: as P↑ As do alternative substrate ⇒ unev]

TABLE 3.4

Period	Beef Price per lb.	Pork Price per lb.	Average Weekly Purchases (lbs. per family)		Elasticity Coefficients	
			Beef	Pork	E_{beef}	$E_{pork/beef}$
I	$0.89	$0.60	2.72	2.25		
					—.64	.52
II	0.68	0.60	3.23	1.96		
III	$0.62	$0.71	3.32	1.57		

Source: Charles J. Zwick, "A Study in the Demand for Meat," unpublished Ph.D. thesis, Harvard University, p. 134, Table 4.7.

Only two elasticity coefficients were computed: the price elasticity of beef for a change in the price of beef from $0.89 to $0.68 and the cross elasticity of demand between beef and pork for the same change in the price of beef. It should be clear to the reader that it would be meaningless to calculate any price elasticity for pork and the price elasticity for beef between periods I and III and II and III and the cross elasticity of demand for beef for a change in the price of pork. In the first two cases, the price of the competing good is not constant; and in the last case, the price of the good itself is not constant so that the net effect of a change in the price of the competing good cannot be isolated. In the cases for which the coefficients were computed, it was implicitly assumed that over the short period under consideration average income was constant, tastes did not change, and prices of other goods remained the same.

Elasticity Coefficients and Tax Policy

Listed in Table 3.5 are some estimates of demand elasticities (at the prevailing prices) for several products (in absolute terms).

TABLE   3.5

Products	Estimates
Automobiles	1.0
Automobile parts and accessories	0.5
Automobile tires and tubes	0.0
Electric light bulbs	0.33
Furs	2.30
Matches	0.0
Motion-picture tickets	0.43
Phonographs and radios	1.5
Safe-deposit boxes	0.0 -

Source: Revenue Revisions of 1950, Hearings before the Committee on Ways and Means of the House of Representatives, 81st Congress, 2nd Session, pp. 980–981.

These coefficients were presented in hearings concerning excise taxes. If the government were interested only in maximizing its tax revenues, the commodities from this list it would choose to tax would be automobile tires and tubes, matches, and safe-deposit boxes, all of which have completely inelastic demands.

It is often contended that goods with high price elasticities are luxuries while those with low coefficients are necessities. What sense does this make in light of these data?

4

THEORY OF DEMAND: CLASSICAL UTILITY APPROACH

Economists have not generally been content with noting the observable general inverse relationship between the price of a commodity and the amount purchased by consumers; nor have they been satisfied simply to postulate negative sloping demand curves based on this evidence. They have attempted, rather, to explain the observable demand phenomena through an analysis of the way in which consumers attempt in some "optimum" sense to spend their incomes on the commodities available to them. We shall review the classical utility approach to consumer equilibrium in this chapter and the indifference curve approach in the following chapter.

TOTAL AND MARGINAL UTILITY

It is assumed that the consumer has a finite money income, I, and that he is faced by n commodities $(a, b, \ldots, n)$ with prices P_a, P_b, $\ldots, P_n$. It is also assumed that the consumer will want to spend his income in such a manner as to maximize the benefit or satisfaction he receives from it.[1] We give the name "utility" to the subjective quantity the individual is assumed to maximize. Given that the individual is consuming quantity q_a of the commodity A per unit of time, he will then be receiving U_a (*total utility*), which is the total satisfaction to him of consuming this amount.

[1] This is the rationality postulate that assumes that the consumer is aware of the alternatives facing him, that he is capable of evaluating them, and that his choices will be consistent.

We may also ask what is the change in total utility at any quantity due to changing quantity consumed by one unit—this measure is called *marginal utility* (MU_a) and is defined for the discrete case as

$$MU_a = \frac{\Delta U_a}{\Delta q_a} \qquad\qquad [4.1]$$

or for continuous functions as

$$MU_a = \frac{dU_a}{dq_a} \qquad\qquad [4.1a]$$

Table 4.1 gives examples of total utility and marginal utility schedules. Total utility and continuous marginal utility are shown graphically in

TABLE 4.1

Total and Marginal Utility Schedules

(1) q_a	(2) U_a	(3) $MU_a = \dfrac{dU_a}{dq_a}$	(4) $MU_a = \dfrac{\Delta U_a}{\Delta q_a}$
0	0		
			100
1	100	95	
			90
2	190	85	
			80
3	270	75	
			70
4	340	65	
			60
5	400	55	
			50
6	450	45	
			40
7	490	35	
			30
8	520	25	
			20
9	540	15	
			10
10	550	5	
			0
11	550	−5	

Column 2 is derived from the equation $U_a = 105q_a - 5q_a{}^2$.
Column 3 is continuous MU that can be derived from the
  equation $dU_a/dq_a = 105 - 10q_a$.
Column 4 is discrete MU and is equal to $\Delta U_a/\Delta q_a$.

Figures 4.1 and 4.2. In graphical terms, MU represents the slope of the total utility schedule.

Notice that the MU column shows MU declining as quantity increases. Although this is the assumption usually made, it is conceivable that for certain goods there is increasing MU over an initial range. For example, if a good is more useful when used in sets, then MU will increase—at least at first.[2]

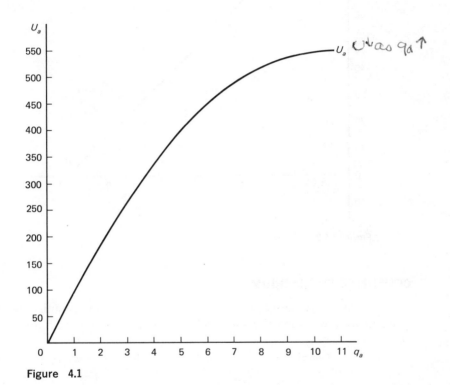

Figure 4.1

The so-called law of diminishing marginal utility—the proposition that as an individual consumes more units of a commodity the increments to his satisfaction due to receiving an additional unit decrease—was generally defended on subjective grounds as being intuitively obvious because the desire for a particular good will become relatively satiated.

The classical utility approach depends on a concept of cardinal utility; that is, it is assumed that the consumer not only knows that he prefers A to B but he can give numerical expression to his desires that permits him to say he prefers A, say, twice as much as B.

[2] Of course, if a single unit of the good is useless by itself, then the correct unit of measurement would be the set—for example, shoes and gloves.

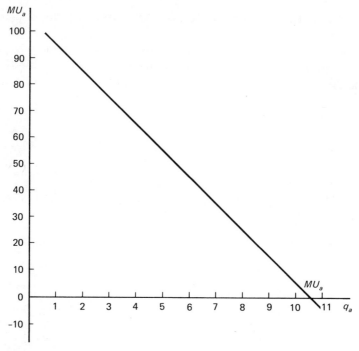

Figure 4.2

CONSUMER EQUILIBRIUM

Given our rationality assumption and the law of diminishing marginal utility, we have the following two equilibrium conditions for the consumer:

$$\text{Condition 1:} \qquad I = q_a P_a + q_b P_b + \cdots + q_n P_n \qquad [4.2]$$

Some of the quantities $q_a \ldots q_n$ may be zero. Further, we may include saving by having as one of our terms the present marginal utility of the future yield of earning assets as a ratio of the current price and by having as another of our terms the marginal utility of idle balances as a ratio of their cost in terms of the forgone rate of return. Condition 1 simply states that all income will be spent.

$$\text{Condition 2:} \qquad \frac{MU_a}{P_a} = \frac{MU_b}{P_b} = \frac{MU_c}{P_c} = \cdots = \frac{MU_n}{P_n} \qquad [4.3]$$

Condition 2 states that in equilibrium the MU's must be in proportion to prices. We have said that the rational consumer will want to maximize his satisfaction, given his income and preferences. Condition 2 will be, therefore, a true equilibrium condition if it is impossible for the consumer, once having achieved this condition, to increase U by rearranging his expenditures. The assumption of diminishing marginal utility guarantees that, when condition 2 is fulfilled, the consumer has indeed a distribution of expenditures where he is maximizing utility. We can see this in an example. Suppose that an individual consumes only A and B, which are substitutes for one another, and that he is allocating his expenditures so that $MU_a/P_a = MU_b/P_b$ and that the numerical values are 50/\$2 = 100/\$4. If the individual removes \$1 from A he will lose 25 utils, but when he increases his consumption of B, MU_b will fall and he will gain something less than 25 utils. Therefore, since the gain is less than the loss, he should not undertake this rearrangement of expenditure—he was already at a maximum.

We can show this point somewhat differently by assuming that the consumer is distributing his expenditures so that $MU_a/P_a \neq MU_b/P_b$. In numerical terms assume 60/\$2 > 80/\$4. In this case the individual is receiving 30 marginal utils per dollar of expenditure on A and 20 utils per dollar of expenditure on B. Clearly, if he shifts a dollar of his expenditure from B to A he will lose 20 utils and gain approximately 30. Hence he will arrange his expenditure so that $MU_a/P_a = MU_b/P_b$, and if we assume diminishing MU this guarantees he is at maximum U.

These utility schedules are assumed to be independent of each other. This, in fact, was the assumption made by the founders of utility theory—Stanley Jevons, Leon Walras, Carl Menger, and Alfred Marshall. If equilibrium conditions 1 and 2 are satisfied, their assumption assures that the individual will indeed be maximizing satisfaction and, further, that he can only be maximizing satisfaction if these conditions are fulfilled.[3] In addition, the independence assumption results in all Engel curves being positively sloped (all goods are superior) and all demand curves negatively sloped.

If the utilities are interdependent, the utility the individual derives from A will depend not only on the quantity of A he consumes but also on the quantities of goods $B \cdots N$ that he consumes. The interdependence between two goods can take the form of either complementarity or rivalry. In terms of utility theory, complementarity may be defined as a relationship between two goods such that an increase in the quantity consumed of one causes the marginal utility schedule of the other to shift upward. Analogously, rivalry exists if the marginal utility schedule of the second good shifts downward when the quantity consumed of the first increases. Thus, the assumption of independence rules out complementarity and rival relationships between commodities.

[3] In mathematical terms, this means that with independent utility functions, conditions 1 and 2 are both necessary and sufficient for maximization of utility. This point is explored further in Appendix 4A.

Despite its obvious limitations, the marginal utility approach assuming independence of utilities did cast revealing light on a paradox that had concerned such eminent economists as Adam Smith and David Ricardo. How is it, they asked, that diamonds, which are not necessary to life, have a higher market value than water, which is necessary to life. This question confuses marginal with total utility; it is the former that is a determinant of value.

DERIVATION OF DEMAND SCHEDULE FROM MU SCHEDULE

Using the concept of marginal utility it is possible to explain the shape of a demand schedule as well as shifts in demand. We demonstrate this with the use of a numerical example. A consumer who spends his entire income on two goods, A and B, has utility schedules for these goods as shown in Table 4.2, where the schedules for good A are the same as those in Table 4.1.

TABLE 4.2

Total and Marginal Utility Schedules

(1) q_a	(2) U_a	(3) MU_a	(4) $\dfrac{MU_a}{P_a\,(=\$5)}$	(5) q_b	(6) U_b	(7) MU_b	(8) $\dfrac{MU_b}{P_b\,(=\$10)}$	(9) $\dfrac{MU_b}{P_b\,(=\$8)}$
1	100	95	$ 19	1	40	38	$ 3.80	$ 4.75
2	190	85	17	2	76	34	3.40	4.25
3	270	75	15	3	108	30	3.00	3.75
4	340	65	13	4	136	26	2.60	3.25
5	400	55	11	5	160	22	2.20	2.75
6	450	45	9	6	180	18	1.80	2.25
7	490	35	7	7	196	14	1.40	1.75
8	520	25	5	8	208	10	1.00	1.25
9	540	15	3	9	216	6	0.60	0.75
10	550	5	1	10	220	2	0.20	0.25
11	550	−5	$−1	11	220	−2	$−0.20	$−0.25

Column 2 is derived from the equation $U_a = 105\,q_a - 5q_a{}^2$.
Column 3 is continuous MU_a derived from the equation $MU_a = 105 - 10q_a$.
Column 6 is derived from the equation $U_b = 42\,q_b - 2q_b{}^2$.
Column 7 is continuous MU_b derived from the equation $MU_b = 42 - 4q_b$.

If the price of good A is initially \$5 and of good B \$10, and if the consumer's income is \$130, the initial equilibrium quantities the consumer will purchase are 10 units of A and 8 units of B. To prove that this is a true equilibrium situation, we show that conditions 1 and 2 are met:

Condition 1: $\quad I = q_a P_a + q_b P_b$

$\$130 = (10)\$5 + (8)\$10$

Condition 2: $\quad \dfrac{MU_a}{P_a} = \dfrac{MU_b}{P_b}$

$$\frac{5}{\$5} = \frac{10}{\$10}$$

$$1 = 1$$

These results can be obtained graphically from Figure 4.3. In the left-hand portion of the graph is plotted $MU_b/\$5$ (with the horizontal axis

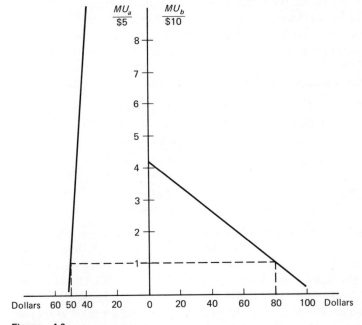

Figure 4.3

read from right to left) and in the right-hand portion, $MU_b/\$10$. Instead of showing these as functions of the quantities of A and B, we have placed dollars on the horizontal axis. Thus, to plot the combination $A = 8$, $MU_a/\$5 = 5$ from Table 4.2, the horizontal axis coordinate is $\$40$, as 8 units of A in dollar terms is $\$40$ ($= \$5 \times 8$ units). Since we assumed an income of $\$130$, equilibrium exists when $MU_a/\$5 = MU_b/\$10$ and the absolute distance between the two schedules is $\$130$ (line AB).[4]

[4] See Appendix 4B for the algebraic solution.

We now assume a change in P_b from $10 per unit to $8. If the consumer desired to continue buying the same quantities of A and B as before, he would be spending $114:

$$q_a P_a + q_b P_b = \text{expenditure}$$
$$(10 \cdot \$5) + (8 \cdot \$8) = \$114$$

Therefore, there has been an increase of $16 in the consumer's purchasing power. Notice that neither equilibrium condition is being fulfilled:

Condition 1: $\$130 > 10 \cdot \$5 + 8 \cdot \$8 = \$114$

Condition 2: $\dfrac{5}{\$5} < \dfrac{10}{\$8}$

As a result of both the change in relative prices and the resulting increase in purchasing power, the consumer must once again redistribute his income of $130 in such a way as to maximize his satisfaction. This new equilibrium position is achieved when the consumer buys (rounded off to three decimal places) 10.325 units of A and 9.797 units of B, because with these quantities both equilibrium conditions are being fulfilled:

Condition 1: $q_a P_a + q_b P_b = I$
$$(10.325)\$5 + (9.797)\$8 = \$51.625 + \$78.376 = \$130$$

Condition 2: $\dfrac{MU_a}{P_a} = \dfrac{MU_b}{P_b}$

$$\dfrac{1.75}{\$5} = \dfrac{2.812}{\$8}$$

$$0.35 = 0.35$$

These results can be obtained approximately from Figure 4.4, where the MU_a/P_a schedule is the same as in Figure 4.3, but the MU_b/P_b is now based on $P_b = \$8$. The line $AB = \$130$; thus equilibrium occurs when $51.625 is spent on A (or $\$51.625/\$5 = 10.325$ units of A) and $78.376 is spent on B (or $\$78.376/\$8 = 9.797$ units of B).[5]

It is possible to derive the demand schedule for good B by assuming a sufficient number of prices for B and then determining the equilibrium quantity of B that the consumer would buy at each of these prices.

Marginal utility analysis explains why a demand curve shifts when a change occurs in the consumer's income or tastes, or in the price of some other commodity. Thus, in our numerical example, when the price of B changed, the demand for A also changed. Analogously, if the individual's income increased, there would be an increase in the demand for both A and B provided they were not inferior goods.[6] A change in tastes would influence the level and shape of the marginal utility curve and, at any

[5] See Appendix 4B for the algebraic solution.
[6] See the final section in this chapter.

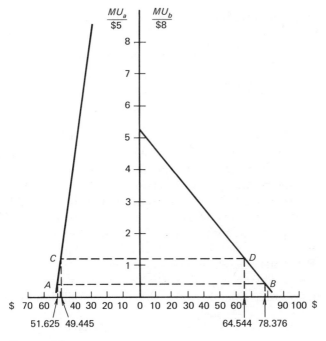

Figure 4.4

particular price, the consumer would desire a different quantity of the commodity affected.

INCOME AND SUBSTITUTION EFFECTS

For analytical purposes it is sometimes useful to break down the effect of the price change into its two parts:

1. The effect due to the change in relative prices alone—*the substitution effect.*
2. The effect due to the change in purchasing power resulting from the change in the price of one good—*the income effect.*

In order to distinguish between these two, we first assume (simply as an expository device) that, after the reduction in price of good B, a tax is levied on the consumer equal to the increase in his purchasing power—$16—and we determine the quantities of goods A and B he would purchase in response to this change in relative prices alone.

After determining these quantities, we next assume that a subsidy of $16 is paid to the consumer. We make this assumption in order to determine what the effects of an increase in income of $16 are on the quantities of A and B purchased if no change in relative prices occurs.

When the $16 tax is levied on the consumer, income again becomes

$114; however, equilibrium is not achieved because the second condition is not being satisfied:

Condition 1: $114 = (10)\$5 + (8)\$8$

Condition 2: $\dfrac{5}{\$5} < \dfrac{10}{\$8}$

$1 < 1.25$

The consumer, by transferring a dollar of expenditure away from A, will lose 1 util; and by spending that dollar on B will gain approximately 1.25 utils. This is a net increase of roughly 0.25 util.

The equilibrium resulting from the efforts of the consumer once again to distribute his expenditures in an optimum fashion would be 9.891 units of A and 8.068 units of B. This is demonstrated in Figure 4.4. When $114 is spent on both goods (line CD) equilibrium is achieved when $49.455 is spent on A (or $49.455/\$5 = 9.891$ units of A) and $64.544 on B (or $64.544/\$8 = 8.068$ units of B).[7]

When the $16 subsidy is paid to the consumer, a new disequilibrium situation arises, this time because the first equilibrium condition is violated:

Condition 1: $130 > (9.891)\$5 + (8.068)\$8 = \$114$

Condition 2: $\dfrac{6.09}{\$5} = \dfrac{9.728}{\$8}$

$1.22 = 1.22$

Clearly, if the individual is to maintain an equality between MU_a/P_a and MU_b/P_b, he must spend more on both A and B.[8] As we saw before, the final new equilibrium position is reached when the consumer buys 10.325 units of A and 9.797 units of B.

Before proceeding further, in Table 4.3 we summarize the income and substitution effects of the decrease in the price of B.

AN ASIDE ON INCOME EFFECTS

For a given good, the substitution effect is always negative: As P decreases, quantity increases, and vice versa. The income effect, however, may be either positive or negative, depending on the consumer's tastes. For most goods, when the consumer experiences an increase in income, he will buy more of the commodity; these are called "superior" goods. There are some goods (oleo, potatoes, bread, subway rides) that are considered "inferior" by many consumers who buy less of the goods when incomes rise.

---

[7] See Appendix 4B for the algebraic solution.
[8] This rests on our assumption of diminishing MU for both goods.

TABLE   4.3

		Quantities	
		Good A	Good B
1	Initial equilibrium	10.000	6.000
2	Equilibrium after reduction in P_b to $8 and compensating decrease in income of $16	9.891	8.068
3	Equilibrium after a subsidy of $16 (final equilibrium)	10.325	9.797
4	Substitution effect = (2) − (1)	−0.109	+2.068
5	Income effect = (3) − (2)	+0.434	+1.729
6	Net effect = (3) − (1) = (4) + (5)	+0.325	+3.797

Because the net effect of a price change is the sum of the income and substitution effects[9] and because the substitution effect is always in the direction of giving negatively sloping demand curves, it is to the income effect that one must look for a positive reaction of quantity to an increase in price. This would clearly occur if a powerful negative income effect (for an inferior good) were to overpower a weaker substitution effect. Such a good, which would have a positively sloping demand curve, is called a Giffen good and is discussed in more detail in Chapter 5.

[9] Alfred Marshall, who was responsible for the fullest development of the utility analysis of demand, avoided the complication of income effects by assuming the commodities under discussion to constitute only a small part of a consumer's budget and that one could safely disregard the consequently unimportant income effects. This was a convenient analytical simplification, but it avoided the problem of income effects instead of solving it. See Appendix 4C.

Appendix 4A

Mathematical Conditions for Consumer Equilibrium

Assume that there are but two commodities, A and B, with prices P_a and P_b and that the individual has an income, I, which he spends on the two commodities.

$$I = q_a P_a + q_b P_b \qquad \text{Income constraint} \qquad \text{[4A.1]}$$

$$U = U(q_a, q_b) \qquad \text{Utility function} \qquad \text{[4A.2]}$$

We may rewrite equation 4A.1 as

$$\frac{I - q_a P_a}{P_b} = q_b \qquad \text{[4A.3]}$$

and then rewrite equation 4A.2 as

$$U = U\left(q_a, \frac{I - q_a P_a}{P_b}\right) \qquad \text{[4A.4]}$$

Let[1]

$$u_a = \frac{\partial U}{\partial q_a}$$

and

$$u_b = \frac{\partial U}{\partial q_b}$$

We now compute

$$\frac{dU}{dq_a} = u_a + u_b\left(-\frac{P_a}{P_b}\right) \qquad \text{[4A.5]}$$

Set this expression equal to zero:

$$u_a + u_b\left(-\frac{P_a}{P_b}\right) = 0 \qquad \text{[4A.6]}$$

$$u_a = u_b\left(\frac{P_a}{P_b}\right) \qquad \text{[4A.7]}$$

or

$$\frac{u_a}{u_b} = \frac{P_a}{P_b} \qquad \text{[4A.8]}$$

[1] For a discussion of partial derivatives, see Appendix 4D.

or

$$\frac{u_a}{P_a} = \frac{u_b}{P_b} \qquad [4A.9]$$

Equation 4A.9, which states that for utility to be maximized the marginal utility of the goods consumed must be proportional to their prices, is a necessary but not a sufficient condition for maximization of utility. This condition ensures only that an extreme—either a maximum or a minimum—has been found. To ensure a maximum a "second order" condition must be fulfilled (that is, a condition involving second partial derivatives).

Let

$$u_{aa} = \frac{\partial^2 U}{\partial q_a{}^2}$$

$$u_{bb} = \frac{\partial^2 U}{\partial q_b{}^2}$$

$$u_{ab} = \frac{\partial^2 U}{\partial q_a \partial q_b}$$

For a maximum to exist, the following must be true

$$\frac{d}{dq_a}\left[\frac{dU}{dq_a}\right] < 0$$

$$\frac{dU}{dq_a} = u_a + u_b\left[-\frac{P_a}{P_o}\right] \cdot \qquad [4A.5]$$

$$\frac{d}{dq_a}\left[\frac{dU}{dq_a}\right] = \frac{d^2U}{dq_a{}^2} = u_{aa} + u_{ab}\frac{dq_b}{dq_a} + \left[u_{ab} + u_{bb}\frac{dq_b}{dq_a}\right]\left[-\frac{P_a}{P_b}\right]$$

We substitute

$$\frac{dq_b}{dq_a} = -\frac{P_a}{P_b}$$

$$\frac{d^2U}{dq_a{}^2} = u_{aa} + u_{ab}\left(-\frac{P_a}{P_b}\right) + u_{ab}\left(-\frac{P_a}{P_b}\right) + u_{bb}\left(-\frac{P_a}{P_b}\right)^2$$

$$\frac{d^2U}{dq_a{}^2} = \left[u_{aa} + 2u_{ab}\left(-\frac{P_a}{P_b}\right) + u_{bb}\left(-\frac{P_a}{P_b}\right)^2\right] < 0$$

$$= \left[u_{aa} + 2u_{ab}\left(-\frac{P_a}{P_b}\right) + u_{bb}\left(\frac{P_a{}^2}{P_b{}^2}\right)\right] < 0 \quad [4A.10]$$

Multiply by $(P_b)^2$ and the inequality remains.

$$[(u_{aa}P_b{}^2) - (2u_{ab}P_aP_b) + (u_{bb}P_a{}^2)] < 0 \qquad [4A.11]$$

If an additive utility function is assumed, so that the utility of each commodity is independent of the utility of the other commodities (this was generally assumed by the founders of utility theory), u_{ab} would be 0.

If then we assume diminishing marginal utility to hold for both commodities, that is $u_{aa} < 0$, $u_{bb} < 0$, then the entire expression on the left is negative and the second condition for a maximum is fulfilled. The role of the assumption of diminishing marginal utility is therefore to ensure that the "second order" condition will be met.

It can be seen, however, that in our general utility function this condition could be fulfilled even if $u_{aa} > 0$ and $u_{bb} > 0$, provided that $u_{ab} > 0$ and the negative middle term were large enough to overpower the end terms. It could also be fulfilled if one commodity displayed diminishing marginal utility and the other did not if the sum of the negative terms were greater (in absolute terms) than the positive terms. On the other hand, if u_{ab} is negative the entire expression may be positive even when $u_{aa} < 0$ and $u_{bb} < 0$. From these considerations it is clear that diminishing marginal utility is necessary and sufficient in order that the second order conditions for maximum total utility be fulfilled only in the case of an additive utility function (a function in which the utilities of the goods are assumed independent).

Indifference curve analysis permits a less restrictive assumption to be made. This will be discussed in Chapter 5.

Appendix 4B

Algebra of Income and Substitution Effects

The initial equilibrium levels of A and B can be determined algebraically in the following way. The equations for the MU schedules are (see Table 4.2)

$$MU_a = 105 - 10q_a \qquad \text{[4B.1]}$$
$$MU_b = 42 - 4q_b \qquad \text{[4B.2]}$$

Therefore,

$$\frac{MU_a}{P_a} = \frac{MU_a}{\$5} = 21 - 2q_a \qquad \text{[4B.3]}$$

$$\frac{MU_b}{P_b} = \frac{MU_b}{\$10} = 4.2 + 0.4q_b \qquad \text{[4B.4]}$$

We assumed that the consumer spends his entire income on these goods:

$$\$5q_a + \$10q_b = \$130 \qquad \text{[4B.5]}$$

or

$$\$5q_a = \$130 - \$10q_b$$
$$q_a = 26 - 2q_b \qquad \text{[4B.6]}$$

Substituting in equation 4B.3, we have

$$\frac{MU_a}{P_a} = 21 - 2(26 - 2q_b) = 21 - 52 + 4q_b = -31 + 4q_b \qquad \text{[4B.7]}$$

In equilibrium $MU_a/P_a = MU_b/P_b$. Therefore,

$$-31 + 4q_b = 4.2 + 0.4q_b \qquad \text{[4B.8]}$$

Solving for q_b, we have

$$4.4q_b = 35.2$$
$$q_b = 8$$

Substituting in equation 4B.6, we have

$$q_a = 26 - 2(8)$$
$$q_a = 10 \qquad \text{[4B.9]}$$

To determine the new equilibrium quantity of A and B after P_b changes from \$10 to \$8, we can follow the same procedure as just given:

$$MU_a = 105 - 10q_a \qquad\qquad\text{[4B.1]}$$

$$MU_b = 42 - 4q_b \qquad\qquad\text{[4B.2]}$$

$$\frac{MU_a}{P_a} = \frac{MU_a}{\$5} = 21 - 2q_a \qquad\qquad\text{[4B.3]}$$

$$\frac{MU_b}{P_b} = \frac{MU_b}{\$10} = 5.25 - 0.5q_b \qquad\qquad\text{[4B.4]}$$

$$\$5q_a + \$8q_b = \$130 \qquad\qquad\text{[4B.5]}$$

or

$$\$5q_a = \$130 - \$8q_b$$

$$q_a = 26 - 1.6q_b \qquad\qquad\text{[4B.6]}$$

$$\frac{MU_a}{P_a} = 21 - 2(26 - 1.6q_b) = 21 - 52 + 3.2q_b = -31 + 3.2q_b \quad\text{[4B.7]}$$

$$-31 + 3.2q_b = 5.25 - 0.5q_b$$

$$3.7q_b = 36.25$$

$$q_b = 9.797 \qquad\qquad\text{[4B.8]}$$

$$q_a = 26 - 1.6(9.797) = 26 - 15.675 \qquad\qquad\text{[4B.9]}$$

$$q_a = 10.325$$

Once again the same method can be used to determine the substitution effect of the decrease in P_b from \$10 to \$8:

$$MU_a = 105 - 10q_a \qquad\qquad\text{[4B.1]}$$

$$MU_b = 42 - 4q_b \qquad\qquad\text{[4B.2]}$$

$$\frac{MU_a}{P_a} = \frac{MU_a}{\$5} = 21 - 2q_a \qquad\qquad\text{[4B.3]}$$

$$\frac{MU_b}{P_b} = \frac{MU_b}{\$8} = 5.25 - 0.5q_b \qquad\qquad\text{[4B.4]}$$

$$\$5q_a + \$8q_b = \$114 \qquad\qquad\text{[4B.5]}$$

or

$$\$5q_a = \$114 - \$8q_b$$

$$q_a = 22.8 - 1.6q_b \qquad\qquad\text{[4B.6]}$$

$$\frac{MU_a}{P_a} = 21 - 2(22.8 - 1.6q_b) = 21 - 45.6 + 3.2q_b = -24.6 + 3.2q_b \quad\text{[4B.7]}$$

$$-24.6 + 3.2q_b = 5.25 - 0.5q_b$$

$$3.7q_b = 29.85$$

$$q_b = 8.068 \qquad\qquad\text{[4B.8]}$$

$$q_a = 22.8 - 1.6(8.068) = 22.8 - 12.909$$

$$q_a = 9.891 \qquad\qquad\text{[4B.9]}$$

Appendix 4C

Marshallian Assumption of Constant Marginal Utility of Money

A consumer purchasing n commodities will fulfill the following condition in equilibrium:

$$\frac{MU_a}{P_a} = \frac{MU_b}{P_b} = \cdots = \frac{MU_n}{P_n} = Z \qquad \text{[4C.1]}$$

Z represents the common ratio of marginal utility to price in equilibrium and has been called the marginal utility of money or the marginal utility of income—the gain in total satisfaction from the marginal dollar of expenditure. Now, if the consumer purchases many commodities and we choose one that represents only a small part of his expenditures, any ordinary change in its price will result in but a small change in purchasing power. Further, when this small change in real income is redistributed among the many commodities the individual buys, there will be very little adjustment of purchases and consequently very little change in Z, the marginal utility of money. Therefore, for a commodity that represents a small part of a consumer's budget, we may, as a simplification, assume Z to be constant; this amounts to ignoring income effects of price changes as being insignificantly small. Now, if Z can be assumed constant, we may write that in equilibrium for commodity A

$$P_a = MU_a \cdot \frac{1}{Z} \qquad \text{[4C.2]}$$

where $1/Z = P_a/MU_a$ and represents the money cost of a marginal util. $MU_a(1/Z)$, therefore, represents marginal utility measured in money terms. The equation states that an individual will purchase a commodity up to the point where the price of the commodity is equal to its marginal utility measured in money terms.

Further, since $1/Z$ is a constant, the demand curve becomes simply the marginal utility curve multiplied by a constant—the reciprocal of the marginal utility of money—that converts it into a marginal utility curve along which MU is measured in dollar units. Further, it is possible to take areas under the MU curve and derive a total utility measure that is also expressed in terms of the MU of money.[1]

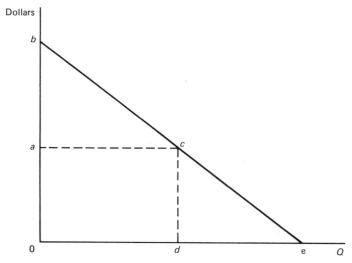

Figure 4.C.1

Under the assumptions just given in Figure 4C.1, if the individual faces a market price of a he will purchase d. His total utility from the commodity (measured in money terms) will be $Obcd$; his expenditures $Oacd$; and he therefore has excess utility of abc, which is called his consumer's surplus. Now the consumer is willing to pay for any unit of the commodity up to its marginal utility (measured in money terms) rather than go without it. This means that by charging for each unit of the commodity the maximum price the consumer will pay, a monopolist can take the consumer's surplus abc unto himself; this is discussed in Chapter 9.

---

[1] Given the function $U = f(q)$ and $MU = f'(q)$, the Marshallian measure gives us $\dfrac{1}{Z}[f'(q)]$. Taking the area under the Marshallian demand curve amounts to

$$\int_0^q \left[\frac{1}{Z}f'(q)\right] dq = \frac{1}{Z}\int_0^q f'(q)dq = \left[\frac{1}{Z}f(q)\right]_0^q$$

Appendix 4D

Partial Derivatives

In Chapter 3 we derived a measure of the effect on the dependent variable of a change in the independent variable. This rate of change we called "slope," the "marginal concept," or—when the changes are infinitesimally small—the "derivative." Most frequently in economics, we deal with a function of more than one independent variable (for example, the utility function) of the form $y = f(x_1 x_2, \ldots, x_n)$. There are many occasions when we wish to measure the effect on the dependent variable of a change in one of the independent variables while holding the rest of the independent variables constant. (This is the *ceteris paribus* assumption we used in our discussion of demand.) These rates of change, called partial derivatives, can best be explained with reference to Figure 4D.1. We desire to find the rate of change of Z with respect to y, holding x constant at the value x_1 in Figure 4D.1a. Holding x constant at x_1 and varying y from y_0 through y_n traces out the curve $Z_n y_n$, which we then show on a two-dimensional diagram in Figure 4D.1b. The procedure to determine this partial derivative is now the same as we used in Chapter 3 except that x (or any number of variables) is held constant. The notion of a partial derivative can be seen as

$$\lim_{\substack{y \to 0 \\ x = \bar{x}_0}} \frac{\Delta f(x, y)}{\Delta y} = \frac{\partial f}{\partial y}$$

The symbol "∂" has the same meaning as "d" except for the constancy of another variable or variables.

An inspection of Figure 4D.1b shows that the slope is becoming greater in absolute terms (or less in algebraic terms). If we want to measure the rate of change of this slope with respect to y, we take the following derivative:

$$\left[\frac{\partial \left(\frac{\partial f}{\partial y} \right)}{\partial y} \right]$$

which is usually written $\dfrac{\partial^2 f}{\partial y^2}$. This measures the rate of change with respect to y of the rate of change of $f(x, y)$ with respect to y. This is called a

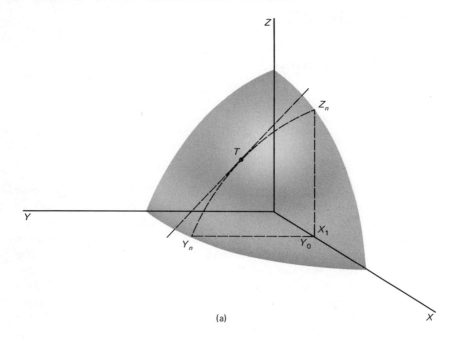

(a)

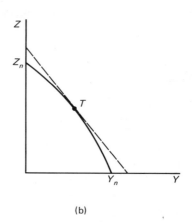

(b)

Figure 4.D.1

second-order partial derivative. This process can be carried on any number of times to generate n-order partial derivatives.

It is obvious that this procedure could have been carried on with respect to x; that is, holding y constant at some level we could calculate $\dfrac{\partial f}{\partial x}$ and all higher-order derivatives.

It is also useful at times to determine how the partial derivative with respect to one variable is effected by a change in another variable. This is called a cross-partial derivative. For example, the effect on $\dfrac{\partial f}{\partial y}$ of a change in x is $\dfrac{\partial\left(\dfrac{\partial f}{\partial y}\right)}{\partial x}$ or in simpler notation $\dfrac{\partial^2 f}{\partial x \partial y}$. Similarly, higher-order cross-partial derivatives can be determined.

5

THEORY OF DEMAND: INDIFFERENCE CURVE APPROACH

INDIFFERENCE CURVES

The indifference curve approach enables us to derive all the theorems concerning consumer behavior that we deduced from utility analysis, using less restrictive assumptions. Furthermore, indifference curve analysis simplifies the solution of certain problems. This analysis depends on the concept of ordinal rather than cardinal utility. *Ordinal utility* is based on the idea that the consumer is capable of ranking quantities according to his preferences without assigning specific preference values to the quantities. In other words, with ordinal utility, the consumer is able to decide whether he prefers combination A to combination B, but not by how much. Because of this virtue, economists prefer the indifference curve approach over the utility approach.

Visualize the following experiment: We endow a consumer with a combination of two goods, X and Y, and ask him a series of questions concerning his preference for alternative combinations of X and Y. For each of the alternative combinations presented to the consumer, he is to decide whether he prefers it to his endowment or if he prefers the endowment to it. We get the results shown in Table 5.1.

If we start with the assumption that X and Y are both commodities (as contrasted with discommodities such as garbage), then clearly the consumer will always prefer a combination that consists of more of both goods to his endowment. Therefore, this particular consumer prefers combinations B, C, D, I, and N to A. Analogously, the consumer will prefer his endowment to all combinations that consist of less of both goods, such as combinations E, F, G, and K.

TABLE 5.1

Combination	X	Y	Ranking (Compared to A)
A (Endowment)	30	15	
B	35	20	$+$
C	40	16	$+$
D	56	25	$+$
E	27	13	$-$
F	15	14	$-$
G	10	13	$-$
H	25	18	$=$
I	50	17	$+$
J	10	45	$=$
K	10	5	$-$
L	6	75	$=$
M	25	16	$-$
N	40	20	$+$
O	50	9	$=$
P	15	30	$=$
Q	45	14	$+$

The consumer's ranking of the combinations containing more of one good and less of the other depends on his individual tastes. Thus, the consumer ranks combinations H, J, L, O, and P equally with his endowment; he prefers the endowment to combination M, while combination Q is ranked as preferable to the endowment.

In Figure 5.1 we plot and label the different combinations of goods X and Y. Notice that all those combinations that are preferable to the endowment appear to the right and above—that is, northeast of—the endowment combination. The combinations less preferred are to the left and below—southwest of—point A. And the combinations that yield the same benefit as the endowment may be connected by a smooth curve if we assume that we have presented to the consumer a sufficient number of combinations to sketch in intermediate points. This curve is called an indifference curve and represents all the combinations of X and Y equally preferred by the consumer—that is, the consumer is indifferent among them. If we had started with a different initial endowment, we would have derived a different indifference curve; thus, an infinite number of these curves could be sketched. Taking any given curve, a curve to its northeast represents a higher level of utility. Conversely, a curve to its southwest would represent a lower level. Any set of numbers can be assigned to these curves that fulfill the condition that moving in a north-

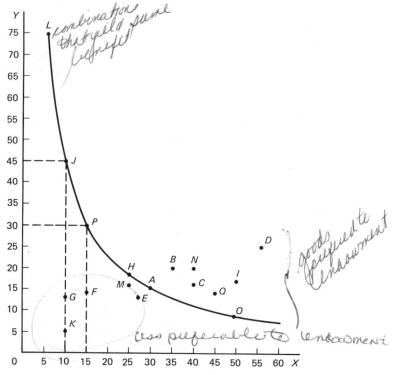

Figure 5.1

east direction results in curves having successively higher numbers. Such a set of numbers is an ordinal index of utility.

With reference to Figure 5.1, we can define the *marginal rate of sub-stitution* between X and Y. MRS_{xy} (which is read "the marginal rate of substitution of X for Y") is the number of units of Y the consumer would be willing to give up for an additional unit of X to maintain the same level of satisfaction. Therefore,[1]

$$MRS_{xy} = \left| \frac{\Delta Y}{\Delta X} \right| \qquad [5.1]$$

and we see that this is the absolute slope of the indifference curve.[2] Between points J and P,

$$MRS_{xy} = \tfrac{15}{5} = 3 \qquad [5.2]$$

[1] We can also define MRS_{yx} as the number of units of X the consumer would be willing to give up for one extra unit of Y; this is equal to $|\Delta X/\Delta Y|$.

[2] Discrete MRS measures the absolute slope between two points on an indifference curve, and continuous MRS measures it in the vicinity of a point.

When a consumer makes comparisons among combinations of X and Y, he must compare a comparable attribute of the commodities. We call this attribute "utility"; and we may express it as a function of the quantities of X and Y consumed:

$$U = f(X, Y) \qquad [5.3]$$

def. of utility

We assume that the utility that a consumer receives from consuming a good A is a function of the quantity of A and also of the quantities of goods $B \cdots N$ that he consumes. In other words, we are now dealing with a generalized, as opposed to an additive, utility function. Assuming just two commodities for ease of exposition, we have a utility function of the form:

$$U = U(X, Y) \qquad [5.4]$$

One possible sketch of this function is shown in Figure 5.2. The student should be aware that although we put certain restrictions on the nature of this function (see the following section), we do not assume a specific form of the function. The indifference curve of Figure 5.1 is assumed to be one of the contour lines of the utility surface shown in Figure 5.2. In Figure 5.3 we present an *indifference map* that shows some of the infinite number of indifference curves corresponding to this utility hill. A contour

def. of indifference map

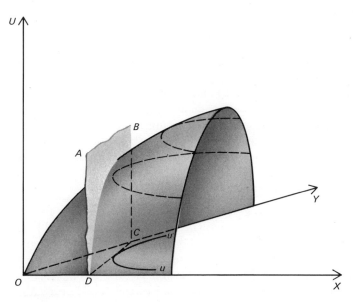

Figure 5.2

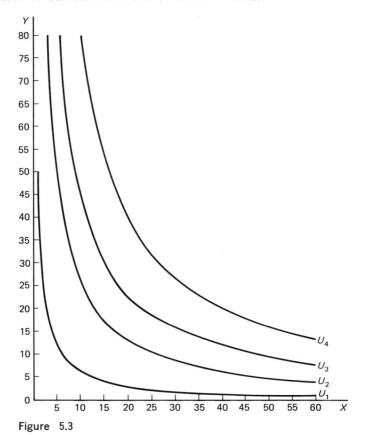

Figure 5.3

line connects points of equal values of some dependent variable—they are used in geology and cartography to indicate equal elevation above sea level and in meteorology to show points of equal atmospheric pressure. With a utility surface, a contour line (indifference curve) connects points of equal utility. However, by the assumption that a consumer can determine whether he is better or worse off, but not by how much, we are able to assign only an ordinal index to the indifference curves.

Properties of Indifference Curves

1. Indifference curves are nonintersecting. This can be demonstrated with the use of Figure 5.4. On U_1, satisfaction yielded by $Y_1 + X_1 =$ satisfaction yielded by $Y_2 + X_2$. On U_2, satisfaction yielded by $Y_1 + X_1 =$ satisfaction yielded by $Y_2 + X_3$. Therefore, satisfaction yielded by $Y_2 + X_2 =$ satisfaction yielded by $Y_2 + X_3$. And so the satisfaction yielded by X_2 is equal to that yielded by X_3; hence it is concluded that the individual receives equal satisfaction from more

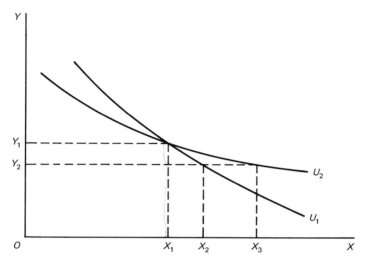

Figure 5.4

and less of commodity X, which is impossible (if X is satisfaction yielding).

2. They must be negatively sloping; that is, $\Delta Y / \Delta X < 0$. A positively sloped indifference curve would imply that as a consumer received more of both commodities, his satisfaction would remain the same. This contradicts our assumption of two utility-yielding goods. In terms of the utility hill, we are assuming the individual to be in the first quadrant of Figure 5.5 where both commodities have positive marginal utilities. This can be shown by holding one commodity constant and increasing the amount of the other; it is seen that the individual moves to successively higher indifference curves. Although this is the normal quadrant, it is possible for the other quadrants to be relevant for other problems, for example, an individual faced with the choice between work and income (keeping income constant and increasing hours of work would result in a movement to successively lower indifference curves). Thus, in quadrant II, the marginal utility of X is negative and in quadrant IV the marginal utility of Y is negative. Quadrant III represents a choice between two discommodities and, therefore, it is unlikely that the individual would ever be in this area. Point S represents the satiation point or the apex of the hill.

3. In the normal case, we assume the MRS_{xy} to be declining; that is, moving along an indifference curve from left to right results in $|\Delta Y / \Delta X|$ decreasing.[3] As we observe the world around us, we note

[3] $MRS_{yx} = |\Delta X / \Delta Y|$ would increase moving from left to right and decrease moving from right to left. (See Appendix 5A.)

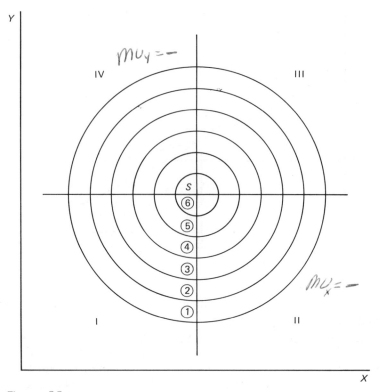

Figure 5.5

that people do not practice monomania (the consumption of merely one commodity); and if we assumed an increasing MRS_{xy}, we would be implying that people acted in this fashion. This will be discussed in detail below.

CASES OF NONNORMAL INDIFFERENCE CURVES

In Figure 5.6a we show a case of concave indifference curves. The MRS_{xy} increases rather than decreases, in moving from left to right along such a curve. This implies that as a consumer acquires more of a commodity, that commodity becomes subjectively more valuable to him so that he is willing to give up ever increasing amounts of the other good for equal increments of the increasingly desirable one. This type of behavior we judge on introspective grounds to be unusual, and we will show below that it leads to market behavior that is empirically rare.

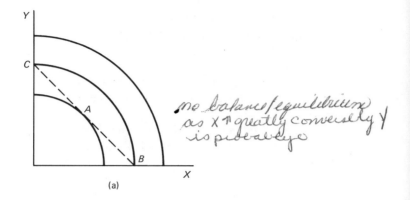

(a)

no balance/equilibrium as X ↑ greatly conversely Y is probably

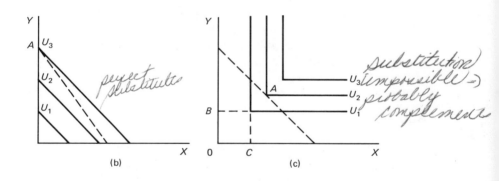

(b)

perfect substitutes

(c)

substitution impossible ⇒ probably complement

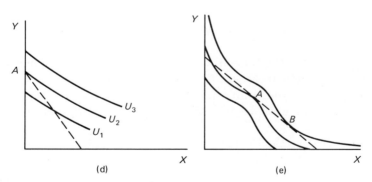

(d)

(e)

Figure 5.6

If two goods are perfect substitutes for one another, an indifference curve for the goods would be of the kind shown in Figure 5.6b. The exact nature of the substitutability is reflected in the slope (MRS_{xy}) of the straight-line indifference curve.[4]

Figure 5.6c represents a case in which substitution is impossible. The two goods must be used in some fixed proportion indicated by the ratio OB/OC.

In Figure 5.6d we show the case in which a consumer regards a minimum amount of one good (good Y) as necessary for a given level of utility but in which no minimum amount of the other good is necessary. If the consumer regarded some minimum amounts of both goods as necessary for a given level of satisfaction, the indifference curves would be parallel to the respective axis (for example, an indifference map between food and clothing).

Figure 5.6e shows an indifference map in which the curves, reading from left to right, are at first convex to the origin and then concave. We shall show below that observable combinations of X and Y for a utility-maximizing individual can only lie in the convex-to-the-origin portions of the indifference curves.

BUDGET LINE[5]

It is obvious that the consumer would like to reach the highest possible indifference curve. Unfortunately, however, he is prevented from doing this because of his limited resources and the positive prices he must pay for the commodities he consumes. In general terms, the budget constraint can be expressed as

$$I = AP_a + BP_b + \cdots + NP_n \qquad [5.5]$$

In three dimensions, the budget constraint is shown as a plane cutting the utility hill, $ABCD$ in Figure 5.2. In his effort to achieve the highest possible altitude on the utility hill the consumer may be pictured as moving up the hill until he hits the wall (plane) that represents the budget constraint.

In two dimensions the budget constraint is a straight line of the form

$$Y = \frac{I}{P_y} - \frac{P_x}{P_y} X \qquad [5.6]$$

[4] If $MRS_{xy} = 1$, we have the uninteresting case of analyzing the substitution between a good and itself. Later in the Chapter, we shall discuss in detail the meaning of substitute and complementary relationships between goods.

[5] The budget line is also called the "consumption possibility schedule," the "line of attainable combinations," and the "price line."

and is presented in Table 5.2 and Figure 5.7 for an income of $300, $P_x = \$5$ and $P_y = \$10$. In general terms, the slope of the budget line, $\Delta Y / \Delta X$, is $-P_x/P_y$. Thus, for this specific one, the slope is $-\$5/\$10$ or $-\frac{1}{2}$.[6]

CONSUMER EQUILIBRIUM AND INDIFFERENCE CURVES

We have said that the consumer desires to move up as high as possible on the utility hill but that he is prevented from doing this by the budget wall. Therefore, in these terms, equilibrium will be achieved when the consumer arrives at the highest possible level on his utility hill permitted by the budget constraint (wall).

In terms of a two-dimensional diagram, because the utility hill is represented by the indifferencè contours and the budget wall by the

---

[6] One can derive the slope of the budget line directly from the accompanying graph. If a consumer is initially purchasing the combination represented by A and then switches to B, he buys more X and less Y at B than at A. But because total expenditure at A is equal to total expenditure at B, we can write

$$-\Delta Y P_y = \Delta X P_x$$

Therefore,

$$\frac{\Delta Y}{\Delta X} = -\frac{P_x}{P_y}$$

The equation for the budget line can also be derived graphically. OY represents the amount of Y purchased if the consumer spends his entire income on Y. Therefore, $OY = I/P_y$ and because the formula for a straight line is $y = a + bx$ (the vertical-axis intercept plus the slope times the x-coordinate), we can write

$$Y = \frac{I}{P_y} - \frac{P_x}{P_y} X$$

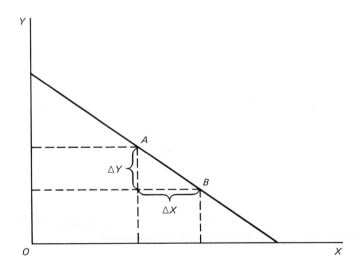

TABLE   5.2

X	Y
0	30
2	29
4	28
6	27
8	26
10	25
12	24
14	23
16	22
18	21
20	20
22	19
24	18
26	17
28	16
30	15 *equilibrium*
32	14
34	13
36	12
38	11
40	10
42	9
44	8
46	7
48	6
50	5
52	4
54	3
56	2
58	1
60	0

The X and Y values were obtained from the equation

$$Y = \frac{\$300}{\$10} - \frac{\$5}{\$10} X = 30 - \tfrac{1}{2}X.$$

budget line, equilibrium will be achieved at the point where the consumer has moved to his highest possible indifference curve within the attainable area delimited by the budget line. We show this in Figure 5.8, in which we have redrawn the indifference map of Figure 5.3 and have super-imposed upon it the budget line of Figure 5.7. The consumer will be in equilibrium when he purchases 30 units of X and 15 of Y. These are the coordinates of the point of tangency between the budget line and U_3—the highest possible indifference curve the consumer can reach. Although

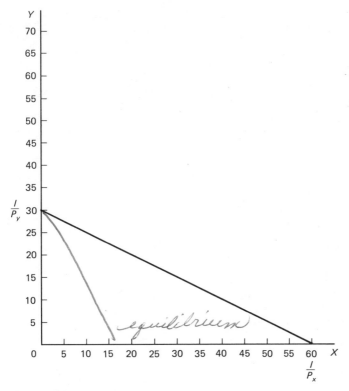

Figure 5.7

there is only one budget line at any given time, there are an infinite number of indifference curves; thus, with normally shaped curves, there will always be such a tangency point.

Another way of showing that the tangency point represents equilibrium is to picture the consumer being first somewhere to the left of equilibrium and then somewhere to the right of equilibrium and then to show how he would always necessarily move toward the tangency point. We may think of the slope of the budget line as being the rate at which the individual can exchange Y for X in the market place. In our example, the slope is $-\$5/\$10$ $(= -P_x/P_y)$, and that means the consumer can exchange $\frac{1}{2}$ unit of Y for 1 unit of X in the market place. The slope of the indifference curve indicates the amount of Y that the consumer would be willing to give up for an additional unit of X. Suppose the consumer is initially at point A and we ask him how much more X he would need in order to be compensated for a loss in Y of 10 units (a change in Y from 25 to 15 units). We find that we would have to give him $6\frac{2}{3}$ units of X to compensate him for this loss of Y. This would bring him from point A

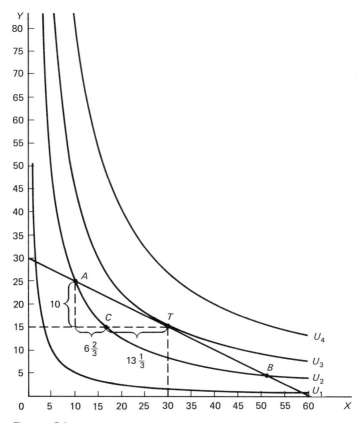

Figure 5.8

to point C along indifference curve U_2. At the prevailing market prices, if the individual were to exchange 10 units of Y, he would be able to receive 20 units of X, which would bring him to point T on the higher indifference curve, U_3. Under these conditions, the consumer will go to the market and move along his budget line to point T, where his subjective valuation of the two goods is the same as the market rate of exchange. To test your understanding of the equilibrium condition, show that if the consumer is initially at point B, he will necessarily move up the budget line to point T.

Similarity between the Indifference Curve and Utility Approaches. We can now show that the equilibrium condition derived from indifference curve analysis is identical with that derived from utility analysis. Moving from left to right between any two points on an indifference curve, the following is true:

$$-\Delta Y \cdot MU_y = +\Delta X \cdot MU_x \qquad [5.7]$$

That is, the loss in utility from consuming fewer units of one good is just matched by the gain from consuming more of the other good. We can rewrite equation 5.7 as

$$\frac{\Delta Y}{\Delta X} = -\frac{MU_x}{MU_y} \qquad [5.8]$$

In words, this states that the slope of the indifference curve is equal to the ratio of the marginal utility of X to the marginal utility of Y. At the point of equilibrium, the slope of the budget line is equal to the slope of the indifference curve.[7]

Slope of budget line: $\quad \dfrac{\Delta Y}{\Delta X} = -\dfrac{P_x}{P_y}$

Slope of indifference curve: $\quad \dfrac{\Delta Y}{\Delta X} = -\dfrac{MU_x}{MU_y}$

or

$$\frac{P_x}{P_y} = \frac{MU_x}{MU_y} \qquad [5.9]$$

which can be rewritten as

$$\frac{MU_x}{P_x} = \frac{MU_y}{P_y} \qquad [5.10]$$

And this is the result we obtained from the utility approach.

Equilibrium Conditions with Nonnormal Indifference Curves. A point of tangency in Figure 5.6a, such as point A, that shows the consumer buying some of each commodity is not a stable equilibrium; it is actually a point of minimum satisfaction.[8] A displacement of the equilibrium at A will cause the individual to move to B or C where he is consuming only one commodity. It is at point B that he will be on the highest possible indifference curve.

In the case of perfect substitutes (Figure 5.6b), if the budget-line slope is equal to the constant MRS_{xy}, then the consumer will be satisfied with any combination of X and Y along the budget line. If the slope of the budget line is not equal to MRS_{xy}, the model predicts monomania. The highest possible indifference curve the consumer can reach will always be on one of the axes, where the consumer is consuming one good to the exclusion of the other; this is indicated by point A in Figure 5.6b. The condition for equilibrium is the same as in the normal case if we restate the equilibrium condition in more general terms: Immediately to the left of equilibrium, $MU_x/MU_y > P_x/P_y$; and immediately to the right of equilibrium, $MU_x/MU_y < P_x/P_y$. In Figure 5.6c, in which substitution

[7] For a proof that the consumer is indeed in equilibrium when the price line and the indifference curve are tangent, see Appendix 4A.

[8] For a more rigorous discussion of this point see Appendixes 4A and 5A.

is not possible, equilibrium will always be at a corner of an indifference curve, such as A. The equilibrium condition is being fulfilled at A because the slope of the vertical segment of the indifference curve is equal to infinity and, therefore, is greater than the slope of the budget line; and the slope of the horizontal segment is zero and, therefore, is less than the slope of the budget line.

Although the indifference map in Figure 5.6d is normal, the slope of the budget line is such that there is no point of tangency and the individual consumes only good Y at point A. Thus, although for substitutable goods, convexity is necessary to ensure a stable nonmonomaniacal equilibrium, convexity in itself does not guarantee that monomania will not occur.

In Figure 5.6e there are two points of tangency, A and B, because of the convex-concave-convex nature of the curves. Clearly, however, given the income constraint, point A represents minimum satisfaction because a movement in either direction away from A would lead the consumer to the convex portion of a higher indifference curve; that is, to the left of point A, $MU_x/MU_y < P_x/P_y$, and to the right, $MU_x/MU_y > P_x/P_y$. Consequently, observable bundles of commodities will always lie on convex sections of indifference curves.

PRICE CONSUMPTION CURVE

The indifference curve technique may be used to develop a demand curve. In order to do this, we first develop a price consumption curve. This procedure will be illustrated with reference to Figure 5.9 and Table 5.3. Let us assume a consumer has a given set of tastes, represented by the indifference map; a given income of $50; and is faced with a constant price for good Y of $2. Furthermore, X and Y are the only two goods that he purchases. Consequently, if he spends his entire income on good Y, he can buy a maximum of 25 units of Y; therefore, no matter what the price of X, as long as income and P_y remain constant, all budget lines will be anchored on the vertical axis at $Y = 25$ units.

The horizontal axis intercept for any P_x represents the maximum amount of X that can be purchased if all the individual's income were spent on X. Therefore, the higher the price of X, the closer will be the horizontal axis intercept to the origin.

If we now vary the price of X (as in Table 5.3) so that we generate a series of budget lines with decreasing slope (that is, a decreasing P_x/P_y, because P_y is a constant), we may find a series of tangency points between these budget lines and various indifference curves. Connecting these points of tangency, we trace out the price consumption curve. In Figure 5.9, we have shown just five such tangency points of the infinite number that trace out the price consumption curve.

TABLE 5.3

(1) P_x	(2) X	(3) TE_x	(4) TE_y	(5) Y
$11	0	$ 0	$50	25
10	1	10	40	20
9	2	18	32	16
8	3	24	26	13
7	4	28	22	11
6	5	30	20	10
5	6	30	20	10
4	7	28	22	11
3	8	24	26	13
2	9	18	32	16
1	10	10	40	20
$ 0	11	$ 0	$50	25

Income is assumed constant at $50 and the price of Y constant at $2. Therefore, columns 3 and 4, which represent total expenditure on X and Y, respectively, must sum to $50; and column 5 can be derived by dividing column 4 by $2.

To derive the demand schedule, we need the locus of price-quantity points. The price consumption curve gives us the locus of (quantity of X) − (quantity of Y) points. However, it is a simple matter to derive the demand curve from the price consumption curve. We shall illustrate this with respect to point A on the price consumption curve and the corresponding point B on the demand curve in Figures 5.10a and b. At point A the equilibrium quantity of X is 4 units; this gives us the quantity coordinate on the demand curve as well. In order to get the price coordinate, we first read the slope of the budget line through A. The slope will give us the ratio of P_x to P_y. However, since we know that the P_y = $2, the price of X follows immediately from the slope of the budget line, that is, the slope of the budget line: $\dfrac{25}{7\frac{1}{7}} = \dfrac{P_x}{$2}$. Thus, P_x must be equal to $7. Similarly, the other price coordinates can be derived.

The reader will remember that the elasticity at the midpoint of a linear demand curve is unitary; at prices above this, $|E| > 1$; and at prices below the midpoint, $|E| < 1$. The behavior of elasticity can be determined from the price consumption curve as well. When P_x = $11, the individual buys none of it but spends his entire income of $50 on Y; and since P_y = $2, he buys 25 units of Y. Moving along the price consumption curve from the vertical axis to point A, the price of X is decreas-

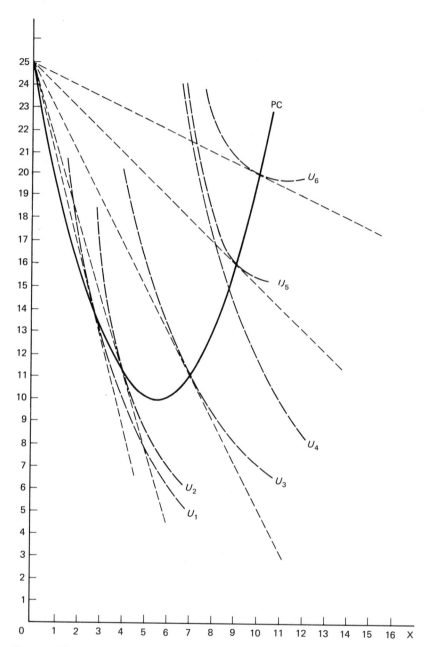

Figure 5.9

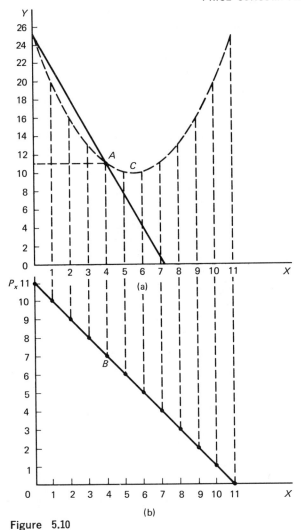

Figure 5.10

ing and the quantity of Y purchased is decreasing. Since P_y is constant, this means that the amount being spent on Y is decreasing. Furthermore, since income is a constant, this means that expenditure on X is increasing. Thus, we can say that as long as the price consumption curve is negatively sloped, expenditure on X increases as P_x falls; or in other words, the absolute elasticity of demand is greater than one. By the same reasoning, we can see that over the upward sloping portion of the price consumption curve, elasticity must be less than one. At point C where X is equal to $5\frac{1}{2}$ units, total expenditure on X is at a maximum and momentarily constant; therefore, elasticity is equal to one. If the price consumption curve is monotonically increasing or decreasing, the curve is inelastic or elastic throughout; and if it is parallel to the horizontal axis, the demand curve will be unitary elastic over its entire range.

It is also a simple matter to determine the sign of the cross elasticity between X and Y. When the price consumption curve is declining, the cross elasticity must be positive; conversely, an upward-sloped price consumption curve implies a negative cross elasticity of demand. (Of course, these implications for cross elasticity hold only in the two good cases.)

The ordinal utility approach is completely general and can be expanded to include any number of goods. We can still make use of two-dimensional representation, but the indifference curve technique as developed so far necessitates using only two commodities. We may, however, conceive of the consumer choosing between a particular good and purchasing power—income—that represents command over all other commodities. Thus, in Figure 5.11 we show good X in the usual fashion on the horizontal axis, and on the vertical axis we plot income, I. The indifference curves drawn show the consumer's preference between good X and I. The vertical axis intercept of the various budget lines is $\bar{I}$, which is the consumer's money income—assumed to be constant.

In general terms, the equation for such budget lines is

$$I = \bar{I} - P_x X \qquad [5.11]$$

where

I = income spent on all goods excluding X
$\bar{I}$ = total money income, assumed to be constant
P_x = price of good X
X = quantity of good X purchased

And the slope is simply $-P_x$.

The five budget lines shown in Figure 5.11 are all based on a constant income, $\bar{I}$, of \$50. For budget line P_{x3}, for example, the X-axis intercept is $12\frac{1}{2}$ units of X—which means P_x is \$4 (that is, \$50/$12\frac{1}{2}$).

A point of tangency, such as A, represents consumer equilibrium; that is, when the consumer's income is \$50 and $P_x = \$4$, he maximizes his satisfaction by consuming 7 units of X and spending \$22 of his income on all other goods.[9] Notice that total expenditures on X (\$4 × 7 units = \$28) can be obtained from the graph as the difference between the vertical axis intercept of the budget line, $\bar{I}$, and the amount spent on all other goods. Thus, \$50 − \$22 = \$28.

[9] It is assumed that the consumer is maximizing his satisfaction not only between X and I but also with regard to the various goods he purchases with I. In other words, $MU_x/MU_I = P_x$ implies

$$\frac{MU_a}{P_a} = \frac{MU_b}{P_b} = \cdots = \frac{MU_x}{P_x}$$

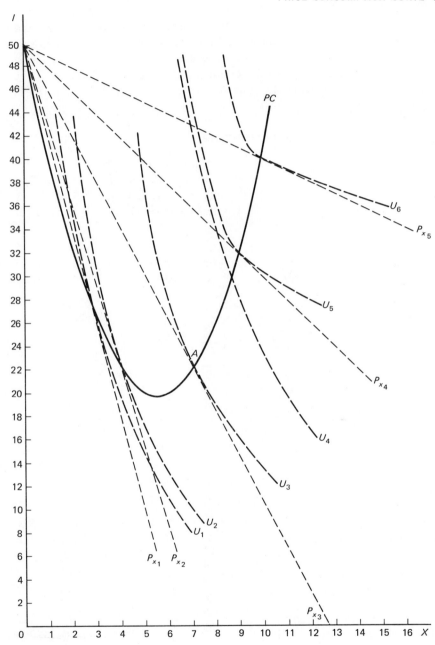

Figure 5.11

With the use of this technique, it is again a fairly simple matter to derive the demand schedule for good X. The only difference between this case and the one where good Y is on the vertical axis is that P_x is given directly by the slope of the budget line. Obviously, the demand curve that could be derived from the price consumption curve in Figure 5.11 is identical to that in Figure 5.10.

INCOME-CONSUMPTION RELATIONSHIP

In drawing a demand schedule, we assume income to be constant at a given level. The level of income is an important factor in determining the quantities that will be purchased at alternative prices. We now investigate this relationship with the aid of Table 5.4 and Figure 5.12.

TABLE 5.4

(1) I	(2) X	(3) P_xX	(4) Y	(5) P_yY
$ 10	0	$ 0	5	$10
20	1	7	$6\frac{1}{2}$	13
30	2	14	8	16
40	3	21	$9\frac{1}{2}$	19
50	4	28	11	22
60	5	35	$12\frac{1}{2}$	25
70	6	42	14	28
80	7	49	$15\frac{1}{2}$	31
90	8	56	17	34
100	9	63	$18\frac{1}{2}$	37
$110	10	$70	20	$40

The constant prices are $P_x = \$7$ and $P_y = \$2$.

In Figure 5.12 we have redrawn the indifference map of Figure 5.9. Assuming that the prices of X and Y are constant at $7 and $2, respectively, we assume higher levels of income, which means in graphical terms a series of budget lines all of which have a slope equal to $7/$2 or in other words, parallel to one another. The income consumption curve is obtained by connecting the successive points of tangency between these budget lines and the relevant indifference curves. Once again, we show only a few of the infinite number of tangencies. The coordinates of these points of tangency are shown in Table 5.4; they represent the equilibrium quantities of X and Y the individual will consume at alternative income levels, with the prices of X and Y held constant. Therefore, the X and Y coordinates on an income-consumption curve correspond to points on different demand curves for X and Y—a different demand

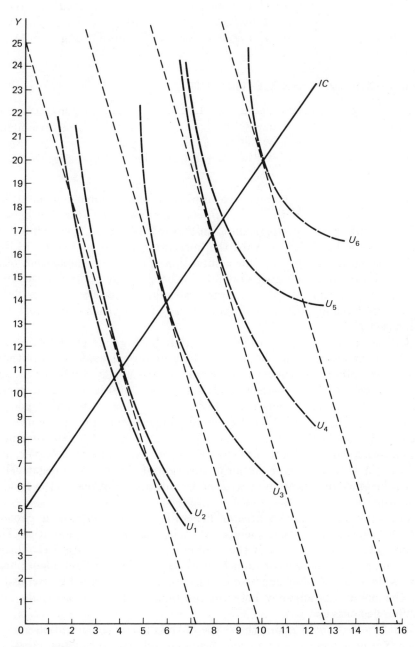

Figure 5.12

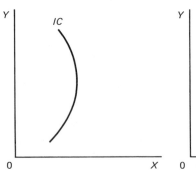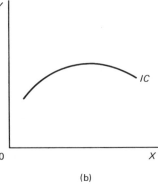

(a)   (b)

Figure 5.13

curve for each level of income. An upward-sloping income-consumption curve indicates that both goods are superior ones. If the curve bends backward toward the vertical axis as in Figure 5.13a, good X is an inferior good; if the curve bends toward the horizontal axis as in Figure 5.13b, good Y is an inferior good. (Our assumption of only two goods rules out the possibility that both goods are inferior because the budget constraint and the assumption of constant prices means that as income rises, less of one good being purchased implies more of the other good must be purchased.)

It is assumed in Figure 5.13a and b that both goods are superior at low levels of income; this is supported by empirical evidence. Another relevant possibility is the case where one of the goods is inferior at all income levels while the other good is superior. In Figure 5.14a, commodity X is inferior throughout; this might be representative of goods such as hamburger and dried beans. The income consumption curve is negatively sloping throughout. Notice that in Figure 5.14b, the income-consumption curve is also negatively sloped throughout; however, in this case, X is superior and Y inferior throughout. Therefore, a negatively sloped income-consumption curve merely indicates that one of the goods is inferior.

Again we may achieve greater generality by considering a choice between one good X and income, that is, all other commodities. In Figure 5.15 we have redrawn the indifference map of Figure 5.11. Once again, we are assuming a constant P_x of \$7 so that the parallel budget lines have a slope of -7. The income-consumption curve is derived by connecting the points of tangency between the budget lines and the relevant indifference curves.

What we have said about the shape of the income-consumption curve when X and Y were the two goods being considered holds when good X is considered against income, except that when X is superior throughout,

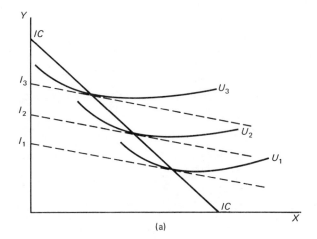

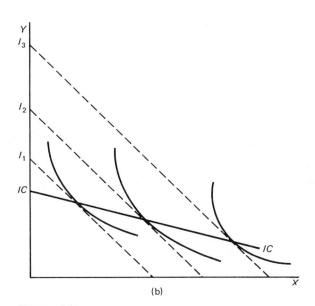

Figure 5.14

as in Figure 5.13b, expenditure on all other commodities decreases as income increases. This means that, although expenditure on some commodities other than X may increase, the net effect of expenditures on all other goods must be a decrease, because the prices of all goods are assumed constant. Although it would be unusual for a consumer to behave in this fashion, one possibility would be for X to be a habit-forming good such as a narcotic.

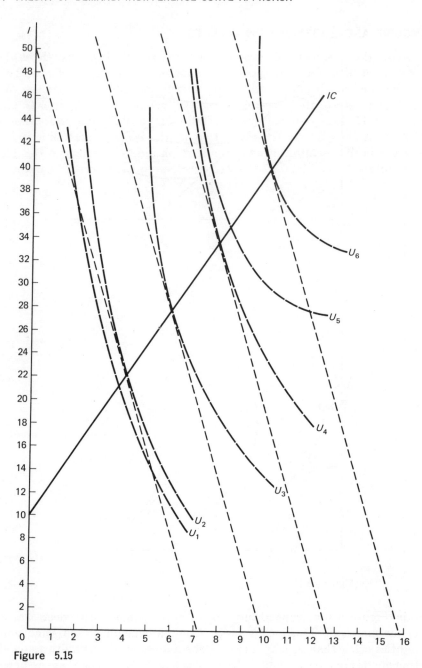

Figure 5.15

INCOME AND SUBSTITUTION EFFECTS

In our discussion of utility we saw that it was useful to break down the total effect of a price change into income and substitution effects. This can be done much more readily with the use of indifference curves. We shall demonstrate the procedure first with reference to Figure 5.16 and then to 5.17. It is assumed that the individual initially has an income of $140, that $P_x = \$2$ and $P_y = \$1$; that is, the initial budget line is KF and the initial equilibrium is at point A on indifference curve U_1. The price of good X is then assumed to decrease to $1, whereupon the new

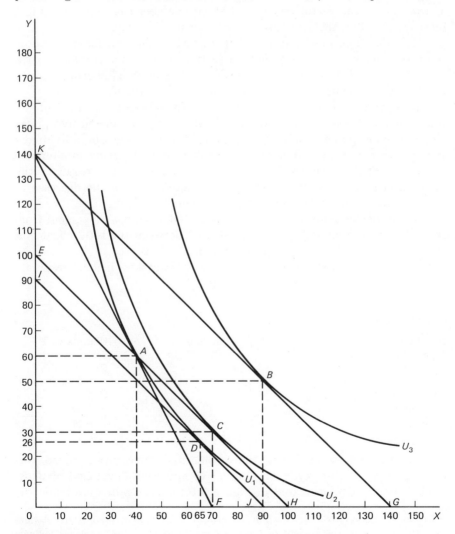

Figure 5.16

budget time is KG and the individual's new equilibrium moves to point B on indifference curve U_3.

Analogous to the procedure used in our utility analysis, we remove from the individual an amount of income equal to the increase in his purchasing power due to the price decrease. His purchasing power increases by the decrease in price times the number of units of good X the individual used to buy [($2 − $1)40 = $40]. In other words, we take away enough income from him so that he is just able to purchase the initial basket of goods at the new price ratio. This is shown graphically by drawing the budget line EH, parallel to the new one KG that goes through point A and intersects the vertical axis at $100. (Remember that parallel budget lines are based on the same price ratio.) Although the consumer can now purchase the same combination as before, we note that he does not choose to do so; because X has become relatively less expensive compared with Y, he would rather consume more of X and less of Y. This brings him to equilibrium at point C on a higher indifference curve, U_2.

The movement from A to C represents the substitution effect of the price change, because it was the result of the change in relative prices alone. The actual change in P_x, however, also increased the individual's purchasing power by $40 so that he arrived at point B on indifference curve U_3. The movement from C to B, therefore, is the result of the increase in real income that occurs as a consequence of the decrease in P_x; this movement, then, is the income effect.

In terms of the sequence of events envisioned, that is, a movement from A to C to B, the income effect is a residual between the total effect and the substitution effect with this approach.

In numerical terms, we can summarize the Slutsky "income-residual" income and substitution effects in Table 5.5.

TABLE 5.5

Initial equilibrium (A)	40 units of X		60 units of Y
Equilibrium after compensated price decrease (C)	70		30
Substitution effect		30 units of X	−30 units of Y
Final Equilibrium (B)	90		50
Income effect		20	20
Total effect		50	−10

This approach to analyzing the income and substitution effects was developed by E. Slutsky.[10] An alternative approach developed by J. R. Hicks[11] is also demonstrated in Figure 5.16. Once again we assume the

[10] Eugen E. Slutsky, *Giornale degli Economisti*, Vol. LI (1915), 1–26. A translation, "On the Theory of the Budget of the Consumer," appears in American Economic Association, *Readings in Price Theory* (Homewood, Ill.: Irwin, 1952), pp. 27–56.
[11] John R. Hicks, *Value and Capital* (revised ed., Oxford University Press, 1946).

consumer is initially in equilibrium at point A and that P_x changes from $2 to $1—or the budget line changes from KF to KG. With the Slutsky approach we changed the individual's *nominal* real income so that he would just be able to buy his original combination of goods at the new price ratio. But we did not, in fact, bring him down to the same level of real income as at point A, because he did not buy the same combination as he bought before the price change and, therefore, ended on a higher indifference curve, U_2. Hicks has suggested that the correct reduction in income in order to compensate for the gain in real income due to the price decrease is one that will bring the consumer to the same indifference curve (this *really* just restores his level of real income) that he was on before, U_1. In the Hicksian analysis, therefore, we take from the individual an amount of income, KI, that brings him to equilibrium at D on indifference curve U_1. Thus, the substitution effect is measured by the movement from A to D and the income effect as the movement from D to B. Table 5.6 summarizes the Hicksian "income-residual" approach in numerical terms.

TABLE 5.6

Initial equilibrium (A)	40 units of X		60 units of Y	
Equilibrium after compensated price decrease (D)	65		26	
Substitution effect		25 units of X		-34 units of Y
Final equilibrium (B)	90		50	
Income effect		25		24
Total effect		50		-10

The Hicksian approach is the theoretically more correct one because it just restores to the individual his initial level of real income, whereas the Slutsky approach "overcompensates" the consumer for his loss of purchasing power by bringing him to a higher indifference curve. The Slutsky method has the virtue of depending only on observable market data, whereas the Hicksian approach necessitates a knowledge of the indifference curves. The Slutsky measure is a good approximation of the Hicksian measure for small price changes. In our example, the difference between the two measures depends on the distance between points C and D, and this distance can be seen to decrease as the change in price approaches zero.

Notice that with both these approaches the income effect is measured as a residual; that is, it is derived by subtracting the substitution effect from the total effect. Notice too that the income and substitution effects for a price increase can also be derived but that this would involve giving the consumer an hypothetical subsidy in order to isolate the substitution effect rather than imposing a hypothetical tax as was done in the case of a price decrease.

An alternative approach derives the income effect directly and obtains the substitution effect as a residual between the total effect and the income effect. This alternative procedure is demonstrated with reference to Figure 5.17, in which the initial and final equilibria are the same as in Figure 5.16. Following the Slutsky approach, we now ask what increment in income would have been necessary to allow the individual to purchase the new basket of goods at point B if the price ratio had not changed, that is, if the price ratio was still given by the slope of the budget line KF. Thus, we draw a new budget line, EH, parallel to the old one, KF, and going through point B. Given the higher income, the individual does not decide to buy the combination of goods at point B but, rather, attains a higher level of satisfaction at point C. Now the income effect is measured as the movement from A to C, and the substitution effect is the residual, that is, the movement from C to B. Notice once again that with the Slutsky approach the consumer is overcompensated because point C lies on a higher indifference curve than point B.

Using the Hicksian approach in Figure 5.17, we give an hypothetical subsidy in lieu of the price decrease that is just sufficient to bring the individual to the indifference curve that he would in fact have reached had there been such a price decrease. This new budget line is IJ, parallel to KF, and is tangent to U_2 at point D. Thus, the income effect is measured as AD and the residual substitution effect as DB. These alternative Slutsky and Hicksian approaches could also be adapted to analyze the income and substitution effects of a price increase. This would involve the use of an hypothetical tax (rather than an hypothetical subsidy) in order to isolate the income effect. Table 5.7 summarizes the numerical results of the "substitution-residual" approaches.

TABLE   5.7

Slutsky Approach

Initial equilibrium (A)	40 units of X		60 units of Y
Equilibrium after compensated price decrease (C)	70		90
Income effect		30 units of X	30 units of Y
Final equilibrium (B)	50		50
Substitution effect	20		−40
Total effect	50		−10

Hicks Approach

Initial equilibrium (A)	40 units of X		60 units of Y
Equilibrium after compensated price decrease (D)	66		85
Income effect		26 units of X	25 units of Y
Final equilibrium (B)	90		50
Substitution effect	24		−35
Total effect	50		−10

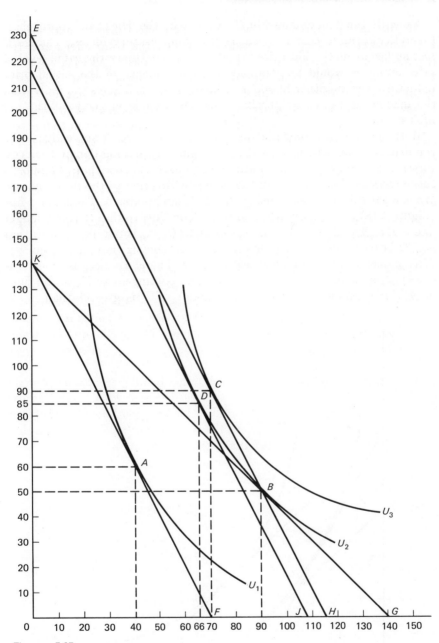

Figure 5.17

As with the "income-residual" approach, the Hicksian approach is theoretically more correct because the compensatory income change is just sufficient at the old prices to afford the consumer the same level of satisfaction as would be attained as a consequence of the actual price reduction. On the other hand, the Slutsky approach gives the individual the income necessary to purchase the new bundle of goods at the old prices.

With the use of income and substitution effects we can investigate the conditions under which we will have negatively sloping demand curves. First, the convexity of the indifference curve ensures that the substitution effect will always be in the opposite direction to the price change. We can see this intuitively using the Hicksian approach. The budget line (Figure 5.18) is originally RS, and then P_x declines so that the new budget line is RT. Equilibrium changes from A to C. PQ is parallel to RT; that is, PQ is based on the new lower P_x. With convex indifference curves, MRS_{xy} declines, moving from left to right. Therefore, because the slope of PQ is less than the slope of RS, PQ must be tangent to U_1 to the right of A (for example, B), where the amount of X is greater than at A.

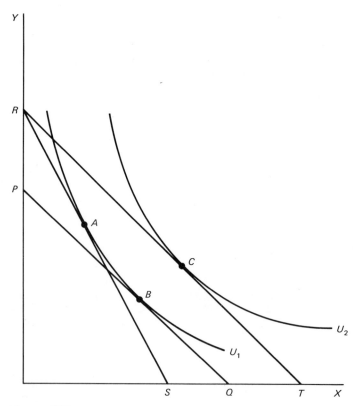

Figure 5.18

Equivalent results could be obtained with the "substitution-residual" approach.

Second, the income effect depends on whether the good is normal or inferior. In our discussions of utility and the income-consumption curve, we saw that the income effect for a superior good will also be in the opposite direction of the price change. Therefore, the net effect (substitution + income) of a price change will always be in the opposite direction of a price change.

We also saw that the income effect for an inferior good is in the same direction as the price change. Therefore, if the income effect is greater than the substitution effect, the net effect will be in the same direction as the price change. In Figure 5.19 we have a case of such a Giffen good. When the consumer is in initial equilibrium at A and then the price decreases from RE to RD, the consumer moves to the new equilibrium, C. Note that at point C the consumer buys less of X even though its price has gone down. This effect, which results in a positively sloped demand curve, is caused by the combination of two circumstances: (1) the good is inferior and (2) the income effect is stronger than the substitution effect; that is, $A \rightarrow B < B \rightarrow C$. Although a Giffen good is a theoretical possibility, an empirical case of such a good has, as yet, not been found.

SUBSTITUTES, COMPLEMENTS, AND RIVALS

The downward slope of an indifference curve implies that goods are substitutes for one another; for example, a consumer is capable of giving

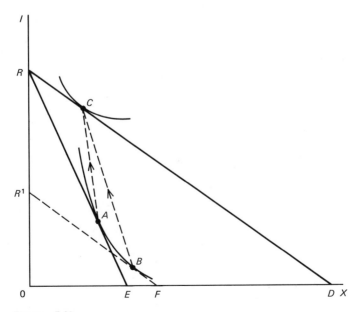

Figure 5.19

up some quantity of one good for some compensating quantity of the other good and still maintain the same level of satisfaction. Substitute goods, however, can be either complements or rivals. Both of these terms refer to the substitution effect between two commodities, that is, what is the effect on the quantity of one good when the price of the other good changes after the consumer has received a compensating variation in income that keeps him at the initial level of satisfaction.

As was discussed in Chapter 3, the usual practice is to classify substitutes and complements on the basis of cross elasticity of demand. When the cross elasticity between two goods is positive, the goods are said to be substitutes, and when the coefficient is negative, the goods are said to be complements. This definition is not analytically precise, which will be made clear with the following example.

Suppose a consumer who purchases two goods, A and B, is faced with an increase in the price of good A. Furthermore, assume that the consumer regards the two goods as "substitutes" for one another in the sense that, to maintain the same level of satisfaction, less of one good can be compensated for by more of the other good. Next, let us suppose that we observe that the consumer buys less of good B after the increase in the price of good A. Judging from the sign of the cross elasticity, we would be led to conclude that the goods are complements. However, the increase in the price of good A has led to a decline in real income; and this decrease in real income (providing the goods are superior) would cause a reduction in the consumption of both goods. If this income effect was sufficiently large, it could more than offset the increase in consumption of good B because of the higher price of good A. To summarize, when we say that cross elasticity is not an analytically precise measure of the relationship between the two goods, we mean that it does not differentiate between effects because of changes in relative prices and those because of changes in real income.

In the light of the above discussion, it is best to reserve the term "substitutes" for two goods whose relationship is described by negatively sloped indifference curves. We then use the terms "complements" and "rivals" to describe the reaction of an individual in his purchases of good B to a change in the price of good A when a compensating income variation has been imposed to remove the income effect of the price change. Good B is complementary to good A if the price of good A has risen (fallen) and a compensating increase (decrease) in income has been given, and, as a result, the purchase of good B decreases (increases). The goods are said to be rivals if the reaction to the compensated price change is in the same direction as the price change.

Appendix 5A

Marginal Rate of Substitution and Marginal Utility

The condition of diminishing absolute MRS_{xy} is not the same as that of diminishing marginal utility; it is less restrictive. By definition, the level of satisfaction along an indifference curve is constant; this means that the total differential is zero. Using some of the symbols used in Appendix 4A, we have

$$u_a dA + u_b dB = 0 \qquad [5A.1]$$

or

$$-\frac{dB}{dA} = \frac{u_a}{u_b} \qquad [5A.2]$$

This simply says that the absolute slope of the indifference curve is equal to the ratio of the marginal utilities of the commodities.

We want to know what happens to MRS_{xy} as we move along the indifference curve, and so we differentiate u_a/u_b again.

Decreasing MRS_{xy} means that

$$\frac{d}{dA}\left(-\frac{dB}{dA}\right) = \left[\frac{1}{u_b^3}\left(u_{aa}u_b^2 - 2u_{ab}u_a u_b + u_{bb}u_a^2\right)\right] < 0 \qquad [5A.3]$$

From Appendix 4A we have

$$u_a = u_b\left(\frac{P_a}{P_b}\right) \qquad [4A.7]$$

We substitute this in equation 5A.3 and obtain

$$\left\{\frac{1}{u_b^3}\left[u_{aa}u_b^2 - 2u_{ab}\left(u_b\frac{P_a}{P_b}\right)u_b + u_{bb}\left(u_b\frac{P_a}{P_b}\right)^2\right]\right\} < 0$$

This simplifies to

$$\left\{\frac{1}{u_b}\left[u_{aa} - 2u_{ab}\left(\frac{P_a}{P_b}\right) + u_{bb}\left(\frac{P_a}{P_b}\right)^2\right]\right\} < 0$$

We now multiply and divide the expression by P_b^2, which leaves the inequality unchanged:

$$\left[\frac{1}{u_b P_b^2}\left(u_{aa}P_b^2 - 2u_{ab}P_a P_b + u_{bb}P_a^2\right)\right] < 0 \qquad [5A.4]$$

The first term of the left must be positive if the commodity is an economic, utility-yielding commodity selling at a positive price. The condition, therefore, that the expression on the left be negative amounts to saying that the second and bracketed expression must be negative. But we have shown in Appendix 4A that this is exactly the second-order condition for maximum utility. Furthermore, we have shown that it does not necessarily imply diminishing marginal utility.

6

THEORY OF PRODUCTION

PRODUCTION FUNCTION

In Chapters 2 to 5 we investigated the determinants of the demand schedule. Thus far we have stated that the shape and position of the supply curve are determined by costs of production. In order to understand fully the relationship between costs of production and supply, it is necessary to understand first the technological conditions facing the firm. The economist summarizes these conditions with the *production function*, which gives the functional relationship between rates of input of factors of production and rates of output per time period. Presumably, this type of information is made available to the firm by engineers and other technical personnel.

In general terms, we may represent a production function as follows:

$$q = q(A, B, C, \ldots, N) \tag{6.1}$$

where $A \cdots N$ represent quantities of productive inputs per time period and q represents output per time period.

For ease of exposition, we shall deal with the case of two homogeneous factors of production that combine to produce a single homogeneous product.[1] Here again, as in the analysis of consumer behavior, we restrict

[1] Most firms produce more than one product. If the firm produces independent goods, it is possible to treat each good in the way we suggest. If the firm produces a main product with by-products in fixed proportions (for example, the production of hides as a consequence of meat slaughtering), then the unit of output is good X plus by-products, adding no other problems. Even when the firm can produce alternative output mixes with a given level of inputs, our results do not change substantially. Therefore, our assumption of a single homogeneous good is not overly restrictive.

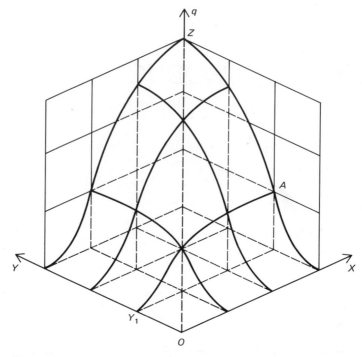

Figure 6.1

ourselves to one dependent and two independent variables permitting the use of two-dimensional diagrams. In functional notation, then, we assume that

$$q = q(X, Y) \tag{6.2}$$

The three-dimensional representation of this function is shown in Figure 6.1; and as we did in Chapter 5, we can reduce this to two-dimensional representation with the use of contour lines, which in the case of the production function are called equal-product curves or *isoquants*. In other words, each contour line in Figure 6.2 is a line of equal output for various combinations of inputs X and Y.

In contradistinction to the indifference map, however, each contour line represents a specific level of output that is assumed to be known because it is based on technological data. Therefore, as we move to higher isoquants, we know that output is increasing as well as by how much.

The data contained in the production function can also be presented in tabular form as in Table 6.1. Thus it will be noted that the output level of 500 units can be produced alternatively with $2X$ and $12.5Y$, $10X$ and

2.5Y, and 20X and 1.25Y.[2] That we assume a given output can be produced with varying factor inputs implies that the technological process permits factor substitution between X and Y; and further, because we draw continuous isoquants, we are also assuming that the factors of production are continuously variable.

The characteristics of an isoquant will be discussed with reference to isoquant 9 (q_9) in Figure 6.2. (Note that successive isoquants are assumed to represent equal increments of output.) We have assumed that the factors are substitutes for one another in the production of the good. *factors = substitutes for one another in production*

[2] Production functions can be presented in tabular form in various ways. We have *production* chosen to show the combinations of X and Y that can be used to produce different given levels of output. (This gives us the contour lines—isoquants—we shall be using subsequently.) An alternative method is to show, for various combinations of X and Y, the different output levels that will be produced.

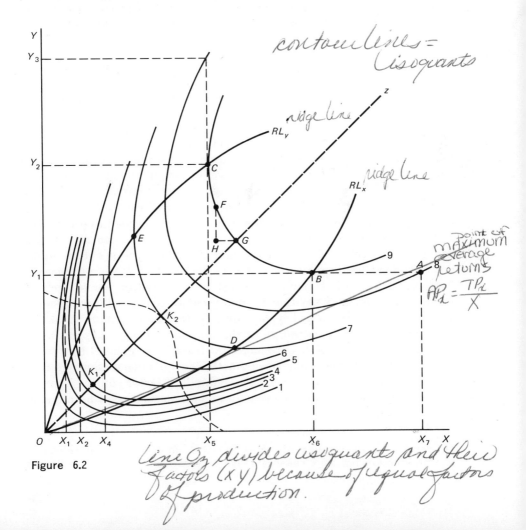

contour lines = (isoquants)
ridge line
ridge line
point of maximum average returns
$AP_x = \dfrac{TP_x}{X}$

Figure 6.2

Line Oz divides isoquants and their factors (xy) because of equal factors of production.

TABLE 6.1

Input of Factor Y Needed with a Given Input of Factor X to Produce a Given Level of Output

Iso-quant Values										
1000	50.000	25.000	16.667	12.500	10.000	8.333	7.143	6.250	5.556	5.000
900	40.500	20.250	13.500	10.125	8.100	6.750	5.786	5.062	4.500	4.050
800	32.000	16.000	10.667	8.000	6.400	5.333	4.571	4.000	3.556	3.200
700	24.500	12.250	8.167	6.125	4.900	4.083	3.500	3.062	2.722	2.450
600	18.000	9.000	6.000	4.500	3.600	3.000	2.571	2.250	2.000	1.800
500	12.500	6.250	4.167	3.125	2.500	2.083	1.786	1.562	1.389	1.250
400	8.000	4.000	2.667	2.000	1.600	1.333	1.143	1.000	0.889	0.800
300	4.500	2.250	1.500	1.125	0.900	0.750	0.643	0.562	0.500	0.450
200	2.000	1.000	0.667	0.500	0.400	0.333	0.286	0.250	0.222	0.200
100	0.500	0.250	0.167	0.125	0.100	0.083	0.071	0.062	0.056	0.050
q										
X	2	4	6	8	10	12	14	16	18	20

However, unless the factors are perfect substitutes (in which case the problem is trivial, because they become in effect the same factor), it is reasonable to expect that a specific level of output requires some minimum amount of each factor. On isoquant 9, at point B, we have the minimum quantity of Y (Y_1) necessary to produce q_9. Similarly, at point C, we have the minimum quantity of X (X_5) needed to produce q_9. If the firm were to acquire a quantity of X greater than X_6 without acquiring any more of Y, it would find that the level of output would decrease or at best remain the same. If the input of X were to increase from X_6 to X_7, with Y remaining constant, then output would decrease from q_9 to q_8. We may say that beyond point B, X is a redundant factor. In order to remain on q_9 beyond point B, the input of both X and Y must be increased. This results in the isoquant's being upward-sloping past B. Analogously, if Y were increased from Y_2 at point C to Y_3 with the quantity of X remaining constant, the level of output would go from q_9 to q_8. Thus, beyond point C, Y is a redundant factor and the isoquant is positively sloped, indicating that to remain on q_9 more of both factors must be used.[3]

---

[3] In drawing the isoquant upward-sloping beyond B and C, we are assuming that the redundant factors become a nuisance; that is, they actually interfere with the pro-

Between points C and B both factors are above their respective minimum requirements for q_9, so that substitution is possible between X and Y: output can be maintained at a given level by increasing one factor and decreasing the other. This is reflected in the downward slope of the isoquant between C and B.

Another characteristic of isoquants is that they are *nonintersecting*. Intersection would mean that a given combination of X and Y could produce two different outputs with given technology.

The curves RL_x and RL_y, called the *ridge lines*, connect points, such as E and C and D and B, where the isoquants become respectively vertical and horizontal. In the area between these ridge lines, the isoquants are negatively sloping and convex to the origin. This means that the $MRTS_{xy}$, the marginal rate of technical substitution between X and Y (the absolute slope of the isoquant, $-\Delta Y/\Delta X$), increases as we move from left to right along an isoquant. The implication of this is that as the firm substitutes X for Y and approaches the minimum quantity of Y necessary to produce a level of output, X becomes a poorer and poorer substitute for Y; therefore it takes more and more X per unit of Y given up to maintain the given level of output.

SHORT RUN — one fixed factor/variable

In the theory of production we define two analytical time periods: the short run and the long run. The *short run* is a period in which at least one factor of production cannot be varied, whereas in the long run all factors of production are presumed to be variable. The calendar time period corresponding to the analytical short-run and long-run periods will vary from industry to industry and among firms within an industry. Thus, the short run for a tailor shop is likely to be a short calendar period, whereas the short run for a steel plant is likely to be fairly lengthy.

In Figure 6.1 assume the firm to be operating in the short run; that is, it has Y_1 of factor Y and can vary its output only through varying the input of factor X. In terms of the diagram, this involves moving along the production surface at the level of Y, Y_1 or, in other words, tracing the curve Y_1A on the production surface. In the two-dimensional terms of Figure 6.2, this amounts to moving along line Y_1A at the level of Y, Y_1, parallel to the X-axis.

Notice that the line Y_1A passes through isoquants that are initially closer and closer together: the distance along Y_1A from the vertical axis

---

duction process. *At* point B, the isoquant is horizontal and *at* point C it is vertical. Later, we shall see that it is at these two points that the marginal productivities of the factors become zero.

If the excess factors do not create a nuisance, then it is more appropriate to draw the isoquant horizontal past B and vertical past C, as the redundant factors add nothing to output.

to q_1 is greater than the corresponding distance between q_1 and q_2, which is greater than the distance between q_2 and q_3. Beyond q_4 the distance between successive isoquants increases. In other words, if the firm uses X_1 along with the fixed Y input of Y_1, output is q_1. Then if the firm increases its input of factor X to X_2 (which means an increase in X of X_1, since $X_1X_2 = OX_1$), the new output level is q_4. Thus, adding the same quantity of the variable input as before has resulted in a greater increase of output; the first increment increased output by 1 unit and the second by 3 units.[4] If the input of the X factor is increased to X_4 (which again represents the same increment: $OX_1 = X_1X_2 = X_2X_4$), we find that output goes to a level somewhat greater than 5 units; the increment of output is less than 3. Clearly, therefore, $\Delta q/\Delta X$ (the marginal product of X) is increasing over the range OX_2 and decreasing thereafter. The first stage is called the stage of increasing returns and the second stage is called the stage of diminishing returns. It should be noted, however, that beyond the point where line Y_1A cuts the ridge line RL_x, it cuts through isoquants that are backward bending and, as we saw before, this means that the factor X is being used to redundancy and output declines; $\Delta q/\Delta X$ becomes negative, and this is called the stage of negative returns. At the ridge line where $\Delta q/\Delta X$ is zero, the firm may be said to be momentarily at zero returns.

In Figure 6.3 is shown the exact relationship between output and the input of factor X, with Y held constant at Y_1. This relationship is called the total product of X (TP_x). In terms of the three-dimensional representation in Figure 6.1, we have sliced the production surface by dropping a plane perpendicular to the X-Y plane at the level of Y, Y_1; and then we have shown how the "altitude" of the slice varies as the input of factor X changes.

Note the following relationships between Figures 6.2 and 6.3. As the horizontal line Y_1A in Figure 6.2 cuts through successive isoquants that are closer and closer together (the stage of increasing returns), TP_x increases at an increasing rate; that is, the curve in Figure 6.3 is convex to the origin from O to X_2. TP_x in the range of X_2 to X_6 is concave to the origin (or, in other words, is rising at a decreasing rate); in Figure 6.2 this corresponds to line Y_1A cutting through successive isoquants that are spaced farther and farther apart. Finally, beyond X_6 where X becomes redundant in Figure 6.2, TP_x declines, showing negative returns. Of course, TP_x is at a maximum at X_6.

The stage of increasing returns exists because too little of the variable factor is being used with the fixed factor; the variable factor is spread "too thin." Therefore, using additional units of the variable factor results in output's increasing at an increasing rate. After the optimum propor-

---

[4] The quantity measure might be units of a hundred or a thousand, not necessarily one. Thus, q_1 might represent 100 units and q_2 200 units, and so on.

tion of the variable factor to the fixed factor has been passed, diminishing returns set in. Finally, when the quantity of the variable factor has increased to such an extent that additional units impede the efficiency of the operation of previous units, output declines.

Increasing and negative returns are probable but may not occur; the fixed factor may be efficient with little of the variable factor, and the variable factor may never become a nuisance. Economists have found, however, that diminishing returns are eventually characteristic of all productive processes in the short run and have consequently formulated the law of diminishing returns, which states: When a variable factor is added to the fixed factor or factors in a productive process, output will increase, but after awhile at a decreasing rate. It is to be noticed that the "law" does not specify when diminishing returns are to set in, but if the "law" is to be anything but a curiosity it must happen within relevant ranges of factor input. It should also be noted that the "law" is valid only under the assumption that factor proportions can be varied, that at least one factor is held fixed, and that technology (the production function) remains the same.

In Figure 6.4 we show the average product of factor X (AP_x) and the marginal product (MP_x) that correspond to the TP_x schedule in Figure 6.3, that is, with Y held constant at Y_1.[5]

$$AP_x = \frac{TP_x}{X} \quad \text{or} \quad \frac{q}{X} \quad \text{(with Y constant at a given level)} \quad [6.3]$$

$$MP_x = \frac{\Delta TP_x}{\Delta X} \quad \text{or} \quad \frac{\Delta q}{\Delta X} \quad \text{(with Y constant at a given level)} \quad [6.4]$$

in the discrete case; in the continuous case, we have

$$MP_x = \frac{\partial q}{\partial X} \quad\quad [6.4a]$$

The usual relationships exist among TP_x, AP_x, and MP_x. First, AP_x at a given level of X can be derived by drawing a line such as OJ from the origin in Figure 6.3 to the appropriate point on the TP_x schedule; thus, AP_x for X_2 units of X is equal to the ratio AX_2/X_2. Therefore, from O to X_2, when TP_x increases at an increasing rate, MP_x rises; from X_2 to X_6, when TP_x increases at a decreasing rate, MP_x declines; and beyond X_6, MP_x becomes negative as TP_x declines. TP_x, can, of course, be derived from either the AP_x or the MP_x schedule in the usual manner. The relationship between AP_x and MP_x can be stated as

$$MP_x = AP_x + \frac{\partial AP_x}{\partial X} X \quad\quad [6.5]$$

[5] It should be noted that there is a different TP_x schedule for every different level of Y held constant and, therefore, different AP_x and MP_x schedules.

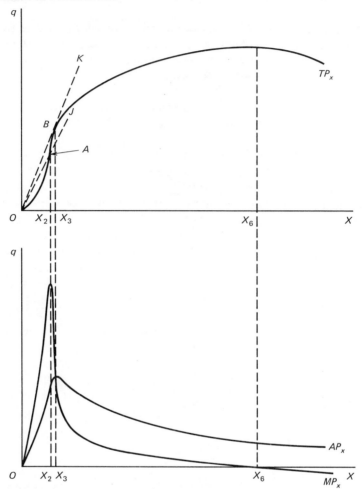

Figure 6.3 (Top)
Figure 6.4 (Bottom)

Slope of the Isoquant as the Ratio of Marginal Products

The slope of an isoquant, $MRTS_{xy}$, is measured as $-\Delta Y/\Delta X$. The slope can also be expressed in terms of the marginal products of the factors. On isoquant 9 in Figure 6.2, F and G represent two of the many different factor combinations that can produce q_9. The factor combination at point H can produce a smaller level of output than q_9. The movement from F to H represents a decrease in input Y while X is held constant. The resulting loss in output can be expressed as $-\Delta Y \cdot MP_y$. The movement from H to G represents an increase in input X with Y being held constant. The resulting increase in output can be expressed as $+\Delta X \cdot MP_x$.

Because output at F and G are the same, the loss in output due to the decrease in Y must equal the gain in output resulting from the use of more X. Therefore,

$$-\Delta Y \cdot MP_y = \Delta X \cdot MP_x \qquad [6.6]$$

or

$$-\frac{\Delta Y}{\Delta X} = \frac{MP_x}{MP_y} \quad \text{and} \quad \frac{MP_x}{MP_y} = MRTS_{xy} \qquad [6.7]$$

This definition of $MRTS_{xy}$ will be useful in our later discussion.[6]

LONG RUN

Whereas in the short run one of the factors of production is assumed fixed at some level (Y_1 in Figure 6.1), in the long run all factors are assumed to be variable. In Figure 6.1, if we assume that factors X and Y are used in a one-to-one ratio, this amounts to slicing the production surface along the line OZ. (We discuss later the determinants of the factor proportion used by the firm in the long run.) In terms of the isoquant map of Figure 6.2, it means moving along line OZ, which is equidistant from the X and Y axes, because we have assumed equal amounts of the factors being used. The cross section obtained can perhaps be better understood with reference to Figure 6.5, in which we show output in relation to "scale." To understand the meaning of the term "scale," consider the production function:

$$q = f(k\bar{X}, k\bar{Y})$$

where $\bar{X}$ and $\bar{Y}$ are initial values of X and Y that fix factor proportions when k, the scale coefficient, equals 1. Thus, k being different from 1 means output changes are due to variations in the quantities of both X and Y that are used, but with the proportion in which they are used remaining the same. For example, suppose a firm consisted only of 5 men and 1 machine; a doubling of scale would involve hiring 5 more men and obtaining 1 more machine. A natural question that arises is what is the effect on output of this change in scale.

In Figure 6.5, OZ shows the variation in output in relation to scale. Using the methods developed in Chapter 3, we derive the curves that are average and marginal to OZ, and these are shown in Figure 6.6. The particular shape of OZ, as depicted in Figure 6.6, shows the following: There are increasing average returns to scale from O to k_2; and thereafter decreasing average returns. Marginal returns increase to k_1, and decrease thereafter.

[6] In continuous notation we can write $-dY/dX = (\partial q/\partial X)/(\partial q/\partial Y) = MP_x/MP_y$. For a more rigorous treatment, see Appendix 5A, where the slope of an indifference curve was derived. The same technique can be used for isoquants: Output is a constant along an isoquant; utility is a constant along an indifference curve.

Increasing returns to scale reflect the opportunities of using specialization of the factors of production (of which division of labor is the most frequently mentioned but by no means the only variant). Decreasing returns to scale arise because of the inefficiencies involved in switching from an entrepreneur to a "management team." For example, doubling the scale of operation would require a doubling of entrepreneurs, but it is highly unlikely that this will double the "entrepreneurial capacity"; that is, with one entrepreneur, there is no communications problem; with two entrepreneurs, two lines of communications are necessary; with three, six lines; and so on.

Although both marginal and average returns to scale can be measured, economists usually mean average returns to scale when they simply discuss returns to scale. As we shall show, the distinction between average and marginal is of crucial importance in explaining the spacing of isoquants along a ray from the origin.

It is simplest to explain the interpretation of returns to scale with regard to average returns by using a homogeneous function. By a "homogeneous function" we mean a relationship between the dependent and the independent variables such that when the independent variables are changed by the same proportion, output changes by a constant proportion. If the production function is

$$q = f(X, Y) \qquad [6.8]$$

then for a homogeneous function, we can write

$$k^i q = f(kX, kY) \qquad [6.9]$$

For example, if $i = 1$, then a doubling, say, of X and Y (that is, $k = 2$) will always cause output to also double. This type of function is called homogeneous of degree one or called a linear homogeneous function. Such a function is said to exhibit "constant returns to scale."

A function that shows "increasing returns to scale" would have i equal a constant greater than one. For example, if $i = 2$ and $k = 2$, then a doubling of all inputs will quadruple output. And in the case of decreasing returns to scale, assume $k = 4$ and $i = \frac{1}{2}$. Then a quadrupling of inputs results in a doubling of output; k^i would be $4^{1/2} = 2$.

For nonhomogeneous functions, i is not a constant, such as that in Figures 6.1 and 6.5. The typical economic production function is not homogeneous, and i usually varies from greater than one, to one, to less than one, that is, successive stages of increasing, constant, and decreasing returns to scale.

As usual, we desire to measure the rate of change of the dependent variable to the independent variable; in this case the rate of change of

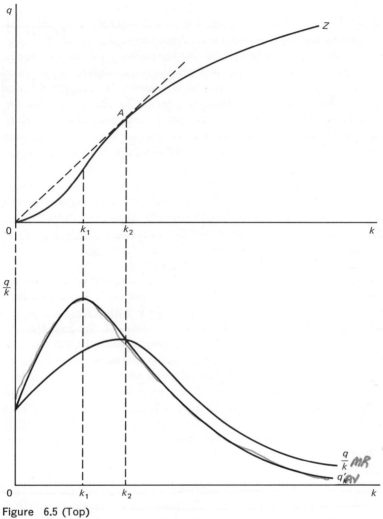

Figure 6.5 (Top)
Figure 6.6 (Bottom)

output to a change in the scale coefficient. Furthermore, as usual, we desire this measure to be independent of units, so we calculate it as an elasticity.

$$\text{Scale elasticity} = \frac{\%\ \text{change in output}}{\%\ \text{change in scale coefficient}}$$

$$E_k = \frac{\dfrac{\partial q}{q}}{\dfrac{\partial k}{k}} = \frac{\dfrac{\partial q}{\partial k}}{\dfrac{q}{k}} \qquad [6.10]$$

The second expression on the right shows (as usual) that scale elasticity is the ratio of marginal to average returns to scale.

We can show that for homogeneous functions, E_k is, in fact, equal to i.[7]

We shall now investigate the relationship among scale elasticity, returns to scale, and the spacing of isoquants. In Figures 6.5 and 6.6, the production function exhibits increasing marginal returns to scale over the range O to k. In terms of the production function viewed in three dimensions (Figure 6.1), this means the surface becomes ever steeper as we move from O to k_1; and in Figure 6.2 it means that along the ray OZ, the isoquants are spaced closer and closer together up to k_1 and then the isoquants are ever further apart, because beyond k_1, marginal returns are decreasing, which means that the surface is becoming continuously flatter. In Figure 6.2, where the isoquants are spaced closer and closer together, it means that for successively equal increments in output, the necessary increments in the factor mix grow smaller; and conversely past k_1, where marginal returns are decreasing.

In Figures 6.5 and 6.6, there are increasing average returns to scale over the range O to k_2. It is just at k_2 in Figure 6.5 that a line from the origin is just tangent to the output curve. In Figure 6.2, if we had assumed various factor proportions (that is, a rotation of the ray OZ through the range $0°$ to $90°$), each ray would have associated with it a point of tangency such as A, that is, a point of maximum average returns. The locus of such points is given by the dashed curve on which k_2 lies. This curve can be called the "horizon" line; the reason for this name can best be seen in Figure 6.1. An individual standing at the origin and scanning up the output hill would be able to see the maximum points on the hill visible (in a linear direction) from the origin. This locus is thus appropriately called the horizon line and represents the locus of maximum average product.

If the production function exhibited constant returns to scale throughout, then the isoquants would be equally spaced along a ray from the origin. A homogeneous production function that displayed increasing

Closer together

[7] Substituting (6.8) in (6.9)

$$q(k\bar{X}, k\bar{Y}) = k^i q(\bar{X}, \bar{Y})$$

$$\frac{\partial q}{\partial k} = i k^{i-1} q(\bar{X}, \bar{Y})$$

$$\frac{q}{k} = \frac{k^i q(\bar{X}, \bar{Y})}{k} = k^{i-1} q(\bar{X}, \bar{Y})$$

$$E_k = \frac{\frac{\partial q}{\partial k}}{\frac{q}{k}} = \frac{i k^{i-1} q(\bar{X}, \bar{Y})}{k^{i-1} q(\bar{X}, \bar{Y})} = i \qquad \text{(a constant)}$$

(decreasing) returns to scale throughout would show isoquants spaced ever closer (ever further apart) along the ray.

It should be emphasized that the spacing of isoquants depends on marginal returns to scale. Notice that between k_1 and k_2 in Figures 6.5 and 6.6, marginal returns to scale are decreasing while average returns are increasing; in other words, between k_1 and k_2, although the isoquants are ever further apart, average returns to scale are increasing.

Homogeneous functions are an important subclass of a group of functions for which the marginal and average returns to scale are in a constant proportion to one another. $E_k = \dfrac{\partial q/\partial k}{q/k}$ and is a constant for a homogeneous function. Therefore, if $E_k = 1$, then the marginal equals the average; if $E_k > 1$, then the marginal exceeds the average and the average is ever-rising; conversely, if $E_k < 1$, then the average continues to fall and the marginal is always less than the average.[8] Thus, it is only in these special cases that a knowledge of either the behavior of average returns to scale or the scale elasticity is sufficient to permit one to infer the spacing of isoquants. In the more general case, it is necessary to have knowledge of the behavior of marginal returns to scale in order to specify the spacing of the isoquants. To summarize for the most general case: when there are (1) increasing average returns to scale followed by (2) momentarily constant returns and then (3) decreasing average returns to scale (as shown in Figures 6.5 and 6.6), the isoquants will in (1) be closer and closer together as long as marginal returns are rising and then become ever further apart as the marginal returns decrease even though average returns are still rising; and in (2) and (3) the isoquants continue to be ever further apart.

SYMMETRY OF THE STAGES

With a linear homogeneous production function, it is instructive to view the short run once again. We have seen that in the initial stages of production, the firm experiences increasing returns as a result of too little of the variable factor being used with the fixed factor; and after a certain quantity of the variable factor is used, diminishing returns set in as a consequence of more than the optimum amount of the variable factor being used with the fixed factor. Finally, we introduced the possibility of negative returns that occur when the variable factor "overwhelms" the fixed factor. We can state with equal validity (1) that increasing returns take place because too much of the fixed factor is being used along with the variable; (2) that diminishing returns occur

[8] See Appendix 6B for a more rigorous treatment of the nature of marginal and average returns to scale.

because less than the optimum amount of the fixed factor is being used with the variable factor; and (3) that negative returns occur because the fixed factor is highly insufficient for the quantity of the variable factor. In other words, the proportions of the factors determine the behavior of output. *Summary of ↑ = ↑↓ returns to scale*

The linear homogeneous production function is particularly interesting in this regard because it is *only* the factor proportions that determine output per "dose" of the inputs. The linear homogeneous production function thus permits us to isolate the effects of proportions of the factors from that of absolute amounts of factor inputs (scale). For example, if 10 units can be produced with 2 units of factor X and 1 of Y, then $2 \times 10 = 20$ units can be produced with $2 \times 2 = 4$ units of X and $2 \times 1 = 2$ of Y; and $\frac{1}{2} \times 2 = 1$ unit of X together with $\frac{1}{2} \times 1 = \frac{1}{2}$ unit of Y can produce 5 units of output. In general then, if we increase (decrease) both inputs by the proportion k, output will increase (decrease) by k. If we know output for any X and Y input combination, then so long as the ratio of X to Y remains constant, we can determine output for any other combination of X and Y inputs. This is demonstrated in Table 6.2.

In section A of the table, we show the behavior of output as the input X is varied from 1 to 14 units with the input of Y held constant at 1 unit. Column 3 shows the proportion of factor inputs, X/Y. In section B of the table, reading from the bottom to the top, we show the behavior of output as Y is varied from 0 to 1 unit with X held constant at 1 unit. Note that the factor proportions listed in column 9 are in terms of the ratio Y/X, not X/Y as in column 3. In other words, even though the factor proportions are the same in both columns, the ones in column 9 appear as the reciprocals of those in column 3.

In column 4 we assume a series of output figures that show increasing and then diminishing returns with respect to increases in the ratio X/Y. This TP_x schedule is plotted in Figure 6.7a. Columns 5 and 6 are derived in the usual fashion and are plotted in Figure 6.7b.

Notice that when we move from left to right in this figure, the ratio X/Y increases, and in moving from right to left, Y/X increases or X/Y decreases. Consequently, column 9 should be read from bottom to top, which is equivalent to reading Figure 6.7 from right to left.

We shall explain the derivation of the figures in column 10 with reference to $Y/X = 1/14$. TP_x was defined as output when X is varied on 1 unit of Y or, in other words, as output for various ratios of X/Y per unit of Y. Similarly, TP_y is defined as output when Y is varied on 1 unit of X or as output for various ratios of Y/X per unit of X. Because we assumed $TP_x = 31$ when 14 units of X are used with 1 unit of Y (a factor ratio of $X/Y = 14/1$), if we desire to maintain this ratio with the X factor now being held at 1 unit, we multiply both inputs and output by

TABLE 6.2

	A							B				
(1) X	(2) Y	(3) X/Y	(4) TP_x	(5) MP_x	(6) AP_x		(7) Y	(8) X	(9) Y/X	(10) TP_y	(11) MP_y	(12) AP_y
1	1	$\frac{1}{1}$	5		5		1	1	$\frac{1}{1}$	5		5
2	1	$\frac{2}{1}$	11	6	$5\frac{1}{2}$		$\frac{1}{2}$	1	$\frac{1}{2}$	$5\frac{1}{2}$	-1	11
3	1	$\frac{3}{1}$	18	7	6	Stage I	$\frac{1}{3}$	1	$\frac{1}{3}$	6	-3	18
4	1	$\frac{4}{1}$	26	8	$6\frac{1}{2}$		$\frac{1}{4}$	1	$\frac{1}{4}$	$6\frac{1}{2}$	-6	26	Stage III
5	1	$\frac{5}{1}$	32	6	$6\frac{2}{5}$		$\frac{1}{5}$	1	$\frac{1}{5}$	$6\frac{2}{5}$	2	32
6	1	$\frac{6}{1}$	37	5	$6\frac{1}{6}$		$\frac{1}{6}$	1	$\frac{1}{6}$	$6\frac{1}{6}$	7	37
7	1	$\frac{7}{1}$	41	4	$5\frac{6}{7}$	Stage II	$\frac{1}{7}$	1	$\frac{1}{7}$	$5\frac{6}{7}$	13	41	Stage II
8	1	$\frac{8}{1}$	43	2	$5\frac{3}{8}$		$\frac{1}{8}$	1	$\frac{1}{8}$	$5\frac{3}{8}$	27	43
9	1	$\frac{9}{1}$	44	1	$4\frac{8}{9}$		$\frac{1}{9}$	1	$\frac{1}{9}$	$4\frac{8}{9}$	35	44
10	1	$\frac{10}{1}$	44	0	$4\frac{2}{5}$		$\frac{1}{10}$	1	$\frac{1}{10}$	$4\frac{2}{5}$	44	44
11	1	$\frac{11}{1}$	43	-1	$3\frac{10}{11}$	Stage III	$\frac{1}{11}$	1	$\frac{1}{11}$	$3\frac{10}{11}$	54	43	Stage I
12	1	$\frac{12}{1}$	41	-2	$3\frac{5}{12}$		$\frac{1}{12}$	1	$\frac{1}{12}$	$3\frac{5}{12}$	65	41
13	1	$\frac{13}{1}$	37	-4	$2\frac{11}{13}$		$\frac{1}{13}$	1	$\frac{1}{13}$	$2\frac{11}{13}$	89	37
14	1	$\frac{14}{1}$	31	-6	$2\frac{3}{14}$		$\frac{1}{14}$	1	$\frac{1}{14}$	$2\frac{3}{14}$	115	31

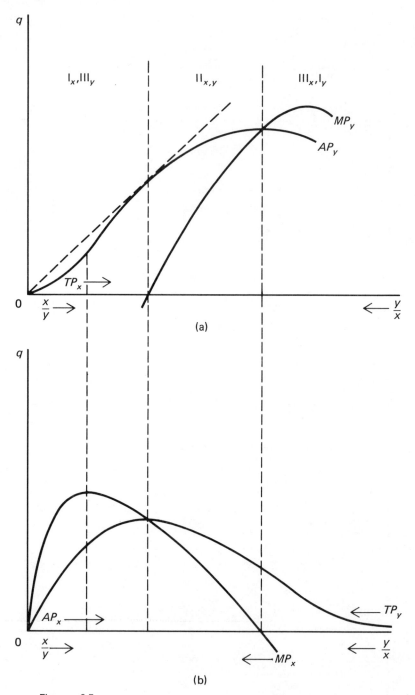

Figure 6.7

$1/14.$[9] Therefore, for a Y input of $1/14$ ($1/14 \times 1 = 1/14$) and an X input of 1 ($1/14 \times 14 = 1$), TP_y is $2\frac{3}{14}$ ($1/14 \times 31 = 2\frac{3}{14}$). The rest of column 10 is derived in analogous fashion. Columns 11 and 12 are derived from column 10 in the usual manner.[10]

[9] The changes in the proportion of the fixed (Y) factor to the variable (X) factor take place through changes in X, the Y factor being indeed *fixed*. Because of the nature of a homogeneous production function, however, we may involve ourselves in a hypothetical experiment in which the proportion of Y to X is kept the same as before but in which it is Y that is being varied, and this permits us to compute the total, the marginal, and the average product of Y. This will perhaps be clearer in the following example. We have assumed that the input of X is varied on a unit of Y and that we know the associated output figures (these are shown in brackets).

X	Y	TP_x	MP_y
[1	1]	5	
2	2	$2 \times 5 = 10$	
			-1.0
[2	1]	11	
3	1.5	$3/2 \times 11 = 16.5$	
			-3.0
[3	1]	18	
4	4/3	$4/3 \times 18 = 24$	
			-6.0
[4	1]	26	
5	5/4	$5/4 \times 26 = 32.5$	
			2.0
[5	1]	32	
6	6/5	$6/5 \times 32 = 38.4$	
			7.0
[6	1]	37	

Thus with 1 unit of X used on 1 unit of Y, 5 units of output are produced. We also know that when input of X is increased to 2 units (keeping Y constant at 1 unit), output goes to 11 units. Now, by definition of a linear homogeneous production function, we know that had both X and Y been doubled (from $1X$ and $1Y$ to $2X$ and $2Y$), output would have doubled from 5 to 10. Therefore, adding one unit of Y causes output to go from 11 to 10 and clearly $MP_y = -1$. We now repeat this process: We know that output for $3X$, $1Y$ is 18. If both X and Y had been increased by 1.5, output would have gone to 16.5. We compute MP_y as follows:

$$\frac{\Delta q}{\Delta Y} = \frac{-1.5}{0.5} = -3.0$$

The other MP_y's are computed in similar fashion.

[10] We may show the variation in the proportions of the factors of production in the short run by holding one of the factors constant at any level and varying the amount of the other factor. If the production function is linear homogeneous, there is symmetry of the stages of production, meaning that when the average product of one of the factors is rising, the marginal product of the other factor is negative, and conversely. However, if the fixed factor is held constant at one unit, we achieve a convenient diagrammatic simplification because the average product of one factor is then the total product of the other, and conversely.

The reader should notice the following symmetry in Figure 6.7, where the numbers from Table 6.2 are plotted. Over the range where AP_x increases, MP_y is negative; conversely, over the range in which AP_y is rising (measured from right to left), MP_x is negative.[11] We have seen that the firm will, if possible, never operate in a stage where a factor is subject to negative returns. Hence the firm will attempt to operate in the stage where neither factor has a negative marginal product (that is, between the ridge lines), which is stage II for both X and Y in Figure 6.7. It should be noted that in stage II_{xy} both factors are subject to both declining marginal and average product.

MULTIPRODUCT FIRM ~~Skip~~

Up to now we have restricted our discussion of production theory to firms producing a single product. We now wish to extend our analysis to the multiproduct firm. Because of ease of graphical exposition, we will consider a firm producing two products; however, the analysis can be extended to any number of products.

Each product is assumed to be produced with two homogeneous factors of production that are combined subject to production functions that exhibit the characteristics discussed above. The production decisions made by the firm are best understood with the use of an Edgeworth box diagram such as the one introduced in Chapter 5.

We assume (in Figure 6.8) the firm has available given quantities of factors X and Y; the amount of X being $O_B D$ and the amount of Y being $O_B E$. The dimensions of the box represent the assumed initial quantities of X and Y. (For every different initial quantity of X and Y, the box will have different dimensions.) The production function for good A is represented by the isoquant map that is convex to the O_A origin; the first isoquant of this set is labelled A_1. Conversely, good B's production function is represented by the isoquants convex to origin O_B, the first of which is labelled B_1.

Assume the producer is initially producing at point Z. We wish to demonstrate that he could produce more efficiently within the elliptical area bounded by ZW; that is, he could produce at least more of one good without a reduction in the other, using the same quantities of factors. We have drawn the curve CC, which connects the points of tangency of the isoquants for the two goods. And if the producer moves to a point such as P that lies both within the elliptical area and on the contract curve, he has achieved the most efficient point of production. In other words, the producer, with a given amount of resources, will always desire

[11] This relationship can be shown as follows: If q/X is rising, a doubling of X must more than double q. But we know that if we double both X and Y, q will just double (the linear homogeneous production function gives constant returns to scale). The effect of increasing the amount of Y must be to decrease output; MP_y is, therefore, negative.

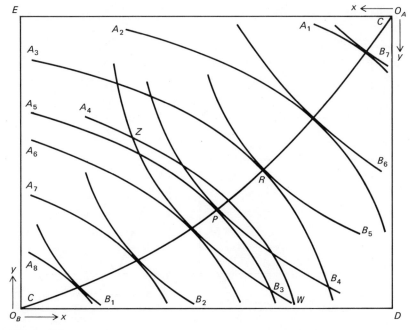

Figure 6.8

to produce at a point along the contract curve because if he is off the curve, he can increase output without a corresponding increase in inputs; and once on the curve, an increase in the production of one good will necessitate a reduction in the output of the other. Therefore, the contract curve is the locus of the most efficient points of production.

From the contract curve, we can derive the production possibility or transformation curve. Each point of tangency between isoquants defines an output pair that is a point on the production possibility curve. For example, at point P in Figure 6.8, the firm is producing A_5 units of good A and B_4 units of B. Thus, in Figure 6.9, point P' represents a plot of the output coordinates of point P on a set of output axes. Each point on curve TT in Figure 6.9 is derived in similar fashion.

To understand further the relationship between Figures 6.8 and 6.9, we refer once again to the tangency condition at point P. The slope of an isoquant for good A is equal to $-\dfrac{MP_x^A}{MP_y^A}$; and for good B, $-\dfrac{MP_x^B}{MP_y^B}$. There-fore, where the isoquants are tangent, $\dfrac{dY}{dX} = \dfrac{MP_x^A}{MP_y^A} = \dfrac{MP_x^B}{MP_y^B}$, or in dis-crete terms, $\dfrac{\Delta Y}{\Delta X} = \dfrac{MP_x^A}{MP_y^A} = \dfrac{MP_x^B}{MP_y^B}$. Now consider a movement along the contract curve from P to R, which can also be represented by a movement from P' to R' on the TT curve, that is, more of good B and

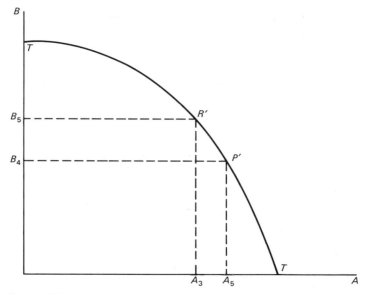

Figure 6.9

less of good A. We may derive the slope of the TT curve and show its relationship to the marginal products of the factors X and Y. We can represent the increase in the quantity of good B as

$$\Delta B = MP_x{}^B \Delta X^B + MP_y{}^B \Delta Y^B \qquad [6.11]$$

where the subscripts denote factors and the superscripts denote products. Similarly, the decrease in production of A can be shown as

$$\Delta A = MP_x{}^A \Delta X^A + MP_y{}^A \Delta Y^A \qquad [6.12]$$

It should be noted that ΔX^B is equal to and opposite in sign to ΔX^A and that ΔY^B is equal and opposite in sign to ΔY^A. The reason for these equalities is that the quantities of X and Y are constant and assumed to be completely utilized.

The slope of the transformation curve (in discrete terms) in Figure 6.9 can be expressed as $\Delta B / \Delta A$. Substituting equations 6.11 and 6.12, we can write

$$\frac{\Delta B}{\Delta A} = \frac{MP_x{}^B \Delta X^B + MP_y{}^B \Delta Y^B}{MP_x{}^A \Delta X^A + MP_y{}^A \Delta Y^A} \qquad [6.13]$$

In addition to the input constraints just mentioned, there is the additional constraint that the firm remain on the contract curve, that is, *on*, not within, the production possibility curve. In other words, it is required that the following condition be fulfilled:

$$\frac{MP_x{}^A}{MP_y{}^A} = \frac{MP_x{}^B}{MP_y{}^B} \qquad [6.14]$$

We next divide equation 6.13 by ΔX^B (which is equal to $-\Delta X^A$).

$$\frac{\Delta B}{\Delta A} = \frac{MP_x{}^B + MP_y{}^B \dfrac{\Delta Y^B}{\Delta X^B}}{-MP_x{}^A - MP_y{}^A \dfrac{\Delta Y^B}{\Delta X^B}} \tag{6.15}$$

From equation 6.14, $MP_x{}^B = MP_y{}^B \dfrac{MP_x{}^A}{MP_y{}^A}$ and $MP_x{}^A = MP_y{}^A \dfrac{MP_x{}^B}{MP_y{}^B}$ and substituting these expressions into equation 6.15 we get

$$\frac{\Delta B}{\Delta A} = \frac{MP_y{}^B \left[\dfrac{MP_x{}^A}{MP_y{}^A} + \dfrac{\Delta Y^B}{\Delta X^B} \right]}{-MP_y{}^A \left[\dfrac{MP_x{}^B}{MP_y{}^B} + \dfrac{\Delta Y^B}{\Delta X^B} \right]}$$

Once again making use of condition 6.14 and cancelling, we get

$$\frac{\Delta B}{\Delta A} = -\frac{MP_y{}^B}{MP_y{}^A} \tag{6.16}$$

If, from equation 6.14, we substitute for $MP_y{}^B$ and $MP_y{}^A$ and then rewrite equation 6.15, the result obtained would be

$$\frac{\Delta B}{\Delta A} = -\frac{MP_x{}^B}{MP_x{}^A} \tag{6.17}$$

The transformation curve drawn in Figure 6.9 is concave to the origin. The concavity represents increasing costs; that is, as more of good A (good B) is produced, the decrements of good B (good A) become ever larger. With the usual assumptions concerning diminishing returns in the short run and decreasing returns to scale in the long run, this is the shape that would result. However, if these assumptions are relaxed, it is possible to have variations in the shape.

LONG-RUN LEAST-COST CONDITIONS

Recall that the isoquant map in Figure 6.2 showed the different combinations of X and Y that the firm could use to produce various levels of output when all factors of production are variable. From a technological point of view, all points along an isoquant represent equal efficiency; that is, the same output can be produced with the different factor combinations. Because a firm must pay positive prices for the factors it employs, the total cost of producing a particular level of output will vary along an isoquant, depending on the factor combination and the factor prices. Thus, although all factor combinations along an isoquant represent equal *technological* efficiency, the combination with which the particular output level can be produced at lowest total cost represents the *economically* most efficient combination. And because firms try to maximize their profits (which are equal to the difference between total revenue and total cost), a firm will try to select the combination of factors that minimizes the total cost for any given level of output. Or, what amounts to the same thing, for a given level of expenditure, the firm will try to maximize output.

Assume that a firm with the production function of Figure 6.2 must pay $1 per unit of X and $2 per unit of Y and that both these factor prices remain the same regardless of the quantities the firm purchases.[12] With these factor prices, we want to determine which factor combination the firm will use to produce each of the output levels included in Figure 6.2. In other words, we wish to find the least cost of producing these outputs.

Nine different *isocost lines* are drawn in Figure 6.10. Each isocost (or equal-cost line) shows the different combinations of factors X and Y the firm *can* produce when $P_x = \$1$ and $P_y = \$2$ for a given level of total expenditure. Thus, along isocost line $TC = \$695$, the firm can purchase the sample quantities of X and Y shown in Table 6.3. Because the factor prices are assumed to be constants, the isocost lines are all parallel with slopes equal to $-P_x/P_y$.[13]

TABLE 6.3

X	Y	P_xX	P_yY	Total Cost
695	0	$695	$ 0	$695
645	25	645	50	695
595	50	595	100	695
545	75	545	150	695
495	100	495	200	695
445	125	445	250	695
395	150	395	300	695
345	175	345	350	695
295	200	295	400	695
245	225	245	450	695
195	250	195	500	695
145	275	145	550	695
95	300	95	600	695
45	325	45	650	695
0	$347\frac{1}{2}$	$ 0	$695	$695

[12] It is also possible that a firm pay either higher or lower per-unit prices for its factors as it increases the quantities of the factors that it purchases or hires. The case of rising factor prices will be considered in Chapter 11.

[13] See page 78, where the slope of the budget line was derived. An isocost line has the same properties as a budget line, as it is based on given prices and a given level of expenditure.

In Figure 6.11 we have redrawn the isoquant map of Figure 6.2 and have superimposed on it the isocost lines of Figure 6.10. From the infinite number of possible isocost lines, we have selected those that are tangent to the isoquants. The coordinates of the point of tangency between isoquant 1 and isocost line 1 (150 units of X and 80 units of Y) are those quantities of X and Y that ensure 100 units of output being produced at minimum cost, which is \$310. We show in Figure 6.11 the least-cost combination of X and Y for the different output levels, and we summarize this information in Table 6.4. The curve drawn connecting these tangency points is called the expansion path of the firm.[14]

[14] For their esthetic appeal, most textbooks show the expansion path and ridge lines as being smooth curves. However, the complexities of the set of choices that the production function summarizes mean that no such regularity in the shape of these curves is necessary.

In pages 112–113 and in Appendix 5A, we showed that the slope of an isoquant was equal to the ratio of marginal products:

$$\frac{dY}{dX} = \frac{MP_x}{MP_y}$$

In Appendix 6A, we show that, with a linear homogeneous production function, the marginal products are functions simply of the factor proportions. If P_x and P_y are constants, the expansion path for this special type of production function will be a straight line. We can see this with reference to the accompanying diagram.

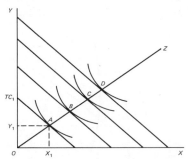

All combinations of X and Y along OZ are in the same proportion. Therefore,

$$\frac{MP_x}{MP_y} \text{ at } A = \frac{MP_x}{MP_y} \text{ at } B = \text{ and so on}$$

If A is the tangency between isoquant 1 and isocost line 1 (that is, X_1 and Y_1 yield the lowest cost to produce q_1), then at A,

$$\frac{MP_x}{MP_y} = \frac{P_x}{P_y}$$

With the assumption of constant P_x/P_y, the slopes of the isocost lines are equal. Therefore, all least-cost combinations (tangency points between isoquants and isocost lines) must lie along line OZ where the slopes of the isoquants, $-MP_x/MP_y$, are all equal to the slope of isoquant q_1 at A.

The ridge lines also will be straight with a linear homogeneous production function. RL_x is the locus of points where $MP_x/MP_y = 0$, RL_y where $MP_x/MP_y = \infty$, and MP_x/MP_y is a function of the factor proportion used.

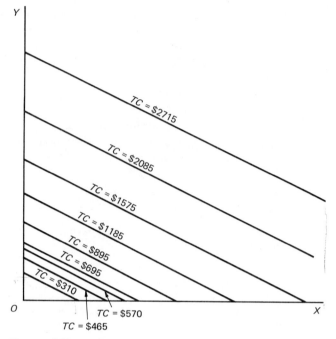

Figure 6.10

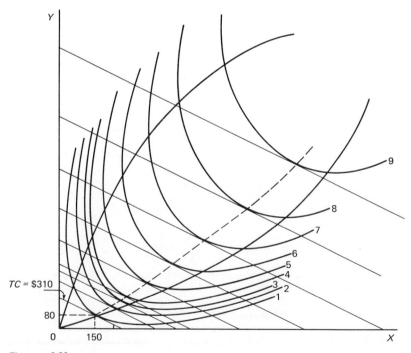

Figure 6.11

TABLE   6.4

(1) q	(2) X	(3) Y	(4) P_xX	(5) P_yY	(6) TC
100	150	80	$150	$160	$310
200	235	115	235	230	465
300	270	150	270	300	570
400	305	195	305	390	695
500	435	230	435	460	895
600	535	325	535	650	1185
700	685	445	685	890	1575
800	905	590	905	1180	2085
900	1125	795	$1125	$1590	$2715

Column 4 = Column 2 × $1
Column 5 = Column 3 × $2
Column 6 = Column 4 + Column 5 = Total cost

It will be recalled that the slope of an isocost line is equal to $-P_x/P_y$ and the slope of an isoquant is equal to $-MP_x/MP_y$. Because at each point of tangency, the slope of the isocost line is equal to the slope of the isoquant, we can state that[15]

$$\frac{MP_x}{MP_y} = \frac{P_x}{P_y} \qquad [6.18]$$

or

$$\frac{MP_x}{P_x} = \frac{MP_y}{P_y} \qquad [6.18a]$$

This tangency condition holds all along the expansion path.

A numerical example should make clear why this tangency condition represents the minimum cost of producing a given level of output or the maximum output for a given level of expenditure. With $P_x = \$1$ and $P_y = \$2$, assume this firm is using a combination of factor quantities such that $MP_x = 10$ and $MP_y = 15$. Then the following inequality would hold:

$$\frac{MP_x}{P_x} > \frac{MP_y}{P_y}; \qquad \frac{10 \text{ units}}{\$1} > \frac{15 \text{ units}}{\$2}$$

or (10 units per $) > ($7\frac{1}{2}$ units per $).

[15] Appendix 4A can be used to demonstrate rigorously that this is a necessary condition if output is to be maximized subject to a given level of total cost. If A and B represent two factors of production, P_a and P_b the given constant prices of those factors, I the given level of total cost, and U the output, the proof is identical with Appendix 4A. (Of course, marginal products would be relevant, rather than the marginal utilities of Chapter 4.) Furthermore, the second-order condition, ensuring that output is at a maximum rather than a minimum is identical with that in Appendix 4A.

If the firm were to spend \$1 less on factor Y, it would lose $7\frac{1}{2}$ units of production; but if the firm kept its expenditure constant by spending the dollar on factor X, it would gain approximately 10 units of output. This means there would be a net increase in output of $2\frac{1}{2}$ units with expenditure the same. Further transfers of expenditure from Y to X would continue to result in additional output as long as $MP_x/P_x > MP_y/P_y$. As discussed previously, however, the use of more X and less Y will cause MP_x to decline and MP_y to increase; and since P_x and P_y are constants, with continuously divisible factors, MP_x/P_x and MP_y/P_y will become equal to each other.

The total cost figures in column 6 of Table 6.4 are the minimum costs for producing the various levels of output. And for each level of output, the factor combination of columns 2 and 3 is the economically most efficient one.

SHORT-RUN EQUILIBRIUM OF THE FIRM

Given the fact that the firm cannot vary all its factors of production, in the short run it will attempt to produce any level of output at the least possible cost. First, we shall consider the short-run situation presented on pages 109–112: Factor X is the only variable factor and Y the only fixed one, which we shall assume is at the level Y_1 (750 units). In Figure 6.2, moving along Y_1A, we can see that for any output a specific input of the one variable factor is necessary if redundancy is to be avoided. In this case the fact that the firm has no technological choice in producing any level of output makes the economically and the technologically most efficient methods of production the same. These conclusions are, however, merely the result of the simplifying assumption that there is only one variable factor of production.

The short-run total product schedule of Figure 6.3 (which was derived from the isoquant map of Figure 6.2 by holding Y constant at $Y_1 = 750$ units) can be converted into a short-run total cost curve. This procedure is demonstrated with reference to Figures 6.12a–c. In Figure 6.12a we merely replot Figure 6.3. In Figure 6.12b we replot the same input-output relationship but with the axes reversed. (Alternatively, this may be described as rotating Figure 6.12a 90 degrees around the O-point as an axis.) In Figure 6.12b the vertical axis gives us the input of the variable factor; and when we have multiplied these factor quantities by the price of the factor (\$1 in this example), we obtain the variable cost for each level of output shown on the horizontal axis. Figure 6.12b with the \$-vertical axis, then, is the variable cost curve of the firm. It is a convention, however, to read positive quantities from left to right. Turning Figure 6.12b over we get Figure 6.12c, which is the same as Figure 6.12b except that the quantity-axis now reads from left to right. Because we

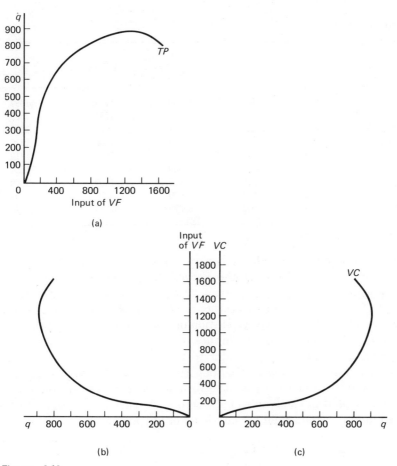

Figure 6.12

have assumed Y constant at 750 units and P_y a constant of \$2 per unit, the "fixed cost" is \$1500. If we were to add this fixed cost to the variable cost at each level of output, we would obtain a new curve, with the same shape as the variable cost curve, but above it by the constant amount of \$1500. This is the short-run total cost curve of the firm. The derivation of these cost curves is summarized in Table 6.5.

Once we make the more realistic assumption that the firm has two or more variable factors, it is again faced with more than one technological alternative and must choose among them on economic grounds. A relationship among three inputs and output is represented by a four-dimensional production surface.[16]

[16] The concept of four dimensions is outside the experience of human beings, who live in a three-dimensional world; it is, however, both mathematically and analytically a useful abstraction to talk about n-dimensional relationships.

TABLE 6.5

X	Y	q	VC (= $1 · X)	FC (= $2 · 750)	TC = VC + FC
90	750	100	$ 90	$1500	$1590
125	750	200	125	1500	1625
150	750	300	150	1500	1650
170	750	400	170	1500	1670
210	750	500	210	1500	1710
300	750	600	300	1500	1800
450	750	700	450	1500	1950
690	750	800	690	1500	2190
1270	750	900	$1270	$1500	$2770

The reader has seen that when we cut a three-dimensional surface at some fixed level of one of the variables, the resulting surface is two-dimensional. Analogously, cutting a four-dimensional surface at a fixed level of one of the variable factors produces a three-dimensional surface. Figure 6.2 might be a representation of a relationship among three inputs and output when one of the inputs is being held constant at some level. The resulting problem is similar to the one considered before in which the firm was operating in the long run with two factors of production. We demonstrated then that the firm would combine its factors in the long run (and in the long run all factors are variable) so that the following equality would hold for any level of output:

$$\frac{MP_a}{P_a} = \frac{MP_b}{P_b} = \cdots = \frac{MP_n}{P_n} \qquad [6.19]$$

OUTPUT AND SUBSTITUTION EFFECTS

In an analogous fashion to the effect upon an individual of a decrease in the price of a product, which may be broken up into income and substitution effects, the decrease in the price of a factor has an effect upon the factor purchases of the firm, which may be broken up into an output and a substitution effect. However, in the treatment of the firm, the firm does not have a fixed income to spend. We may, however, discuss the output and input decisions of the firm for a given cost. The second difference is that there cannot be a Giffen factor so that the firm will always buy more of a relatively lower-cost factor. We now illustrate this with regard to Figure 6.13.

Assume the price of X declines so that the isocost line changes from FG to FB, with the initial least-cost equilibrium at A and the new equilibrium at B. Once again, we may hypothetically decompose the total

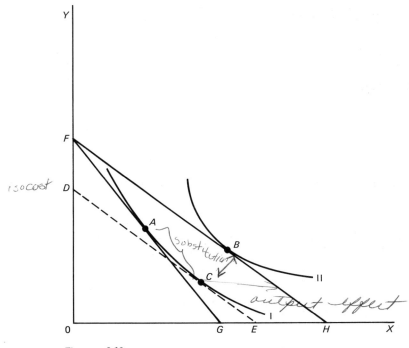

Figure 6.13

movement from A to B into the components: AC, the substitution effect and CB the output effect. The isocost line DE is derived by the firm hypothetically decreasing its expenditure at the new factor price ratio so that it is just able to produce its previous output level, represented by isoquant I. It is to be noted that the new factor combination is represented by C, where the firm uses more of the now-cheaper factor X. In fact, the firm moves to point B on the higher isoquant II; thus, the movement from C to B is the output effect.[17]

[17] For a discussion of the possibility of an inferior factor, *see* J. R. Hicks, *Value and Capital*, 2d. ed., Oxford, 1946, pp. 93–96.

Appendix 6A

Some Characteristics of Homogeneous Production Functions

A homogeneous function of degree i can be written as

$$k^i q = f(kX, kY) \tag{6A.1}$$

Since k is any number, we can define it to be equal to $1/X$. Therefore, we can write:

$$\frac{1}{X^i} q = f\left(1, \frac{Y}{X}\right)$$

$$\frac{q}{X^i} = g\left(\frac{Y}{X}\right)$$

$$q = X^i g\left(\frac{Y}{X}\right) \tag{6A.2}$$

$$\frac{q}{X} = X^{i-1} g\left(\frac{Y}{X}\right) \tag{6A.3}$$

It is obvious that $\dfrac{q}{Y} = Y^{i-1} h\left(\dfrac{X}{Y}\right)$.

Note that for a homogeneous function, q/X (that is, the AP_x) is a function solely of the factor proportion Y/X. Furthermore, the degree of AP_x is $i - 1$ or one degree less than the production function; that is, if both X and Y were doubled, $g\left(\dfrac{Y}{X}\right)$ will remain unchanged but q/X will increase by the multiple $(2)^{i-1}$.

It is also true that the marginal products depend only on factor proportions and are homogeneous of the degree $i - 1$. Differentiating equation 6A.2 with respect to Y, we get

$$MP_x = \frac{\partial q}{\partial X} = X^{i-1} g\left(\frac{Y}{X}\right) + X^{i-2} g'\left(\frac{Y}{X}\right)\left(-\frac{Y}{X^2}\right)$$

or

$$= X^{i-1} g\left(\frac{Y}{X}\right) + X^{i-1} g'\left(\frac{Y}{X}\right)\left(-\frac{Y}{X}\right) \tag{6A.4}$$

Notice that the usual marginal-average relationship holds so that equation 6A.4 could have been obtained directly from 6A.3.

Rewriting equation 6A.4 we get

$$\frac{\partial q}{\partial X} = X^{i-1}\left[g\left(\frac{Y}{X}\right) + g'\left(\frac{Y}{X}\right)\left(-\frac{Y}{X}\right)\right] \qquad [6A.5]$$

The expression within the square brackets depends solely on the factor proportion; thus, changing both factors by the proportion α will not effect this value. However, X^{i-1}, which multiplies this expression, will change by α^{i-1}, thus changing $\partial q/\partial X$ by the same proportion.

Another interesting characteristic of homogeneous functions may be derived as follows, given the homogeneous production function $q = f(X, Y)$. Now the partial derivative $\partial q/\partial X$ gives the infinitesimal increment in output due to an infinitesimal change in the use of factor X, with the quantity of factor Y being held constant. If we multiply this rate by an infinitesimal change in the quantity of X, dX, we obtain an approximate value of the change in output resulting from the increment in X. The same reasoning holds for factor Y, with X held constant. Thus the total change in output may be written as:

$$dq = \frac{\partial q}{\partial X}\,dX + \frac{\partial q}{\partial Y}\,dY \qquad [6A.6]$$

Assume that X and Y are changed in the same proportion; that is, $dX/X = dY/Y$. Because $X = k\bar{X}$ and $Y = k\bar{Y}$, this means $dX/X = dY/Y = dk/k$. Substituting in equation 6A.6:

$$dq = \frac{\partial q}{\partial X}\frac{dk}{k}X + \frac{\partial q}{\partial Y}\frac{dk}{k}Y$$

$$dq = \frac{dk}{k}\left(\frac{\partial q}{\partial X}X + \frac{\partial q}{\partial Y}Y\right)$$

$$\frac{dq}{\frac{dk}{k}} = \frac{\partial q}{\partial X}X + \frac{\partial q}{\partial Y}Y$$

Dividing the numerator of the left-hand term by q and multiplying the entire left-hand term by q (which leaves the entire expression unchanged in value):

$$q\frac{\frac{dq}{q}}{\frac{dk}{k}} = \frac{\partial q}{\partial X}X + \frac{\partial q}{\partial Y}Y$$

However,

$$\frac{\frac{dq}{q}}{\frac{dk}{k}} = E_k$$

Therefore,

$$qE_k = \frac{\partial q}{\partial X} X + \frac{\partial q}{\partial Y} Y \qquad \text{[6A.7]}$$

This is the Wicksell-Johnson theorem.

In the special case where $E_k = 1$ (that is, a linear homogeneous production function), equation 6A.7 reduces to

$$q = \frac{\partial q}{\partial X} X + \frac{\partial q}{\partial Y} Y \qquad \text{[6A.8]}$$

which is known as Euler's theorem. This says that the sum of the marginal products of the inputs multiplied by their respective quantities is equal to the output. This will be an important theorem in our discussion of factor pricing and distribution. However, at this point, Euler's theorem may be used to illuminate our previous discussion of the symmetry of the stages of production.

Expression 6A.8 can be rewritten as either

$$\frac{q}{X} - \frac{\partial q}{\partial X} = \frac{\partial q}{\partial Y} \cdot \frac{Y}{X} \qquad \text{[6A.9]}$$

or

$$\frac{q}{Y} - \frac{\partial q}{\partial Y} = \frac{\partial q}{\partial X} \cdot \frac{X}{Y} \qquad \text{[6A.10]}$$

The first stage for X is defined as the output interval over which AP_x is rising. Over this stage, then, $MP_x > AP_x$; that is, $\partial q/\partial X > q/X$. In equation 6A.9, this means that the left-hand side is negative; and since Y/X is positive, $\partial q/\partial Y$ must be negative: Factor Y is in the redundant area, stage III. Analogously, using equation 6A.10, we can show that when AP_y is rising, $\partial q/\partial X$ is negative. When X is in stage II, $\partial q/\partial X > 0$, and $q/X > \partial q/\partial X$, which means $\partial q/\partial Y > 0$. In equation 6A.10, then, $q/Y > \partial q/\partial Y$, which, together with $\partial q/\partial Y > 0$, means Y is also in stage II.

A form of the linear homogeneous production function that has frequently been used in economics is the Cobb-Douglas function, which is of the form $q = AL^\alpha C^{1-\alpha}$ where L and C represent labor and capital, A is a constant, and the exponents α and $1 - \alpha$ sum to the scale elasticity of the function (that is, 1). The student might show that the Cobb-Douglas has the characteristics just proved that hold for all linear homogeneous functions.

Appendix 6B

Scale Elasticity and the Spacing of Isoquants

In order to show the relationship between scale elasticity and the spacing of isoquants, we begin with the definition of scale elasticity:

$$E_k = \frac{\dfrac{\partial q}{\partial k}}{\dfrac{q}{k}} \qquad [6B.1]$$

Differentiating with respect to k:

$$\frac{dE_k}{dk} = \frac{d}{dk}\left[\frac{\partial q}{\partial k}\cdot\frac{k}{q}\right] = \frac{\partial^2 q}{\partial k^2}\frac{k}{q} + \frac{1}{q}\frac{\partial q}{\partial k} - \frac{k}{q^2}\left[\frac{\partial q}{\partial k}\right]^2$$

Substituting equation 6B.1 in the previous equation, we have

$$\frac{dE_k}{dk} = \frac{\partial^2 q}{\partial k^2}\frac{k}{q} + \frac{1}{q}\frac{\partial q}{\partial k}(1 - E_k) \qquad [6B.2]$$

For homogeneous functions, E_k is a constant, and therefore, $dE_k/dk = 0$. In addition, we assume $k > 0$ and $\partial q/\partial k > 0$. It follows from equation 6B.2 that

$$\frac{\partial^2 q}{\partial k^2}\frac{k}{q} = -\frac{1}{q}\frac{\partial q}{\partial k}(1 - E_k)$$

and

$$\frac{\dfrac{\partial^2 q}{\partial k^2}}{\dfrac{\partial q}{\partial k}} = \frac{E_k - 1}{k} \qquad [6B.3]$$

Thus, when $E_k > 1$,

$$\frac{\partial^2 q}{\partial k^2} > 0 \qquad \text{(isoquants are ever closer)}$$

when $E_k = 1$,

$$\frac{\partial^2 q}{\partial k^2} = 0 \qquad \text{(isoquants are equally spaced)}$$

when $E_k < 1$,

$$\frac{\partial^2 q}{\partial k^2} < 0 \qquad \text{(isoquants are ever farther apart)}$$

These relationships also hold for nonhomogeneous functions for which average and marginal returns to scale always increase and decrease together.[1]

Next we consider the most general case: nonhomogeneous functions. We investigate first the case where scale elasticity is positive and increasing, that is, $dE_k/dk > 0$. Again we assume $k > 0$ and $\partial q/\partial k > 0$. From equation 6B.2:

$$\frac{dE_k}{dk} = \frac{\partial^2 q}{\partial k^2}\frac{k}{q} + \frac{1}{q}\frac{\partial q}{\partial k}(1 - E_k) > 0$$

and

$$\frac{\dfrac{\partial^2 q}{\partial k^2}}{\dfrac{\partial q}{\partial k}} > \frac{E_k - 1}{k} \qquad\qquad \text{[6B.4]}$$

If $E_k > 1$,

$$\frac{\partial^2 q}{\partial k^2} > 0$$

if $E_k = 1$,

$$\frac{\partial^2 q}{\partial k^2} > 0$$

and if $E_k < 1$,

$$\frac{\partial^2 q}{\partial k^2} \gtrless 0$$

Of more importance for economic analysis is $dE_k/dk < 0$; that is, a stage of increasing returns to scale followed by constant and/or decreasing returns to scale. Our assumptions are now $dE_k/dk < 0$, $k > 0$, and $\partial q/\partial k > 0$. Then equation 6B.2 gives

$$\frac{dE}{dk} = \frac{\partial^2 q}{\partial k^2}\frac{k}{q} + \frac{1}{q}\frac{\partial q}{\partial k}(1 - E_k) < 0$$

$$\frac{\dfrac{\partial^2 q}{\partial k^2}}{\dfrac{\partial q}{\partial k}} < \frac{E_k - 1}{k} \qquad\qquad \text{[6B.5]}$$

[1] For a further discussion, see F. W. McElroy, "Returns to Scale and the Spacing of Isoquants: Comment," *American Economic Review* (March 1967), 223–224.

If $E_k > 1$,

$$\frac{\partial^2 q}{\partial k^2} \gtreqless 0$$

if $E_k = 1$,

$$\frac{\partial^2 q}{\partial k^2} < 0$$

and if $E_k < 1$,

$$\frac{\partial^2 q}{\partial k^2} < 0$$

7

COSTS OF PRODUCTION

SHORT-RUN COSTS

In this section we shall consider the costs of the firm in the short run, when at least one factor of production is fixed.[1] We now derive the average and marginal cost curves.

Variable costs (VC) are the costs that vary with the output of the firm and that will be zero when output is zero.

Fixed costs (FC) are the costs that remain constant as output varies and are incurred even if output is zero.[2]

Total cost (STC) is the sum of variable plus fixed costs.[3]

$$STC = VC + FC \qquad [7.1]$$

[1] It has been pointed out that the "fixed factor" is many times fixed in cost but, within the fixed cost, the entrepreneur has built a flexible plant adaptable to a wide range of outputs. For instance, he may build ten small machines that can be brought into use as needed to produce a wide range of outputs, rather than a single large machine of equal cost that, although more efficient in producing large outputs, is not as flexible. For a full discussion of this point, see George J. Stigler, "Production and Distribution in the Short Run," *Journal of Political Economy*, Vol. XLVII (1939), 105–127; reprinted in A.E.A., *Readings in Income Distribution* (Homewood, Ill.: Irwin, 1951).

[2] Another category of short-run costs is quasifixed costs. These are costs that are zero when output is zero but that assume a certain value when output is increased above zero and that then remain at that level for all outputs above the initial one.

[3] Included in all the cost concepts are not only the explicit or expenditure cost but also the cost of forgone opportunities—or implicit cost. For example, the wages lost by the entrepreneur when he works for his own firm rather than in his most remunerative alternative occupation are included as implicit costs.

Marginal cost (SMC) is the rate of change of total cost with respect to changes in output. In the continuous case,

$$SMC = \frac{dSTC}{dq} \qquad [7.2a]$$

and in the discrete case,

$$SMC = \frac{\Delta STC}{\Delta q} \qquad [7.2b]$$

Because the difference between total cost and variable cost is a constant (fixed cost), marginal cost can also be computed as

$$SMC = \frac{dVC}{dq} \qquad \text{or} \qquad SMC = \frac{\Delta VC}{\Delta q} \qquad [7.2c]$$

TABLE 7.1

(1) X	(2) Y	(3) q	(4) VC	(5) FC	(6) STC	(7) AP_x	(8) AVC	(9) MP_x	(10) SMC	(11) AFC	(12) SAC
0	750	0	$ 0	$1500	$1500					$→∞	$→∞
								1.11	$0.90		
90	750	100	90	1500	1590	1.11	$0.90			15.00	15.90
								2.86	0.35		
125	750	200	125	1500	1625	1.60	0.625			7.50	8.125
								4.00	0.25		
150	750	300	150	1500	1650	2.00	0.50			5.00	5.50
								5.00	0.20		
170	750	400	170	1500	1670	2.35	0.425			3.75	4.175
								2.50	0.40		
210	750	500	210	1500	1710	2.38	0.42			3.00	3.42
								1.11	0.90		
300	750	600	300	1500	1800	2.00	0.50			2.50	3.00
								0.67	1.50		
450	750	700	450	1500	1950	1.56	0.6428			2.14	2.785
								0.42	2.40		
690	750	800	690	1500	2190	1.16	0.8625			1.88	2.737
								0.17	$5.80		
1270	750	900	$1270	$1500	$2770	0.71	$1.411			$ 1.67	$ 3.077

(1), (2), and (3) were obtained from Figure 6.12a
(4) = (1) × $1 (see Figure 6.12c)
(5) = (2) × $2
(6) = (4) + (5)
(7) = (3) ÷ (1)
(8) = (4) ÷ (1)
(9) = Δ(3) ÷ Δ(1) = discrete MP_x
(10) = Δ(4) ÷ Δ(3) = Δ(6) ÷ Δ(3) = discrete MC
(11) = (5) ÷ (3)
(12) = (8) + (11) = (6) ÷ (3)

Average variable cost (AVC) is the variable cost per unit of output:

$$AVC = \frac{VC}{q} \tag{7.3}$$

Average fixed cost (AFC) is the fixed cost per unit of output:

$$AFC = \frac{FC}{q} \tag{7.4}$$

Average total cost (SAC) is the total cost per unit of output:

$$SAC = \frac{STC}{q} = \frac{VC}{q} + \frac{FC}{q} = AVC + AFC \tag{7.5}$$

We now derive the relationships just defined for the cost data that was obtained from the production function on page 108, where $P_x = \$1$ and $P_y = \$2$. With reference to Table 7.1, the student should note the following relationships: When AP_x rises, $MP_x > AP_x$, and when AP_x declines, $MP_x < AP_x$ (columns 7 and 9). When AP_x rises, AVC falls, and when AP_x declines, AVC increases (columns 7 and 8). Because X is the only variable factor and its price is a constant, when the average productivity of X rises (that is, increasing returns to X), the cost per unit of output (AVC) must decline. There is an analogous relationship between MP_x and SMC (columns 9 and 10). When the marginal productivity of X rises, the extra cost per unit of output (SMC) must fall.[4]

Therefore, if there is an initial stage of increasing returns, followed by a stage of decreasing returns, the AVC curve will be **U** shaped; it declines, reaches a minimum, and then rises. Analogously, the SMC curve will be **U** shaped. The usual relationship holds between the AVC and SMC curves and is shown graphically in Figure 7.1: When AVC declines,

---

[4] These relationships can be shown as follows:

$$\frac{q}{X} = AP_x$$

If q/X rises, X/q falls and $(X/q)P_x$, with P_x constant, falls. If $\Delta q/\Delta X$ rises, $\Delta X/\Delta q$ falls, and $(\Delta x/\Delta q)P_x$ falls, with P_x constant.

Figure 7.1 does not show the segments of the cost curves that correspond to the range of output where X is the redundant factor or, in other words, that correspond to the dashed portion of the VC curve in Figure 6.12c. It is to be noted that the VC curve turns back toward the vertical axis. Consequently, AVC is no longer a single-valued function of q, which means that for any output value, there will be both a low and high value of average variable cost. Obviously, because X is variable, the firm will never utilize a sufficient amount of X to produce a given output at the higher AVC. Because VC rises with decreases in output in this redundant area, SMC must be negative in this area. This creates a discontinuity at the point where total product is a maximum. For a full discussion of this point, see Om P. Tangri, "Omissions in the Treatment of the Law of Variable Proportions," *The American Economic Review* (June 1966), 484–493.

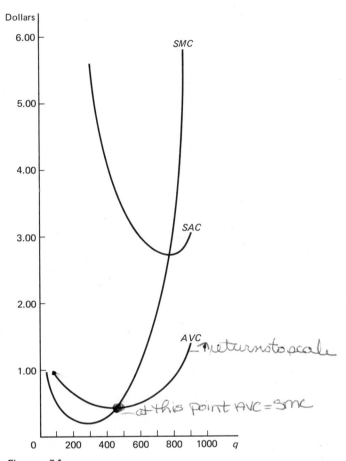

Figure 7.1

SMC lies below *AVC*; when *AVC* rises, *SMC* lies above *AVC*; and when *AVC* is at its minimum level, it is equal to *SMC*.

We show the *AFC* schedule (column 11 in Table 7.1) in Figure 7.2. Fixed costs being constant, *AFC* continuously declines as output is increased. When output reaches high levels, *AFC* approaches zero but, of course, must remain positive.[5] In graphical terms, then *AFC* is a rectangular hyperbole.

The shape of the *SAC* schedule in Figure 7.1 (column 12) depends on the shapes of the *AVC* and *AFC* schedules because $SAC = AVC + AFC$. Over the range of output where *AVC* is declining (up to 500 units in Table 7.1), *SAC* will also fall, because *AFC* always declines. However,

[5] We have seen that $AFC = FC/q$; clearly, also $AFC \times q = (FC/q)q = FC =$ constant. In graphical terms, this means that the rectangles cut off by the ordinates and abscissas of the points of the *AFC* curve must all have areas equal to *FC*.

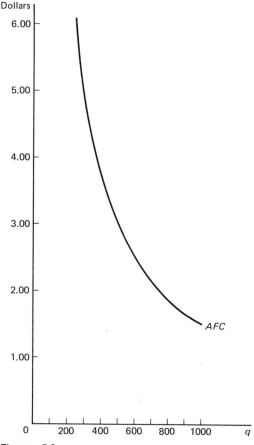

Figure   7.2

when AVC starts to increase, SAC can continue to decline, if the decrease in AFC more than offsets the increase in AVC. Thus, in our example, SAC declines up to 800 units of output. SMC has the same relationship to SAC as it does to AVC, because $SMC = \Delta STC/\Delta q = \Delta VC/\Delta q$; that is, when SAC declines, $SMC < SAC$; when SAC increases, $SMC > SAC$; and $SMC = SAC$ when SAC is at its minimum level. This relationship is shown in Figure 7.1.

For some firms, evidence indicates the variable costs of production increase at a constant rate over a range of outputs. This situation is presented in Table 7.2 for the range of outputs between 4 and 8 units. Thus, AVC reaches a minimum of \$7 at 4 units; but instead of rising as output expands, AVC remains at \$7 through 8 units and rises thereafter. Note that because SMC is equal to AVC at the minimum level of AVC, SMC and AVC are coincident over a range of outputs. With a flat-bottomed

AVC curve, SAC will still be $\mathbf{U}$ shaped; SAC will decline while AVC is a constant and will rise when the increases in AVC start to outweigh the decreases in AFC. The cost schedules of Table 7.2 are drawn in Figure 7.3.

TABLE 7.2

q	VC	FC	STC	SMC	AVC	AFC	SAC
0	$ 0	$10	$ 10			$\to \infty$	$\to \infty$
				$10			
1	10	10	20		$10	10.00	20.00
				8			
2	18	10	28		9	5.00	14.00
				6			
3	24	10	34		8	3.33	11.33
				4			
4	28	10	38		7	2.50	9.50
				7			
5	35	10	45		7	2.00	9.00
				7			
6	42	10	52		7	1.67	8.67
				7			
7	49	10	59		7	1.43	8.43
				7			
8	56	10	66		7	1.25	8.25
				16			
9	72	10	82		8	1.11	9.11
				$18			
10	$90	$10	$100		$ 9	$ 1.00	$10.00

LONG-RUN COSTS

Because in the long run all factors of production can be varied, the relevant cost concepts are *total cost* (LTC, which is the same as total variable cost) and the corresponding average and marginal costs.

Marginal cost (LMC) is the rate of change of total cost with respect to changes in output:

$$LMC = \frac{dLTC}{dq} \quad \text{(continuous)} \qquad [7.6a]$$

$$LMC = \frac{\Delta LTC}{\Delta q} \quad \text{(discrete)} \qquad [7.6b]$$

Average cost (LAC) is the total cost per unit of output:

$$LAC = \frac{LTC}{q} \qquad [7.7]$$

The relationships that exist among LTC, LAC, and LMC are the same as the short-run ones. This is demonstrated with respect to Table 7.3 and

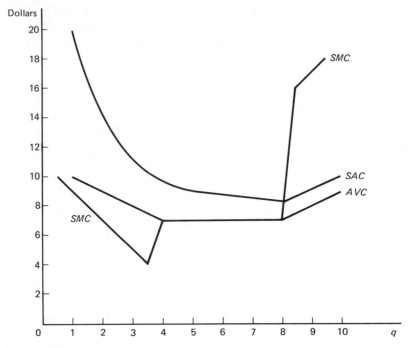

Figure 7.3

TABLE 7.3

q	LTC	LMC	LAC
0	$ 0		
		$3.10	
100	310		$3.10
		1.55	
200	465		2.32
		1.05	
300	570		1.90
		1.25	
400	695		1.74
		2.00	
500	895		1.79
		2.90	
600	1185		1.90
		3.90	
700	1575		2.25
		5.10	
800	2085		2.61
		$6.30	
900	$2715		$3.02

Source: Table 6.6.

Figure 7.4. When *LTC* increases at a decreasing rate, *LMC* falls; and *LMC* rises when *LTC* increases at an increasing rate. Observe how the declining stage of *LMC* is over the range of outputs where the isoquants were closer and closer together in Figure 6.7. Similarly, for the outputs

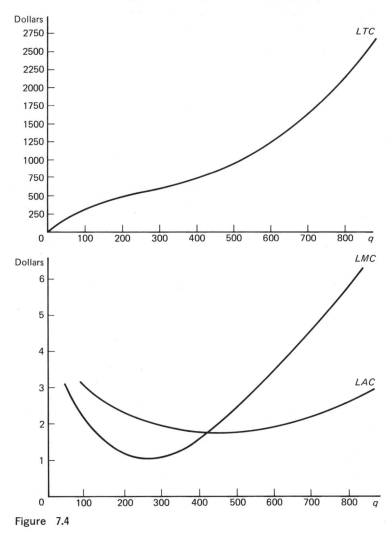

Figure 7.4

where the isoquants were drawn farther and farther apart in Figure 6.7, *LMC* increases. When *LAC* decreases, *LMC* < *LAC*; when *LAC* increases, *LMC* > *LAC*; and when *LAC* is at its minimum level, *LMC* = *LAC*.

If there is a wide range of output over which there are constant returns to scale, the *LAC* curve will be flat-bottomed and the *LMC* curve will coincide with *LAC* over this portion.

RELATIONSHIP BETWEEN LONG-RUN AND SHORT-RUN COSTS

We have seen above that, depending on the period that the firm has available to adjust its size of plant, either the firm will be able to achieve a completely optimum combination of factors, when all factors are variable (the long run), or it will achieve a less than optimum combination because of the constraint of some fixed factor or factors (the short run).

At any moment in time, the firm will be operating in the short run. However, if we conceive of a firm that has not yet entered an industry or of an operating firm planning for the future over a time period long enough so that all factors affecting operations can be varied, then the relevant production and cost data for the decision making of the firm are the long-run ones.

In Figure 7.5 we assume the firm to be producing q_1 in the short run with Y_1 of the fixed factor and X_1 of the variable factor. If it became necessary for the firm to increase output to q_2 in the short run, it would produce q_2 using its fixed factor, Y_1, and X_3 of the variable factor. It would move from point L on isoquant q_1 to point M on isoquant q_2. On the other hand, if the firm were planning to increase output to q_2 in the long run, it would choose to do so by utilizing Y_2 of the now variable Y factor and X_2 of the X factor. This amounts to a movement from L on isoquant q_1 to J on isoquant q_2, along the expansion path. Analogously, if the firm were to increase output from q_2 to q_3, in the short run it would move from J to K, and in the long run from J to G on the expansion path.

It should be noted that if the firm happens to have Y_1 of the fixed factor in the short run and desired to produce q_1, it will, of necessity, use X_1 of the variable factor. And this is the factor combination that will be used in the long run. In the same way, if the firm happened to have Y_2 of the fixed factor in the short run, it would be forced to utilize X_2 to produce q_2. Finally, if fortuitously the firm had Y_3 of the fixed factor in the short run, it would end using X_3 of the variable factor to produce q_3; and this is just the combination the firm would choose in the long run. In other words, points L, J, and G lie on the long-run expansion path and, therefore, on the long-run output curve of the firm; and these points also lie on the respective short-run product curves cut out by Y_1A, Y_2B, and Y_3C.

In Figure 7.6 we first show the long-run total cost curve derived from the expansion path in Figure 7.5. We also show the short-run total cost curves tangent to the LAC curve at q_1, q_2, and q_3. STC_1 corresponds to the short run in which the fixed factor is at the level Y_1; STC_2 corresponds to the short run in which the fixed factor is at the level Y_2; and

STC_3 corresponds to the short run in which the fixed factor is at the level Y_3. Clearly, for each point on the LTC curve there will correspond a point of tangency with an STC curve. Another way of stating this is that the LTC curve consists of the minimum cost points for particular outputs on an infinite number of STC curves.

[margin note: explains 7.6 (diagram)]

The same relationship can be explained in terms of the average and marginal schedules in Figure 7.7. Like the relationship between LTC and STC, the SAC curve consists of the minimum per unit cost points for particular outputs on an infinite number of SAC curves. The LAC curve is called an envelope curve to the SAC curves because no point on an SAC curve can ever lie below the LAC curve. In other words, each point on the LAC curve represents the absolute minimum per unit cost of producing a given output when all factors are variable. We have assumed that the Y factor can be varied continuously and so get a smooth envelope curve. If Y can be varied only discretely, the envelope curve would give a scalloped effect.

We have assumed that the X-Y combination at point J in Figure 7.5 represents not only the least-cost combination of inputs for producing q_2 but also the minimum per unit cost of producing any output in the long run. Therefore, in Figure 7.6, a line drawn from the origin is tangent to the LTC curve at q_2; as a consequence, LAC in Figure 7.7 is at a minimum and equal to LMC at q_2. Furthermore, since $STC_2 = LTC$ to produce q_2, $SAC_2 = LAC$ and $SMC_2 = LMC$. Therefore, $SAC_2 = SMC_2$; or, in other words, at q_2, SAC_2 is at its minimum and $SAC = SMC = LMC = LAC$.

It will be noticed that for all outputs less than that at which LAC is a minimum, the tangency with an SAC curve occurs to the left of the minimum SAC on the relevant SAC curve. And for outputs greater than q_2, the tangencies take place at outputs greater than the respective minimum SAC. This means that when a firm is operating subject to increasing returns to scale (from 0 to q_2), it can achieve minimum SAC by building plants larger than those that would produce given outputs at their minimum cost points and underutilizing these plants (that is, at outputs less than those that result in minimum SAC). Similarly, for outputs greater than q_2, where the firm experiences decreasing returns to scale, the firm will achieve lowest SAC for a particular level of output by building plants smaller than those that would produce a given output at minimum SAC and by overutilizing them. To summarize, a firm is not interested in achieving the minimum cost output for a given plant but is interested in producing a given output at minimum cost.

A concrete example will perhaps make it easier to see why the firm may choose to operate plants at other than minimum cost outputs. Suppose that a housewife has 10 pounds of wash per day that can be done

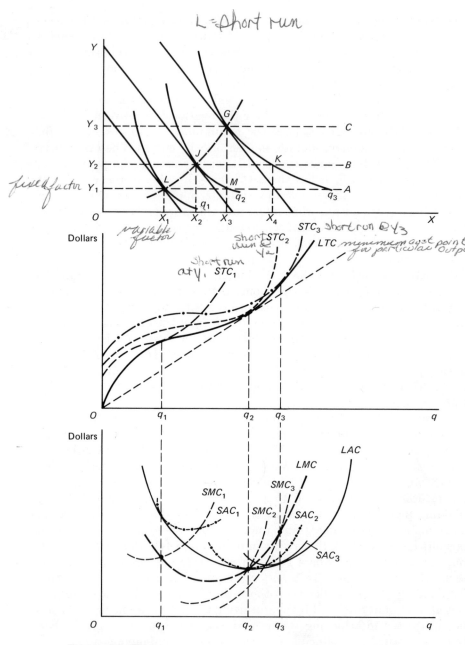

L = short run [handwritten]

fixed factor [handwritten, left of Y_1]

variable factor [handwritten]

short run at Y_1 STC$_1$ [handwritten]

short run STC$_2$ [handwritten]

STC$_3$ short run @Y_3 [handwritten]

LTC = minimum cost points for particular outputs [handwritten]

Figure 7.5 (Top)
Figure 7.6 (Center)
Figure 7.7 (Bottom)

by hand, be washed in a machine, or be sent to a steam laundry. The following are the relevant long-run cost data:

Cost per Pound If Done by Hand	Cost per Pound If Done by Washing Machine	Cost per Pound If Done by Laundry
10¢	10 lbs. (1 hr.): 6¢ 50 lbs. (5 hrs.): 5¢	10 lbs.: 7¢ 50 lbs.: 4.2¢

Based on the fact that her cost per pound is minimized this way, she chooses to buy a washing machine and run it one hour a day. A friend points out that if she were to run the machine the maximum time per day permitted by the landlord (5 hours) and wash 50 pounds, her per-pound cost would be reduced to 5¢. She replies that she is interested in washing 10 and not 50 pounds of laundry per day, and for 10 pounds the washing machine gives the lowest unit cost; and that if she wanted to wash 50 pounds per day, the steam laundry would be more economical, because its unit cost for this quantity is lower than that of the washing machine.

Appendix 7A

Relationship between LMC and SMC and LAC and SAC

Assume that in Figure 7A.1 a firm is producing q_2 using X_3 of X and Y_2 of Y. We want to demonstrate that, if the firm were to expand output to

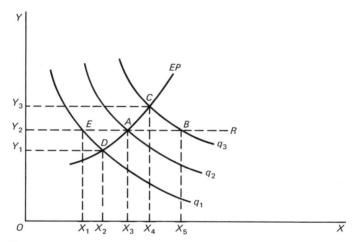

Figure 7A.1

q_3 (assuming that $q_3 - q_2$ represents a small increase), $SMC > LMC$. At point A,

$$\frac{MP_{x_3}}{MP_{y_2}} = \frac{P_x}{P_y} \qquad [7A.1]$$

which we can rewrite as

$$\frac{MP_{x_3}}{P_x} = \frac{MP_{y_2}}{P_y} \qquad [7A.2]$$

Because these ratios are equal, their reciprocals are equal:

$$\frac{P_x}{MP_{x_3}} = \frac{P_y}{MP_{y_2}} \qquad [7A.3]$$

Note that

$$\frac{P_x}{MP_x} = \frac{P_x}{\Delta q / \Delta X} = \frac{\Delta TC}{\Delta q} = MC$$

Since $P_x/MP_x = P_y/MP_y$ along the expansion path, the addition to cost will be the same no matter which factor is used to produce a small increment of output. Therefore, at A,

$$\frac{P_x}{MP_{x_3}} = \frac{P_y}{MP_{y_2}} = LMC \qquad [7A.4]$$

Similarly, in the short run, if the firm employs only one variable factor of production,

$$\frac{P_x}{MP_x} = SMC$$

Therefore, at A, along line Y_2R,

$$\frac{P_x}{MP_{x_3}} = SMC \qquad [7A.5]$$

and at A, therefore,

$$LMC = SMC \qquad [7A.6]$$

If the firm expanded output to q_3 and was free to vary both X and Y, it would produce at C on the expansion path. At C,

$$\frac{P_x}{MP_{x_4}} = \frac{P_y}{MP_{y_3}} = LMC \qquad [7A.7]$$

If the firm operates in the short run with Y_2 of Y, it would produce q_3 at B where

$$\frac{P_x}{MP_{x_5}} = SMC \qquad [7A.8]$$

Note that, if we exclude the possibility of the firm's operating in an area where a factor is redundant,

$$MP_{x_4} > MP_{x_5} \qquad [7A.9]$$

since at B there is more X and less Y than at C. If

$$MP_{x_4} > MP_{x_5}, \qquad \frac{P_x}{MP_{x_4}} < \frac{P_x}{MP_{x_5}}$$

and, therefore, from equations 7A.7 and 7A.8 we see that

$$LMC < SMC \qquad [7A.10]$$

We can use the same procedure to demonstrate that if the firm were to decrease output from q_2 to q_1, $SMC < LMC$. If the firm could vary X and Y, it would produce at D on the expansion path. At D,

$$\frac{P_x}{MP_{x_2}} = \frac{P_y}{MP_{y_1}} = LMC \qquad [7A.11]$$

If the firm had a fixed amount of Y, Y_1, it would produce q_1 at E. At E,

$$\frac{P_x}{MP_{x_1}} = SMC \qquad\qquad [7A.12]$$

Since at E there is less X and more Y than at D,

$$MP_{x_1} > MP_{x_2} \qquad\qquad [7A.13]$$

Thus,

$$\frac{P_x}{MP_{x_1}} < \frac{P_x}{MP_{x_2}}$$

And, following from equations 7A.11 and 7A.12,

$$SMC < LMC \qquad\qquad [7A.14]$$

8

PRICING AND OUTPUT
DECISIONS UNDER
PERFECT COMPETITION

PROFIT MAXIMIZATION

$Profit = TR - TC$

In his model of the firm, the economist assumes that a firm will attempt to maximize its profits (or minimize its losses), that is, maximize the difference between total revenue and total cost. The economist does not mean to say that this is the only motive influencing the behavior of the firm. There are other factors based on sociological, political, and psychological considerations. However, for contemporary, free-market economies, the economist does claim that the assumption of profit maximization is the crucial one; furthermore, in this system, the other considerations are many times measured in monetary terms. For example, if a firm were operating with the purpose of maximizing the prestige of the entrepreneur, it would probably attempt, in our type of economy, to maximize its profit because wealth and prestige are highly correlated. If the behavior of the firm is expressed as follows:

Economic behavior $= f$ (profits and sociological, political, and other factors)

the economist assumes that predictions as to the behavior of the firm, based on the assumption of profit maximization, will yield better predictions than those based on any other variable or variables, given the difficulty of measuring these other variables and of incorporating them into a model of firm behavior. The profit maximization assumption will stand or fall depending on its ability to predict more accurately than any alternative assumption.

In this chapter we deal with profit maximization under conditions of perfect competition; and in the following chapters, we deal with various other market structures.

DEMAND FACING A PERFECTLY COMPETITIVE FIRM

The demand schedule facing an individual producer shows the quantities he can sell at various alternative prices. The nature of this demand schedule depends on the structure of the industry of which the producer is a member. We may classify market structures according to the number of sellers in the industry and the degree of homogeneity of the good. Pure monopoly and perfect competition are the extremes of market organization. In this chapter we deal with perfect competition.

A perfectly competitive industry is one in which a large number of firms sell a homogeneous product. To investigate the nature of the demand schedule facing one of these firms, consider a numerical example.

Aggregate demand for the product of a competitive industry is given by the equation $Q_d = 11,000,000 - 100,000P$. There are 10,000 firms within this industry, all with the supply schedule $q_s = P$; thus, the industry supply schedule is $Q_s = 10,000P$. The equilibrium price is \$100 per unit and the equilibrium quantity is 1 million units, with each firm supplying 1/10,000 of aggregate output or 100 units. We now wish to determine the effect on equilibrium price and quantity if one firm should stop producing. The industry supply schedule becomes $Q_s = 9999P$ and the new equilibrium price and quantity are approximately (to four decimal places) \$100.0009 and 999,908.9991 units. The initial equilibrium situation is shown in Figure 8.1a. The area in the vicinity of the equilibrium point is magnified in Figure 8.1b in order to show the effects of the shift on supply and the new equilibrium.

We can now derive the demand curve facing the individual perfect competitor, which is shown in Figure 8.2a. When the firm produces no output, the price it faces is \$100.0009; and when the firm produces 100 units, it can sell at \$100 per unit. The elasticity of this demand curve at \$100 is computed as follows (the price change being rounded to -0.001):

$$\frac{\Delta q}{\Delta P} \cdot \frac{P}{q} = \frac{100}{-0.001} \cdot \frac{100}{100} = -100,000 \qquad [8.1]$$

The elasticity of the aggregate demand curve at \$100 is

$$\frac{\Delta Q}{\Delta P} \cdot \frac{P}{Q} = \frac{91}{-0.001} \cdot \frac{100}{1,000,000} = -9.1 \qquad [8.2]$$

Notice that the slopes (and, therefore, the reciprocals of the slopes) of the total demand curve and that of the individual firm are not very different; it does not appear this way graphically because of the difference in scales that are used. However, the fact that the elasticity coeffi-

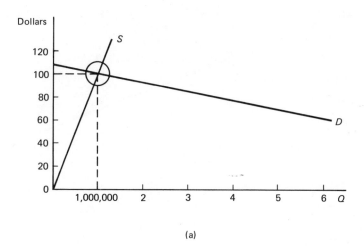

(a)

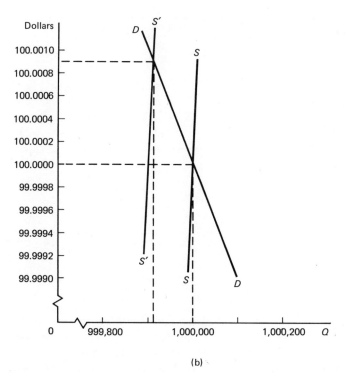

(b)

Figure 8.1

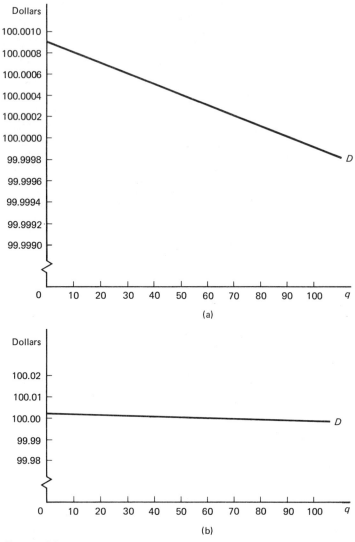

Figure 8.2

cients are quite different is based on the difference in the magnitude of output of the entire industry as compared with that of a single firm. The usual practice is to draw the demand curve facing the individual firm as being horizontal and to say that the coefficient of elasticity is infinite. What is implied by this is that the individual competitive firm has no influence on the market price and can sell as much as it can produce at the price given it. We can see from the above discussion that the correct statement should be that the individual competitive firm has only an imperceptible influence on the market price, that the demand curve for its output is "highly" elastic, and that when drawn upon the industry price scale it cannot be distinguished from a horizontal line. For example, in Figure 8.2b, with the price-axis fairly elongated, in pennies, the demand curve appears almost horizontal. If the price-axis scale of Figure 8.1a had been used, it would be virtually impossible to distinguish the demand curve from a horizontal line.

It is important to make this distinction in order to understand the mechanism by which the equilibrium market price is arrived at in a perfectly competitive industry. When there is a disequilibrium situation in a market, say, an excess of supply over demand, the equilibrium price would be arrived at by a process of competitive price shading. In our current example we can see that if the 10,000th firm were not able to sell its output at the market price of $100.0009, it would need to shade the price by only $.0009 in order to dispose of its output and to bring the market into equilibrium.[1]

We can now utilize the relationship among average revenue, marginal revenue, and elasticity derived in Chapter 3 to show the relationships among them for perfect competition. The relationship derived was:

$$MR = AR\left(1 + \frac{1}{E_d}\right), \qquad \text{where } E_d < 0$$

or

$$MR = AR + \frac{AR}{E_d}, \qquad \text{where } E_d < 0$$

For the perfectly competitive firm, elasticity approaches infinity; therefore, the term $1/E_d$ approaches zero and may be disregarded. It follows that $MR = AR\ (\equiv P)$ and that the demand curve and the marginal revenue curves facing the perfect competitor are coincident (or approximately so).

PROFIT MAXIMIZATION IN THE SHORT RUN

We have seen that a perfectly competitive firm accepts the going market price as a given; in other words, the demand schedule faced by the perfectly competitive firm has elasticity approaching infinity. As we have argued, this type of demand curve will appear visually as a horizontal line at the market price. Further, since $TR = P \times q$, the TR schedule of the perfectly competitive firm will be q times the constant P. This will appear graphically as a straight line from the origin with slope (MR) equal to price (which is average revenue).

[1] The student should be warned that we shall keep the conventions of drawing horizontal demand curves facing individual competitive firms and stating that the elasticity of these demand curves is infinite; but these are only convenient approximations that are true at the limit when the number of firms approaches infinity.

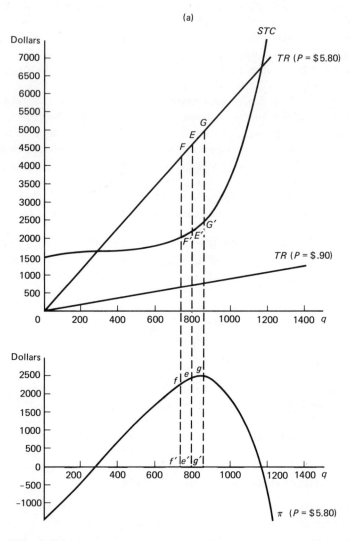

Figure 8.3

In Figure 8.3a we show the STC schedule from Table 8.1 and the TR schedule corresponding to an assumed market price of \$5.80 per unit. Since profit (π) is measured as

$$\pi = TR - STC \qquad [8.3]$$

in graphical terms, it is measured as the vertical distance between the TR and STC curves. This vertical distance will be a maximum when the

TABLE 8.1

(1) q	(2) VC	(3) STC	(4) AVC	(5) SAC	(6) SMC	(7) TR (P = $5.80)	(8) π (P = $5.80)	(9) Mπ (P = $5.80)	(10) TR (P = $0.90)	(11) π (P = $0.90)	(12) Mπ (P = $0.90)	(13) TR (P = $0.30)	(14) π (P = $0.30)	(15) Mπ (P = $0.30)
0	$0	$1500		$→ ∞		$0	$−1500		$0	$−1500		$0	$−1500	
100	90	1590	$0.90	15.90	$0.90	580	−1010	$4.90	90	−1500	$0	30	−1560	$−0.60
200	125	1625	0.625	8.125	0.35	1160	−465	5.45	180	−1445	0.55	60	−1565	−0.05
300	150	1650	0.50	5.50	0.25	1740	90	5.55	270	−1380	0.65	90	−1560	+0.05
400	170	1670	0.425	4.175	0.20	2320	650	5.60	360	−1310	0.70	120	−1550	+0.10
500	210	1710	0.42	3.42	0.40	2900	1190	5.40	450	−1260	0.50	150	−1560	+0.10
600	300	1800	0.50	3.00	0.90	3480	1680	4.90	540	−1260	0	180	−1620	−0.60
700	450	1950	0.6428	2.785	1.50	4060	2110	4.30	630	−1320	−0.60	210	−1740	−1.20
800	690	2190	0.8625	2.737	2.40	4640	2450	3.40	720	−1470	−1.50	240	−1950	−2.10
900	1270	2770	1.411	3.077	5.80	5220	2450	0	810	−1960	−4.90	270	−2500	−5.50
1000	2270	3770	2.27	3.77	10.00	5800	2030	−4.20	900	−2870	−9.10	300	−3470	−9.70
1100	3770	5270	3.427	4.791	15.00	6380	1110	−9.20	990	−4280	−14.10	330	−4940	−14.70
1200	$6070	$7570	$5.058	$6.308	$23.00	$6960	$−610	$−17.20	$1080	$−6490	$−22.10	$360	$−7210	$−22.70

Source: Although the output levels through 900 give the same cost schedules as those in Table 7.1, the function from which this table is derived is different from the one in Table 7.1, since here total output continues to increase beyond q = 900.

slope of the TR curve is equal to the slope of the STC curve; in other words, where $P \equiv MR = MC$. These vertical distances (profits) such as FF', EE', and GG' are shown in Figure 8.3b, where it will be seen that they reach a maximum at approximately 850 units.

Thus far we have established that a necessary condition for profit maximization is that $P \equiv MR = MC$. As we pointed out in Chapter 3, a *stable* equilibrium requires that any movement from equilibrium sets up forces such that there is a movement back to the equilibrium. In Table 8.1, $P \equiv MR = SMC$ between 800 and 900 units of output, that is, when SMC is at \$5.80 (the constant MR). Note that for smaller outputs, $SMC < MR \equiv P$. Consequently, marginal profit, which is defined as $MR - MC$, is positive. This means that if the entrepreneur were to expand output, the increment to his revenue would exceed the increment to his cost; or, in other words, total profit would increase.

Furthermore, for larger than the equilibrium output, $SMC > MR \equiv P$ and marginal profit is negative. Thus, if the entrepreneur were to decrease his output level back toward the equilibrium, the reduction of total revenue would be less than the reduction from total cost, and consequently total profit would be increased. Thus, movements away from the stable equilibrium point create incentives for movements back to that point.

These points can also be made with reference to Figure 8.3a and b. In graphical terms, marginal profit is the slope of the total profit schedule. Notice that to the right of e in Figure 8.3b, the total profit schedule is declining; its slope is negative (marginal $\pi = MR - SMC < 0$). To the left, total profit is increasing; the slope of the total profit curve is positive (marginal $\pi = MR - SMC > 0$).[2]

We may summarize our discussion of the necessary and sufficient conditions for competitive firm output equilibrium as follows: At the profit-

---

[2] When profit is being maximized, the slope of the profit curve is momentarily zero (at about 850 units in Figure 8.3b). Since $\pi = TR - TC$, we can write the slope of the profit curve in continuous terms as

$$\frac{d\pi}{dq} = \frac{dTR}{dq} - \frac{dTC}{dq}$$

When profit is being maximized,

$$\frac{d\pi}{dq} = 0 \text{ or } \frac{dTR}{dq} - \frac{dTC}{dq} = 0$$

Therefore,

$$\frac{dTR}{dq} = \frac{dTC}{dq}$$

However, both the minimum and the maximum of a curve have zero slope. To ensure a maximum, the second derivative of the profit curve must be negative; that is,

$$\frac{d^2\pi}{dq^2} = \frac{d^2TR}{dq^2} - \frac{d^2TC}{dq^2} < 0 \text{ or } \frac{dMR}{dq} - \frac{dMC}{dq} < 0 \text{ or } \frac{dMR}{dq} < \frac{dMC}{dq}$$

maximizing level of output, (1) $MR = MC$ and (2) the slope of the MR curve is less than the slope of the MC curve. Another way of stating this condition is (1) for outputs greater than the equilibrium one, $MC > MR$; (2) for outputs less than the equilibrium one, $MR > MC$.

We can arrive at these same results in Table 8.1. In column 7, TR is computed at the assumed price of $5.80, and in column 8, profit is the difference between TR and STC (column 7 − column 3). The highest profit is attained at 850 units. Note that in Table 8.1 total profit is $2450 at both 800 and 900 units of output. However, the discrete nature of the data hides the actual maximum profit point that lies between 800 and

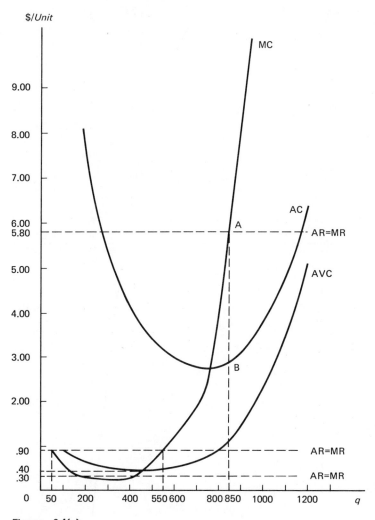

Figure   8.4(a)

900 units of output. This may be seen from the second order condition just discussed.

Another way of viewing profit maximization is in terms of the marginal and average schedules. In Figure 8.4a we plot the AVC, SAC, and SMC schedules from Table 8.1. In addition we show the demand (and MR) schedule facing the firm with the assumed price of $5.80. Since

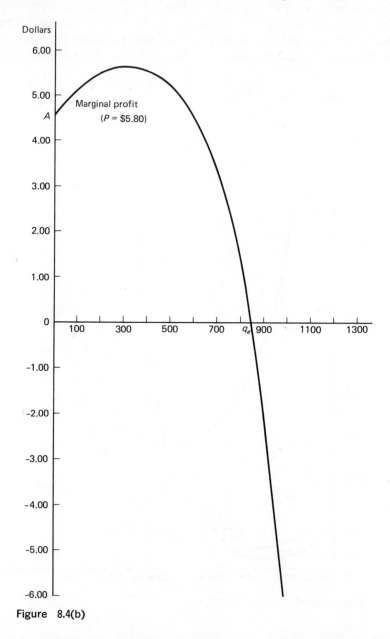

Figure 8.4(b)

profits are maximized when $MR = MC$ (or $P = MC$ with perfect competition since $P \equiv MR$), the firm will produce at the output level of approximately 850 units. In column 9 of Table 8.1 and in Figure 8.4b, we show marginal profit $(M\pi)$, which is equal to $MR - MC$. As long as $M\pi > 0$, the firm can increase its total profit by increasing output; and when $M\pi < 0$, the firm can increase total profit by decreasing output; and when $M\pi = 0$, the firm is maximizing its profit. If output is discontinuous, the firm will stop producing at the level of output where marginal profit is as close to zero as possible without becoming negative.

Total profit can be measured in Figure 8.4a by taking the difference between price (AR) and SAC at the profit-maximizing level of output and then multiplying this profit per unit by the level of output. In algebraic terms, this can be written as follows:

$$\frac{TR}{q} - \frac{STC}{q} = \frac{\pi}{q} \qquad [8.4]$$

$$\frac{\pi}{q}(q) = \pi \qquad [8.5]$$

Thus, in Figure 8.4a we can measure profits as follows:

$$
\begin{aligned}
\pi &= AB \times 850 \text{ units} \\
&= (\$5.80 - \$2.80)850 \text{ units} \\
&= \$3.00 \times 850 \text{ units} \\
&= \$2550
\end{aligned}
$$

Although it is not as frequently used, an alternate method of graphically measuring total profit is to take the area under the marginal profit curve.[3] In Figure 8.4b, this amounts to measuring the area OAq_e under the marginal profit curve. Note that the equilibrium quantity is always given by the point at which the marginal profit curve cuts the horizontal axis from above.

Next, we assume the price facing the firm is \$0.90 per unit, and we determine the profit-maximizing output. In Figure 8.3a we draw the new TR schedule. At no output does TR lie above STC. This means, of course, that the firm cannot make a positive profit at any level of output. The problem then becomes one of minimizing loss rather than one of maximizing profit.[4] We follow the same procedure as before and choose the output at which the slope of the TR curve (MR) is equal to the slope of the STC curve (SMC). This occurs at 550 units of output.

[3] This amounts to integrating the following expression:

$$\frac{d\pi}{dq} = \frac{dTR}{dq} - \frac{dTC}{dq}, \int_0^{q_e}\left[\frac{dTR}{dq} - \frac{dTC}{dq}\right]dq$$

where q_e is profit-maximizing output. This gives $TR - TC = \pi$.

[4] If $STC > TR$ at every level of output, then losses are minimized when $STC - TR$ is a minimum. Algebraically, this is the same as stating that $TR - STC$ should be a maximum and we demonstrated before that this occurs when $MR = SMC$.

In Figure 8.4a we show the new horizontal demand (and MR) curve at $0.90. It will be noticed that in applying our rule for profit maximization (or loss minimization), we are faced with a conundrum: there are two outputs at which $MR = SMC$, 50 units and 550 units. But if the firm desires to produce 50 units, it is not minimizing its loss; if it were to increase output beyond 50, $MR > SMC$ (in other words, $M\pi > 0$), and the firm could reduce its loss. If the firm decreased output below 50 units, $SMC > MR$, and the firm's losses would be smaller. Thus, at 50 units, the firm would be better off either expanding output or cutting back to zero. In fact, at 50 units, it is maximizing its losses (or minimizing its profit). On the other hand, at an output of 550 units, if the firm were to expand output, $SMC > MR$ and marginal profit would be negative; or if it were to decrease output, $MR > SMC$, marginal profit would be positive and this would mean a positive loss of profit.[5]

Column 11 in Table 8.1 lists profits at the different output levels when the price faced by the firm is $0.90. The minimum loss occurs between 500 and 600 units of output, and Figure 8.4a shows the minimum loss (of approximately $1255) to occur at 550 units.

We have now investigated a case in which the firm is not making profits; the best it can do is to minimize losses. The natural question then is this: How large must losses be in the short run before the firm will leave the industry?

Our definition of fixed costs makes them, in effect, the unavoidable costs: the costs that would exist even if output were to fall to zero. Variable costs, on the other hand, are the avoidable costs: those that vary with output and would be zero if output were zero. In the short run, because only variable costs can be avoided by shutting down, it is these costs that must be covered if the firm is to stay in the industry. A numerical example will make this clear.

In the previous case with the price being $0.90, the best the firm can do is to take a loss of $1255. Now suppose the firm decides to leave the industry; its fixed or unavoidable cost (loss) would be $1500. Clearly, the firm will find it preferable to remain in operation because in this fashion it reduces its losses by approximately $245 ($1500 − $1255). These conclusions are valid only so long as the $1500 cost remains unavoidable, that is, in the short run.

As our last example, we assume a price of $0.30 per unit, and once again we see that positive profits are impossible. Column 14 in Table 8.1

---

[5] In note 2 we proved that for the output at which $MR = SMC$ to be a maximum profit (or minimum loss) output, the slope of the MR curve must be less than the slope of the SMC curve. At 50 units of output, this condition is not fulfilled: The slope of the MR curve is zero, while the slope of the SMC curve is less than zero. However, at 550 units, the slope of $SMC > 0$ and the slope of MR is still zero and, therefore, the condition is fulfilled.

indicates that losses are minimized when the firm produces nothing; so it would be better off to cease operation.

We have seen that, in the short run, the firm would be willing to stay in the industry at a loss when the price was $0.90 but would not be willing to stay when the price was $0.30. In the first instance, the loss at the optimum output was less than the fixed, unavoidable cost, and in the second instance, it was greater than the fixed cost at every output. We may then ask, What is the minimum price at which the firm would stay in the industry? It must be the price at which the firm would at least cover its avoidable, variable costs. If it just covers variable costs, its losses will equal fixed, unavoidable costs, which would be incurred even if output were zero. Therefore, the minimum price at which the firm will remain in the industry is that at which variable costs are being covered by total revenue (to put it another way, where $P = $ minimum AVC). In terms of Figure 8.4a, this minimum price is $0.40. For prices above this level, it will produce the quantity given by the intersection of the price ordinate with the SMC curve above minimum AVC. At a price equal to minimum AVC, the firm will incur the same loss whether it shuts down or produces where $SMC = P$. Here the firm is indifferent between staying in or leaving the industry as far as short-run variables are concerned; the decision will be based on expectations for the long run.

Note that what we have said concerning the output decision of the firm for prices above minimum AVC amounts to the assertion that the SMC curve, above minimum AVC, gives us the output that the firm will produce for various prices. In other words, this portion of the SMC curve is the supply curve of the perfectly competitive firm in the short run.

If we know the SMC for each of the many firms within the perfectly competitive industry, and if we assume these SMC curves are stable for changes in industry output, we can derive the industry short-run supply curve by summing horizontally. If all firms are identical, then the industry's short-run supply curve would have the same shape as the individual firm's short-run supply curve with the quantity axis multiplied by the number of firms.

If this industry is only one of many that employ the same factors of production, then an increase in industry output, resulting in an increased demand for these factors of production, will have only slight effect on the prices of the factors.[6] In other words, our assumption of stable SMC curves with changes in industry output will be valid.

If, however, the industry purchases enough of a factor to have a substantial effect upon price, the industry's short-run supply curve cannot be obtained by a simple summation of the firms' supply curves. The

[6] In effect, the supply curves of these factors of production are approximately horizontal to the firm. See Chapter 11.

reason for this is illustrated in Figure 8.5 (where we assume an industry composed of 1000 identical firms). Assume the price to be P_1 with the firm producing the profit-maximizing output of q_1. Then assume an increase in industry demand that results in an increase in price to P_2. If factor prices remained constant, the firm would increase its output along SMC_1 to q_2. But under the assumption that changes in the industry's demand for factors of production increase the prices of these factors, the SMC curve is assumed to shift to SMC_2.[7] Now the new profit-maximizing output for the firm will be q_2'. Note that the firm's output at P_1 and P_2 is read from two different SMC curves; we cannot simply add the firms' SMC curves in order to obtain the supply of the industry. It is possible, however, to find the output of the industry at various prices by adding together the quantities produced at $P_1, P_2, \ldots, P_n$, which would be at points such as $A, B, \ldots, N$, on a succession of SMC curves.[8]

PROFIT MAXIMIZATION IN THE LONG RUN

In the long run as in the short run, the firm finds its profit-maximizing output by equating marginal cost to marginal revenue. In the long

[7] These shifts in the cost curves should not be confused with the movements along cost curves due to the output decisions of the firm; these were discussed in Chapters 6 and 7. The shifts take place because of changes in variables not under the control of the firm.

[8] For the individual firm, it is possible in the accompanying diagram for the SMC curve to shift to a position such as SMC_2 so that B' lies to the right of A and $q_2' > q_1$;

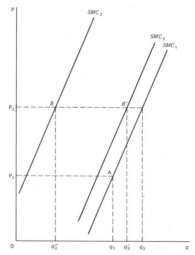

it is also possible for the curve to shift to a position such as SMC_3 and consequently for B to lie to the left of A and for $q_1 > q_2''$. However, for the industry as a whole, the supply curve must be positively sloping; otherwise there would have been no increase in output and no consequent increase in cost. This means that on balance the sum of outputs at B must be greater than at A.

run, however, all costs are variable; therefore, the firm must cover total cost in order to remain in the industry. We illustrate long-run profit maximization in Table 8.2 and Figure 8.6. If the firm faces a price of $2 per unit, $MR = LMC$ at 450 units in Table 8.2 and Figure 8.6.

Maximum profit in Table 8.2 is seen to be in excess of $105 at 450 units.

TABLE 8.2

q	LTC	LAC	LMC	TR $(P = \$2)$	π $(P = \$2)$
0	$0			$0	$0
			$3.10		
100	310	$3.10		200	−110
			1.55		
200	465	2.32		400	−65
			1.05		
300	570	1.90		600	30
			1.25		
400	695	1.74		800	105
			2.00		
500	895	1.79		1000	105
			2.90		
600	1185	1.98		1200	15
			3.90		
700	1575	2.25		1400	−175
			5.10		
800	2085	2.61		1600	−485
			$6.65		
900	$2715	$3.02		$1800	$−915

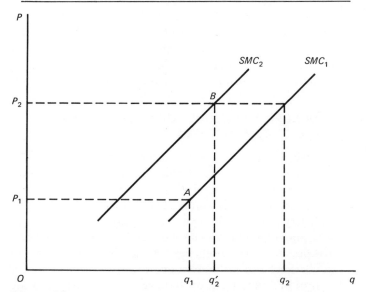

Figure 8.5

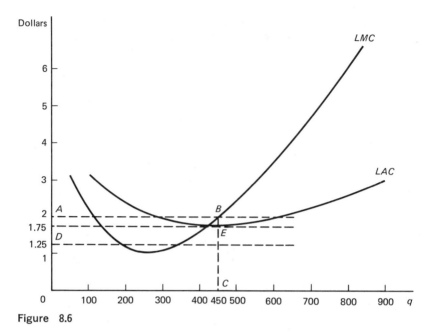

Figure 8.6

According to Figure 8.6, $\pi = \$112.50$. This can be calculated in the following way:

$$TR = OABC = \$2.00 \times 450 \text{ units} = \$900.00$$
$$LTC = ODEC = \$1.75 \times 450 \text{ units} = \$787.50$$
$$\pi = DABE = \$0.25 \times 450 \text{ units} = \$112.50$$

Next we consider the price of $\$1.25/\text{unit}$ in Figure 8.6 and see that the price is below LAC at all levels of output. All costs being variable in the long run, the firm will leave the industry; for all prices below minimum LAC, the firm will leave the industry. Thus, the long-run supply curve of the perfectly competitive firm is the portion of LMC that lies above LAC.

THE LONG-RUN SUPPLY SCHEDULE OF THE PERFECTLY COMPETITIVE INDUSTRY

When we derived the industry's short-run supply curve, we simply horizontally summed the firms' short-run supply curves on the assumption that changes in industry output do not change factor prices. With the assumption that factor prices (and, therefore, the firms' cost curves) change as industry output changes, the industry's supply curve was derived by summing horizontally the short-run profit-maximizing outputs for alternative prices, after the changes in the firms' cost curves.

Because in the long run all factors of production can be varied, there can be entry into and exit from an industry. In deriving the industry's long-run supply curve, it will not do to add the firms' profit-maximizing outputs at different prices when the number of firms within the industry is a variable.

Before we demonstrate the derivation of the long-run supply curve, consider the meaning of economic profit. Recall that costs of production include not only the expenditure (or explicit) costs of the firm but also the nonexpenditure (or implicit) costs. Thus, when $\pi = TR - LTC = 0$, it does not mean that the entrepreneurs of the firm are not "making any money"; $\pi = 0$ means that the earnings of the entrepreneurs are equal to what their factors (labor and capital) could earn in alternative occupations. Thus, their remuneration is just sufficient to keep them in the industry. In fact, as we shall see later, the meaning of long-run equilibrium for the perfectly competitive firm is that $\pi = 0$.

We shall derive the long-run supply schedule for a hypothetical industry. We assume, for the present, that all firms in this industry, as well as potential firms, have identical cost schedules and that changes in industry output do not affect these cost schedules.

Figure 8.7a depicts a representative firm in long-run equilibrium ($\pi = 0$), producing q_1 at a price of P_1, as well as the relevant SAC and SMC curves for the initial equilibrium point. In Figure 8.7b we show the corresponding short-run industry supply curve, SRS_1, with the equilibrium output of Q_1 and the price of P_1. Now let demand increase to D_2 and the resulting change in price to P_2. Industry output expands in the short run to Q_2. The individual firm moves along its SMC curve, adjusting output as best it can with existing capacity, to q_2. When the firm is producing q_2 at P_2, its profit is $(P_2 - SAC)q_2$.

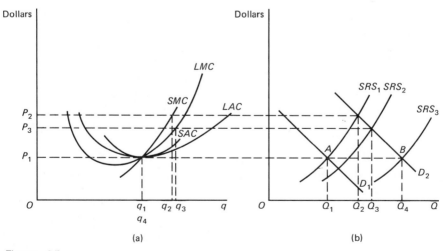

(a) (b)

Figure 8.7

If we assume that demand does not change in the long run, there will be two long-run reactions to this increase in price: (1) Existing firms will adjust capacity so as to produce a given output most efficiently; that is, they will base their output decisions on long-run costs. (2) Potential firms will enter the industry in response to the positive profits. For the sake of simplicity, we shall assume that the individual firms' adjustments precede the entry of new firms into the industry.

As the firms increase output along LMC (and produce on new SMC curves to the right of the initial SMC curve), industry supply increases to SRS_2 and the new short-run equilibrium output is Q_3. This, however, reduces price to P_3, and the firm's output is q_3. At this new price, profits are still being made by the firm, however, so that potential firms now enter the industry and continue to enter as long as positive profits exist. Long-run equilibrium will not occur until price has fallen to P_1 or until the new industry short-run supply schedule is SRS_3.

It will be noted that the individual firm's new long-run equilibrium is at the output at which LAC is a minimum, q_1. Further, the output of the industry in the long run has grown through an increase in the number of firms, not by an increase in output of existing firms, although in the adjustment period, the existing firms' outputs did increase.

If we connect points such as A and B, which represent long-run equilibriums, we obtain the long-run supply curve for the industry. In this case, it is a horizontal line at the level of minimum LAC, showing that industry output can be increased by any amount in the long run at this constant price. This is called a constant-cost industry.

We now change the assumption that alterations in industry output have no effect on costs of production to the new assumption that, as industry output expands, the costs of the individual firms change.

One example of a situation resulting in increasing cost curves for the firm has already been discussed; when an industry is an important enough buyer of a particular factor of production, increased industry demand for this factor will raise its price. Another possible situation leading to increasing costs occurs when an industry is communication oriented (that is, there are advantages to be obtained from being located near one another; some examples are the garment and publishing industries in New York City). As the specific location becomes crowded, the location costs to individual firms rise.

One possible source of decreasing costs is created by firms that locate near a spatially concentrated industry to provide needed materials and services; and they produce these auxiliary goods and services at lower costs than the individual firms within the major industry can produce. For example, the garment industry of New York is inhabited by many small firms buffetted by continuous style changes. Consequently, it is imperative for firms in this industry to maintain flexibility; and this is permitted to a large degree by the existence of large numbers of firms parasitic to the industry, which provide materials, buttons, and machine parts and which consequently minimize the inventories to which the garment firms must commit themselves at any moment.

There is no necessity that external economies or diseconomies be reversible. We shall illustrate this by two examples. The first concerns an industry that grows up in an area because of the availability of needed raw materials. When the density of firms has reached a certain point, a railroad spur is built to connect this area to the main line, thereby reducing the per-unit transportation costs of the firms. If the number of firms (and industry output) decreases as a result of a reduction in industry demand, it is probable that the spur will remain and, therefore, the reduction in per-unit costs will continue. (The long run for a railroad is substantially longer than for most other industries because of the durability of equipment. But, of course, if the spur is unprofitable for the railroad over a period long enough for the equipment to be depreciated, then it will abandon the spur and, at that time, per-unit transportation costs would revert to their original level.)

Our second example concerns surface mining in a locality. As a result of an increase in the demand for the mineral, new firms enter the industry. As long as the density of firms is such that when surface deposits are exhausted, a firm can move to virgin land, inexpensive strip-mining techniques will continue to be used. However, if no virgin land is available, then more expensive and intensive methods of mining will become necessary. Now, suppose that after these intensive methods have been utilized for a time, the demand for output declines and firms leave the industry. The remaining firms will still need to use the intensive techniques because surface deposits have been exhausted. Clearly, the external diseconomies in this case are not reversible.

To return to our new assumption, again for the sake of simplicity, let costs change only as a result of substantial changes in industry output—in other words, when firms enter or leave. We shall once again show the derivation of the industry's long-run supply curve under these new conditions.

In Figure 8.8a, q_1 and P_1 represent the firm's long-run equilibrium, and, in Figure 8.8b, Q_1 is the corresponding industry equilibrium output when the demand curve is D_1. If demand increases to D_2, the industry will increase output to Q_2, and the firm will maximize its short-run profit by producing q_2 at the price of P_2. In the long run, the firm will adjust capacity so as to produce profit-maximizing output most efficiently. This increase in output is reflected in the increase of the industry short-run supply curve to SRS_2. Thus, industry output is Q_3, price is P_3, and the individual firm produces q_3. Profits are still greater than zero. Therefore, new firms enter the industry and keep doing so until $\pi = 0$.

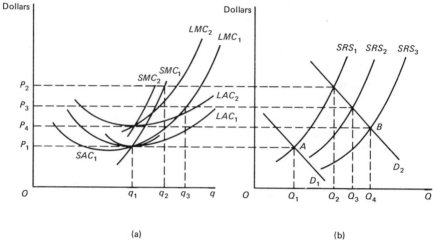

(a)   (b)

Figure 8.8

By our assumption of increasing costs as industry output expands, the cost curves of the individual firms shift upward;[9] this involves short-run adjustments of output of the type discussed before. We show, however, only the final long-run equilibrium, which is at P_4 and Q_4 for the industry and at q_4 for the firm.

Note that long-run changes are now of three types: (1) the increase in output of the existing firms; (2) the entry of new firms into the industry and the resulting increase in output; and (3) the shift upward of the cost curves of the firms that results in the new long-run equilibrium price being greater than the original.

Note also that the new long-run equilibrium quantity for the firm is the same as the old equilibrium quantity. The reason for this is that, in deriving the new cost curves, we implicitly assumed the same percentage increase in all factor prices. Therefore, minimum LAC is at the same level of output as it was before.[10] If all factor prices do not change proportion-

[9] To avoid cluttering the diagrams, we shift only the long-run cost curves, but short-run costs increase as well.

[10] This can be seen by considering the least-cost condition for selecting the optimum factor proportions:

$$\frac{MP_a}{P_a} = \frac{MP_b}{P_b} = \cdots = \frac{MP_n}{P_n}$$

At the initial equilibrium, this condition must have been fulfilled. If we multiply all factor prices by a constant, k, the equality still holds:

$$\frac{MP_a}{kP_a} = \frac{MP_b}{kP_b} = \cdots = \frac{MP_n}{kP_n}$$

Other cases will be considered in Chapter 11.

ately, there is no necessity for the cost curves to shift parallel to themselves, and output of the individual firm can either increase or decrease.

To get the long-run industry supply curve, we once again connect points such as A and B and find that we have a positively sloping long-run supply curve for the industry; such an industry is called an increasing-cost industry.

Turning to the case of external economies (decreasing-cost industry), we assume the industry initially to be in long-run equilibrium, producing Q_1 at P_1 (Figure 8.9b), and the firm's initial long-run equilibrium to be at q_1 (Figure 8.9a). As a result of an increase in demand to D_2, the price in the short run rises to P_2 and the firm increases output to q_2 along SMC_1. The long-run adjustment of the firm is to produce along LMC_1; this shifts the industry's short-run supply curve to SRS_2, the price falls to P_3, and the firm produces q_3.

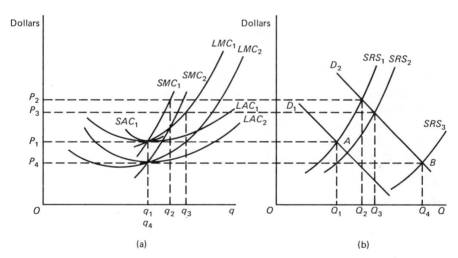

(a)   (b)

Figure 8.9

In response to the still-existing profits, new firms enter the industry; and with the assumption of decreasing costs, the cost schedules of the firms fall. New firms continue to enter until long-run profit is zero and the new long-run equilibrium price is P_4. Once again we have assumed that the new equilibrium output of the firm is the same as before. When we connect points such as A and B, we find the long-run industry supply curve to be downward sloping and we have a decreasing-cost industry.

It should be obvious that, if an industry is initially in equilibrium, a decrease in demand will result in losses; and in the long run, adjustments through exit of firms from the industry will result.

Until this point we have assumed all firms to be identical, and, therefore, it has been correct to say that when price reached the level of minimum LAC for one firm, all firms had zero profit. Even if all firms are not identical, it is still true that the LAC for all firms, when costs are properly defined, will be at the same level. Under conditions of perfect competition, differences between firms due to superior knowledge and lower factor prices are ruled out. However, it is possible for a firm to have a unique factor of production. But with perfect knowledge, the superior productivity of this factor will be known to the industry, and other firms will bid for the services of the factor. As long as the differential between this factor's remuneration and the payments to comparable factors of lesser productivity is less than the new revenue that the superior factor adds to the total revenue of the firm that utilizes it, firms will continue to bid for its services. This will drive up its rate of remuneration until it is just equal to the differential value of its service. Therefore, the firm that does use this factor will have a cost curve at the same level as the firms that do not use the factor. The cost curve of the former will, however, include a rental element to a superior factor.[11] A simple numerical example will explicate this point. Assume an industry in which all firms but one have average costs of $10 at an output level of 100 units. The other firm, because of a superior factor, has an average cost of $9 for the same output level. Therefore, the superior factor gives rise to a differential of $1 $\times$ 100 units of output = $100. Competitive bidding will, therefore, force up the factor's remuneration until it is $100 higher than that for ordinary comparable factors. This will raise the average cost of the firm utilizing this factor by $100/100 units, or $1, so that the new average cost at 100 units will be $9 + $1 = $10, which is the same as average cost for the other firms.

[11] See Chapter 12.

Appendix 8A

Stability Conditions under Perfect Competition

We now investigate the possibility of a negatively sloping supply curve. This can intersect a negatively sloping demand curve in one of two ways shown in Figure 8A.1.

Which of these represents a stable equilibrium? Marshall considered Figure 8A.1b stable and Figure 8A.1a unstable. He argued that to the left of the intersection, demand price is greater than supply price and output will expand; to the right of the intersection, supply price is greater than demand price and, consequently, supply will contract. Walras considered the situation shown in Figure 8A.1a to be stable and 8A.1b

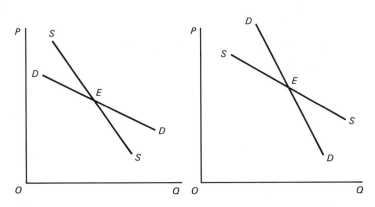

Figure 8A.1

unstable. To the left of the intersection, quantity supplied is greater than quantity demanded at any price and price must fall; to the right of the intersection, quantity supplied is less than quantity demanded and price must rise.

Actually, both figures represent stable equilibriums, but for different time periods. Walras was thinking of the short run in which the burden of adjustment is upon price; thus, in Figure 8A.1a an excess of supply to the left of E will drive the price down, and an excess of demand over supply to the right of E will drive the price up. Marshall, on the other hand, was concerned with the long run. An excess of demand price over supply price to the left of E in Figure 8A.1b could cause an expansion of output, and a reduction of price and an excess of supply price over demand price in the long run will result in a contraction of output and an increase in price.

The comparison of these seemingly contradictory positions is important because it demonstrates how important it is to specify the process involved in achieving an equilibrium. Simply comparing two static equilibriums is not enough, as was just made clear.

9

PRICING AND OUTPUT
DECISIONS UNDER
MONOPOLY

PURE MONOPOLY

Monopoly exists when the following conditions are fulfilled:
1. There is a single seller of a homogeneous good.
2. There are no close substitutes for the good.
3. Effective barriers to entry into the industry exist for one or more of the following reasons:

   a. The market is limited and will not support more than one firm.
   b. The existing firm follows a price policy calculated to reduce the attractiveness of entry.
   c. The firm has control over strategic raw materials or an important process through ownership of patent rights.
   d. The firm operates through government licensing or the imposition of trade barriers such as tariffs and quotas.

The demand schedule facing the monopolist is coincident with the industry demand.

The principles of profit maximization for monopoly are the same as for perfect competition. Thus, in general, profit will be maximized where $MR = MC$ and the slope of MC is greater than the slope of MR at the point of intersection. The second condition can be stated as $MR > MC$ for outputs less than the profit-maximizing one, and $MR < MC$ for greater outputs.

Profit maximization in the short run is shown in Figure 9.1. Notice that $P > MR$. The student is reminded of the following relationship:

$$MR = AR + \frac{AR}{E} = AR\left(1 + \frac{1}{E}\right) \qquad \text{(where } E < 0\text{)} \qquad [9.1]$$

Under conditions of perfect competition, $E \to -\infty$, and, therefore, $(1/E) \to 0$ and $MR \equiv AR$. However, E is finite under monopoly, which means that $-\infty < 1/E < 0$. Thus, MR is less than AR by the amount $AR(1/|E|)$.

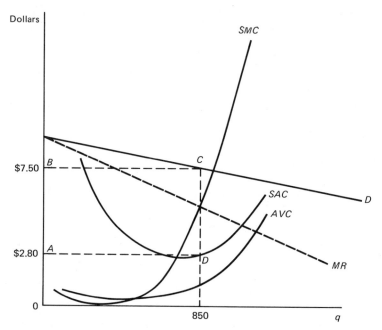

Figure 9.1

We may look at this relationship another way. MR is defined as the change in total revenue due to producing and selling an extra unit of output. When a perfect competitor sells at a given market price, the additional revenue he receives for selling an extra unit is equal to the market price. But, because a monopolist faces a downward-sloping demand curve, the price must be reduced in order to sell an additional unit. If the monopolist sells a homogeneous good in a market that cannot be segmented, then a reduction in price on the $(n + 1)$ unit must result in a similar price reduction on the previous n units. This can be summarized by the following relationship, which we derived in Chapter 3.

$$MR = AR + \frac{dAR}{dq}q \qquad [9.2]$$

or in discrete terms,

$$MR = AR_2 + \frac{\Delta AR}{\Delta q} q_1 \qquad [9.2a]$$

For the competitive firm, $dAR/dq \equiv dP/dq$ (the slope of the demand schedule) $= 0$; therefore, $MR = AR$. For the monopolist, $dP/dq < 0$ and, therefore, $MR < P$.

Figure 9.1 and Table 9.1 illustrate the determination of profit-maximizing output and price for the monopolist in the short run. The output produced will be 850 units, which is the level at which SMC intersects MR from below. The price for that output is then found by going vertically up to the demand curve. Thus, $7.50 is the equilibrium price and the short-run profit is $ABCD = \$3995$.

TABLE 9.1

(1) q	(2) STC	(3) AVC	(4) SAC	(5) SMC	(6) P	(7) TR	(8) MR	(9) π
0	$1500		$→ ∞		$9.20	$0		−$1500
				$0.90			$9.00	
100	1590	$0.90	15.90		9.00	900		−690
				0.35			8.60	
200	1625	0.625	8.125		8.80	1760		135
				0.25			8.20	
300	1650	0.50	5.50		8.60	2580		930
				0.20			7.80	
400	1670	0.425	4.175		8.40	3360		1690
				0.40			7.40	
500	1710	0.42	3.42		8.20	4100		2390
				0.90			7.00	
600	1800	0.50	3.00		8.00	4800		3000
				1.50			6.60	
700	1950	0.64	2.785		7.80	5460		3510
				2.40			6.20	
800	2190	0.86	2.74		7.60	6080		3890
				5.80			5.80	
900	2770	1.41	3.08		7.40	6660		3890
				10.00			5.40	
1000	3770	2.27	3.77		7.20	7200		3430
				15.00			5.00	
1100	5270	3.43	4.79		7.00	7700		2330
				$23.00			4.60	
1200	$7570	$5.06	$6.31		$6.80	$8160		$590

Source: Columns 1–5 are from Table 8.1.

It is of interest to note that although the perfect competitor has only one decision alternative (that is, he must make an output decision on the basis of a given price), the monopolist has two decision alternatives. He can set the price and allow profit-maximizing output to be determined; or he can set output and then charge the price that will maximize profits. In either case there is only one price-output combination that is optimum for profit maximization.

Long-run profit maximization is achieved when $LMC = MR$. The extent of monopoly power in the long run will probably be less than in the short run. One reason for this is the likelihood that demand will be more elastic in the long run than in the short run because people have more opportunity to adjust to prices and to seek appropriate substitutes. Another reason is that the threat of potential entry exists in the long run. A monopolist, concerned with maximizing profit in the long run, may in the short run forgo the temporary advantages to be gained from maximizing short-run profit. This may happen because of the fear of attracting punitive legislation (such as antitrust), new firms into the industry, and foreign rivals into the domestic market.

Unlike the case of perfect competition, the marginal cost curve is not the supply curve of the monopolist. A supply curve shows the amount a producer is willing to sell at any given price. The general condition for finding the profit-maximizing level of output is $MR = MC$. Because in perfect competition, P and MR are the same, for any given price ($\equiv MR$) that the firm faces, the profit-maximizing output can be read from the MC curve. However, for the monopolist, a knowledge of price is insufficient to determine the equilibrium quantity; it is the equality of MR and MC that determine output, and any particular price can correspond to different values of MR, depending on the elasticity of demand. This can be demonstrated by Figure 9.2. The MC curve is assumed common to two monopolists and a perfectly competitive firm faced with the demand curves D_1, D_2, and D_c, respectively. Notice that in all three cases, MR cuts MC at the same point and, consequently, the profit-maximizing output is q. However, the profit-maximizing price is different for the three firms. Only for the competitive firm is a knowledge of the price and marginal cost curve sufficient to determine the equilibrium output; for the monopolists, further information regarding either marginal revenue or elasticity is required. In summary then, because the monopolist equates MC and MR, the MC curve of the monopolist may be said to give a relationship between MR and output rather than between price and output, as is true of the perfect competitor. There are an infinite number of prices corresponding to each MR; the particular price corresponding to any MR depends on the elasticity as shown in

$$P = \left(\frac{E}{E + 1}\right) MR$$

Therefore, no supply schedule of the ordinary kind exists for the monopolist.

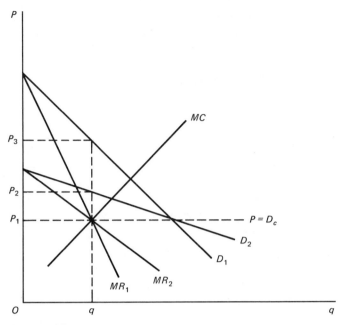

Figure 9.2

Note further that it is only under conditions of perfect competition that there is an equality between the price that consumers are willing to pay for an additional unit and the incremental cost necessary to produce that unit. In addition, with the assumption of a given cost schedule, the perfectly competitive firm produces the given output at the lowest price. We shall further compare monopoly and perfect competition in Chapter 10.

An interesting difference between the perfectly competitive industry and the monopoly firm (which is the industry itself) is that the equilibrium output can exist at any point along the demand curve facing the competitive industry, whereas the profit-maximizing output for the monopolist can never be on the inelastic portion of the demand curve. This can be seen from

$$MR = P\left(1 + \frac{1}{E}\right)$$

which can be written as

$$MR = P\left(1 - \frac{1}{|E|}\right)$$

When $|E| < 1$, $(1/|E|) > 1$, and $MR < 0$. Since MC must be positive, profit maximization cannot exist. Should the monopolist blunder onto the inelastic section of his demand curve, a reduction in output will at the same time increase revenue and reduce costs and, therefore, necessarily increase profits.

AN ASIDE ON AVERAGE COST PRICING

Based on the fact that businessmen generally set price by adding a markup to an estimate of average cost, some individuals have attacked the relevance of marginal-cost pricing in explaining price behavior. There are two main lines of counterattack. First, as we pointed out in the beginning of Chapter 8, the validity of a model does not depend on its descriptive accuracy but on its ability to predict behavior more accurately than alternative models. Second, on the basis of empirical evidence concerning the shape of typical cost curves, markup pricing can give approximately the same results as marginal-cost pricing.

The empirical evidence indicates that long-run average cost curves are flat-bottomed over a wide range of output. As we showed in Chapter 7, this means that LMC and LAC are coincident over the flat-bottomed portion. With marginal-cost pricing, the following long-run equilibrium condition exists:

$$LMC = MR \qquad [9.3]$$

For a firm that is not a perfect competitor,

$$MR = P(1 + 1/E) \qquad [9.4]$$

where

$$E \leq -1$$

Therefore, in equilibrium,

$$LMC = P\left(\frac{E + 1}{E}\right) \qquad [9.5]$$

or

$$P = LMC\left(\frac{E}{E + 1}\right) \qquad [9.6]$$

Over the range where LAC is flat-bottomed, $LAC = LMC$, so that in equilibrium

$$P = LAC\left(\frac{E}{E + 1}\right) \qquad [9.7]$$

Now suppose $E = -3$. Then

$$P = LAC\left(\frac{-3}{-3 + 1}\right) = 1.5 LAC \qquad [9.8]$$

In other words, the markup would be 50 percent. Furthermore, notice that the greater the inelasticity (the smaller the coefficient in absolute terms), the greater will be the markup.

If, in the short run, the firm were to mark up on average variable cost, and AVC was flat-bottomed (and the empirical evidence indicates it often is), then the results obtained would be the same as those obtained with marginal-cost pricing. If, however, as is much more likely, business-men mark up on the basis of SAC, a discrepancy arises between average-cost pricing and marginal-cost pricing, the size of which is based on the magnitude of AFC.

PRICE DISCRIMINATION

Price discrimination exists when a seller charges different prices for units of a commodity produced at equal marginal cost. The following conditions must be fulfilled if price discrimination is to be practiced:

1. The seller has some degree of monopoly power.
2. The seller is able to segment his market. Segmentation exists when consumers who buy at a low price are not able to resell the commodity at a higher price. Segmentation can arise because of the physical characteristics of the good (for example, physicians' services or electricity) or because of such barriers as transport costs and tariffs.

Take-It-or-Leave-It Price Discrimination. Ordinarily, the monopolist sets a profit-maximizing price and permits buyers to purchase as much as they wish at that price. Under perfect price discrimination the monopolist deals with each buyer separately and instead of permitting him to buy all that he wants to at a stated price, the monopolist specifies both the quantity the buyer can receive of the good and the total amount of money he must pay to get it. The monopolist in effect makes the buyer pay the maximum amount that he will, for the amount that the monopolist decides to supply to him, under threat of denying the good to him alto-gether; he gives him a take-it-or-leave-it choice. This kind of discrimina-tion is called perfect because it permits the seller to squeeze the greatest revenue from the buyer for any given output.

In effect, then, the demand curve of the consumer becomes the marginal revenue curve facing the monopolist.[1] This is shown in column 3 of Table 9.2, where we show the original demand schedule considered by the monopolist to be his MR schedule (with the MR figures placed at the midpoints of their respective intervals) and, corresponding to this MR schedule, we show an "all-or-nothing" demand schedule P'. The total revenue collected by the monopolist for four units with perfect discrimina-tion can be found as the sum of the MR figures up to and including MR

---

[1] This is true only when the practice of perfect price discrimination by the monopolist does not reduce the consumer's purchasing power enough to cause him to reduce his purchase of all goods, including the one subject to take-it-or-leave-it price discrimina-tion. This will generally be true if expenditure on the good in question is a small pro-portion of his total expenditures. If the good should have an important place in the consumer's budget, the perfect discrimination curve will be somewhat below the ordinary demand curve. For further discussion of this point, see Appendix 4C.

TABLE 9.2

(1) P	(2) Q	(3) MR'	(4) TR	(5) TR'	(6) P'
6	0		0	0	
		$5\frac{1}{2}$			
5	1		5	$5\frac{1}{2}$	$5\frac{1}{2}$
		$4\frac{1}{2}$			
4	2		8	10	5
		$3\frac{1}{2}$			
3	3		9	$13\frac{1}{2}$	$4\frac{1}{2}$
		$2\frac{1}{2}$			
2	4		8	16	4
		$1\frac{1}{2}$			
1	5		5	$17\frac{1}{2}$	$3\frac{1}{2}$
		$\frac{1}{2}$			
0	6		0	18	3

Columns 1 and 2 are the ordinary demand schedules.
Column 4 is the ordinary TR schedule: (1) $\times$ (2).
Column 3 is the perfect discriminator's MR when the consumer is forced to pay the maximum price he is willing to pay for each unit.
Column 5 shows the total revenue corresponding to MR'.
Column 6 is derived as $TR'/q = (5)/(2)$.

for the fourth unit $(5\frac{1}{2} + 4\frac{1}{2} + 3\frac{1}{2} + 2\frac{1}{2} = \$16)$ or as $P' \times 4$ units ($\$4.00 \times 4 = \$16$).

The MR' and P' schedules of Table 9.2 are shown in Figure 9.3. In this diagram we demonstrate graphically the calculation of TR by using both these schedules. Using the P' schedule, TR is simply measured as the rectangle $OBDF$ (4 units $\times$ \$4) or \$16. Alternately, TR can be measured as the area under the MR' curve up to 4 units, that is, $OACEF$.

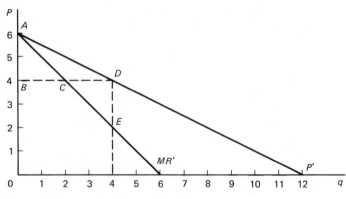

Figure 9.3

We can show that this area is equivalent to $OBDF$. Note first that both these areas have the section $OBCEF$ in common. Second, the two triangles ABC and CDE are equal in area.[2] It follows that the two methods of measuring TR yield the same result.[3]

The monopolist attempting to practice take-it-or-leave-it discrimination would find it extremely difficult to discriminate perfectly along a consumer's demand schedule, because he would be charging different prices for each unit for infinitesimal increments of output sold to the consumer. In practice, perfect discrimination is usually "lumpy." For example, electricity rates are often quoted on the basis of different prices

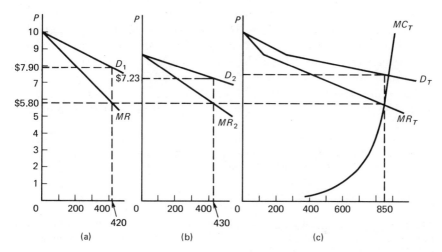

Figure 9.4

for successive "lumps" of the service rather than declining continuously as the consumer uses more electricity.

Imperfect Discrimination. In order to demonstrate imperfect discrimination, we assume a monopolist sells in two separate markets, each with its own demand schedule. We also assume that the marginal cost of supplying a unit of output to either market is the same. In Figures 9.4a–c we demon-

---

[2] Using the basic axioms of geometry $\angle ACB = \angle ECD$ and $\angle ABC = \angle EDC$; and since the absolute slope of MR is twice the absolute slope of P' (see p. 24 in Chapter 3), $BC = CD$. These equalities are sufficient for $\triangle ABC \cong \triangle EDC$, or in other words, the area of the two triangles are equal.

[3] Mathematically, we can see this as follows: If the original demand schedule or MR' is given by $P = a + bq$, then the "all-or-nothing" demand schedule would be $P' = a + \dfrac{b}{2}q$. For a given q, TR can be determined as

$$Pq = aq + \frac{b}{2}q^2 \quad \text{or} \quad \int_0^q (a + bq)dq = aq + bq^2$$

strate the determination of the equilibrium price and quantity for each market. Figures 9.4a and b show the demand and marginal revenue schedules for the respective markets. Figure 9.4c shows the aggregate demand (D_T) and its corresponding MR schedule (MR_T). The aggregate demand, marginal-revenue, and marginal-cost curves in Figure 9.4c are the same as the ones we assumed for the nondiscriminating monopolist discussed in the first section previously.

The monopolist determines his optimum output of 850 units in the usual fashion by equating MR_T to MC_T (Figure 9.4c). Once the monopolist has decided to produce a given output at a given cost, he can maximize his total revenue (and, therefore, his profit) by allocating the output between the two markets in such a way that the marginal revenues are equal; that is, $MR_1 = MR_2 = MR_T = MC_T = \$5.80.$[4] For example, if sales had been allocated in such a way that $MR_1 = \$7$ and $MR_2 = \$2$, then transferring a unit from the second market to the first would result in an increase in total revenue of approximately $5.

Therefore, the monopolist will sell 420 units in market 1 and charge $7.90 per unit, and in market 2 he will sell 430 units at a price of $7.23.

---

[4] If we assume the cost of supplying the commodity to the two markets 1 and 2 to be the same, then the firm will maximize total revenue (and total profits) for any given output by dividing its sales between the two markets so that

$$\text{(a)} \qquad MR_1 = P_1\left(1 + \frac{1}{E_1}\right) = MR_2 = P_2\left(1 + \frac{1}{E_2}\right)$$

The firm will be producing the maximum profit output where $MR_1 = MR_2 = MC$ in which MC is the marginal cost (the same for both markets) of producing a unit of output. In equilibrium, then,

$$\begin{aligned}\frac{P_1}{P_2} &= \left[\frac{(E_2 + 1)/E_2}{(E_1 + 1)/E_1}\right] \\ \text{(a')} \qquad &= [(E_2 + 1)/E_2][E_1/(E_1 + 1)]\end{aligned}$$

A more general formulation that makes no assumptions about costs in the two markets states that in each market the firm will equate MR to MC. In equilibrium, then,

$$\text{(b)} \qquad \begin{aligned} MC_1 &= MR_1 = P_1[(E_1 + 1)/E_1] \\ MC_2 &= MR_2 = P_2[(E_2 + 1)/E_2] \\ \frac{P_1}{P_2} &= \frac{MC_1[E_1/(E_1 + 1)]}{MC_2[E_2/(E_2 + 1)]} \end{aligned}$$

If $MC_1 = MC_2$ as assumed in (a), then,

$$\frac{P_1}{P_2} = [E_1/(E_1 + 1)][(E_2 + 1)/E_2]$$

and this is the same result as that obtained in (a'). If $E_1 = E_2$, then,

$$\frac{P_1}{P_2} = \frac{MC_1}{MC_2}$$

It should be noted that $q_1 + q_2$ is equal to q_T in Figure 9.4;[5] that is, $420 + 430 = 850$.

Some examples of imperfect price discrimination include different prices for theater tickets, based on the location of the seats in the theater, when the cost differential is significantly smaller than the price dif-

[5] We can prove this relationship as follows: Assume linear demand curves in both markets, represented by

$$P_1 = a + bq_1 \quad \text{and} \quad P_2 = c + dq_2$$

or

$$q_1 = \frac{P_1}{b} - \frac{a}{b} \quad \text{and} \quad q_2 = \frac{P_2}{d} - \frac{c}{d}$$

where b and d are the slopes and a and c are the vertical-axis intercepts. The total demand schedule can be written as

$$q_T = \frac{P_1}{b} + \frac{P_2}{d} - \frac{a}{b} - \frac{c}{d}$$

The corresponding marginal revenue schedules can be derived by using the following demand equations:

$$P_1 = a + bq_1$$
$$P_2 = c + dq_2$$
$$P_T = \frac{bdq_T}{b+d} + \frac{ad}{b+d} + \frac{cb}{b+d}$$

Express total revenue for the three demand equations:

$$TR_1 = aq_1 + bq_1^2$$
$$TR_2 = cq_2 + dq_2^2$$
$$TR_T = \left(\frac{bd}{b+d}\right)q_T^2 + \left(\frac{ad}{b+d}\right)q_T + \left(\frac{cb}{b+d}\right)q_T$$

The MR equations are then

$$MR_1 = a + 2bq_1$$
$$MR_2 = c + 2dq_2$$
$$MR_T = 2q_T\left(\frac{bd}{b+d}\right) + \left(\frac{ad}{b+d}\right) + \left(\frac{cb}{b+d}\right)$$

We can now state

$$q_1 = \frac{MR_1}{2b} - \frac{a}{2b}$$

$$q_2 = \frac{MR_2}{2d} - \frac{c}{2d}$$

$$q_T = \frac{MR_T}{2d} + \frac{MR_T}{2b} - \frac{a}{2b} - \frac{c}{2d}$$

Therefore, when $MR_1 = MR_2 = MR_T$

$$q_1 + q_2 = q_T \quad \text{since} \quad \frac{MR}{2d} + \frac{MR}{2b} - \frac{a}{2b} - \frac{c}{2d} = \frac{MR}{2b} - \frac{a}{2b} + \frac{MR}{2d} - \frac{c}{2d}$$

ferential; different prices for different classes of service charged by steamship and airline companies, when the price differences outweigh the cost differences; and different electricity rates charged to commercial and residential users.

We can show the loss in utility that results from price discrimination with the use of the Edgeworth box diagram discussed at the end of Chapter 5. Assume initially in Figure 9.5 that price discrimination exists, that individual A is being charged price P_a, and is therefore in equilibrium at Z on U_{a1}; and assume that B is being charged a price P_b

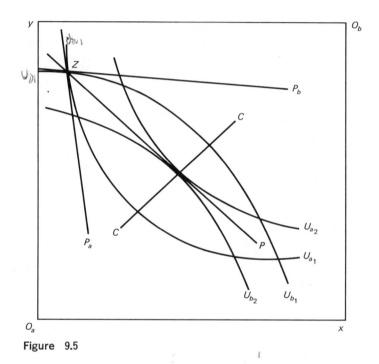

Figure 9.5

and is in equilibrium at Z on U_{b1}. If price discrimination is removed and a uniform price (represented by ZP) is charged, each individual will adjust his purchases so that when he is at his new equilibrium, the price line ZP is tangent to his highest possible indifference curve. But when the indifference curves of A and B are tangent to a common price line, they are tangent to each other; and thus the common equilibrium point lies on the contract curve. We saw in Chapter 5 that a move from an equilibrium off the contract curve to one on the curve represents a gain in utility for at least one individual; we see in Figure 9.5 that A moves from U_{a1} to U_{a2}, and B moves from U_{b1} to U_{b2}.

REGULATED MONOPOLIES

There are some industries in which economies of scale are so substantial (for example, many public utilities) that, in a sense, they are "natural" monopolies. The per-unit cost of providing the commodity declines substantially as the firm increases production so that the most efficient form of organization is that of monopoly. In the case in which the government permits the existence of a monopoly to achieve economies of scale, it is generally, in the United States, accompanied by government regulation to protect the public from undue exercise of monopoly power. We shall discuss several of the many alternative methods that government uses to control monopolies.

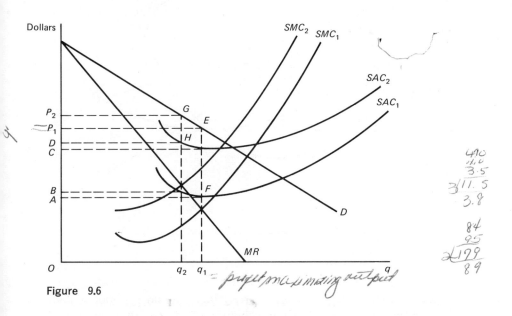

Figure 9.6

Indirect Government Control through Taxation. We assume that a *specific tax* of AC per unit is levied on the monopolist shown in Figure 9.6. Prior to the imposition of the tax, the monopolist's profit-maximizing output was q_1, the price was P_1, and profits were AP_1EF.

The tax raises the STC schedule by the amount of the tax; thus, we show an upward shift in both the SAC and SMC curves by the amount of the tax. Profit-maximizing output is now q_2, the price is P_2, and the profits are reduced to DP_2GH. Profits must be smaller with the tax because the monopolist was originally maximizing his profits by producing q_1; therefore, selling q_2 must result in a before-tax profit of less than the q_2

profit. In addition, the monopolist must pay a tax from these smaller profits.[6]

The degree to which a monopolist can shift a per-unit tax depends in part on the elasticity of demand facing him. Because the demand for the product of monopolist tends to be relatively inelastic, in all likelihood a good portion of the tax will be shifted to the consumer; and, therefore, the tax revenue collected by the government will represent mainly a burden on the consumer rather than a reduction in the gains from monopoly power.[7]

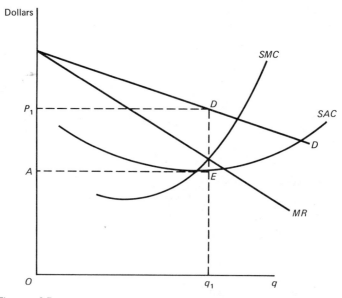

Figure 9.7

We next analyze the effects of a *profits tax* upon the monopolist. We assume the original equilibrium in Figure 9.7 to be q_1 units of output, the price to be P_1, and the profits to be AP_1DE. A tax equal to a certain percentage of total profits will not result in any change in the equilibrium price and output. If t is the tax (in percentage terms) and q_1 is the *profit-maximizing* output prior to the tax, then $(1 - t) \times q_1(P_1A)$ (that is, the

[6] Since q_1 was the profit-maximizing output before the tax,

$$q_1(P_1A) > q_2(P_2B)$$

With the tax, the SAC for q_2 units increases from OB to OD. Therefore,

$$q_1(P_1A) > q_2(P_2D)$$

[7] The exact effects of a specific tax on a monopolist are discussed in detail in Appendix 9A.

percentage of profits kept after the tax) is the largest after-tax profit obtainable by the firm.[8]

Direct Government Control through Price Regulation. We shall discuss two major kinds of price regulation. In one the government sets a ceiling price at the level where $LMC = P$. This is the price P_2 in Figure 9.8. In the absence of regulation, the monopolist would produce q_1 at a price of P_1. With the ceiling price, the effective demand curve becomes P_2AD; the corresponding MR curve is coincident with the demand curve over the range P_2A, is discontinuous at A, and then becomes CD. The profit-maximizing output is q_2, since at greater outputs, $LMC > MR$, and at smaller outputs, $LMC < MR$. The monopolist is thus forced to produce more at a lower price.

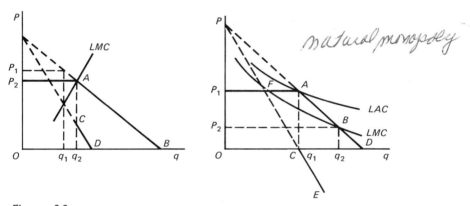

Figure 9.8

If, however, as is implied by natural monopoly, the LAC curve is downward sloping over the entire relevant range of outputs (see Figure 9.9), then attempting to set a price equal to LMC will result in losses to the monopolist. For example, at the price P_2, average revenue will be less than LAC. Therefore, unless the government is willing to subsidize the firm, this type of regulation is not feasible.

In this case, the usual procedure is to permit the firm to make a "fair" return on invested capital. If the opportunity cost of invested capital is included in the cost schedules, this procedure is the same as setting a price such that profits are zero. In Figure 9.9 this amounts to setting the

[8] As currently constituted, the corporation profits tax is not a true profits tax. This is so because dividends are treated as a distribution of pure profits, whereas the payment to the owners is really made up of two components: (1) a return on invested capital, that is, the opportunity cost of the funds tied up in the firm by the owners, and (2) pure profit, if any. This creates an incentive for the corporation to raise new funds through the bond market rather than from the sale of new stock, because bond interest is a cost that can be deducted before computation of taxable income.

price P_1 so that the demand schedule becomes P_1AB and the marginal revenue schedule is coincident with demand over the range P_1A, is discontinuous at A, and thereafter is CE. At the price of P_1, the firm will produce q_1, since $MR < LMC$ for greater outputs and $MR > LMC$ for smaller outputs.[9] Another way of stating this is to say that LMC cuts MR in its discontinuous segment.[10]

---

[9] It should be noted that the intersection of MR and LMC at point F does not represent an equilibrium, because for smaller outputs, $LMC > MR$, and for greater outputs, $MR > LMC$.

[10] It is sometimes possible for the government to force an output where $LMC = P$ even with continuously declining LAC, by permitting the monopolist to practice price discrimination. An example of this is the different rates charged by electrical utility companies to the different markets of commercial and residential consumers.

Appendix 9A

Effects of a Specific Tax on a Monopolist and a Perfectly Competitive Industry

We wish to show the impact of a specific tax on the output, price, and profit of a monopolist; and in addition we wish to compare these effects with the impact of a tax on a perfectly competitive industry. For the sake of simplicity, throughout this appendix we assume linear demand and cost schedules. Assume the following schedules:

Demand:	$P = a + bq;$	$b \leq 0$	[9A.1]
Marginal revenue:	$MR = a + 2bq$		[9A.2]
Average cost:	$AC = c + \dfrac{d}{2} q$		[9A.3]
Marginal cost:	$MC = c + dq$		[9A.4]

For the monopolist, we determine the equilibrium values as follows: For output, equate equation 9A.2 to equation 9A.4:

$$a + 2bq = c + dq$$

which gives

$$q_1 = \frac{a - c}{d - 2b} \qquad [9A.5]$$

Substituting equation 9A.5 in equation 9A.1,

$$P = a + b \left(\frac{a - c}{d - 2b} \right) \qquad [9A.6]$$

In order to compute total profit, we first compute total revenue:

$$TR = a \left(\frac{a - c}{d - 2b} \right) + b \left(\frac{a - c}{d - 2b} \right)^2 \qquad [9A.7]$$

Next, we obtain $TC = AC \times q$. First substituting equation 9A.5 in equation 9A.3 and then multiplying by equation 9A.5 yields

$$TC = c \left(\frac{a - c}{d - 2b} \right) + \frac{d}{2} \left(\frac{a - c}{d - 2b} \right)^2 \qquad [9A.8]$$

195

Thus, profit can be derived as $\pi = TR - TC$. Subtracting equation 9A.8 from 9A.7:

$$\pi_1 = (a - c)\left(\frac{a - c}{d - 2b}\right) - \left(\frac{d - 2b}{2}\right)\left(\frac{a - c}{d - 2b}\right)^2$$

$$= \frac{1}{2}\left(\frac{a - c}{d - 2b}\right)^2 \qquad [9A.9]$$

Now let us suppose a specific tax to be imposed on the monopolist. This can be shown as either an increase in MC or a reduction in the price per unit received by the monopolist, that is, a parallel shift downward in the demand schedule. Using the latter device, the new demand schedule facing the firm becomes

$$P = a - t + bq \qquad [9A.10]$$

and

$$MR = a - t + 2bq \qquad [9A.11]$$

As before, by equating MR to MC, we can solve for the post-tax equilibrium quantity.

$$q_2 = \frac{a - t - c}{d - 2b} \qquad [9A.12]$$

Substituting in equation 9A.9, the price retained by the monopolist after payment of the tax is

$$P_2 = a - t + b\left(\frac{a - t - c}{d - 2b}\right) \qquad [9A.13]$$

The new price paid by consumers is P_2 plus the tax. Profits after the tax are given by

$$\pi_2 = \frac{1}{2}\left(\frac{a - c}{d - 2b}\right)^2 + \frac{1}{2}t\left[\frac{t - 2a + 2c}{d - 2b}\right] \qquad [9A.14]$$

Taking the difference between the post-tax and pretax equilibrium quantities, we obtain

$$\Delta q = q_2 - q_1 = (9A.11) - (9A.5)$$

$$\Delta q = -\frac{t}{d - 2b} \qquad [9A.15]$$

The rate at which quantity changes with respect to the tax is given by

$$\frac{\Delta q}{\Delta t} = -\frac{1}{d - 2b} \qquad [9A.16]$$

Taking the difference between post-tax and pretax equilibrium prices, we get

$$\Delta P = P_2 - P_1 = (9A.11) - (9A.6)$$

$$\Delta P = \frac{t(b - d)}{d - 2b} \qquad [9A.17]$$

And the rate at which price changes with respect to the tax is given by

$$\frac{\Delta P}{\Delta t} = \frac{b - d}{d - 2b} \qquad \text{[9A.18]}$$

The difference in the prices paid by consumers is given by equation 9A.17 plus the tax or

$$\Delta P' = -\frac{tb}{d - 2b} \qquad \text{[9A.19]}$$

To calculate the change in profits, we compute

$$\Delta \pi = \pi_2 - \pi_1 = (9A.14) - (9A.9)$$

$$\Delta \pi = t \left[\frac{\dfrac{t}{2} - a + c}{d - 2b} \right] \qquad \text{[9A.20]}$$

The rate at which profits change with respect to the tax can be determined as

$$\frac{\Delta \pi}{\Delta t} = \frac{\dfrac{t}{2} - a + c}{d - 2b} \qquad \text{[9A.21]}$$

Using the previous generalized relationships, we may summarize the effect on quantity, price, and profits of the shape of the marginal cost schedule.

	$\dfrac{\Delta q}{\Delta t}$	$\dfrac{\Delta p}{\Delta t}$	$\dfrac{\Delta \pi}{\Delta t}$
(1) Constant MC $(d = 0)$	$-\dfrac{1}{2|b|}$	$-\dfrac{1}{2}$	$\dfrac{1}{4}\dfrac{t}{|b|} - \left(\dfrac{a - c}{2|b|}\right)$
(2) Nonconstant MC $(d \neq 0)$	$-\dfrac{1}{d + 2|b|}$	$\dfrac{-[|b| + d]}{d + 2|b|}$	$\dfrac{\dfrac{t}{2} - a + c}{d + 2|b|}$

The usual assumption is that marginal cost rises with increases in output; thus, on line 2, $d > 0$. Note that $\dfrac{\Delta q}{\Delta t}$ is negative on both lines 1 and 2; however, $\left|\dfrac{\Delta q}{\Delta t}\right|$ when $d = 0$ is greater than $\left|\dfrac{\Delta q}{\Delta t}\right|$ when $d > 0$. In other words, for the same tax change, the decrease in output is smaller when MC is rising. It is intuitively clear that the smaller decline in output in the case of rising MC is attributable to the countervailing effect of declining MC with decreased output on marginal profit in the face of the downward shift in MR.

The effect of the tax on the price retained by the monopolist when MC is constant is simply equal to $-\frac{1}{2}$; thus a tax of \$1 would result in a price decline of \$.50. On the assumption of rising MC, line 2 shows that the monopolist will suffer a price decline of more than $\frac{1}{2}$.

The effect on profits of the tax, whatever the shape of the MC curve, is a reduction. This must be the case because the initial position was a profit-maximizing one; the tax has pushed the monopolist away from this point, and in addition he must pay the tax.[1] Although we have shown that the imposition of the tax reduces profits when MC is constant and rising, it is impossible to show, prima facie, in which case the reduction will be greater.

We next investigate the case where $d < 0$. In similar manner we may show that, compared to constant MC, with falling MC the decline in output due to a given tax is greater, the decline in price kept by the monopolist is less; and once again, it is not possible to tell in which case profits decline more.[2]

We now compare the results we obtained with those that would be obtained by assuming a tax imposed on a perfectly competitive industry. Now assume that equation 9A.1 represents the demand schedule facing the industry and equation 9A.4 represents the supply schedule of the industry. Equating supply and demand, the equilibrium quantity is given by

$$q_1 = \frac{a - c}{d - b} \qquad [9A.22]$$

Substituting in equation 9A.1, we determine price.

$$P_1 = a + b \left[\frac{a - c}{d - b} \right] \qquad [9A.23]$$

After the tax is imposed, using the new demand equation 9A.10, we obtain

$$q_2 = \frac{a - c - t}{d - b} \qquad [9A.24]$$

---

[1] From an inspection of lines 1 and 2, it is not obvious that $\Delta\pi/\Delta t$ must be negative. However, it can be shown quite easily that this is true. For both lines 1 and 2, $\Delta\pi/\Delta t$ must be negative because the following inequality holds in both cases: $c < \left(a - \frac{t}{2} \right)$. This inequality must hold because (1) c represents the vertical axis intercept of the MC curve and (2) a represents the vertical axis intercept of the MR curve. Because the MR curve is downward sloping and MC is upward sloping, if these linear schedules are to intersect, $c < a$. Furthermore, $a - t$ represents the vertical axis intercept of the after-tax MR schedule; and, once again, if there is to be an equilibrium point, $c < (a - t)$. Finally, it follows that if $c < (a - t)$, $c < \left(a - \frac{t}{2} \right)$.

[2] Once again, profits must decline. Although both MR and MC are now declining, stable equilibrium now requires that $c < a$.

and

$$P_2 = a - t + b \left[\frac{a - c - t}{d - b} \right] \qquad \text{[9A.25]}$$

Thus,

$$\Delta q = - \frac{t}{d - b} \qquad \text{[9A.26]}$$

and

$$\frac{\Delta q}{\Delta t} = - \frac{1}{d - b} \qquad \text{[9A.27]}$$

Finally,[3]

$$\Delta P = - \frac{dt}{d - b} \qquad \text{[9A.28]}$$

and

$$\frac{\Delta P}{\Delta t} = - \frac{d}{d - b} \qquad \text{[9A.29]}$$

Comparison with monopoly shows that, in the case of constant cost, the decrease in quantity per unit change in tax for the monopolist is one half the decrease for the competitive industry; there is no change in price for the competitive industry compared to $\Delta P/\Delta t = 1/2$ for the monopolist. (Note that it is meaningless to compare profits because in the competitive industry in the long run there will be no profits.)

In the case of increasing costs, a comparison of equations 9A.16 and 9A.27 shows that the decline in output, per-unit change in tax, will be greater under competition, whereas expressions 9A.18 and 9A.29 indicate that $\Delta P/\Delta t$ is greater for the competitive industry. (This last statement can be verified by subtracting equation 9A.29 from equation 9A.18 and noticing the sign of the difference.)

By subtracting equation 9A.27 from equations 9A.16 and by subtracting equation 9A.29 from equation 9A.18, we can see that, in the case of decreasing costs, $\Delta q/\Delta t$ is larger for the monopolist while $\Delta P/\Delta t$ is greater for the competitor.

---

[3] It is interesting to note that in the case of a downward-sloping competitive industry supply curve, the price paid by consumers after the imposition of a tax rises by more than the amount of the tax. This is because of the induced change in industry costs caused by the reduction in output.

10

PRICING AND OUTPUT DECISIONS UNDER MONOPOLISTIC COMPETITION AND OLIGOPOLY

MONOPOLISTIC COMPETITION

Monopolistic competition is a market situation in which there are a large enough number of firms selling differentiated goods so that there is no interdependence among them; that is, the action taken by one firm will not have any appreciable effects upon the other firms. In a sense each firm is a monopolist because it is the only seller of the good, narrowly defined. The nature of the demand schedule facing an individual monopolistic competitor depends, first, on the number of sellers of the broad category of goods and, second, on the degree of differentiation (that is, uniqueness) of the seller's particular good. Because the individual monopolistic competitor has some degree of "monopoly" power based on the fact that consumers consider his product to be in some sense different,[1] he is able to increase the price of his product without running the risk of losing his entire market, as would a perfect competitor.

An example of monopolistic competition may help to clarify the concept. Assume a large number of barber shops in a community and assume that consumers are indifferent among the haircuts and other services offered in the respective shops. We would consider this a competitive industry. Suppose, alternatively, that the owner of shop A is a raconteur, that the owner of shop B is capable of a critique of last night's opera, that the owner of shop C is a fount of baseball scores, and so on for the rest of the firms. Although each barber provides haircuts, consumers—with varying

[1] This difference can be real or imagined on the part of consumers and can be created through advertising.

tastes for chitchat—will prefer one barber to the others. Each barber may charge a price somewhat, but not too, different from the others and still retain his customers. Clearly, however, at a substantial price difference, haircuts with baseball talk (perhaps one could take along some plugs of cotton) would compete with haircuts with opera talk.

The demand schedule facing a monopolistic competitor will be somewhat downward sloping. The degree of monopoly power will depend on the degree of differentiation, because all the other conditions of perfect competition are being fulfilled. Of course, if a high degree of differentiation is achieved, the appropriate model is no longer monopolistic competition but is monopoly. On the other hand, if the degree of differentiation is minute, then for many problems the appropriate model is perfect competition. The monopolistic competitive model is mainly useful for explaining certain phenomena, such as advertising and selling costs, in industries considered "substantially" competitive, which are not predicted by the perfectly competitive model.

The notion of an equilibrium price loses its uniqueness in monopolistic competition. Because the goods are not perfect substitutes for one another, there may be more than one price at a time.

MONOPOLISTIC COMPETITION: SHORT-RUN EQUILIBRIUM

Short-run, profit-maximizing price and output are determined in the usual fashion. Thus, in Figure 10.1, $MR = SMC$ at 850 units and the price charged will be $6.65. Because the gap between P and MR is determined by

$$MR = AR \left(1 + \frac{1}{E}\right)$$

the difference between P and SMC at the equilibrium output will be relatively small under conditions of monopolistic competition.[2]

The products sold by the monopolistic competitors within an industry may differ from one another physically, but it is more likely that the differentiation is based on attendant services and amenities (for example, the conversational abilities of the barbers just described, packaging, convenience of location, and branding of product).

Although the perfect competitor has no incentive to advertise or to carry on other sales promotion activities, the monopolistic competitor will use these devices in an effort to differentiate further his good so that

[2] For purposes of comparison, it was assumed that the monopolist in Figure 9.1 and the monopolistic competitor in Figure 10.1 have the same cost schedules and produce the same profit-maximizing output. At the profit-maximizing output of 850 units, the gap between P and SMC for the monopolist is $1.70 ($7.50 − $5.80); whereas for the monopolistic competitor, P exceeds SMC by $0.85 ($6.65 − $5.80).

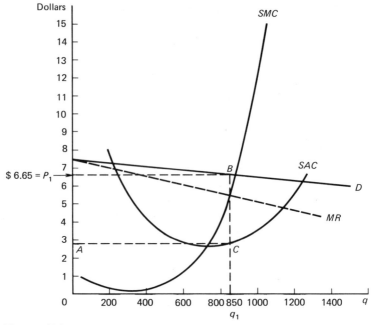

Figure 10.1

the demand he faces will increase as well as become more inelastic. As a limit, he attempts to achieve the gains of monopoly. An increase in selling activities will shift the average and marginal costs of the firm upward, and they are undertaken in an attempt to shift the demand and marginal revenue schedules upward. The profitability of the selling activities will be indicated by $\Delta TR_s - \Delta TC_s$, where the subscript s represents "due to a per-unit change in selling activities."

MONOPOLISTIC COMPETITION: LONG-RUN EQUILIBRIUM

The usual situation under monopolistic competition is free entry into and exit from the industry in the long run. When profits are being earned in the short run, they present an incentive to potential firms to enter the industry. If we assume that the total demand for the products remains constant and that the degree of differentiation among firms is such that consumers consider the products of the various firms to be substitutes in a broad sense, then with new firms entering, customers will be drawn from the existing firms to the new ones. Thus, as new firms enter, the demand schedule facing each member of the industry will shift downward. This downward shift in demand will continue as long as positive profits exist. Thus, in Figure 10.2 long-run equilibrium is shown as Oq_1 and OP_1. At

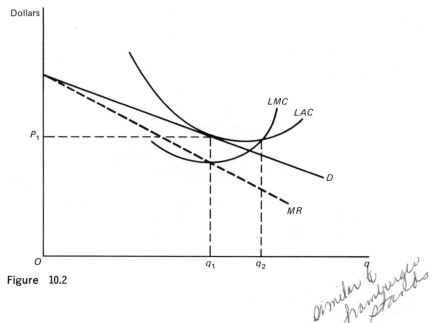

Figure   10.2

this output, price is just equal to LAC; thus, $\pi = 0$. Note also that at Oq_1, where the demand schedule is tangent to LAC, $MR = LMC$.[3]

Note that if the firm were operating in a perfectly competitive industry, it would be in long-run equilibrium at an output of Oq_2, where it would be operating at minimum LAC. The monopolistic competitive firm stops short of this output. Therefore, the monopolistic competitor does not operate at the most efficient point on his LAC curve. In other words, excess capacity exists in the long run. This model casts some light on the phenomenon of several barber shops in close proximity, with one or a few chairs rarely occupied, as well as similar situations with gas stations, drugstores, neighborhood grocery stores, and the like, all of which fulfill the conditions of monopolistic competition and exhibit excess capacity.

In Figure 10.3 we show long-run equilibrium when entry into the industry is blocked. When potential firms cannot enter the industry freely in response to positive profits, the existing firms are able to retain profits in the long run. In Figure 10.3 the long-run profits are AP_1BC.

[3] This can be proven as follows:

$$E_d = \frac{dq}{dp} \cdot \frac{p}{q} \qquad \text{and} \qquad E_{LAC} = \frac{dq}{dLAC} \cdot \frac{LAC}{q}$$

At Oq_1, $P = LAC$ and $dp/dq = dLAC/dq$. Therefore, $E_d = E_{LAC}$ at Oq_1. The relationship between MR and P is $MR = P(1 + 1/E_d)$ and the relationship between LMC and LAC is $LMC = LAC(1 + 1/E_{LAC})$. Therefore, since $P = LAC$ and $E_d = E_{LAC}$ at Oq_1, $MR = LMC$.

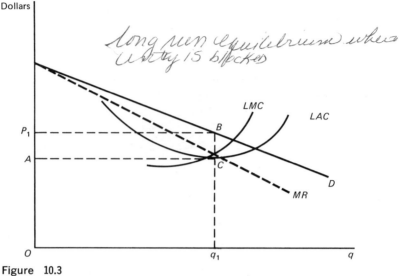

Figure 10.3

Because the initial costs of entering a typical monopolistic competitive industry are relatively low, if barriers to entry exist, they are likely to be artificial, such as licensing or other government regulations. For example, in New York City there are a fixed number of taxi medallions that are required in order to run a cab within the city. Another example of blocked entry is the licensing of liquor stores in many states.

Most monopolistic competitive industries, however, do have free entry. This fact, together with the small initial cost of entering, tends to result in a high birth rate of new firms in these industries. The death rate will tend also to be high, partially because of the excess capacity in these industries and partially because of the fact that "hope springs eternal" when it is shrouded by ignorance: Many potential small entrepreneurs have little or no experience in operating their own businesses.

It should be noted that the concept of the industry under conditions of monopolistic competition becomes somewhat fuzzy. Firms may be said to be in the same industry when they sell a homogeneous good; that is, the cross elasticities among the products are infinite. Thus, in perfect competition and monopoly, the concept of the industry is precise. Because in monopolistic competition, firms sell products that are different, at least in some degree, it becomes difficult to define precisely what we mean by an industry. One method of determining industry boundaries is to place with high positive cross elasticities into the same industry. However, what constitutes a "high" coefficient of cross elasticity is entirely arbitrary.

OLIGOPOLY

The identifying characteristic of oligopoly is interdependence among the firms in the industry. By this is meant that the number of firms is small enough so that the action of any one firm will affect the others. Each firm considers how its actions will affect the policies of its rivals. The oligopolist is like the man who is playing chess: Before taking any action, he must consider the possible reactions on the part of his opponent and how to counter them.

Oligopoly does not lend itself readily to theoretical analysis of the sort we have been using because there are an infinite number of reaction patterns. At one extreme is an oligopoly situation in which the firms decide to act in collusion and, therefore, achieve a monopoly solution to pricing and output decisions. At the other extreme is the situation in which the individual oligopolist changes his price and output without regard to the reactions of his rivals because he has a misguided notion about their stupidity and/or ignorance or because he is persuaded that their reaction lag is great enough to permit him to gain a temporary advantage from these changes. Between these extremes there are, if not an infinite, at least a large number of possibilities. In our discussion we shall consider several of the more interesting ones.

It should also be noted that the product of an oligopolistic industry can be either homogeneous or differentiated. The former is likely to exist in producer goods industries such as steel, cement, and copper, and the latter in consumer goods industries such as automobiles and cigarettes. The reason for the lack of differentiation in the producer goods industries is that these are goods usually purchased according to engineering specifications. In the examples that we shall be cons dering, we shall assume pure (or homogeneous) oligopoly.

As in monopolistic competition, the greater the degree of differentiation, the less the interdependency among the oligopolists. When an oligopolistic industry achieves a mature status and when firms realize the consequences of competitive price cutting, they tend to revert to non-price competition (such as advertising and "quality" changes). The effort is to increase profits through a shift in their demand curves and an increased inelasticity of demand in the relevant price range.

OLIGOPOLY WITH ABSOLUTE COLLUSION

The firms in an oligopolistic industry realize that total industry profits can be fully maximized by collusion; that is, price and output are determined for the industry by equating MR, corresponding to the aggregate demand facing the industry, to MC of the industry. The industry marginal cost schedule is the horizontal summation of the member firms' MC

schedules. Once the industry profit-maximizing output is determined, each firm's contribution to the total output is determined in such a way that

$$MC_1 = MC_2 = \cdots = MC_n \qquad [10.1]$$

In other words, the MC for producing a unit of output must be the same for all firms if the profit-maximizing output is to be produced at minimum cost.

In Figure 10.4d, the profit-maximizing output is 1100 units, because at that level $MR_T = MC_T$ ($1.10 = $1.10). Thus, to ensure the lowest cost for 1100 units, firm 1 will produce 550 units, firm 2 will produce 330 units, and firm 3 will produce 220 units. It will be noted that $q_1 + q_2 + q_3 = Q_T$ (550 + 330 + 220 = 1100).[4]

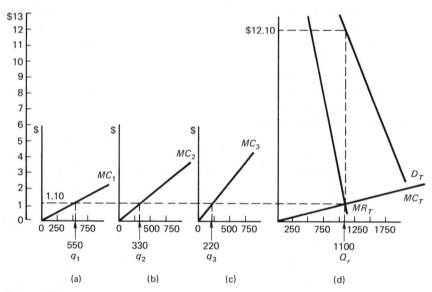

Figure 10.4

There is the additional problem of allocating the now larger industry profits among the member firms. If these profits are distributed in such a way that each firm receives the same percentage of industry profit as it did prior to collusion, then each firm's profits will increase as a result of collusion. The actual method used for allocating profits depends on the relative bargaining strengths of the firms, the history of the industry, and so on. Clearly, the firm will be willing to participate in the cartel only if it will be at least as well off as it was before.[5]

---

[4] See note - in Chapter 9.

[5] In the next section, we shall compare profits obtained under the monopoly solution with those obtained when there is less-than-complete collusion of the oligopolists.

OLIGOPOLY WITH TACIT COLLUSION

In the United States overt collusion is illegal. One form of tacit collusion among oligopolists is reflected by the *kinky demand curve*. This type of demand curve expresses the view of the oligopolist that his rivals will follow his price cuts but not his price increases. Under this assumption the demand curve facing the oligopolist will be highly elastic at prices above the prevailing market price and relatively inelastic at prices below this one. This type of demand curve is shown in Figure 10.5; it is "kinked" at

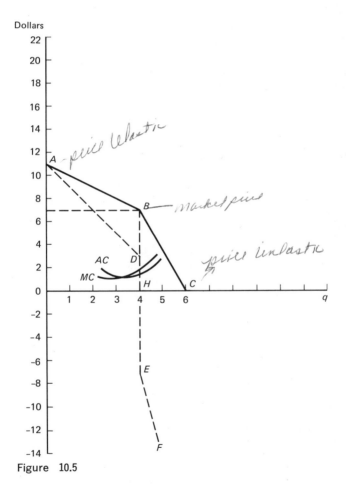

Figure 10.5

the prevailing market price ($7). The demand curve faced by the oligopolist at a price above $7 is relatively elastic because the other firms in the industry will not follow a price rise so that consumers have available several fairly good substitutes at lower prices. Below the prevailing price the demand curve is shown to be relatively inelastic. Because the other firms follow a price cut, the only increase in sales the price-cutting firm experiences is its proportionate share of the increase in quantity demanded along the industry demand curve. Although the kinky demand curve describes a particular attitude, it does not say anything about the determinants of the attitude, nor does it explain the current price at which the kink is presumed to be. Once the current price has been arrived at by some historical process of interaction among the oligopolists (perhaps disastrous experiences with competitive price cutting), the kinky demand curve helps to explain future behavior.

With the given cost schedules of the firm in Figure 10.5, the equilibrium output is 4 units and the price is $7, because for outputs greater than 4 units, $MC > MR$ and for smaller outputs, $MR > MC$.

It is often said that the kinky oligopoly demand curve results in rigid prices: The price remains stable over long periods of time. This is a consequence of two factors: (1) each firm believes that little is to be gained by a price rise and that a price cut will lead to a "price war" and (2) because the MC curve cuts the discontinuous section of the MR curve, substantial shifts in the MC and AC curves can take place and, depending on the length of the discontinuity, the firm will still find its optimum output to be the same as it was at the kink price. For example, in Figure 10.5, if MC shifts within the range DH, no change in price or output will result, because MR will still be greater than MC for smaller outputs and because MC will be greater than MR for larger outputs.

Empirical evidence seems to indicate that the kinky oligopoly demand curve does not accurately describe the most common form of oligopoly behavior. It is believed that oligopolists act in collusion and attempt to achieve a monopoly solution rather than behave as posited by the kinky demand curve.[6] Recent antitrust action in the electrical equipment and steel industries tends to support this belief.

Another possible form of tacit collusion is *price leadership on the part of the low-cost oligopolist* in the industry. In Figures 10.6a–c we assume three firms in an industry and show the equilibrium price and output under the assumption that the firms have agreed to share the market equally.[7] Firm 1 would like to charge $11.91 and sell 373 units; firm 2 would like to sell 365 units at $12.15 per unit; and firm 3 would like to sell 355 units at $12.45. However, firm 1, being the lowest-cost firm, charges a price lower than that charged by the other two firms. If there is no overt agreement among the firms as to price policy, firms 2 and 3

[6] For a further discussion of this point, see George J. Stigler, "The Kinky Oligopoly Demand Curve and Rigid Prices," *Journal of Political Economy*, Vol. LV (October 1947), 432–449.
[7] Thus, the horizontal sum of the three demand curves represents the aggregate demand facing the industry.

will be forced to charge \$11.91 and sell 373 units each or be faced with the danger of losing their share of the market.

It should be noted that the horizontal sum of the demand curves in Figure 10.6 is equal to the market demand that we assumed to face the cartel in Figure 10.4d; that is,

$$q_1 = 770 - 33\tfrac{1}{3}P$$
$$q_2 = 770 - 33\tfrac{1}{3}P$$
$$q_3 = 770 - 33\tfrac{1}{3}P$$
$$\overline{Q_T = 2310 - 100P \text{ or } P = 23.10 - 0.01Q_T}$$

Therefore, it is possible to compare the total profit earned by the cartel to industry profit with price leadership.

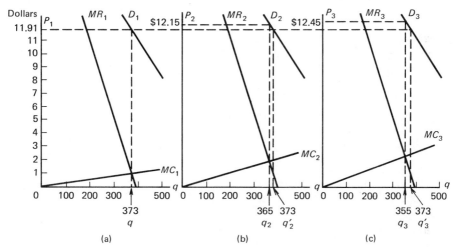

Figure 10.6

Still another type of tacit collusion is called "umbrella price leadership," which occurs when a dominant firm in the industry sets price at the level at which it can sell its profit-maximizing output and then permits the smaller firms in the industry to sell all they profitably can at that price. One of the reasons why this may be done is the desire to retain the appearance of a competitive industry in the presence of anti-trust laws. We demonstrate this type of behavior in Figure 10.7, in which MC_S represents the horizontal sum of the smaller firms' MC curves and in which MC_L represents the large firms' marginal cost. We shall assume that all the small firms have identical cost schedules and that there are 20 of them in the industry. Because the small firms accept the price set by the dominant firm, their MC curves are their supply curves (in the same way that the MC curve of the perfectly competitive firm is its supply curve because it accepts the price set by the market) and MC_S is, therefore, the total supply curve of the small firms. The demand curve facing the large firm can be derived by taking the horizontal difference at any price between the total demand and the amount supplied by the small firms. This demand is shown as D_L and the corresponding marginal revenue curve is MR_L. Thus the large firm will produce 972 units at the point where $MC_L = MR_L$ and it will set a price of $4.46. At this price the small firms will supply a total of 892 units, or each firm will produce 44.6 units.

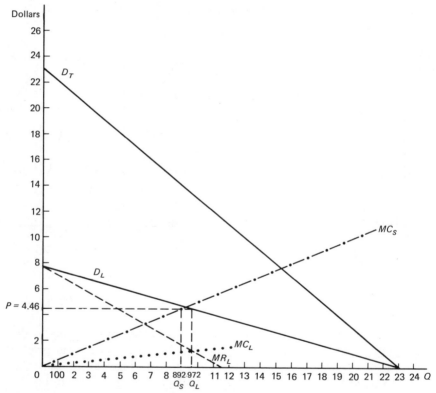

Figure 10.7

OLIGOPOLY WITHOUT COLLUSION

In this section we shall discuss unsophisticated oligopoly behavior. By "unsophisticated" we mean either that an oligopolist does not realize he and his rivals are interdependent or that he realizes this but makes no effort to establish any form of collusion with them. In the first case, we assume an oligopolist who is not aware of this interdependence or, if he is aware of it, misjudges its magnitude. We may describe this variant of oligopolistic behavior as immature, because, unless the oligopolist suffers from colossal stupidity, he will at some point learn the lessons of experience: He cannot disregard the effect that his rivals' reactions to his own actions will have upon him. For example, suppose that an oligopolist who was maximizing profit experiences a decrease in costs and, in order to achieve new maximum profits, reduces price and increases his output. His rivals discover that, as a result of this price reduction, their demand schedules shift downward; they will react to this by reducing price and output, causing reductions in their maximum profits. But this reaction shifts the demand schedule of the first oligopolist; and thus his price and output will change. But this shifts the demand curves facing his rivals, and so on and on. This type of behavior will deteriorate into a competitive price-cutting war. When the oligopolists have learned the lesson from their experiences, their behavior may be better described by the kinky demand curve or by one of the other forms of tacit collusion.

An example of unsophisticated oligopoly behavior, when the oligopolist realizes he is interdependent, was described by Augustin Cournot.[8] We shall present Cournot's treatment of the oligopoly solution for the two-firm case (duopoly), but the reasoning can be extended to several firms. Assume that the aggregate demand facing an industry is given by

$$Q_d = 10 - P \qquad \text{(Figure 10.8a)} \qquad [10.2]$$

and that the costs of production are zero. (Cournot's two firms were owners of mineral springs producing identical mineral water.) Thus, a firm maximizing profits will produce where its TR is a maximum; in other words, where $MR = MC = 0$. Let us initially assume that there is one firm in the industry. Acting as a monopolist, it will produce 5 units at $P = \$5$, as is shown in Figure 10.8b, and its profits will be \$25.

Next, we assume that the second firm enters the industry and that its assumption concerning the behavior of the existing firm is that that firm's output will remain at 5 units regardless of its own behavior. Therefore, the second firm takes its demand equation to be

$$q_2 = (10 - P) - 5$$

or

$$q_2 = 5 - P \qquad [10.3]$$

Figure 10.8c shows the determination of equilibrium price and output for the second firm; thus, $P = \$5/2$, $q_2 = 5/2$, and maximum profits are therefore \$6.25 ($5/2 \times \$5/2 = \$25/4$).

[8] Augustin Cournot, *Researches into the Mathematical Principles of Wealth*, trans. N. Bacon and Irving Fisher (New York: The Macmillan Company, 1897).

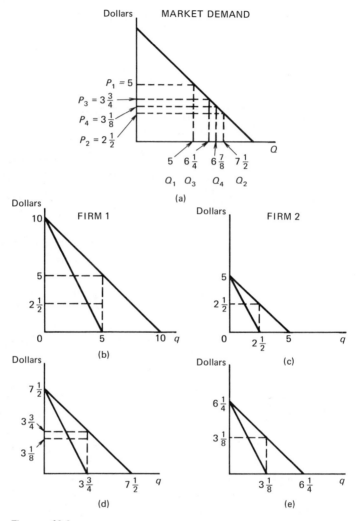

Figure 10.8

Total industry output is now $7\frac{1}{2} = q_1 + q_2 = 5 + 2\frac{1}{2}$. According to the total demand curve of Figure 10.8a, market price will become $5/2. Therefore, firm 1 will now be able to sell its 5 units at $P = \$5/2$; and its profits are reduced to one half their former level—$12.50.

If the first firm suffers from the same form of myopia as the second firm, it will assume that the 5/2 units being sold by the second firm are fixed, and the first firm then will re-estimate its demand curve, based on this assumption. This new demand curve will be

$$q_1 = (10 - P) - 2\tfrac{1}{2} = 7\tfrac{1}{2} - P \qquad [10.4]$$

In Figure 10.8d, the new profit-maximizing output is 15/4, $P = \$15/4$, and profits have been increased temporarily from \$12.50 to \$14.06 ($15/4 \times \$15/4 = \$225/16$).

Firm 2 will now regard the 15/4 units as constant, and its demand curve becomes

$$q_2 = (10 - P) - \frac{15}{4} = \frac{25}{4} - P \qquad [10.5]$$

Figure 10.8e shows the equilibrium values of $q_2 = 25/8$ and $P = \$25/8$, and profits increased to \$9.77 ($25/8 \times \$25/8 = \$625/64$) from \$6.25.

The new market price becomes \$25/8 and the first firm's profits are now \$11.72 ($30/8 \times \$25/8 = \$750/64$).

This process continues, with the fluctuations becoming progressively smaller, and the values of P, q_1, and q_2 approach limits. The limits they approach can be determined in the following manner: Since total demand is given by $Q_T = 10 - P$ and $Q_T = q_1 + q_2$, the demand facing firm 1 can be written as

$$q_1 = (10 - P) - q_2 \qquad [10.6]$$

which can also be written as

$$P = (10 - q_2) - q_1 \qquad [10.7]$$

Firm 1 regards firm 2's output as a given; thus, the term $(10 - q_2)$ is a constant, and equation 10.7 can be written as

$$P = \alpha - q_1 \qquad [10.8]$$

where α is a constant equal to $(10 - q_2)$.

Because equation 10.8 represents a linear demand curve, the corresponding marginal revenue curve will have twice the absolute slope of the demand curve. Thus,

$$MR_1 = \alpha - 2q_1 \qquad [10.9]$$

or

$$MR_1 = 10 - q_2 - 2q_1 \qquad [10.10]$$

Analogously, the marginal revenue curve for firm 2 can be derived as

$$MR_2 = 10 - q_1 - 2q_2 \qquad [10.11]$$

Since we have assumed zero marginal costs, the equilibrium output for firm 1 can be determined as

$$MR_1 = 10 - q_2 - 2q_1 = 0$$
$$2q_1 = 10 - q_2$$
$$q_1 = 5 - \tfrac{1}{2}q_2 \qquad [10.12]$$

And for firm 2, we have

$$MR_2 = 10 - q_1 - 2q_2 = 0$$
$$q_2 = 5 - \tfrac{1}{2}q_1 \qquad\qquad [10.13]$$

Equations 10.12 and 10.13 are the expressions for the reaction curves of the respective duopolists; that is, each expresses the behavior of a duopolist as a function of the behavior of his rival (based on the assumption that the rival's output will remain constant).

Clearly, the duopolists will be in equilibrium when each has no motive to change his output behavior, that is, when each has his expectations as to the other's behavior fulfilled. This will only be true when the two reaction equations are simultaneously satisfied. Thus, equilibrium can be determined as the solution to the simultaneous equations 10.12 and 10.13; or in graphical terms, it is represented by the intersection of the two reaction curves. The simultaneous solution proceeds as follows:

$$q_1 = 5 - \tfrac{1}{2}q_2 \qquad\qquad [10.12]$$
$$q_2 = 5 - \tfrac{1}{2}q_1 \qquad\qquad [10.13]$$

Substituting equation 10.13 into equation 10.12, we get

$$q_1 = 5 - \tfrac{1}{2}[5 - \tfrac{1}{2}q_1]$$
$$q_1 = 5 - \tfrac{5}{2} + \tfrac{1}{4}q_1$$
$$\tfrac{3}{4}q_1 = \tfrac{5}{2}$$
$$q_1 = \tfrac{10}{3} \qquad\qquad [10.14]$$

We can substitute in equation 10.13 and get $q_2 = \tfrac{10}{3}$. To determine market price, we substitute in the aggregate demand equation:

$$q_1 + q_2 = Q_T = 10 - P \qquad\qquad [10.15]$$
$$\tfrac{20}{3} = 10 - P$$
$$P = \tfrac{10}{3} \qquad\qquad [10.16]$$

The graphical solution is shown in Figure 10.9.

To demonstrate that E is a stable equilibrium, consider duopolist 1 entering the market unaware of the existence of duopolist 2. He would produce the output that would maximize his profits, which can be seen to be 5 units, at point A. However, duopolist 2 then produces at point B along his reaction curve; which is $2\tfrac{1}{2}$ units. Then duopolist 1 becomes aware of the existence of duopolist 2 and produces $3\tfrac{3}{4}$ units at point C on his reaction curve. And this causes a movement to point D on duopolist 2's reaction curve, and so on. We can see that the movement from A to B to C to D is rapidly converging to the equilibrium point E. It could be shown in like manner that if we had initially assumed that duopolist 2 was unaware of duopolist 1 and was, therefore, producing 5 units, the solution in Figure 10.9 would converge downward to point E.

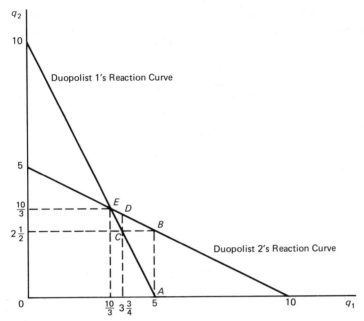

Figure 10.9

We can generalize the Cournot solution in order to show the effect on price and output of an increase in the number of oligopolists. Let us assume n firms and again assume zero marginal costs for all. We assume the demand facing the industry is

$$P = a - bQ_T \qquad [10.17]$$

where

$$Q_T = q_1 + q_2 + \cdots + q_n \qquad [10.18]$$

Thus the total revenue schedule for firm 1 is

$$TR_1 = q_1P = q_1[a - b(q_1 + q_2 + \cdots + q_n)] \qquad [10.19]$$

and the demand schedule facing firm 1 is

$$\frac{TR_1}{q_1} = a - bq_1 - bq_2 - \cdots - bq_n \qquad [10.20]$$

Since all the q's are constant except for q_1, equation 10.20 can be written as

$$P_1 = [a - bq_2 - \cdots - bq_n] - bq_1 \qquad [10.21]$$

or

$$P_1 = \beta - bq_1 \qquad [10.22]$$

where β is a constant. Thus, we have a linear demand curve with the corresponding marginal revenue curve:

$$MR_1 = \beta - 2bq_1 \tag{10.23}$$

or

$$MR_1 = [a - bq_2 - \cdots - bq_n] - 2bq_1 \tag{10.24}$$

Setting MR_1 equal to zero, we get the reaction curve for firm 1.

$$q_1 = \frac{a}{2b} - \frac{1}{2}(q_2 + q_3 + \cdots + q_n) \tag{10.25}$$

And similarly for the other firms, we get

$$q_2 = \frac{a}{2b} - \frac{1}{2}(q_1 + q_3 + \cdots + q_n) \tag{10.26}$$

$$q_3 = \frac{a}{2b} - \frac{1}{2}(q_1 + q_2 + \cdots + q_n) \tag{10.27}$$

$$\vdots \qquad\qquad\qquad\qquad \vdots$$

$$q_n = \frac{a}{2b} - \frac{1}{2}(q_1 + q_2 + \cdots + q_{n-1}) \tag{10.28}$$

In equilibrium each of these equations must be satisfied, so that we sum to obtain the equilibrium industry output.

$$\Sigma\,(q_1 + q_2 + \cdots + q_n) = Q_T$$

$$Q_T = \frac{na}{2b} - \frac{1}{2}[(n-1)q_1 + (n-1)q_2 + \cdots + (n-1)q_n] \tag{10.29}$$

$$Q_T = \frac{na}{2b} - \left(\frac{n-1}{2}\right)[q_1 + q_2 + \cdots + q_n] = \frac{na}{2b} - \left(\frac{n-1}{2}\right)Q_T$$

$$Q_T + \left(\frac{n-1}{2}\right)Q_T = \frac{na}{2b}$$

$$Q_T\left[1 + \frac{n-1}{2}\right] = \frac{na}{2b} = Q_T\left[\frac{n+1}{2}\right]$$

$$Q_T = \frac{na}{2b}\frac{2}{n+1} = \frac{n}{n+1}\frac{a}{b} \tag{10.30}$$

By our assumption of equal marginal costs, each firm will produce $\frac{1}{n}Q_T$ or

$$\frac{1}{n}\left[\frac{n}{n+1}\frac{a}{b}\right] = \frac{1}{n+1}\frac{a}{b} \tag{10.31}$$

To determine industry price, we can substitute for Q_T in the industry demand equation 10.17:

$$P = a - b\left[\frac{n}{n+1}\frac{a}{b}\right] = a - \frac{an}{n+1} = \frac{an + a - an}{n+1} = \frac{a}{n+1} \quad [10.32]$$

To demonstrate these results, we apply them to our previous duopoly problem. In that example, $a = 10$, $b = 1$, and $n = 2$. Thus,

$$q_1 = \frac{1}{n+1}\frac{a}{b} = \frac{1}{3}\frac{10}{1} = \frac{10}{3} = q_2$$

$$Q_T = \frac{n}{n+1}\frac{a}{b} = \frac{2}{3}\frac{10}{1} = \frac{20}{3}$$

$$P = \frac{a}{n+1} = \frac{10}{3}$$

COMPARISON OF PERFECT AND IMPERFECT COMPETITION

The existence of antitrust legislation in many countries implies a judgment that competition is in some sense more socially desirable than other market structures. In this section we shall compare the various market structures we have discussed as to differences in price, output, and efficiency under similar conditions. The only completely accurate comparison that can be made is between perfect competition and monopoly, because in the in-between cases, a host of particular assumptions can be made concerning the exact degree of monopoly power that exists and the way in which it is exercised.

Perfect Competition vs. Monopoly: Short-Run Price and Output

In Figure 10.10, ΣSMC is the short-run supply of a perfectly competitive industry (that is, it is the sum of the SMC curves of the individual member firms) and D is the aggregate demand for the output of the industry. Thus, the market price will be OP_C and the equilibrium output OQ_C.

Let us assume that a monopolist buys all the firms in the industry and operates them as individual plants and that, as a result of this purchase, no changes take place in the costs of the individual plants. If the monopolist maximizes his profits, he will equate MR to ΣSMC, and the monopoly price will be OP_M and monopoly output OQ_M. As a result of the monopolization of the industry, price is higher and quantity less than under perfect competition.

Notice also that under perfect competition $P = MC$. This means that the price to the consumer for an extra unit of output is just equal to the value of the factors of production that society must surrender in order to produce the extra unit of output. Under monopoly, however, $P >$

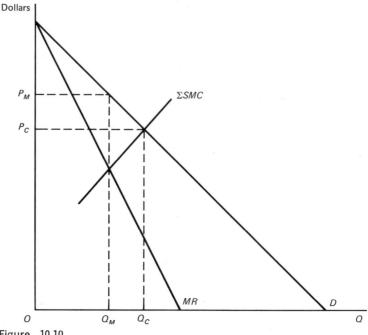

Figure 10.10

$MR = MC$, so that the price to the consumer is in excess of the value to society of the resources used up. And although the consumer is willing to pay more for an additional unit of output than the cost to society for producing that unit of output, no further output is forthcoming from the monopolist. This means that a shift of the resources needed to produce one unit of output from a competitive industry to a monopolistic one (with the same marginal costs) will increase the total money value of output produced with the same resources. If we measure economic efficiency as

$$\frac{\text{value of output}}{\text{value of input}}$$

for the economy as a whole, then if such shifts of resources can profitably take place, the ratio has not been maximized and maximum economic efficiency has not been attained.

Perfect Competition versus Monopoly: Long-Run Price and Output

We saw in Chapter 8 that when the perfectly competitive firm is in long-run equilibrium, it produces at the minimum point of its LAC

curve and has no profit. This is shown in Figure 10.11a. This means that the perfectly competitive firm produces where its per-unit cost is the lowest possible; in other words, it has taken advantage of all economies of scale and has not yet incurred any diseconomies of scale. On the other hand, as Figure 10.11b indicates, the monopolist is not subject to pressure from entering firms, and thus there is no necessity for him

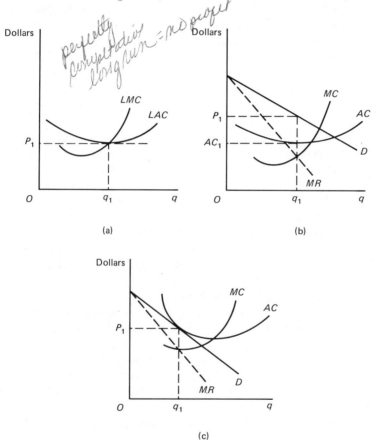

perfectly competitive long run = no profit

(a)

(b)

(c)

Figure 10.11

to produce at minimum LAC or to make zero profit. Even if, by chance, the monopolist makes no profit, he still does not produce where LAC is a minimum (see Figure 10.11c). In summary, we can state that a competitive firm will utilize the optimum plant in the most efficient manner in the long run and that the competitive entrepreneur will earn only the opportunity costs of his factors of production. The monopolist, on the other hand, need not build the optimum-size plant in the long run, and may receive returns in excess of opportunity costs. It will be recalled that this excess is wasteful in the sense that it is not necessary to retain the factors of production in the industry in the long run.

Some Other Considerations

In our comparison of perfect competition and monopoly, we assumed that the industry could be either competitive or monopolistic. However, let us consider the situation where market price in a competitive industry is such that losses are made in the short run. This will result in firms leaving the industry in the long run. And it may happen that price does not reach minimum LAC until relatively few firms remain in the industry. Under these conditions, perfect competition could not exist. Or consider the case in which LAC continues to decline until a single firm's output represents a very large proportion of total industry demand. Again, perfect competition will not be possible.

The fact that many firms do control a substantial portion of their respective industry outputs, in spite of antitrust laws, seems to indicate an attitude in the law that it is not the existence of market power that constitutes a violation of antitrust regulations but rather the "undue" exercise of this power, however the court may define it. All forms of imperfect competition represent some degree of market power, monopoly being the ultimate. The inefficiencies ascribed to monopoly are therefore ascribable in part to other forms of imperfect competition, the exact degree being dependent on where they lie on the continuum between perfect competition and pure monopoly.

In Figure 10.10 we assumed that the monopolization of the industry did not result in a change in costs. It is possible, though, for the monopolization of the industry to result in either an increase or a decrease in costs. An increase in costs can occur because (1) there are inefficiencies associated with the attempt of the monopolist to run all the plants that were formerly part of the competitive industry and (2) the monopolist becomes lax and does not act as a true profit maximizer in the sense that he allows costs to rise above the minimum attainable level because he is not subjected to competitive pressures.

It may be argued that monopolization can result in a decrease in costs if the monopolist uses part of his monopoly profit for research and development with the aim of reducing his costs of production. It has also been argued that the "neighborhood effects" of this research and development are substantial: The benefits of new knowledge accrue to society as a whole. On the other hand, it cannot be argued that, simply because a firm possessing market power has lower per-unit costs than comparable firms in a competitive industry, the cost difference represents a gain of technological efficiency due to monopolization. This difference can be due to the fact that the monopolist, because of his size, is capable of exerting pressure on suppliers of factors of production and to effect a transfer of income from these suppliers by extorting a noneconomically justified reduction in factor prices.

A further point that must be taken into consideration in comparing perfect with imperfect competition concerns the difference in the types of goods produced. For example, monopolistic competition affords the consumer a wide variety of choices among similar goods, whereas with perfect competition, homogeneous goods are produced. Therefore, if the satisfaction of consumers is increased as a result of the differentiation of goods, the inefficiencies ascribable to this form of imperfect competition cannot be compared in absolute terms with the efficiencies of perfect competition.

11

DETERMINATION OF FACTOR PRICES

So far our discussion has been concerned mainly with the determination of product prices, with factor prices being taken as given. In this chapter, we turn our attention to the factor markets. We shall deal with the supply of and demand for factors of production and their interaction in the determination of factor prices under alternative market conditions.

SOME BASIC CONCEPTS

The total expenditure on a factor of production X may be written:

$$TC_x = P_x X \qquad [11.1]$$

The average cost of a factor is defined as

$$AC_x = \frac{TC_x}{X} = \frac{P_x X}{X} = P_x \qquad [11.2]$$

In other words, the average cost of a factor is identical to the factor's price.

The factor's marginal cost is defined as

$$MC_x = \frac{\Delta TC_x}{\Delta X} \qquad [11.3]$$

in discrete terms; and in continuous terms as

$$MC_x = \frac{dTC_x}{dX} \qquad [11.3a]$$

The usual relationship between the average cost and the marginal cost of a factor holds; that is,

$$MC_x = P_x + \frac{dP_x}{dX} X \qquad [11.4]$$

in continuous terms; and

$$MC_x = P_{x_2} + \frac{\Delta P_x}{\Delta X} X_1 \qquad [11.4a]$$

in discrete terms.

Note that if $dP_x/dX = 0$, then $MC_x = P_x$; if $dP_x/dX > 0$, $MC_x > P_x$; and if $dP_x/dX < 0$, $MC_x < P_x$. These three cases are illustrated in Figure 11.1a–c.

ISOCOST LINES

The isocost lines of Chapters 6 and 7 were based on factor supplies of the kind shown in Figure 11.1a. If the firm is using two factors of production, X and Y, the equation for a given level of expenditure would be $TC = P_xX + P_yY$ where P_x and P_y are constants and the isocost

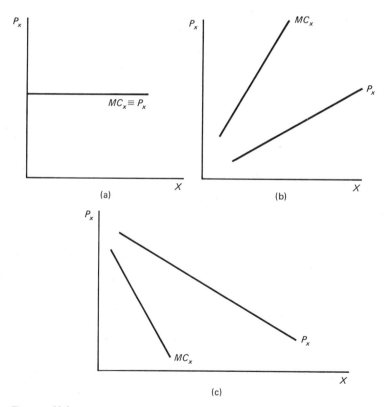

Figure 11.1

lines are consequently linear. In this chapter, we wish to generalize the cost constraint to encompass all variants of factor supply; and thus we write

$$C = g(X, Y) \qquad [11.5]$$

where C is a constant (a given level of expenditure).

Table 11.1 summarizes the likely combination of supply conditions for factors X and Y and the consequent isocost patterns that result. In order to understand the possible shapes of the isocost maps, we first

TABLE 11.1

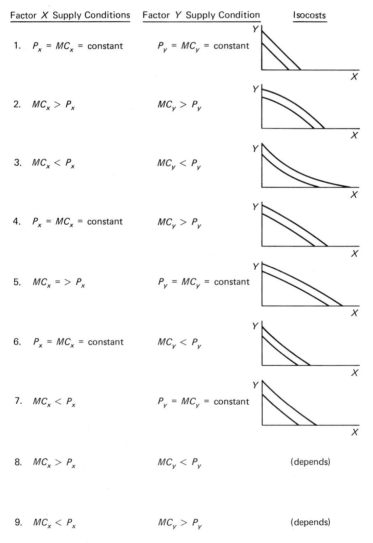

Factor X Supply Conditions	Factor Y Supply Condition	Isocosts
1. $P_x = MC_x$ = constant	$P_y = MC_y$ = constant	
2. $MC_x > P_x$	$MC_y > P_y$	
3. $MC_x < P_x$	$MC_y < P_y$	
4. $P_x = MC_x$ = constant	$MC_y > P_y$	
5. $MC_x => P_x$	$P_y = MC_y$ = constant	
6. $P_x = MC_x$ = constant	$MC_y < P_y$	
7. $MC_x < P_x$	$P_y = MC_y$ = constant	
8. $MC_x > P_x$	$MC_y < P_y$	(depends)
9. $MC_x < P_x$	$MC_y > P_y$	(depends)

derive the slope of an isocost curve.[1] Since total cost is a constant all along an isocost curve, we may write

$$\Delta C = \frac{\Delta C}{\Delta X} \Delta X + \frac{\Delta C}{\Delta Y} \Delta Y = 0 \qquad [11.6]$$

In words this means that any change in costs that occur is due to the marginal cost of factor X multiplied by the change in the quantity of X plus the marginal cost of factor Y multiplied by the change in the quantity of Y. However, since the expenditure along an isocost curve is a constant, $\Delta C = 0$. Therefore,

$$\frac{\Delta Y}{\Delta X} = - \frac{\dfrac{\Delta C}{\Delta X}}{\dfrac{\Delta C}{\Delta Y}} = - \frac{MC_x}{MC_y} \qquad [11.7]$$

In case 1 of Table 11.1, $\dfrac{\Delta Y}{\Delta X} = - \dfrac{P_x}{P_y}$ since we assumed P_x and P_y were both constants and this means $MC_x = P_x$ and $MC_y = P_y$. And as we have seen, this results in linear isocost curves.

In case 2 in Table 11.1, the supply curves of both factors are rising. Consequently, as we move down the isocost curve from left to right (which means more X and less Y), MC_x increases while MC_y declines. Therefore, the absolute slope, MC_x/MC_y increases; the isocost curves are concave to the origin.

The converse case is case 3, in which both factors have negatively sloping supply curves. Here, moving down the isocost curve results in the MC_x going down and the MC_y going up; thus, MC_x/MC_y decreases and the isocosts are convex to the origin. Cases 4 to 7 are variants of the ones discussed in which one of the factors is supplied at a constant price and the other at a varying price. This results in a general shape of the isocost map similar to the ones in which both factors move in the same direction except that the slope of the isocosts is flatter (on the assumption that one factor rises or declines at the same rate as in cases 2 or 3 in Table 11.1 and the other factor is supplied at a constant price). This is true because the curvature now depends solely on one factor.

In cases 8 and 9, it is not possible to determine, prima facie, whether the isocosts are convex or concave to the origin. We shall demonstrate this with respect to case 8; the demonstration would proceed similarly for case 9. Moving from left to right along an isocost curve, MC_x rises and MC_y also rises. Since both the numerator and denominator of the absolute slope, MC_x/MC_y, are rising, whether the fraction itself is rising or not depends on the relative rates of increase of MC_x and MC_y.

[1] A more rigorous treatment is in Appendix 11A.

EQUILIBRIUM CONDITIONS

Before proceeding to the generalized least-cost equilibrium conditions, we first review the case of perfect competition. The condition was

$$\frac{MP_x}{MP_y} = \frac{P_x}{P_y}$$

or, in words, the slope of the isoquant is equal to the slope of the isocost. This is the necessary condition; the sufficient condition (to ensure that output is a maximum for a given level of expenditure or that expenditure is a minimum for a given level of output) is simply that the isoquants be convex to the origin, because constant factor prices (linear isocost curves) are assumed.[2]

In the general case, the first-order condition is the same, that is, that the isocost and isoquant be tangent to each other. However, now the slope of an isocost is not necessarily the constant $-P_x/P_y$ but can be expressed as $-MC_x/MC_y$. Thus, at the point of tangency, we have

$$\frac{MP_x}{MP_y} = \frac{MC_x}{MC_y} \qquad [11.8]$$

or

$$\frac{MP_x}{MC_x} = \frac{MP_y}{MC_y} \qquad [11.9]$$

We may illustrate the meaning of this equilibrium condition by Figure 11.2. The firm, for the given level of expenditure, represented by isocost curve C_1C_1, desires to maximize output. Clearly, this can be done only at point A, where the isocost curve is tangent to the highest obtainable isoquant.

Still with reference to Figure 11.2, for point A to represent a maximum output rather than a minimum output (the second-order condition), the following inequalities must hold:

$$\text{to the left of point } A: \quad \left| \frac{MP_x}{MP_y} \right| > \left| \frac{MC_x}{MC_y} \right|$$

$$\text{to the right of point } A: \quad \left| \frac{MP_x}{MP_y} \right| < \left| \frac{MC_x}{MC_y} \right| \qquad [11.10]$$

Another way of stating these inequalities is to say that at point A, the curvature of the isoquant must be greater than the curvature of the isocost in algebraic terms. That this must be true can be demonstrated with reference to the perfectly competitive case as well as Figure 11.2. First of all, isoquants are convex to the origin, and the convexity means that in moving from left to right, the absolute slope is decreasing, which

[2] See note 14 in Chapter 6.

means that in algebraic terms the slope is increasing. (Remember, in algebraic terms, $-2 > -5$.) The linear isocost curve has a constant slope; thus its curvature is zero. At the point of tangency then, the second-order condition is obviously fulfilled. For the concave isocost curve of Figure 11.2, the curvature of the isoquant is again positive; the slope of the isocost is becoming increasingly negative or the curvature is negative. And once again, the second-order condition is fulfilled.

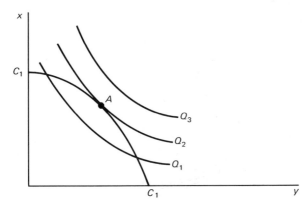

Figure 11.2

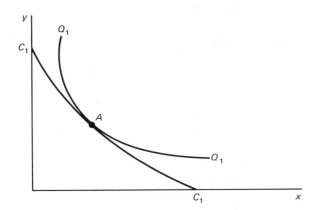

Figure 11.3

The case of convex isocost curves is slightly more complex, as we can see with reference to Figures 11.3 and 11.4. In both diagrams, tangency is at point A; however, the least-cost condition is being fulfilled in Figure 11.3 but not in Figure 11.4. The reason for this is that in Figure 11.3 the curvature of the isoquant at point A is greater than the curvature of the isocost. Or alternatively, it may be verified by the reader that equation 11.10 holds.

In Figure 11.4 at point A, the curvature of the isoquant is less than that of the isocost. Or in other words, equation 11.10 is being violated. That point A is clearly not a maximum output equilibrium can be seen by considering point B, which represents a greater output for the same level of costs, C_1. But point B is also not an equilibrium because there will be an intersection of the isocost curve with a still-higher isoquant. Under these conditions, equilibrium will occur at a point along one of the ridge lines.[3]

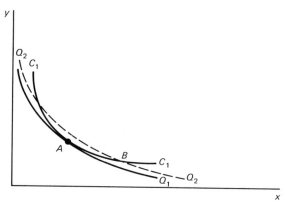

Figure 11.4

DETERMINATION OF EQUILIBRIUM FACTOR HIRE

The least-cost equilibrium condition determines factor proportions along an expansion path. However, it does not tell us at what point along the expansion path the firm will produce, and, therefore, it does not tell us the absolute quantities of the factors that the firm will hire.

In determining the quantity of a factor that it will hire, the firm will compare the increment to its revenue produced by the factor to the increment to its cost arising from hiring the factor. The increment to its revenue is determined by multiplying the marginal product of the factor by the marginal revenue that results from selling an incremental unit of output. We may call this incremental revenue the marginal revenue product of the factor (MRP_i). Thus,

$$MRP_i = MP_i \cdot MR \qquad [11.11]$$

Clearly, so long as the marginal revenue product exceeds the marginal cost of the factor, the firm will find it profitable to increase its hire of the factor. Conversely, if the factor's marginal cost exceeds its marginal

[3] For a rigorous treatment of the equilibrium conditions, see Appendix 11A.

revenue product, the firm will reduce its employment of the factor and increase its profit. In summary then,

If $MRP_i > MC_i$, increase employment of factor I
If $MRP_i < MC_i$, decrease employment of factor I [11.12]
If $MRP_i = MC_i$, maintain current level of employment of factor I

Alternatively, we can state the factor hire equilibrium condition as

$$MP_i \cdot MR \equiv MRP_i = MC_i \qquad [11.13]$$

or

$$\frac{MP_i \cdot MR}{MC_i} \equiv \frac{MRP_i}{MC_i} = 1 \qquad [11.13a]$$

This discussion of equilibrium factor hire holds for all variable inputs that the firm employs.

RELATIONSHIP BETWEEN EQUILIBRIUM FACTOR HIRE AND EQUILIBRIUM OUTPUT DETERMINATION

It is clear that once the firm has decided on its equilibrium compliment of factors, it has also determined its equilibrium output. In order for our theory to be internally consistent, the equilibrium quantity determined in this fashion must be identical with the equilibrium output that would be determined by the $MR = MC$ condition derived in Chapters 8 and 9.

The equilibrium condition, equation 11.9, can be generalized for more than two factors of production as follows:

$$\frac{MP_a}{MC_a} = \frac{MP_b}{MC_b} = \cdots = \frac{MP_n}{MC_n} \qquad [11.14]$$

In discrete terms, any one of these ratios can be written as

$$\frac{\dfrac{\Delta q_i}{\Delta I}}{\dfrac{\Delta TC_i}{\Delta I}} = \frac{\Delta q_i}{\Delta I} \cdot \frac{\Delta I}{\Delta TC_i} = \frac{\Delta q_i}{\Delta TC_i} \qquad [11.15]$$

where i represents any one of the inputs.

Equation 11.11, which must hold in long-run equilibrium, means that the increment in output, per unit increase in factor cost, must be the same for all factors. Therefore, in equation 11.12, if we invert the ratio, we have

$$\frac{\Delta TC_i}{\Delta q_i} = MC \qquad [11.16]$$

where the MC is the incremental cost of producing a unit with any factor increment. Thus, to summarize, we can rewrite equation 11.11 as

$$\left[\frac{MP_a}{MC_a} = \frac{MP_b}{MC_b} = \cdots = \frac{MP_n}{MC_n}\right] = \frac{1}{MC} \qquad [11.17]$$

Multiplying both sides of equation 11.17 by MR, we obtain

$$\left[\frac{MP_a \cdot MR}{MC_a} = \frac{MP_b \cdot MR}{MC_b} = \cdots = \frac{MP_n \cdot MR}{MC_n}\right] = \frac{MR}{MC} \qquad [11.18]$$

Assuming the firm is in factor market equilibrium, we can substitute equation 11.13 into equation 11.18. Each ratio within the parentheses on the left is equal to 1, and we consequently have

$$\frac{MR}{MC} = 1 \qquad \text{or} \qquad MR = MC \qquad [11.19]$$

And this is the product market profit-maximization condition derived earlier. It is obvious from equation 11.18 that had we assumed product market equilibrium, this would have resulted in equation 11.12 as a condition for factor market equilibrium.

SHORT-RUN DEMAND FOR A FACTOR WITHIN A FIRM

In addition to the marginal revenue product that we have already defined, there are three other measures that are important in understanding a firm's demand for a factor.

The *total revenue product* of a factor I is defined as the revenue accruing to the firm due to selling the output from hiring I units of the factor— (TRP_i).

The *average revenue product* of a factor is defined as the average product multiplied by the average revenue (price) of the product. Thus,

$$ARP_i = AP_i \cdot AR \qquad [11.20]$$

Or,

$$ARP_i = \frac{Q}{I} \cdot \frac{TR}{Q} = \frac{TR}{I} \qquad [11.21]$$

It also follows that

$$TRP_i = ARP_i \cdot I \qquad [11.22]$$

To review, the *marginal revenue product* is defined as the marginal product of the factor multiplied by the marginal revenue of the product.

$$MRP_i = MP_i \cdot MR \qquad [11.23]$$

Or

$$MRP_i = \frac{\Delta Q}{\Delta I} \cdot \frac{\Delta TR}{\Delta Q} = \frac{\Delta TR}{\Delta I} \qquad [11.24]$$

in discrete terms. And

$$MRP_i = \frac{\partial Q}{\partial I} \cdot \frac{\partial TR}{\partial Q} = \frac{\partial TR}{\partial I} \qquad [11.25]$$

in continuous terms.

Finally, the *value of the marginal product* of a factor is defined as the marginal product of the factor multiplied by the average revenue (price) of the product.

$$VMP_i = MP_i \cdot AR \qquad [11.26]$$

Or

$$VMP_i = \frac{\Delta Q}{\Delta I} \cdot \frac{TR}{Q} \qquad [11.27]$$

in discrete terms. And

$$VMP_i = \frac{\partial Q}{\partial I} \cdot \frac{TR}{Q} \qquad [11.28]$$

in continuous terms.

It should be remembered that under competitive conditions in the product market, the price and the marginal revenue of the good are identical. Therefore, equations 11.23 and 11.26 give the same results; or, in other words, the marginal revenue product and the value of the marginal product are identical. Of course, this identity does not hold under noncompetitive conditions. The relationship among ARP, MRP, and VMP for the competitive firm in the product market is demonstrated in Figure 11.5. For expository purposes we assume labor is the factor in question, and in this short run, it is the only variable factor.

The reader should note that the usual average-marginal relationship holds between ARP_L and MRP_L and, furthermore, that Figure 11.5 looks very much like the average and marginal product diagrams of Chapter 6. This is, of course, because the curves of Figure 11.5 are merely the AP_L and MP_L curves multiplied by the constant product price. That is,

$$ARP_L = AP_L \cdot AR$$
$$MRP_L = MP_L \cdot MR \qquad \text{with} \qquad MR \equiv AR$$

Thus, when AP_L reaches a maximum, so does ARP_L, and it is at this level of labor that $AP_L = MP_L$ and that $ARP_L = MRP_L$. As long as ARP_L rises, MRP_L lies above it; when ARP_L declines, MRP_L lies below it; and when ARP_L is at its maximum, MRP_L is equal to it. This can be summarized by stating[4]

$$MRP_L = ARP_L + \frac{dARP_L}{dL} L \qquad [11.29]$$

---

[4] This result can be derived directly as follows:

$$TRP_L = ARP_L \cdot L$$
$$MRP_L = \frac{\partial TRP_L}{\partial L} = ARP_L + \frac{\partial ARP_L}{\partial L} L$$

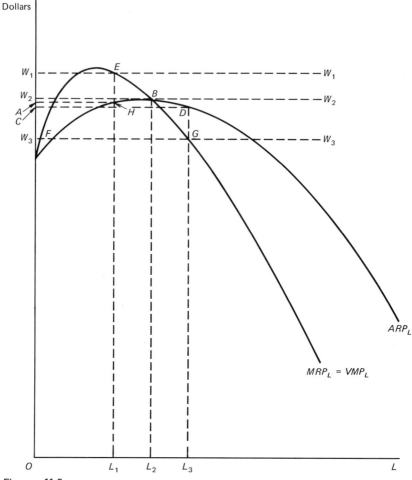

Figure 11.5

In addition to assuming that the firm is a perfect competitor in the product market, we assume it has no effect on the price of labor that it hires; that is, it hires labor in a perfectly competitive market. Assume the wage W_3 to face the firm. We know from our previous discussion that the firm will hire until $MRP_L = P_L$ (or the wage rate) and the MRP_L schedule cuts the supply curve of labor from above. (This is the equivalent of equation 11.12.) Furthermore, we know that, in this case, $W \equiv MC_L$. Therefore, for the given wage rate, W_3 the equilibrium intersection is at point G where the firm hires L_3 of labor. (Note that although at point F, $MRP_L = W_3$, this is not an equilibrium, because equation

11.12 is being violated; this means that a movement from F in either direction will increase profits.)

Although we know that point G represents the maximum profit or the least loss level of factor hire, this might be inferior to a zero level of factor hire (and consequent zero output). This is the factor dimension implied by the problem of deciding to produce or shut down in the short run (which was discussed in Chapter 8). The average revenue product schedule permits a comparison of the average revenue from and average cost of the factor. At L_3, ARP_L is L_3D, and W_3 can be measured as L_3G; and profit per unit of labor is measured as GD. Or alternatively, total cost of the factor can be measured as OW_3GL_3, and the total revenue derived from hiring the factor (TRP_L) is measured as the area $OCDL_3$. The difference between these areas, the excess of revenue over avoidable (variable) costs, is given by W_3CDG. It is obvious, based on our discussion in Chapter 8, that revenue must at least cover variable costs—in this case, the cost of labor—in order for the firm to remain in business. Note that this does not imply that total revenue must cover total cost (that is, the sum of variable and fixed cost); and because Figure 11.5 does not include fixed costs, we cannot measure profits.

Next let us assume that the wage rate faced by the firm is W_2, the equilibrium is at B, and the employment level is L_2. Thus, TC_L is OW_2BL_2, TRP_L is OW_2BL_2, and the excess of revenue over variable cost is zero. The firm, therefore, suffers a loss equal to its fixed cost that cannot be avoided in the short run. Thus, its decision to remain in the industry will be based on its predictions as to future profits.

Finally, we consider the firm faced by a wage rate of W_1. Point E is now the equilibrium intersection; L_1 is the amount of labor, OW_1EL_1 is total labor cost, and TRP_L is $OAHL_1$. Therefore the area AW_1EH represents a loss in addition to the loss of fixed cost, and the firm will definitely leave the industry.

The demand curve for a factor of production relates the alternative quantities of the factor the firm will hire to the various prices of the factor. It should be clear that the MRP_L curve that lies below the ARP_L curve gives just such a relationship between the wage rate and the quantities demanded of labor. In general we say that, for a firm faced with horizontal factor supply curves, the demand for a particular factor is that factor's MRP curve below the corresponding ARP curve. For a firm that is also a competitor in the product market (as in Figure 11.5), the demand curve is the VMP curve because $VMP \equiv MRP$. Thus the demand for the product determines the level of demand for the factor that the firm hires; that is, the demand for a factor is a derived demand (derived from the demand for the product).

The relationship between the demand for the product and the derived demand for the factor can also be seen by examining the determinants of the elasticity of derived demand. These determinants were first presented by Alfred Marshall[5] and are given below in the formulation of A. C. Pigou.[6]

1. The demand for a factor is likely to be more elastic the more readily substitutes can be obtained. (A measure of the ease of substitution is the elasticity of substitution that is discussed later.)
2. The demand for a factor is likely to be less elastic the less important is the part played by the cost of the factor in total production cost.
3. The demand for a factor is likely to be more elastic the more elastic is the supply of co-operant agents of production.
4. The demand for a factor is likely to be more elastic the more elastic the demand for the product.

The first determinant is simply an example of an observation we made earlier in connection with the elasticity of demand for a good. The elasticity of substitution, σ, is a measure of the ease of substitution between factors and is defined as

$$\sigma = \frac{d\left(\dfrac{Y}{X}\right)}{\dfrac{Y}{X}} \Bigg/ \frac{dMRS_{xy}}{MRS_{xy}} \qquad [11.30]$$

This is a ratio of (1) the relative change in the factor proportion to (2) the relative change in the marginal rate of substitution.[7]

The elasticity of substitution is illustrated in discrete terms graphically in Figure 11.6. Moving from G to H along the isoquant results in a change in factor proportion measured as the change in the slope of a ray from the origin to the relevant points on the isoquant, that is, the difference in slope between rays OA and OB. The difference in the slope of the isoquant at points G and H is measured as the difference in the slopes of the tangent lines CE and DF. These measures, in relative terms, represent respectively the numerator and the denominator of the elasticity of substitution.[8]

The second determinant has sometimes been referred to as "the importance of being unimportant." To explain this determinant, let us

[5] Alfred Marshall, *Principles of Economics* (8th ed.; New York: Macmillan, 1920), Book V, Chap. 6.
[6] See J. R. Hicks, *The Theory of Wages* (2d ed.; New York: Macmillan, 1964), p. 242.
[7] Intuitively it seems that a more meaningful definition would be the reciprocal of what was defined as σ, that is, the ratio of (1) the change in the curvature of the isoquant to (2) a change in the relative factor proportion. However, in the literature, it is generally defined as just given for reasons that will become clear in our discussion of distribution; thus, we have decided to retain this definition.
[8] A mathematical treatment of the elasticity of substitution is to be found in Appendix 11B.

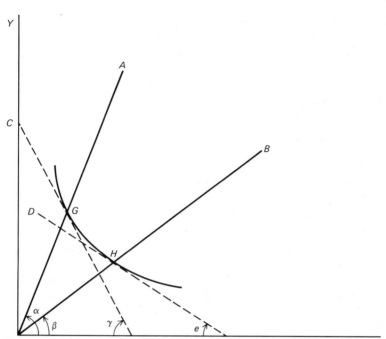

Figure   11.6

assume a production process using two factors, X and Y. Let k represent the percentage of total cost going to factor X and let $1 - k$ be the percentage spent on factor Y. Now let us assume an increase in the price of X with the price of Y remaining constant. There are two types of substitution that will result from this price increase: (1) commodity substitution; an increase in the factor price causes an increase in total cost that leads to a higher commodity price resulting in consumers substituting relatively less expensive goods for the one whose price has increased and (2) factor substitution; the firm will attempt to substitute the now relatively cheaper factor Y for X.

Assume that the elasticity of demand for the good is greater than the elasticity of substitution. The extent of commodity substitution will depend on the product elasticity as well as on k. A given increase in the price of X will cause a larger change in the product price the greater is k and, consequently, the greater is the commodity substitution for a given elasticity of demand. On the other hand, the extent of factor substitution depends solely on the size of σ. In fact, the smaller is k, the smaller is the elasticity of derived demand, because commodity substitution will be directly related to the size of k. If we assume, conversely, that σ is greater than the elasticity of demand, the elasticity of derived demand becomes inversely related to k.

Assume now that k is large and that the elasticity of substitution is greater than the elasticity of demand for the good; that is, $\sigma > \eta$. Then, because the possibilities of substitution are relatively great, by assumption, the size of k must be due to the employment of a large quantity of X rather than a high price of X. The large size of k means that there will be two offsetting effects on commodity substitution. The relatively large size of k will tend to increase commodity substitution while the relatively small size of η will tend to decrease commodity substitution. Factor substitution will tend to be great because of the size of σ. However, because a large quantity of X is being employed, the proportional increase of X due to the price increase will tend to be small.

On the other hand, when k is small, there are no longer offsetting effects on commodity substitution; this tends to be small, but factor substitution is relatively great by assumption, and the small quantity of X employed means that the relative change in the quantity of X will tend to be large.[9]

Although it is true that it is "important for a factor to be unimportant" (provided that $\eta > \sigma$), the more narrowly we define a factor of production (that is, the smaller k becomes), the greater generally does σ become. In this case, k and σ move in opposite directions. Thus, it is not possible to state unequivocally what the effect of the size of k will be unless one knows something about the factor classification that is reflected in both k and σ.

To demonstrate the third determinant of elasticity, let us once again assume that the price of factor X rises and that the firm attempts to substitute the now relatively cheaper factor Y for X. Given the elasticity of substitution, the ease with which the firm can substitute Y for X is determined by the elasticity of supply of factor Y. To illustrate, let us assume the elasticity of supply of factor Y is inelastic, that is, less than one. In this case, the price of Y rises substantially compared to the vertical shift in the demand curve. Thus the firm will be severely limited in the extent to which it is profitable to substitute Y for X. On the other hand, if the supply elasticity is great, the firm's ability to substitute will be limited by the technical possibilities, that is, the elasticity of substitution.

The fourth determinant is simple to explain. The more inelastic the product demand, the more difficult it will be for commodity substitution to take place and, thus, the less elastic will be the demand for the factor.

By way of summarizing, we point out some of the similarities between the derivations of (1) the firm's demand curve for a factor and (2) the firm's supply curve of a good: the maximum profit (minimum loss) point

[9] For a rigorous mathematical proof that Marshall's proposition holds only when $\eta > \sigma$, see Appendix 11C.

occurs for (1) when $MRP_L = MC_L$ and $MRP_L > MC_L$ for smaller L and $MRP_L < MC_L$ for greater L; and for (2) when $MR = SMC$ with $MR > SMC$ for smaller outputs and $MR < SMC$ for greater outputs. The demand in (1) is the MRP_L curve below ARP_L and in (2) the short-run supply curve is SMC above AVC.

We shall now demonstrate, with a numerical example, the determination of equilibrium factor employment within the perfectly competitive firm of Chapter 8. In Table 11.2 we list various input levels and

TABLE 11.2

(1)	(2)	(3)	(4)	(5)	(6)	(7)
			$MR \equiv P$	VMP_x $\equiv MRP_x$		$\dfrac{P_x}{MP_x}$
X	q	MP_x	$= \$5.80$	$= [(3) \cdot (4)]$	SMC	$= \dfrac{\$1}{MP_x}$
0	0					
		1.11	$5.80	$6.438	$0.90	$0.90
90	100					
		2.86	5.80	16.588	0.35	0.35
125	200					
		4.00	5.80	23.20	0.25	0.25
150	300					
		5.00	5.80	29.00	0.20	0.20
170	400					
		2.50	5.80	14.50	0.40	0.40
210	500					
		1.11	5.80	6.438	0.90	0.90
300	600					
		0.67	5.80	3.886	1.50	1.50
450	700					
		0.42	5.80	2.436	2.40	2.40
690	800					
		0.17	5.80	0.986	5.80	5.80
1270	900					
		0.02	$5.80	$0.116	$10.00	$10.00
6270	1000					

show output at these levels. In column 3 we show the marginal product of the factor X, MP_x. Because we assume the firm is a perfect competitor in the product market, $P \equiv MR$, in this case $5.80, and this is shown in column 4. In column 5 we show $VMP_x \equiv MRP_x$. In column 6 we reproduce the SMC figures of Table 8.1. We assume the same constant P_x of $1 as we did in Chapters 6 to 8; and based on this price, in column 7 we compute the ratios P_x/MP_x.

The firm will continue to increase its hire of the factor until MRP_x ($\equiv VMP_x$) $= P_x$. This occurs between 800 and 900 units of output, or at 850 units. The equilibrium quantity of the factor lies between 690 and 1270 units. Due to the discrete nature of the data, it is not possible to determine from the Table the exact level of X. However, from the function giving the relationship between X and q, we can determine the exact level as being 880 units.

A comparison of columns 4 and 6 and of columns 4 and 7 confirms our earlier proof that equilibrium viewed in terms of the product market is identical to equilibrium in terms of the factor market. Indeed a comparison of the profit calculated in terms of the product market in Chapter 8 to the profit in terms of the factor market indicates the identical figure of $2550. For the product market, we have

$$P \equiv MR = \$5.80$$
$$q = 850 \text{ units}$$
$$TR = \$4930$$
$$STC = \$2380$$
$$\pi = \$2550$$

And for the factor market, we have

$$X = 880$$
$$TC_x = \$880$$
$$q = 850 \text{ units}$$
$$TRP_x = \$4930$$
$$TC = TC_x + FC = \$880 + \$1500 = \$2380$$
$$\pi = \$2550$$

With the aid of Figure 11.7, we now derive the demand for a factor within a firm that has monopoly power in the product market. Since $P > MR$ in this case, $VMP_L > MRP_L$. The demand curve for the factor is still the MRP_L below ARP_L, and the VMP_L curve is superfluous in the determination of equilibrium factor hire. Note further that $VMP_L \neq P_L$; this implies an inefficient allocation of resources that will be discussed later.[10]

---

[10] In Figure 11.7, while $ARP_L = MRP_L$ at the maximum point of ARP_L, this no longer occurs at the labor quantity where $AP_L = MP_L$ as was true in Figure 11.5. The reason can be seen in terms of the two definitions:

$$ARP_L = AP_L \cdot AR$$
$$MRP_L = MP_L \cdot MR$$

Since $AR > MR$, for ARP_L to equal MRP_L, $AP_L < MP_L$. And this can occur only when AP_L is rising. However, the point of intersection of VMP_L and ARP_L is at the quantity of labor where $AP_L = MP_L$ since

$$VMP_L = MP_L \cdot AR$$
$$ARP_L = AP_L \cdot AR$$

If the firm in Figure 11.7 faces a wage rate of W_1 (that is, the horizontal supply curve of labor that it faces is represented by W_1W_1), the equilibrium intersection would be C with L_1 the equilibrium quantity of labor, L_1C (W_1) the given wage rate, L_1B the value of the marginal product, and L_1E the marginal revenue product. $VMP_L > W_1$ by CB.

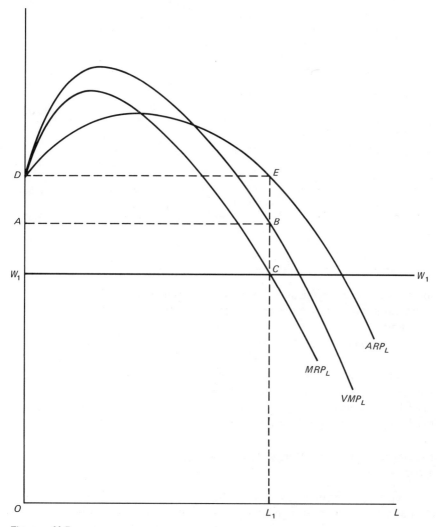

Figure 11.7

In Table 11.3 we list the relevant data for the determination of the factor market equilibrium of the monopolist of Chapter 9. We assumed there that the firm hired its variable factor at $1.00 per unit. Therefore, as with the perfectly competitive firm of Table 11.2, we approximate the

TABLE 11.3

(1) X	(2) q	(3) MP_x	(4) P	(5) VMP_x	(6) MR	(7) MRP_x
0	0		$9.20			
		1.11		$10.10	$9.00	$10.00
90	100		9.00			
		2.86		25.45	8.60	24.57
125	200		8.80			
		4.00		34.80	8.20	32.80
150	300		8.60			
		5.00		42.50	7.80	39.00
170	400		8.40			
		2.50		20.75	7.40	18.50
210	500		8.20			
		1.11		9.00	7.00	7.78
300	600		8.00			
		0.67		5.29	6.60	4.40
450	700		7.80			
		0.42		3.23	6.20	2.58
690	800		7.60			
		0.17		1.28	5.80	1.00
1270	900		7.40			
		0.02		$0.15	$5.40	$0.108
6270	1000		$7.20			

equilibrium factor input as 880 units; and once again, if we compare this equilibrium with the one shown in Figure 9.1, we will find they are equivalent.

To derive the aggregate demand for this factor, we horizontally sum the MRP_x curves (which for the competitive firm is the same as its VMP_x curve) of all firms that are users of the factor. And the intersection of this aggregate demand schedule with the total supply schedule of the factor determines the market price of the factor, which the firms then accept as the going factor price.[11]

DETERMINATION OF FACTOR HIRE EQUILIBRIUM UNDER MONOPSONY

Monopoly power may exist in the factor market as well as in the product market. When a single firm is the only user of a specific factor of production, it is called a *monopsonist;* if it is one of several firms using

[11] The MRP curve is the demand curve for a factor only under the assumption that it is the only variable factor. If there was more than one variable factor in the short run, it would be necessary to take into account the adjustments of the quantities of the other factors to a change in the quantity of the first factor and to take into account the consequent shift in the MRP curve of this first factor. This analysis will be pursued in detail in our analysis of the long run.

the factor, it is an *oligopsonist*. In our discussion of monopsony power, we shall assume the firm is a pure monopsonist.

Just as the monopolist faces the total demand for the product he sells, the monopsonist faces the entire supply schedule of the factor he employs. Therefore, the monopsonist must consider the effect of a change in his employment of the factor on the price of the previous units employed, just as a monopolist must consider the effect of selling the $n + 1$ unit on the price of the previous n units per time period.

Whether the firm is a perfect competitor or a monopsonist in the factor market, the equilibrium condition for factor hire is the same: The firm will continue to employ the factor as long as the extra revenue received from the sale of the extra output produced by the extra unit of the factor (MRP_L) exceeds the extra outlay necessary to acquire the extra factor unit (MC_L). Thus, we can state the equilibrium condition as:

If $MRP_L > MC_L$, the firm will increase its employment of L [11.31a]
If $MRP_L < MC_L$, the firm will decrease its employment of L [11.31b]

In other words, equilibrium factor employment occurs when

$$MRP_L = MC_L \qquad [11.32]$$

provided that equation 11.31a holds to the left of equilibrium and equation 11.31b holds to the right.

When the firm is a perfect competitor in the factor market, $MC_L \equiv P_L$, so that in equilibrium, $MRP_L = MC_L \equiv P_L$. However, if the firm is a monopsonist, $MC_L > P_L$, and in equilibrium, then

$$MRP_L = MC_L > P_L \qquad [11.33]$$

With the aid of Figure 11.8 and Table 11.4, we shall demonstrate the determination of factor hire equilibrium for the firm that is a perfect competitor in the product market and is a monopsonist in the factor market. Note that in Figure 11.8, the MC_L curve lies above the S_L curve. Since the S_L curve shows for each labor quantity the price per unit at which that quantity will be forthcoming, from the following relationship, we would expect the MC_L curve to lie above it:

$$MC_L = P_L + \frac{dP_L}{dL} L \qquad [11.34]$$

Since the slope of the S_L curve is positive, $\frac{dP_L}{dL} L$ is positive and $MC_L >$ P_L. Furthermore, since the S_L curve is linear, dP_L/dL is a constant; as we move along the horizontal axis, L increases. Thus, the gap between MC_L and P_L widens moving along the horizontal axis.

$MRP_L = MC_L$ at point B. Thus, the firm would like to hire L_1 units of labor at a wage of W_1 per unit. It should be noted that the $MRP_L >$

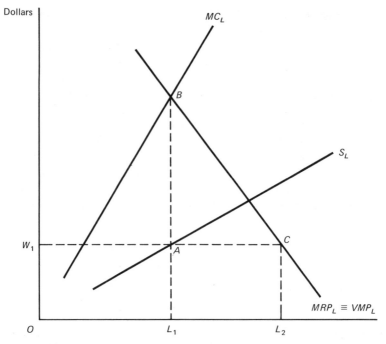

Figure 11.8

W_1, whereas if the firm were a perfect competitor in the factor market, $MRP_L = W_1$. Furthermore, because it is assumed that the firm is a perfect competitor in the product market, $MRP_L \equiv VMP_L$ and $VMP_L > W_1$. This means that labor is not receiving the value of its marginal product. This inequality is symptomatic of a misallocation of resources, and this will be discussed later.

TABLE 11.4

(1) P_L	(2) L	(3) TC_L	(4) MC_L	(5) MRP_L
$27.50	10	$275.00	$30.00	$90.00
30.00	20	600.00	35.00	80.00
32.50	30	975.00	40.00	70.00
35.00	40	1400.00	45.00	60.00
37.50	50	1775.00	50.00	50.00
40.00	60	2400.00	55.00	40.00
42.50	70	2975.00	60.00	30.00
$45.00	80	$3600.00	$65.00	$20.00

$$P_L = 25 + \tfrac{1}{4}L$$
$$MC_L = 25 + \tfrac{1}{2}L$$
$$MRP_L = 100 - L$$

For the monopsonist, the MRP_L curve is not a demand curve in the usual sense; that is, from this curve we can not read the alternative labor quantities the firm will hire at various wage rates. For example, if the firm were faced with a given wage rate of W_1, it would like to hire L_2 units of labor. But because the firm is faced with a rising supply curve of labor, it maximizes its profits by hiring L_1 units; and L_1 is not read from the intersection of the MRP_L with the S_L curve, but rather the intersection of the MRP_L and MC_L curves determines the point on the S_L curve that determines L_1. This is analogous to the situation under monopoly in that at the equilibrium price the monopolist would like to sell more (if that price were to remain constant) but desists because of the effect on marginal revenue.

In Table 11.4, columns 1 and 2 represent the upward sloping supply curve faced by the monopsonist. Columns 4 and 5 show continuous MC_L and MRP_L as derived from the equations in the Table. Equilibrium occurs at 50 units of L with $P_L = \$37.50$. Notice that at 50 units of L, $VMP_L \equiv MRP_L > P_L$; that is, $\$50 > \$37.50$. Also, if the firm thought it could hire all it wanted at the wage of $\$37.50$, it would want to hire 62.5 units of labor.

We now consider a firm with monopoly power in the product market and monopsony power in the factor market. In Figure 11.9, the equilib-

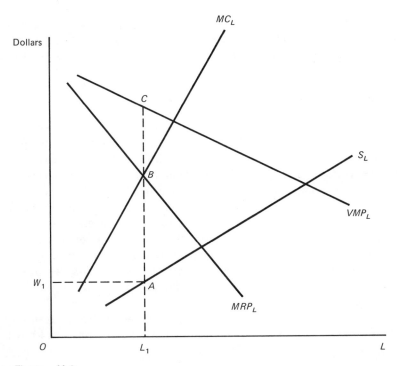

Figure 11.9

rium intersection is at point B, with L_1 units of labor being employed at a wage rate of W_1. Notice that, once again, $VMP_L > P_L$, but now there are two reasons for this. First, because the firm is a monopolist, $VMP_L > MRP_L$; second, because the firm is a monopsonist, $MC_L > P_L$. Again the firm would want to hire more labor if it could obtain it at W_1. A numerical example representing monopoly-monopsony is given in Table 11.5.

TABLE 11.5

(1) P_L	(2) L	(3) TC_L	(4) MC_L	(5) MRP_L	(6) VMP_L
$27.50	10	$275.00	$30.00	$90.00	$95.00
30.00	20	600.00	35.00	80.00	90.00
32.50	30	975.00	40.00	70.00	85.00
35.00	40	1400.00	45.00	60.00	80.00
37.50	50	1775.00	50.00	50.00	75.00
40.00	60	2400.00	55.00	40.00	70.00
42.50	70	2975.00	60.00	30.00	65.00
$45.00	80	$3600.00	$65.00	$20.00	$60.00

$$P_L = 25 + \tfrac{1}{4}L \qquad VMP_L = 100 - \tfrac{1}{2}L$$
$$MC_L = 25 + \tfrac{1}{2}L \qquad MRP_L = 100 - L$$

At 50 units of L, $MC_L = MRP_L$, $VMP_L > MRP_L$ ($75.00 > $50.00), and $MC_L > P_L$ ($50.00 > $37.50). Thus, $VMP_L > P_L$ ($75.00 > $37.50) and labor does not receive the value of its marginal product for two reasons.

RELEVANCE OF MONOPSONY

One of the best historical examples of monopsony in the United States is the "factory town," in which one concern was the chief source of employment. With the advent of the automobile and other cheap methods of transportation, this type of regional monopsony has become less likely. Even if a firm possesses monopoly power in the product market, it is unlikely that it will be able to achieve monopsony power in the factor market. For example, the largest automobile producers possess market power on the selling side; but because they are in competition for factors not only with other firms in the Detroit area but with firms in the surrounding factor market (which encompasses a much wider area than merely Detroit), if they do possess monopsony power, it is only to a small degree.

Furthermore, monopsony power has been reduced as a result of increased knowledge on the part of the workers. The increase in knowledge has been made possible by the expansion of government employment offices, recruitment by firms over a wider geographical area, and wider circulation of media that provide employment information. The improved and expanded transportation and communications facilities have also resulted in increased mobility on the part of labor. This too, of course, has the effect of lessening regional monopsony.

DOWNWARD-SLOPING SUPPLY CURVES FACING THE FIRM

A firm can face a downward-sloping supply curve of a factor if that factor is an intermediate one produced under one of the following conditions:

1. The factor supplying firm has monopoly power and is producing under conditions of decreasing cost.
2. The industry supplying the intermediate factor is a perfectly competitive one that is subject to economies of scale.

Two examples of this are illustrated in Figures 11.10 and 11.11; the first shows a firm that is a perfect competitor in the product market, and the second shows a firm with monopoly power in the product market.

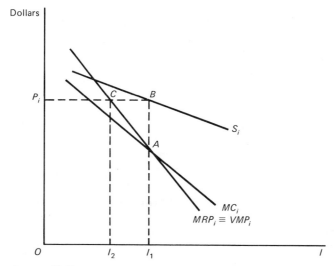

Figure 11.10

In Figure 11.10, the equilibrium intersection is point A, the wage is P_i, and the equilibrium factor employment level is I_1. Once again, there is a disparity between P_i and VMP_i, but now $P_i > VMP_i$; and because $VMP_i \equiv MRP_i$, $P_i > MRP_i$. Note also that if P_i were a constant, the firm would want to employ I_2 of factor I. The reason for the firm's employment of I_1 is that, as it increases its factor use, the marginal cost of the factor declines. This fact accounts also for $P_i > MC_i$ and, therefore, for $P_i > MRP_i$ in equilibrium. A numerical example will help clarify this point. Assume that when a firm is using n units of a factor, it is paying $10 per unit for the factor. It now employs the $n + 1$ unit, and because it faces a falling supply curve, it pays $9 for the $n + 1$ unit and for all previous units of the factor, because we are assuming homogeneous factors.[12] The change in costs will be: $+9 for the $n + 1$ unit $+$ $(-1 \cdot n$ units). Clearly, this change in cost (MC_i) will be less than the new factor price of $9; and this impels the firm to use more of the factor than it would if the factor's marginal cost were $9.

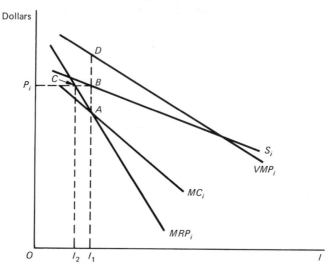

Figure 11.11

The situation in Figure 11.11 differs from that of Figure 11.10 only in that $VMP_i > MRP_i$. Thus, whereas $P_i > MRP_i$, with linear curves, $P_i > VMP_i$. Again, if P_i were a constant, the firm would buy less of the factor.[13] The various short-run equilibrium conditions are summarized in Table 11.6.

COMPETITIVE FIRM'S DEMAND FOR A FACTOR WHEN MORE THAN ONE INPUT IS VARIABLE

To this point we have considered only the demand for a factor when that factor was the only variable one. We now turn our attention to the

[12] In fact, in our entire discussion of factor pricing, we have implicitly assumed that factors are homogeneous and, therefore, that they receive equal remuneration. However, impediments to the equalization of the per-unit remuneration of homogeneous factors may exist in the short run due to temporarily fixed contractural obligations. This just means that the adjustment process will not be as smooth as assumed before.
[13] Notice that in Figures 11.10 and 11.11 we have drawn the MC_i curve less steep in absolute terms than the MRP_i curve. The student should be able to demonstrate that this relationship is necessary for a stable equilibrium.

case of the long run where all factors are variable and (what is basically the same case) of the short run when more than one factor is variable.

Remember that for an economically efficient allocation of resources, the following least-cost, profit-maximizing conditions must be fulfilled:

$$\frac{MP_a}{MC_a} = \frac{MP_b}{MC_b} = \cdots = \frac{MP_n}{MC_n} = \frac{1}{MC} = \frac{1}{MR} \qquad [11.35]$$

where for a competitive firm, $MC_a = P_a$; $MC_b = P_b$; and so on.

TABLE 11.6

Summary of Short-Run Equilibrium Conditions

	Equilibrium Conditions	
	Gain to Firm from Hiring Extra Unit of Factor	Cost to Firm due to Hiring Extra Unit of Factor
General case	$MRP_i = MC_i$	
Perfect competition in both markets	$VMP_i \equiv MRP_i = MC_i \equiv P_i$	
Monopolist in product; perfect competitor in factor market	$VMP_i > MRP_i = MC_i \equiv P_i$	
Perfect competitor in product; monopsonist	$VMP_i \equiv MRP_i = MC_i > P_i$	
Monopolist-monopsonist	$VMP_i > MRP_i = MC_i > P_i$	
Perfect competitor in product; falling factor supply curve	$VMP_i \equiv MRP_i = MC_i < P_i$	
Monopolist; falling factor supply curve	$VMP_i > MRP_i = MC_i < P_i$	

For ease of exposition, we assume two variable factors of production, A and B. (This may be either the long run, where A and B are the only inputs, or a short run in which the firm can vary only A and B but there are other factors.) In Figure 11.12, the firm is initially faced with the price P_{a1} and we assume that the relevant marginal revenue product schedule is MRP_{a1}. Therefore, the initial equilibrium intersection is at B with A_1 units of the factor being employed. Now we assume that because of, say, a change in factor supply, the price of A changes to P_{a2}. Assume a sequential pattern of reactions, although in reality the individual steps might merge. In order to understand the sequence of events, it is necessary to understand that an individual marginal revenue product curve, such as MRP_{a1}, is drawn on the assumption of given quantities of the other factors.

When the price of A changes from P_{a1} to P_{a2}, the firm will move along MRP_{a1} to point C where $P_{a2} = MRP_{a1}$. However, this violates equation 11.35, because a change in the quantity of A used will alter the marginal product of B. Thus, in order to restore equilibrium, the firm will change the quantity of B because P_b is constant. But this will in turn cause a change in the marginal product of A, which in turn will cause an adjustment in B, and so on. We assume that the ultimate effect of these tandem

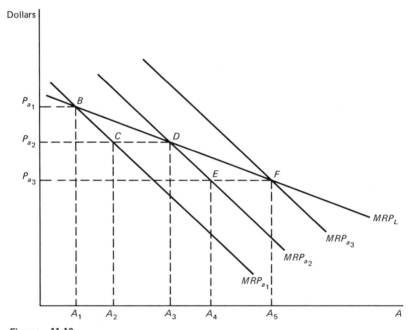

Figure 11.12

adjustments will be a shift in the marginal product schedule of A such that the new MRP_a curve is MRP_{a2}. Furthermore, the new equilibrium intersection is at D with A_3 units of the factor employed at the new given price of P_{a2}.

Analogously, should the price of A change to P_{a3}, the sequence of events would entail a movement from D to E and ultimately to F. If we connect points such as B, D, and F, we derive a marginal revenue product (demand) curve for A that is based on the assumption that the prices for the other factors of production are fixed but their quantities are varied to achieve efficient factor utilization as expressed in equation 11.35.

Two interesting points are worth noting. The first point has to do with the relationship between the two factors. We can define substitute factors as being either complements or rivals. Two factors are complementary if, given an increase in the quantity of one factor, the marginal product schedule of the other factor shifts upward. Conversely, two factors are rivals if the increased quantity of one causes the other factor's marginal product schedule to shift downward.

Although it is not intuitively obvious, the shifts in the MRP curve of Figure 11.12 will be in the same direction, whether the factors are rivals or complements. This can be seen as follows: Assume A and B are complementary factors and that P_a declines, leading to an increased use of A. This causes the marginal product of B to increase and, on the basis of constant product prices, MRP_b also increases; and to restore equilibrium, more B will be used. This in turn raises the marginal product of A and, therefore, causes a shift to the right of the MRP_a curve and a consequent further increase in the use of A.

Now assume A and B to be rivals and again assume that P_a declines with more A being used. The increased quantity of A causes the marginal product of B (and the MRP_b) to decline, resulting in the use of less B. The decreased quantity of B leads to an increase in the marginal product of A and MRP_a and thus an increase in the equilibrium quantity of A. Once again, the MRP_a curve shifts to the right.

The second point is that the MRP_L curve must be more elastic than the unadjusted MRP_a schedules. This can be seen by comparing the change in the equilibrium quantity of A, due to a decline in P_a, along MRP_{a1} with the change along MRP_L. Just as the long-run supply curve is more elastic than the short-run one, because the firm has more flexibility in adjusting factor proportions, the long-run demand for a factor will be more elastic for the same reason.

Appendix 11A

Generalized Least-Cost Conditions for Production

We consider a firm using two homogeneous factors of production, X and Y, and faced with the production function

$$q = f(X, Y) \qquad [11A.1]$$

and the cost function

$$C = g(X, Y) \qquad [11A.2]$$

The slope of an isocost curve can be determined as follows: Along an isocost curve, expenditure is a constant. We may, therefore, write

$$dC = \frac{\partial g}{\partial X} dX + \frac{\partial g}{\partial X} dY = 0 \qquad [11A.3]$$

Thus,

$$\frac{dY}{dX} = -\frac{\dfrac{\partial g}{\partial X}}{\dfrac{\partial g}{\partial Y}} = -\frac{MC_x}{MC_y} \qquad [11A.4]$$

Similarly, for the production function, output is a constant along an isoquant, and we may write

$$dq = \frac{\partial f}{\partial X} dX + \frac{\partial f}{\partial Y} dY = 0 \qquad [11A.5]$$

Therefore,

$$\frac{dY}{dX} = -\frac{\dfrac{\partial f}{\partial X}}{\dfrac{\partial f}{\partial Y}} = -\frac{MP_x}{MP_y} \qquad [11A.6]$$

Dividing equation 11A.5 by dX, we obtain

$$\frac{dq}{dX} = \frac{\partial f}{\partial X} + \frac{\partial f}{\partial Y}\frac{dY}{dX} = 0 \qquad [11A.7]$$

Next we substitute equation 11A.4 into equation 11A.7.

$$\frac{dq}{dX} = \frac{\partial f}{\partial X} - \frac{\partial f}{\partial Y} \left(\frac{\dfrac{\partial g}{\partial X}}{\dfrac{\partial g}{\partial Y}} \right) = 0 \qquad [11A.8]$$

We introduce the following notation:

$$\frac{\partial g}{\partial X} = g_x{}'$$

$$\frac{\partial g}{\partial Y} = g_y{}'$$

$$\frac{\partial f}{\partial X} = f_x{}'$$

$$\frac{\partial f}{\partial Y} = f_y{}'$$

Rewriting equation 11A.8, we get

$$f_x{}' - f_y{}' \left(\frac{g_x{}'}{g_y{}'} \right) = 0 \qquad [11A.9]$$

And,

$$\frac{g_x{}'}{g_y{}'} = \frac{f_x{}'}{f_y{}'} \qquad [11A.10]$$

This is the first-order condition for least-cost equilibrium, that is, the tangency between an isoquant and isocost.

To derive the second-order condition that ensures that the tangency represents a maximum output for a given level of expenditure (or minimum expenditure for a given level of output), we first take the derivative of equation 11A.8 with respect to X.

$$\frac{d^2q}{dX^2} = \frac{d}{dX} (f_x{}') - \frac{d}{dX} \left[f_y{}' \left(\frac{g_x{}'}{g_y{}'} \right) \right] \qquad [11A.11]$$

To ensure maximum output, equation 11A.11 must be less than zero.

$$\frac{d}{dX} (f_x{}') - \frac{d}{dX} \left[f_y{}' \left(\frac{g_x{}'}{g_y{}'} \right) \right] < 0$$

Or,

$$\frac{d}{dX} \left[f_y{}' \left(\frac{g_x{}'}{g_y{}'} \right) \right] > \frac{d}{dX} (f_x{}') \qquad [11A.12]$$

Taking the derivatives as indicated in equation 11A.12, we get

$$f_y{}' \left[\frac{d}{dX} \left(\frac{g_x{}'}{g_y{}'} \right) \right] + \left(\frac{g_x{}'}{g_y{}'} \right) \left[\frac{d}{dX} (f_y{}') \right] > \frac{d}{dX} (f_x{}') \qquad [11A.13]$$

Rearranging terms in equation 11A.13 gives us

$$f_y'\left[\frac{d}{dX}\left(\frac{g_x'}{g_y'}\right)\right] > \frac{d}{dX}(f_x') - \left(\frac{g_x'}{g_y'}\right)\left[\frac{d}{dX}(f_y')\right]$$

Dividing both sides by f_y', we get:

$$\frac{d}{dX}\left(\frac{g_x'}{g_y'}\right) > \frac{\dfrac{d}{dX}(f_x') - \left(\dfrac{g_x'}{g_y'}\right)\left[\dfrac{d}{dX}(f_y')\right]}{f_y'} \qquad [11A.14]$$

The term on the left represents the curvature of the isocost curve, the slope of the absolute slope of the isocost. Furthermore, we now show that the term on the right is the curvature of the isoquant.

The slope of the isoquant is given by

$$\frac{dY}{dX} = -\frac{f_x'}{f_y'} \qquad \text{or} \qquad \left|\frac{dY}{dX}\right| = \frac{f_x'}{f_y'} \qquad [11A.15]$$

Therefore,

$$\frac{d}{dX}\left(\frac{f_x'}{f_y'}\right) = \frac{f_y'\left[\dfrac{d}{dX}(f_x')\right] - f_x'\left[\dfrac{d}{dX}(f_y')\right]}{(f_y')^2} \qquad [11A.16]$$

Dividing numerator and denominator of the right-hand side of equation 11A.16, we get

$$\frac{d}{dX}\left(\frac{f_x'}{f_y'}\right) = \frac{\left[\dfrac{d}{dX}(f_x')\right] - \left(\dfrac{f_x'}{f_y'}\right)\left[\dfrac{d}{dX}(f_y')\right]}{f_y'} \qquad [11A.17]$$

From equation 11A.10 we can substitute $\dfrac{g_x'}{g_y'}$ for $\dfrac{f_x'}{f_y'}$ and obtain

$$\frac{d}{dX}\left(\frac{f_x'}{f_y'}\right) = \frac{\left[\dfrac{d}{dX}(f_x')\right] - \left(\dfrac{g_x'}{g_y'}\right)\left[\dfrac{d}{dX}(f_y')\right]}{f_y'} \qquad [11A.18]$$

which is the right-hand side of the second-order condition of equation 11A.14.

It should be noted that equation 11A.14 is equivalent to the second-order condition obtained intuitively in the text; that is, for maximum output at a given level of expenditure, the curvature of the isocost curve must exceed the curvature of the isoquant at the point of tangency.

Appendix 11B

Elasticity of Substitution[1]

Given the production function

$$q = f(X, Y) \tag{11B.1}$$

we get from this a system of isoquants

$$q = f(X, Y) = k, \text{ a constant} \tag{11B.2}$$

If we let $f_x = \partial q/\partial X$ and $f_y = \partial q/\partial Y$, we have along the isoquant

$$f_x dX + f_y dY = 0 \tag{11B.3}$$

The slope of the isoquant is therefore

$$\frac{dY}{dX} = -\frac{f_x}{f_y} = -\frac{MP_x}{MP_y} \tag{11B.4}$$

And MRS_{xy}, or r, is defined as

$$r = -\frac{dY}{dX} = \frac{f_x}{f_y} \tag{11B.5}$$

Equation 11B.5 gives the marginal rate of substitution of Y for X in the production of q; it measures the number of units of factor Y that must be used to compensate for the loss of a unit of factor X in the production of q.

Along the isoquant, $d(Y/X)$ represents the change in the relative use of Y compared with X, and $dr = d(f_x/f_y)$ represents the corresponding change in the marginal rate of substitution. The ratio of these differentials (expressed in relative terms to make them independent of units) is defined as the *elasticity of substitution* between the factors at any point:

$$\sigma = \left[\frac{d\left(\dfrac{Y}{X}\right)}{\dfrac{Y}{X}} \middle/ \frac{dr}{r} \right] = \frac{\dfrac{X}{Y} d\left(\dfrac{Y}{X}\right)}{\dfrac{1}{r} dr} \tag{11B.6}$$

---

[1] This derivation and discussion follows R. G. D. Allen, *Mathematical Analysis for Economists* (New York: Macmillan, 1956), pp. 341–343.

The value of σ can be written in terms of the partial derivatives of r (the marginal rate of substitution) where $r = g(X, Y)$, or the value of σ can be written in terms of the partial derivatives of the production function itself.

$$d\left(\frac{Y}{X}\right) = \frac{X\,dY - Y\,dX}{X^2} \tag{11B.7}$$

$$d(r) = \frac{\partial r}{\partial X}\,dX + \frac{\partial r}{\partial Y}\,dY \tag{11B.8}$$

Now:

$$\frac{dY}{dX} = -\frac{f_x}{f_y} \quad \text{or} \quad dY = -\frac{f_x}{f_y}\,dX \quad \text{and} \quad r = \frac{f_x}{f_y} \quad \text{so} \quad dY = -r\,dX$$

Substituting into equations 11B.7 and 11B.8, we get

$$d\left(\frac{Y}{X}\right) = \left(\frac{-Xr + Y}{X^2}\right)dX \tag{11B.9}$$

$$dr = \frac{\partial r}{\partial X}\,dX + \frac{\partial r}{\partial Y}\,(-r\,dX) = dX\left[\frac{\partial r}{\partial X} - \frac{\partial r}{\partial Y}\,r\right] \tag{11B.10}$$

$$= -\left(r\frac{\partial r}{\partial Y} - \frac{\partial r}{\partial X}\right)dX$$

Substituting into equation 11B.6, we have

$$\sigma = \frac{\dfrac{X}{Y}\left(-\dfrac{Xr + Y}{X^2}\right)dX}{\dfrac{1}{r}\left[-\left(r\dfrac{\partial r}{\partial Y} - \dfrac{\partial r}{\partial X}\right)dX\right]} = \frac{r}{XY}\left(\frac{Xr + Y}{r\dfrac{\partial r}{\partial Y} - \dfrac{\partial r}{\partial X}}\right) \tag{11B.11}$$

Since $r = f_x/f_y$,

$$\frac{\partial}{\partial X}r = \frac{\partial}{\partial X}\left(\frac{f_x}{f_y}\right) = \frac{f_y f_{xx} - f_x f_{xy}}{f_y{}^2} \tag{11B.12}$$

and

$$\frac{\partial}{\partial Y}r = \frac{\partial}{\partial Y}\left(\frac{f_x}{f_y}\right) = \frac{f_y f_{xy} - f_x f_{yy}}{f_y{}^2} \tag{11B.13}$$

Substituting equations 11B.12 and 11B.13 into equation 11B.11, we have:

$$\sigma = \frac{\dfrac{f_x}{f_y}}{XY}\left[\frac{X\dfrac{f_x}{f_y} + Y}{\dfrac{f_x}{f_y}\left(\dfrac{f_y f_{xy} - f_x f_{yy}}{f_y{}^2}\right) - \left(\dfrac{f_y f_{xx} - f_x f_{xy}}{f_y{}^2}\right)}\right] \tag{11B.14}$$

The denominator of the expression in brackets in equation 11B.14 simplifies to

$$\frac{f_x f_{xy} - \dfrac{f_x{}^2}{f_y}f_{yy}}{f_y{}^2} - \frac{f_y f_{xx} - f_x f_{xy}}{f_y{}^2} \tag{11B.15}$$

This may be written

$$\frac{2f_x f_{xy} - \dfrac{f_x{}^2}{f_y} f_{yy} - f_y f_{xx}}{f_y{}^2} \qquad \text{[11B.16]}$$

Now invert this expression and multiply it by the numerator of equation 11B.14:

$$\sigma = \frac{f_x}{f_y} \left[\frac{(f_y)^2 \left(X \dfrac{f_x}{f_y} + Y \right)}{XY \left(2f_x f_{xy} - \dfrac{f_x{}^2}{f_y} f_{yy} - f_y f_{xx} \right)} \right] \qquad \text{[11B.17]}$$

Multiply the denominator by f_y and the numerator by f_x. Then,

$$\sigma = \frac{Xf_x{}^2 f_y + Yf_x f_y{}^2}{XY(2f_x f_y f_{xy} - f_x{}^2 f_{yy} - f_y{}^2 f_{xx})}$$

or

$$\sigma = \frac{f_x f_y(Xf_x + Yf_y)}{XY(2f_x f_y f_{xy} - f_x{}^2 f_{yy} - f_y{}^2 f_{xx})} \qquad \text{[11B.18]}$$

This is a symmetrical expression and shows that although σ has been defined for the substitution of Y for X, it has the same value when defined for the substitution of X for Y. We now find an expression for σ in terms of r: $\dfrac{d}{dX}\left(\dfrac{dY}{dX}\right) = -\dfrac{d}{dX} r$ gives the curvature, or rate of change of the slope of the isoquant. Now $r = g(X, Y)$, so $-\dfrac{d}{dX} r =$ $-\left(\dfrac{\partial r}{\partial X} + \dfrac{\partial r}{\partial Y}\dfrac{dY}{dX}\right)$. Since $\dfrac{dY}{dX} = r$, we have

$$-\frac{d}{dX}(r) = r\frac{\partial r}{\partial Y} - \frac{\partial r}{\partial X} \qquad \text{[11B.19]}$$

We may now rewrite equation 11B.11 as

$$\sigma = \frac{Xr^2 + Yr}{XY} \cdot \frac{1}{r\dfrac{\partial r}{\partial Y} - \dfrac{\partial r}{\partial X}}$$

or

$$\sigma = \frac{Xr^2 + Yr}{XY} \cdot \frac{1}{\dfrac{d}{dX}\left(\dfrac{dY}{dX}\right)} \qquad \text{[11B.20]}$$

Thus σ is a positive multiple of the reciprocal of the rate of change of the slope of the isoquant. That is, it is positive and inversely proportional to the curvature of the isoquant. The larger the value of σ, the flatter is the isoquant and the more slowly does r increase as Y is substituted for X. The magnitude of σ is thus a measure of the ease with which production can be maintained by substituting Y for X.

As may be seen from note 14 of Chapter 6 and Appendix 5A, $\dfrac{d^2Y}{dX^2} =$ $(2f_x f_y f_{xy} - f_x{}^2 f_{yy} - f_y{}^2 f_{xx})$; and, of course, this is precisely what we have in the denominator of equation 11B.18.

If X and Y are perfect substitutes, so that output can be maintained by increasing Y in proportion as X decreases, then the isoquant is a straight line, $\dfrac{d^2Y}{dX^2}$ is zero, and σ is infinite. If X and Y cannot be substituted, the isoquants are right angled at the unique factor proportion, $\dfrac{d^2Y}{dX^2} = \infty$, and σ is zero. As σ increases from zero to ∞, substitution between the factors becomes increasingly easier.

In Appendix 6A we derived the following relationship for linear homogeneous functions:

$$X \frac{\partial q}{\partial X} + Y \frac{\partial q}{\partial Y} = q \tag{11B.21}$$

This is an identity—true for any value of X and Y. The partial derivatives of one side will therefore be equal to the partial derivatives of the other side.

$$\frac{\partial}{\partial X} \left(X \frac{\partial q}{\partial X} + Y \frac{\partial q}{\partial Y} \right) = \frac{\partial q}{\partial X}$$

$$X \frac{\partial^2 q}{\partial X^2} + \frac{\partial q}{\partial X} \frac{\partial X}{\partial X} + Y \frac{\partial^2 q}{\partial X \partial Y} + \frac{\partial q}{\partial Y} \frac{\partial Y}{\partial X}$$

Now, $\dfrac{\partial X}{\partial X} = 1$ and $\dfrac{\partial Y}{\partial X} = 0$, since Y is a constant when partially differentiating with respect to X. We thus have

$$X \frac{\partial^2 q}{\partial X^2} + \frac{\partial q}{\partial X} + Y \frac{\partial^2 q}{\partial X \partial Y} = \frac{\partial q}{\partial X}$$

$$\frac{\partial^2 q}{\partial X^2} = -\frac{Y}{X} \frac{\partial^2 q}{\partial X \partial Y}$$

$$f_{xx} = -\frac{Y}{X} f_{xy} \tag{11B.22}$$

We may also show in like manner that

$$\frac{\partial^2 q}{\partial Y^2} = -\frac{X}{Y} \frac{\partial^2 q}{\partial X \partial Y}$$

$$f_{yy} = -\frac{X}{Y} f_{xy} \tag{11B.23}$$

The denominator of expression (11B.18) for σ was

$$XY(2f_x f_y f_{xy} - f_x{}^2 f_{yy} - f_y{}^2 f_{xx})$$

We substitute the expressions for f_{xx} and f_{yy} derived for the linear homogeneous function (equations 11B.22 and 11B.23), into the above:

$$XY\left(2f_x f_y f_{xy} + \frac{X}{Y}f_x{}^2 f_{xy} + \frac{Y}{X}f_y{}^2 f_{xy}\right) = (XY2f_x f_y f_{xy} + X^2 f_x{}^2 f_{xy} + Y^2 f_y{}^2 f_{xy})$$

$$= f_{xy}(XY2f_x f_y + X^2 f_x{}^2 + Y^2 f_y{}^2)$$

$$= f_{xy}(Xf_x + Yf_y)^2$$

Therefore,

$$\sigma = \frac{f_x f_y (Xf_x + Yf_y)}{f_{xy}(Xf_x + Yf_y)^2} = \frac{f_x f_y}{f_{xy}(Xf_x + Yf_y)} \qquad [11B.24]$$

But by Euler's theorem, $Xf_x + Yf_y = q$. Thus,

$$\sigma = \frac{f_x f_y}{f_{xy}q} = \frac{\dfrac{\partial q}{\partial X}\cdot\dfrac{\partial q}{\partial Y}}{q\dfrac{\partial^2 q}{\partial X \partial Y}} \qquad [11B.25]$$

Thus, when there are constant returns to scale, σ is inversely proportional to the second-order partial derivatives of the linear homogeneous production function.

If $\dfrac{\partial^2 q}{\partial X \partial Y}$ is negative (factor rivalry), then σ would be negative. Thus,

$$\left[\frac{r}{\dfrac{Y}{X}}\cdot\frac{d\left(\dfrac{Y}{X}\right)}{dr}\right] < 0$$

If we assume that $\dfrac{\partial q}{\partial X}$ and $\dfrac{\partial q}{\partial Y}$ are positive (we are within the ridge lines), so that $r = -\dfrac{dY}{dX} = \dfrac{f_x}{f_y} > 0$, then $\sigma < 0$ implies

$$\left[\frac{d\left(\dfrac{Y}{X}\right)}{d\left(-\dfrac{dY}{dX}\right)}\right] < 0$$

which means that as the absolute slope of the isoquant increases $\left(-\dfrac{dY}{dX}\right.$ increases), the ratio of Y/X must decrease. This implies a concave isoquant and implies that only one factor will be used.[2]

[2] *See* Chapter 11, p. 228.

Appendix 11C

Elasticity of Derived Demand[1]

The elasticity of demand for a factor of production on the part of a competitive industry may be derived as follows.

Given a production function,

$$X = f(a, b) \qquad [11C.1]$$

η is the elasticity of demand for the product:

$$\eta = -\frac{dX}{dP_x} \cdot \frac{P_x}{X} = \frac{-P_x}{X \dfrac{dP_x}{dX}} \qquad [11C.2]$$

e is the elasticity of supply of b:

$$e = \frac{db}{dP_b} \cdot \frac{P_b}{b} = \frac{P_b}{b \dfrac{dP_b}{db}} \qquad [11C.3]$$

λ is the elasticity of demand for a:

$$\lambda = -\frac{da}{dP_a} \cdot \frac{P_a}{a} = \frac{-P_a}{a \dfrac{dP_a}{da}} \qquad [11C.4]$$

Competition is assumed so that factors are paid the value of their marginal products:

$$P_a = P_x \frac{\partial X}{\partial a} \qquad [11C.5a]$$

$$P_b = P_x \frac{\partial X}{\partial b} \qquad [11C.5b]$$

Assuming constant returns to scale for the industry (that is, a linear homogeneous production function for the industry) and competition, we have

$$P_x X = P_a a + P_b b \qquad [11C.6]$$

---

[1] See J. R. Hicks, *The Theory of Wages*, (2d ed.; New York: Macmillan, 1964), pp. 241–246.

or

$$X = a \frac{\partial X}{\partial a} + b \frac{\partial X}{\partial b} \qquad \text{[11C.7]}$$

Differentiating equation 11C.7 partially with respect to b (remember that partial differentiation with respect to b means a = constant, so $\frac{\partial a}{\partial b} = 0$ and $\frac{\partial b}{\partial b} = 1$), we get

$$\frac{\partial X}{\partial b} = a \frac{\partial^2 X}{\partial a \partial b} + b \frac{\partial^2 X}{\partial b^2} + \frac{\partial X}{\partial b}$$

Thus,

$$b \frac{\partial X^2}{\partial b^2} = -a \frac{\partial^2 X}{\partial a \partial b} \qquad \text{[11C.8]}$$

We now take the total differential of equation 11C.1:

$$dX = \frac{\partial X}{\partial a} da + \frac{\partial X}{\partial b} db \qquad \text{[11C.9]}$$

Substituting equations 11C.5a and 11C.5b into equation 11C.9, we get

$$dX = \frac{P_a}{P_x} da + \frac{P_b}{P_x} db$$

And multiplying both sides by P_x, we have

$$P_x dX = P_a da + P_b db \qquad \text{[11C.10]}$$

The condition of equality of receipts and expenditures must be satisfied after a small change in P_a, which results in a small change in a. Thus we take the differential of equation 11C.6:

$$P_x dX + X dP_x = P_a da + a dP_a + P_b db + b dP_b \qquad \text{[11C.11]}$$

Now, substituting equation 11C.10 into equation 11C.11, we get

$$X dP_x + P_a da + P_b db = P_a da + a dP_a + P_b db + b dP_b$$

Thus,

$$X dP_x = a dP_a + b dP_b \qquad \text{[11C.12]}$$

From equation 11C.2 we have

$$\eta = \frac{-P_x}{X \dfrac{dP_x}{dX}}$$

Thus,

$$\frac{P_x dX}{\eta} = P_x dX \left(\frac{X \dfrac{dP_x}{dX}}{-P_x} \right) = -X dP_x \qquad \text{[11C.13]}$$

From equation 11C.3 we have

$$e = \frac{P_b}{b \dfrac{dP_b}{db}}$$

Thus,

$$\frac{P_b db}{e} = P_b db \frac{b \dfrac{dP_b}{db}}{P_b} = b dP_b \qquad [11C.14]$$

From equation 11C.4 we have

$$\lambda = \frac{-P_a}{a \dfrac{dP_a}{da}}$$

Thus,

$$\frac{P_a da}{\lambda} = P_a da \left(\frac{-a \dfrac{dP_a}{da}}{P_a} \right) = -a dP_a \qquad [11C.15]$$

Substituting equations 11C.13, 11C.14, and 11C.15 into equation 11C.12, we have

$$-\frac{P_x dX}{\eta} = -\frac{P_a da}{\lambda} + \frac{P_b db}{e}$$

or

$$\frac{P_x dX}{\eta} = \frac{P_a da}{\lambda} - \frac{P_b db}{e} \qquad [11C.16]$$

Now, from equation 11C.3 we have

$$e = \frac{db}{dP_b} \cdot \frac{P_b}{b}, \qquad \frac{b}{P_b} e = \frac{db}{dP_b}, \qquad \text{or} \qquad db = \frac{be}{P_b} dP_b \qquad [11C.17]$$

From equation 11C.5b we substitute into equation 11C.17:

$$db = \frac{be}{P_b} d \left(P_x \frac{\partial X}{\partial b} \right)$$

$$= \frac{be}{P_b} \left[P_x d \left(\frac{\partial X}{\partial b} \right) + \frac{\partial X}{\partial b} dP_x \right]$$

$$= \frac{be}{P_b} \left[P_x \left(\frac{\partial^2 X}{\partial a \partial b} da + \frac{\partial^2 X}{\partial b^2} db \right) + \frac{\partial X}{\partial b} dP_x \right] \qquad [11C.18]$$

From equation 11C.8 we have

$$b \frac{\partial^2 X}{\partial b^2} = -a \frac{\partial^2 X}{\partial a \partial b}$$

and thus

$$\frac{\partial^2 X}{\partial b^2} = -\frac{a}{b} \frac{\partial^2 X}{\partial a \partial b}$$

Now, substituting into equation 11C.18, we get

$$db = \frac{be}{P_b}\left\{P_x\left[\frac{\partial^2 X}{\partial a \partial b}\,da + \left(-\frac{a}{b}\frac{\partial^2 X}{\partial a \partial b}\right)db\right] + \frac{\partial X}{\partial b}\,dP_x\right\} \qquad [11C.19]$$

$$db = \frac{be}{P_b}\left[P_x\frac{\partial^2 X}{\partial a \partial b}\left(da - \frac{a}{b}\,db\right) + \frac{\partial X}{\partial b}\,dP_x\right] \qquad [11C.20]$$

Now, in equation 11C.5b we have

$$P_b = P_x\frac{\partial X}{\partial b} \qquad \text{so} \qquad \frac{P_b}{P_x} = \frac{\partial X}{\partial b}$$

Thus,

$$\frac{\partial X}{\partial b}\,dP_x = \frac{P_b}{P_x}\,dP_x$$

Now,

$$\frac{P_b dX}{\eta X} = \frac{P_b dX}{\dfrac{-P_x}{X\dfrac{dP_x}{dX}}X} = P_b dX\left(\frac{-X\dfrac{dP_x}{dX}}{XP_x}\right) = -\frac{P_b}{P_x}\,dP_x$$

Substituting in equation 11C.20, we have

$$db = \frac{be}{P_b}\left\{-\frac{P_b dX}{X\eta} + P_x\frac{\partial^2 X}{\partial a \partial b}\left(da - \frac{a}{b}\,db\right)\right\} \qquad [11C.21]$$

We saw in Appendix 11B that the elasticity of substitution for a linear homogeneous function may be written

$$\sigma = \frac{\dfrac{\partial X}{\partial a}\cdot\dfrac{\partial X}{\partial b}}{X\dfrac{\partial^2 X}{\partial a \partial b}}$$

Now substitute from equations 11C.5a and 11C.5b, $\dfrac{\partial X}{\partial a} = \dfrac{P_a}{P_x}$ and $\dfrac{\partial X}{\partial b} = \dfrac{P_b}{P_x}.$

$$\sigma = \frac{P_a P_b}{P_x^2 X\dfrac{\partial^2 X}{\partial a \partial b}}$$

Let $k = \dfrac{P_a a}{P_x X}$, and $1 - k = \dfrac{P_b b}{P_x X}.$ Now multiply out equation 11C.21:

$$db = -\frac{ebdX}{X\eta} + \frac{P_x be}{P_b}\frac{\partial^2 X}{\partial a \partial b}\left(da - \frac{a}{b}\,db\right)$$

$$\frac{ebdX}{X\eta} = -db + \frac{P_x be}{P_b}\frac{\partial^2 X}{\partial a \partial b}\left(da - \frac{a}{b}\,db\right)$$

Multiplying both sides by $\dfrac{XP_x}{eb}$, we get

$$\frac{P_x dX}{\eta} = -\frac{XP_x}{eb}\,db + \frac{XP_x{}^2}{P_b}\frac{\partial^2 X}{\partial a \partial b}\left(da - \frac{a}{b}\,db\right) \qquad \text{[11C.22]}$$

Now the first term on the right in equation 11C.22 may be written as

$$-\frac{XP_x}{b}\,db\left(\frac{1}{e}\right)$$

Now, $\dfrac{1}{1-k} = \dfrac{P_x X}{P_b b}$. Thus, $\dfrac{1}{1-k}(db\,P_b) = \dfrac{P_x X}{b}\,db.$

The first term on the right of equation 11C.22 may therefore be written as

$$-\frac{P_b db}{1-k}\left(\frac{1}{e}\right) \qquad \text{[11C.23a]}$$

Multiply out the second half of equation 11C.22:

$$\frac{XP_x{}^2}{P_b}\frac{\partial^2 X}{\partial a \partial b}\,da - \frac{XP_x{}^2}{P_b}\frac{\partial^2 X}{\partial a \partial b}\left(\frac{a}{b}\,db\right) \qquad \text{[11C.23b]}$$

Now multiply the first expression in equation 11C.23b by P_a in the numerator and denominator.

$$P_a da\,\frac{P_x{}^2 X\,\dfrac{\partial^2 X}{\partial a \partial b}}{P_a P_b}$$

By our definition of σ in equation 11C.21, we see that this may be written as

$$\frac{P_a da}{\sigma} \qquad \text{[11C.23c]}$$

The second part of equation 11C.23b can be written as

$$-\left(\frac{aP_x}{P_b}\right)\left(\frac{\partial^2 X}{\partial a \partial b}\right)\left(\frac{P_x X}{b}\,db\right)$$

or

$$-\left[\frac{P_x\,\dfrac{\partial^2 X}{\partial a \partial b}}{P_b}\,a\right]\left[\frac{P_x X}{b}\,db\right]$$

We multiply and divide this expression by P_a, $P_x X$, and P_b:

$$-\left[\frac{P_x{}^2 X\,\dfrac{\partial^2 X}{\partial a \partial b}}{P_a P_b}\,\frac{P_a a}{P_x X}\right]\left[P_b\left(\frac{P_x X}{P_b b}\right)db\right]$$

And using our definitions of σ and k, this can be rewritten as

$$- \left[\frac{1}{\sigma}k\right]\left[\frac{P_bdb}{1-k}\right] \qquad [11\text{C}.23\text{d}]$$

Now combining equations 11C.23a, 11C.23c, and 11C.23d, we get

$$\frac{P_xdX}{\eta} = \frac{P_ada}{\sigma} - \frac{P_bdb}{1-k}\left(\frac{1}{e}+\frac{k}{\sigma}\right) \qquad [11\text{C}.24]$$

We now use equations 11C.10, 11C.16, and 11C.24 to eliminate da, db, dX, P_a, P_b, and P_x. Taking equation 11C.10 and 11C.16 we have

$$\frac{P_ada}{\eta} + \frac{P_bdb}{\eta} = \frac{P_ada}{\lambda} - \frac{P_bdb}{e}$$

$$\frac{P_ada}{\eta} - \frac{P_ada}{\lambda} = -\frac{P_bdb}{e} - \frac{P_bdb}{\eta}$$

$$\frac{P_ada}{\lambda} - \frac{P_ada}{\eta} = \frac{P_bdb}{e} + \frac{P_bdb}{\eta}$$

$$\frac{\eta(P_ada)}{\lambda\eta} - \frac{\lambda(P_ada)}{\lambda\eta} = \frac{\eta(P_bdb)}{e\eta} + \frac{e(P_bdb)}{e\eta}$$

$$\frac{P_ada(\eta-\lambda)}{\lambda\eta} = \frac{(P_bdb)(\eta+e)}{e\eta} \qquad [11\text{C}.25]$$

Now take equations 11C.16 and 11C.24 and equate them:

$$\frac{P_ada}{\lambda} - \frac{P_bdb}{e} = \frac{P_ada}{\sigma} - \frac{P_bdb}{1-k}\left(\frac{1}{e}+\frac{k}{\sigma}\right)$$

$$\frac{P_ada}{\lambda} - \frac{P_ada}{\sigma} = \frac{P_bdb}{e} - \frac{P_bdb}{1-k}\left(\frac{1}{e}+\frac{k}{\sigma}\right)$$

$$\frac{\sigma(P_ada)}{\lambda\sigma} - \frac{\lambda P_ada}{\lambda\sigma} = \frac{(1-k)P_bdb}{(1-k)e} - \frac{e(P_bdb)\left(\frac{1}{e}+\frac{k}{\sigma}\right)}{(1-k)e}$$

$$\frac{(\sigma-\lambda)(P_ada)}{\lambda\sigma} = \frac{P_bdb\left(\dfrac{-k(\sigma+e)}{\sigma}\right)}{(1-k)e} \qquad [11\text{C}.26]$$

Divide equation 11C.26 by equation 11C.25:

$$\left[\frac{(\sigma-\lambda)(P_ada)}{\lambda\sigma}\right]\left[\frac{\lambda\eta}{P_ada(\eta-\lambda)}\right] = \left[\frac{P_bdb\left(-k\dfrac{(\sigma+e)}{\sigma}\right)}{(1-k)e}\right]\left[\frac{e\eta}{(P_bdb)(\eta+e)}\right]$$

Thus,

$$\frac{(\sigma-\lambda)\eta}{\sigma(\eta-\lambda)} = \left(\frac{-k\left(\dfrac{\sigma+e}{\sigma}\right)}{1-k}\right)\left(\frac{\eta}{\eta+e}\right)$$

Multiply both sides by $-\dfrac{\sigma}{\eta}$:

$$\frac{\lambda - \sigma}{\eta - \lambda} = \frac{k}{1 - k}\left(\frac{e + \sigma}{e + \eta}\right) \qquad \text{[11C.27]}$$

$\left(\text{Note that when } e = \infty, \dfrac{e + \sigma}{e + \eta} = 1.\right)$

Next, multiply out equation 11C.27:

$$\lambda - \sigma = (\eta - \lambda)\left(\frac{k}{1 - k}\right)\left(\frac{e + \sigma}{e + \eta}\right)$$

$$\lambda - \sigma = \left(\frac{\eta k}{1 - k}\right)\left(\frac{e + \sigma}{e + \eta}\right) - \left(\frac{\lambda k}{1 - k}\right)\left(\frac{e + \sigma}{e + \eta}\right)$$

$$\lambda = \frac{\eta k(e + \sigma)}{(1 - k)(e + \eta)} - \frac{\lambda k(e + \sigma)}{(1 - k)(e + \eta)} + \frac{\sigma(1 - k)(e + \eta)}{(1 - k)(e + \eta)}$$

$$\frac{\lambda(1 - k)(e + \eta)}{(1 - k)(e + \eta)} + \frac{\lambda k(e + \sigma)}{(1 - k)(e + \eta)} = \frac{\eta k(e + \sigma)}{(1 - k)(e + \eta)} + \frac{\sigma(1 - k)(e + \eta)}{(1 - k)(e + \eta)}$$

$$\frac{\lambda(e + \eta - ke - k\eta + ke + k\sigma)}{(1 - k)(e + \eta)} = \frac{\eta k(e + \sigma)}{(1 - k)(e + \eta)} + \frac{\sigma(1 - k)(e + \eta)}{(1 - k)(e + \eta)}$$

Divide by the second term on the left:

$$\lambda = \frac{\eta k(e + \sigma) + \sigma(1 - k)(e + \eta)}{[e + \eta - k(\eta - \sigma)]}$$

We multiply out the numerator of the expression:

$$\lambda = \frac{\eta ke + \eta k\sigma + \sigma e(1 - k) + \sigma\eta(1 - k)}{[e + \eta - k(\eta - \sigma)]}$$

$$\lambda = \frac{\eta ke + \eta k\sigma + \sigma e - k\sigma e + \sigma\eta - k\sigma\eta}{[e + \eta - k(\eta - \sigma)]}$$

$$\lambda = \frac{\sigma(\eta + e) + ke(\eta - \sigma)}{\eta + e - k(\eta - \sigma)} \qquad \text{[11C.28]}$$

Now Marshall's results, based on the special case where $e = \infty$, may be derived from equation 11C.27 in which on the right-hand side, $\dfrac{e + \sigma}{e + \eta} = 1$, since both numerator and denominator are equal to ∞. Thus, we have

$$\frac{\lambda - \sigma}{\eta - \lambda} = \frac{k}{1 - k} \qquad \text{[11C.27']}$$

Cross multiply and we get

$$k(\eta - \lambda) = (1 - k)(\lambda - \sigma)$$
$$\lambda = k\eta + \sigma - k\sigma$$
$$\lambda = k(\eta) + (1 - k)\sigma \qquad \text{[11C.28']}$$

In order to assess the effect of σ, k, e, and η on λ, we now differentiate equation 11C.28 with respect to each of these four variables:

$$\frac{\partial \lambda}{\partial \sigma} = \frac{[\eta + e - k(\eta - \sigma)][\eta + e - ke] - [\sigma(\eta + e) + ke(\eta - \sigma)](k)}{[\eta + e - k(\eta - \sigma)]^2}$$

With simplification this gives

$$\frac{\partial \lambda}{\partial \sigma} = (1 - k) \left[\frac{e + \eta}{\eta + e - k(\eta - \sigma)} \right]^2 \qquad [11C.29]$$

$$\frac{\partial \lambda}{\partial k} = \frac{[\eta + e - k(\eta - \sigma)][e(\eta - \sigma)] - [\sigma(\eta + e) + ke(\eta - \sigma)][\sigma - \eta]}{[\eta + e - k(\eta - \sigma)]^2}$$

With simplification this gives

$$\frac{\partial \lambda}{\partial k} = [(\eta - \sigma)(\eta + e)(e + \sigma)] \left[\frac{1}{\eta + e - k(\eta - \sigma)} \right]^2 \qquad [11C.30]$$

$$\frac{\partial \lambda}{\partial e} = \frac{[\eta + e - k(\eta - \sigma)][\sigma + k\eta - k\sigma] - [\sigma(\eta + e) + ke(\eta - \sigma)]}{[\eta + e - k(\eta - \sigma)]^2}$$

With simplification this gives

$$\frac{\partial \lambda}{\partial e} = k(1 - k) \left[\frac{\eta - \sigma}{\eta + e - k(\eta - \sigma)} \right]^2 \qquad [11C.31]$$

$$\frac{\partial \lambda}{\partial \eta} = \frac{[\eta + e - k(\eta - \sigma)][\sigma + ke] - [\sigma(\eta + e) + ke(\eta - \sigma)][1 - k]}{[\eta + e - k(\eta - \sigma)]^2}$$

With simplification this gives

$$\frac{\partial \lambda}{\partial \eta} = k \left[\frac{(e + \sigma)}{\eta + e - k(\eta - \sigma)} \right]^2 \qquad [11C.32]$$

Equation 11C.29 must be positive because the squared term is necessarily positive, and $1 - k$ must be positive because $k < 1$. Equation 11C.31 must also be positive for a comparable reason, as must equation 11C.32. However, equation 11C.30 may be positive or negative depending on $\eta \lessgtr \sigma$.

Appendix 11D

Elasticity of Substitution in the Theory of Demand[1]

It is interesting to show an analog to the income and substitution effects of a price change in terms of the elasticity of demand, income elasticity of demand, and elasticity of substitution. We can derive the elasticity of substitution along an indifference curve in an analogous fashion to the elasticity of substitution along an isoquant, as given in Appendix 11B.

Let σ_x be the partial elasticity of substitution with respect to X, defined as

$$\sigma_x = \frac{\dfrac{\partial X}{X}}{\dfrac{\partial R}{R}} \qquad [11\text{D}.1]$$

Analogously, let σ_y be the partial elasticity of substitution with respect to Y:

$$\sigma_y = \frac{\dfrac{\partial Y}{Y}}{\dfrac{\partial R}{R}} \qquad [11\text{D}.2]$$

We then define the reciprocals of these measures as

$$S_x = \frac{1}{\sigma_x} = -\frac{\partial R}{\partial X}\frac{X}{R} \qquad [11\text{D}.3]$$

$$S_y = \frac{1}{\sigma_y} = \frac{\partial R}{\partial Y}\frac{Y}{R} \qquad [11\text{D}.4]$$

To make clear the meaning of the partial elasticity of substitution and to compare it with the (total) elasticity of substitution, we present Figure 11D.1.

σ measures the ratio of (1) the change in the factor ratios in moving from point A to point B, that is, the change in the slope of a ray from the origin to the point as we move from A to B (the change in the slope of ray Oa as it rotates to Ob) to (2) the change in the marginal rate of

[1] This appendix is based on J. R. Hicks and R. G. D. Allen, "A Reconstruction of The Theory of Value," *Economica* 1, 52-76 and 196-219.

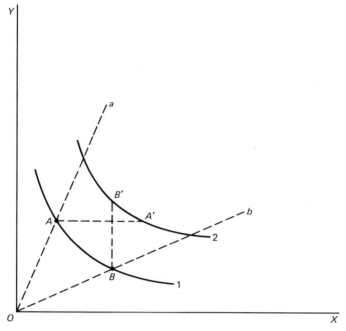

Figure 11D.1

substitution in going from A to B. In computing σ_x we hold the quantity of Y constant and change the quantity of X, moving to an adjacent contour line as in going from A to A'. σ_x measures the change in the factor ratio for this movement as a proportion of the change in the MRS in moving from A to A', and σ_y is an analogous measure for a movement from B to B'.

Let

$$k_x = \frac{XP_x}{M} \qquad\qquad [11\text{D}.5]$$

and

$$k_y = \frac{YP_y}{M} \qquad\qquad [11\text{D}.6]$$

represent the proportion of income spent on goods X and Y, with

$$k_x + k_y = 1 \qquad\qquad [11\text{D}.7]$$

The equilibrium conditions are

$$XP_x + YP_y = M \qquad\qquad [11\text{D}.8]$$

$$R = \frac{P_x}{P_y} = \frac{\dfrac{\partial U}{\partial X}}{\dfrac{\partial U}{\partial Y}} \qquad\qquad [11\text{D}.9]$$

In equilibrium, σ can be expressed as

$$\sigma = \frac{XR^2 + YR}{XY\left(R\dfrac{\partial R}{\partial Y} - \dfrac{\partial R}{\partial X}\right)} = \frac{X\left(\dfrac{P_x}{P_y}\right)^2 + Y\left(\dfrac{P_x}{P_y}\right)}{XY\left(\dfrac{P_x}{P_y}\dfrac{\partial R}{\partial Y} - \dfrac{\partial R}{\partial X}\right)}$$

$$\sigma = \frac{\dfrac{P_x}{P_y}\left(X\dfrac{P_x}{P_y} + Y\right)}{XY\left(\dfrac{P_x}{P_y}\dfrac{\partial R}{\partial Y} - \dfrac{\partial R}{\partial X}\right)} = \frac{\dfrac{P_x}{P_y}\left(\dfrac{M - YP_y}{P_y} + Y\right)}{XY\left(\dfrac{P_x}{P_y}\dfrac{\partial R}{\partial Y} - \dfrac{\partial R}{\partial X}\right)}$$

$$\sigma = \frac{\dfrac{P_x}{P_y}\left(\dfrac{M}{P_y} - Y + Y\right)}{XY\left(\dfrac{P_x}{P_y}\dfrac{\partial R}{\partial Y} - \dfrac{\partial R}{\partial X}\right)} = \frac{\dfrac{P_x}{P_y}\left(\dfrac{M}{P_y}\right)}{XY\left(\dfrac{P_x}{P_y}\dfrac{\partial R}{\partial Y} - \dfrac{\partial R}{\partial X}\right)}$$

Multiply each term by P_y:

$$\sigma = \frac{\dfrac{P_x}{P_y}\dfrac{M}{XY}}{P_x\dfrac{\partial R}{\partial Y} - P_y\dfrac{\partial R}{\partial X}} \qquad [11\text{D}.10]$$

In equilibrium, the reciprocals of the partial elasticities of substitution can be expressed as

$$S_x = -\frac{\partial R}{\partial X}\frac{X}{R} = -\frac{\partial R}{\partial X}X\frac{P_y}{P_x} \qquad [11\text{D}.11]$$

$$S_y = \frac{\partial R}{\partial Y}\frac{Y}{R} = \frac{\partial R}{\partial Y}Y\frac{P_y}{P_x} \qquad [11\text{D}.12]$$

We define the income elasticities as follows:

$$e_x = \frac{\partial X}{\partial M}\frac{M}{X} \qquad [11\text{D}.13]$$

$$e_y = \frac{\partial Y}{\partial M}\frac{M}{Y} \qquad [11\text{D}.14]$$

These expressions can be written as

$$\frac{\partial X}{\partial M} = e_x\frac{X}{M} \qquad [11\text{D}.15]$$

$$\frac{\partial Y}{\partial M} = e_y\frac{Y}{M} \qquad [11\text{D}.16]$$

We differentiate equilibrium condition 11D.8 with respect to M:

$$\frac{\partial X}{\partial M}P_x + \frac{\partial Y}{\partial M}P_y = 1$$

Substitute for $\dfrac{\partial X}{\partial M}$ and $\dfrac{\partial Y}{\partial M}$ from equations 11D.15 and 11D.16:

$$e_x \frac{X}{M} P_x + e_y \frac{Y}{M} P_y = 1$$

$$e_x X P_x + e_y Y P_y = M \qquad \text{[11D.17]}$$

Next, we differentiate equilibrium condition 11D.9 also with respect to M:

$$\frac{\partial R}{\partial X} \frac{\partial X}{\partial M} + \frac{\partial R}{\partial Y} \frac{\partial Y}{\partial M} = 0$$

Substitute for $\dfrac{\partial X}{\partial M}$ and $\dfrac{\partial Y}{\partial M}$ from equations 11D.15 and 11D.16:

$$\frac{\partial R}{\partial X} e_x \frac{X}{M} + \frac{\partial R}{\partial Y} e_y \frac{Y}{M} = 0$$

$$\frac{\partial R}{\partial X} e_x X + \frac{\partial R}{\partial Y} e_y Y = 0 \qquad \text{[11D.18]}$$

Thus, we have two equations in the two unknowns, e_x and e_y:

$$X P_x e_x + Y P_y e_y = M \qquad \text{[11D.17]}$$

$$\frac{\partial R}{\partial X} X e_x + \frac{\partial R}{\partial Y} Y e_y = 0 \qquad \text{[11D.18]}$$

We can solve for these unknowns using determinants. Let

$$D = \begin{vmatrix} X P_x & Y P_y \\ X \dfrac{\partial R}{\partial X} & Y \dfrac{\partial R}{\partial Y} \end{vmatrix}$$

$$D = X P_x Y \frac{\partial R}{\partial Y} - Y P_y X \frac{\partial R}{\partial X}$$

$$D = XY \left(P_x \frac{\partial R}{\partial Y} - P_y \frac{\partial R}{\partial X} \right) \qquad \text{[11D.19]}$$

Solving for e_x, we get

$$D_x = \begin{vmatrix} M & Y P_y \\ 0 & Y \dfrac{\partial R}{\partial Y} \end{vmatrix}$$

$$D_x = M Y \frac{\partial R}{\partial Y} \qquad \text{[11D.20]}$$

$$e_x = \frac{D_x}{D} = \frac{M Y \dfrac{\partial R}{\partial Y}}{XY \left(P_x \dfrac{\partial R}{\partial Y} - P_y \dfrac{\partial R}{\partial X} \right)}$$

$$e_x = \frac{\dfrac{\partial R}{\partial Y} \dfrac{M}{X}}{P_x \dfrac{\partial R}{\partial Y} - P_y \dfrac{\partial R}{\partial X}} \qquad \text{[11D.21]}$$

Multiply the equilibrium values for S_y and σ.

$$\frac{\partial R}{\partial Y} Y \frac{P_y}{P_x} \left(\frac{\dfrac{P_x}{P_y} \dfrac{M}{XY}}{P_x \dfrac{\partial R}{\partial Y} - P_y \dfrac{\partial R}{\partial X}} \right) = \frac{\dfrac{\partial R}{\partial Y} \dfrac{M}{X}}{P_x \dfrac{\partial R}{\partial Y} - P_y \dfrac{\partial R}{\partial X}} \qquad [11\text{D}.22]$$

Thus,

$$e_x = S_y \sigma \qquad [11\text{D}.23]$$

In an analogous fashion, we solve for e_y.

$$D_y = \begin{vmatrix} XP_x & M \\ X \dfrac{\partial R}{\partial X} & 0 \end{vmatrix}$$

$$D_y = -MX \frac{\partial R}{\partial X} \qquad [11\text{D}.24]$$

$$e_y = \frac{D_y}{D} = \frac{-MX \dfrac{\partial R}{\partial X}}{XY \left(P_x \dfrac{\partial R}{\partial Y} - P_y \dfrac{\partial R}{\partial X} \right)}$$

$$e_y = \frac{-\dfrac{M}{Y} \dfrac{\partial R}{\partial X}}{P_x \dfrac{\partial R}{\partial Y} - P_y \dfrac{\partial R}{\partial X}} \qquad [11\text{D}.25]$$

Multiply the equilibrium values for S_x and σ:

$$-\frac{\partial R}{\partial X} X \frac{P_y}{P_x} \left(\frac{\dfrac{P_x}{P_y} \dfrac{M}{XY}}{P_x \dfrac{\partial R}{\partial Y} - P_y \dfrac{\partial R}{\partial X}} \right) = \frac{-\dfrac{M}{Y} \dfrac{\partial R}{\partial X}}{P_x \dfrac{\partial R}{\partial Y} - P_y \dfrac{\partial R}{\partial X}} \qquad [11\text{D}.26]$$

Thus,

$$e_y = S_x \sigma \qquad [11\text{D}.27]$$

From equations 11D.5 and 11D.6, $XP_x = k_x M$ and $YP_y = k_y M$. Thus, equation 11D.17 can be written as

$$k_x M e_x + k_y M e_y = M$$

or

$$k_x e_x + k_y e_y = 1 \qquad [11\text{D}.28]$$

Substituting equations 11D.23 and 11D.27 into equation 11D.28, we can write

$$k_x S_y \sigma + k_y S_x \sigma = 1$$

or

$$k_x S_y + k_y S_x = \frac{1}{\sigma} \qquad [11\text{D}.29]$$

Next, we define price elasticities as follows:

$$E_x = -\frac{\partial X}{\partial P_x}\frac{P_x}{X} \qquad [11D.30]$$

$$E_{xy} = -\frac{\partial Y}{\partial P_x}\frac{P_y}{Y} \qquad [11D.31]$$

These can also be written as

$$\frac{\partial X}{\partial P_x} = -E_x \frac{X}{P_x} \qquad [11D.32]$$

$$\frac{\partial Y}{\partial P_x} = -E_{xy} \frac{Y}{P_x} \qquad [11D.33]$$

To determine these elasticities, first differentiate equilibrium condition 11D.8 with respect to P_x, with M and P_y constant:

$$X + P_x \frac{\partial X}{\partial P_x} + P_y \frac{\partial Y}{\partial P_x} = 0$$

or

$$-P_x \frac{\partial X}{\partial P_x} - P_y \frac{\partial Y}{\partial P_x} = X$$

Substituting equations 11D.32 and 11D.33, we get

$$E_x X + P_y E_{xy} \frac{Y}{P_x} = X$$

Multiplying by P_x, we have

$$XP_x E_x + YP_y E_{xy} = XP_x \qquad [11D.34]$$

Now differentiate equilibrium condition 11D.9 with respect to P_x:

$$\frac{\partial R}{\partial X}\frac{\partial X}{\partial P_x} + \frac{\partial R}{\partial Y}\frac{\partial Y}{\partial P_x} = \frac{P_y}{P_y{}^2} = \frac{1}{P_y}$$

Substituting equations 11D.32 and 11D.33 results in

$$-\frac{X}{P_x}\frac{\partial R}{\partial X}E_x - \frac{Y}{P_x}\frac{\partial R}{\partial Y}E_{xy} = \frac{1}{P_y}$$

Multiply by $-P_x$:

$$X\frac{\partial R}{\partial X}E_x + Y\frac{\partial R}{\partial Y}E_{xy} = -\frac{P_x}{P_y} \qquad [11D.35]$$

Thus, we have two equations in the two unknowns E_x and E_{xy}:

$$XP_x E_x + YP_y E_{xy} = XP_x \qquad [11D.34]$$

$$X\frac{\partial R}{\partial X}E_x + Y\frac{\partial R}{\partial Y}E_{xy} = -\frac{P_x}{P_y} \qquad [11D.35]$$

We use determinants to solve for these unknowns. First, we determine E_x:

$$D = \begin{vmatrix} X & YP_y \\ X\dfrac{\partial R}{\partial X} & Y\dfrac{\partial R}{\partial Y} \end{vmatrix}$$

$$D = XYP_x\frac{\partial R}{\partial Y} - XYP_y\frac{\partial R}{\partial X} \qquad [11D.36]$$

$$E_x = \frac{1}{D}\begin{vmatrix} XP_x & YP_y \\ -\dfrac{P_x}{P_y} & Y\dfrac{\partial R}{\partial Y} \end{vmatrix}$$

$$E_x = \frac{1}{D}\left(XYP_x\frac{\partial R}{\partial Y} + P_xY \right)$$

$$E_x = \frac{XYP_x\dfrac{\partial R}{\partial Y} + P_xY}{XYP_x\dfrac{\partial R}{\partial Y} - XYP_y\dfrac{\partial R}{\partial X}} = \frac{P_x\dfrac{\partial R}{\partial Y} + \dfrac{P_x}{X}}{P_x\dfrac{\partial R}{\partial Y} - P_y\dfrac{\partial R}{\partial X}}$$

From equation 11D.10,

$$P_x\frac{\partial R}{\partial Y} - P_y\frac{\partial R}{\partial X} = \frac{\dfrac{P_x}{P_y}\dfrac{M}{XY}}{\sigma}$$

Thus,

$$E_x = \left(P_x\frac{\partial R}{\partial Y} + \frac{P_x}{X} \right)\left(\frac{\sigma}{\dfrac{P_x}{P_y}\dfrac{M}{XY}} \right)$$

or

$$E_x = \sigma P_x\frac{\partial R}{\partial Y}\frac{P_y}{P_x}\frac{XY}{M} + \sigma\frac{P_x}{X}\frac{P_y}{P_x}\frac{XY}{M}$$

From equation 11D.12,

$$S_y = \frac{\partial R}{\partial Y}Y\frac{P_y}{P_x}$$

Thus,

$$E_x = \sigma P_x S_y\frac{X}{M} + \sigma P_y\frac{Y}{M}$$

From equations 11D.5 and 11D.6, $\dfrac{P_xX}{M} = k_x$ and $\dfrac{P_yY}{M} = k_y = 1 - k_x$, and from equation 11D.23, $S_y\,\sigma = e_x$. Therefore,

$$E_x = e_xk_x + (1 - k_x)\sigma \qquad [11D.37]$$

We solve in an analogous fashion for E_{xy}:

$$E_{xy} = \frac{1}{D} \begin{vmatrix} XP_x & XP_x \\ X\dfrac{\partial R}{\partial X} & -\dfrac{P_x}{P_y} \end{vmatrix}$$

$$E_{xy} = \frac{1}{D}\left(-\frac{P_x^2}{P_y}X - X^2 P_x \frac{\partial R}{\partial X} \right) \qquad [11D.38]$$

$$E_{xy} = \frac{-\dfrac{P_x^2}{P_y}X - X^2 P_x \dfrac{\partial R}{\partial X}}{XY\left(P_x \dfrac{\partial R}{\partial Y} - P_y \dfrac{\partial R}{\partial X}\right)} = \frac{-\dfrac{P_x^2}{P_y Y} - \dfrac{XP_x}{Y}\dfrac{\partial R}{\partial X}}{P_x \dfrac{\partial R}{\partial Y} - P_y \dfrac{\partial R}{\partial X}}$$

$$E_{xy} \doteq \left(-\frac{P_x^2}{P_y Y} - \frac{XP_x}{Y}\frac{\partial P}{\partial X}\right)\left(\frac{\sigma}{\dfrac{P_x}{P_y}\dfrac{M}{XY}}\right)$$

$$E_{xy} = -\frac{P_x^2 \sigma}{P_x \dfrac{M}{X}} - \frac{\sigma XP_x \dfrac{\partial R}{\partial X}}{P_x \dfrac{M}{P_y}\dfrac{}{X}} = -\frac{P_x X}{M}\sigma - \frac{XP_x \dfrac{\partial R}{\partial X}\sigma P_y X}{P_x M}$$

Substituting from equation 11D.11, $S_x = -\dfrac{\partial R}{\partial X} X \dfrac{P_y}{P_x}$, and from equation 11D.5, $\dfrac{P_x X}{M} = k_x$:

$$E_{xy} = -k_x\sigma + S_x k_x\sigma$$

And from equation 11D.27, $e_y = S_x\,\sigma$. Therefore,

$$E_{xy} = k_x e_y - k_x\sigma \qquad [11D.39]$$

We now wish to determine the effect of a change in P_y on Y and X. We first define the following price elasticities:

$$E_y = -\frac{P_y}{Y}\frac{\partial Y}{\partial P_y} \qquad [11D.40]$$

$$E_{yx} = -\frac{P_y}{X}\frac{\partial X}{\partial P_y} \qquad [11D.41]$$

These expressions can be rewritten as

$$\frac{\partial Y}{\partial P_y} = -E_y \frac{Y}{P_y} \qquad [11D.42]$$

$$\frac{\partial X}{\partial P_y} = -E_{yx}\frac{X}{P_y} \qquad [11D.43]$$

Next, differentiate equilibrium condition 11D.8 with respect to P_y:

$$P_x \frac{\partial X}{\partial P_y} + Y + P_y \frac{\partial Y}{\partial P_y} = 0$$

$$P_x \frac{\partial X}{\partial P_y} + P_y \frac{\partial Y}{\partial P_y} = -Y$$

Substituting equations 11D.42 and 11D.43, we get

$$-P_x \frac{X}{P_y} E_{yx} - P_y \frac{Y}{P_y} E_y = -Y$$

or

$$P_x X E_{yx} + P_y Y E_y = P_y Y \qquad [11D.44]$$

Now differentiate equilibrium condition 11D.9 with respect to P_y:

$$\frac{\partial R}{\partial X} \frac{\partial X}{\partial P_y} + \frac{\partial R}{\partial Y} \frac{\partial Y}{\partial P_y} = -\frac{P_x}{P_y{}^2}$$

Again substituting equations 11D.42 and 11D.43, we get

$$-\frac{\partial R}{\partial X} \frac{X}{P_y} E_{yx} - \frac{\partial R}{\partial Y} \frac{Y}{P_y} E_y = -\frac{P_x}{P_y{}^2}$$

or

$$\frac{\partial R}{\partial X} X E_{yx} + \frac{\partial R}{\partial Y} Y E_y = \frac{P_x}{P_y} \qquad [11D.45]$$

We, again, have two equations in two unknowns, E_y and E_{yx}:

$$P_x X E_{yx} + P_y Y E_y = P_y Y \qquad [11D.44]$$

$$\frac{\partial R}{\partial X} X E_{yx} + \frac{\partial R}{\partial Y} Y E_y = \frac{P_x}{P_y} \qquad [11D.45]$$

Following the same procedure as above, we have

$$D = \begin{vmatrix} P_y Y & P_x X \\ \dfrac{\partial R}{\partial Y} Y & \dfrac{\partial R}{\partial X} X \end{vmatrix}$$

$$D = \frac{\partial R}{\partial X} X P_y Y - \frac{\partial R}{\partial Y} Y P_x X \qquad [11D.46]$$

Solving for E_y:

$$E_y = \frac{1}{D} \begin{vmatrix} P_y Y & P_x X \\ \dfrac{P_x}{P_y} & \dfrac{\partial R}{\partial X} X \end{vmatrix}$$

$$E_y = \frac{1}{D} \left[\frac{\partial R}{\partial X} X P_y Y - \frac{(P_x)^2}{P_y} X \right] \qquad [11D.47]$$

$$E_y = \frac{\dfrac{\partial R}{\partial X} X P_y Y - \dfrac{(P_x)^2}{P_y} X}{\dfrac{\partial R}{\partial X} X P_y Y - \dfrac{\partial R}{\partial Y} Y P_x X} = \frac{\dfrac{\partial R}{\partial X} P_y - \dfrac{(P_x)^2}{P_y Y}}{\dfrac{\partial R}{\partial X} P_y - \dfrac{\partial R}{\partial Y} P_x}$$

From equation 11D.10,

$$\frac{\partial R}{\partial X} P_y - \frac{\partial R}{\partial Y} P_x = \frac{-\sigma}{\dfrac{P_x}{P_y} \dfrac{M}{XY}}$$

Thus,

$$E_y = \left[\frac{\partial R}{\partial X} P_y - \frac{(P_x)^2}{P_y Y} \right] \left(\frac{-\sigma}{\dfrac{P_x}{P_y} \dfrac{M}{XY}} \right)$$

$$E_y = - \frac{\sigma \dfrac{\partial R}{\partial X} P_y P_y XY}{P_x M} + \frac{\sigma (P_x)^2 P_y XY}{P_x P_y YM}$$

From equation 11D.11, $S_x = - \dfrac{\partial R}{\partial X} X \dfrac{P_y}{P_x}$, and from equations 11D.5

and 11D.6, $k_x = \dfrac{XP_x}{M}$ and $k_y = \dfrac{YP_y}{M}$. Thus, we can substitute

$$E_y = \sigma S_x k_y + \sigma k_x$$

And from equation 11D.27, $e_y = S_x \sigma$. Therefore,

$$E_y = e_y k_y + (1 - k_y)\sigma \qquad [11\text{D}.48]$$

Last, solving for E_{yx}:

$$E_{yx} = \frac{1}{D} \begin{vmatrix} P_y Y & P_y Y \\ \dfrac{\partial R}{\partial Y} Y & \dfrac{P_x}{P_y} \end{vmatrix}$$

$$E_{yx} = \frac{1}{D} \left(P_x Y - \frac{\partial R}{\partial Y} P_y YY \right) \qquad [11\text{D}.49]$$

$$E_{yx} = \frac{P_x Y - \dfrac{\partial R}{\partial Y} P_y YY}{\dfrac{\partial R}{\partial X} XP_y Y - \dfrac{\partial R}{\partial Y} YP_x X} = \frac{\dfrac{P_x}{X} - \dfrac{\partial R}{\partial Y} P_y \dfrac{Y}{X}}{\dfrac{\partial R}{\partial X} P_y - \dfrac{\partial R}{\partial Y} P_x}$$

Substituting from equation 11D.10:

$$E_{yx} = \left(\frac{P_x}{X} - \frac{\partial R}{\partial Y} P_y \frac{Y}{X} \right) \left(\frac{-\sigma}{\dfrac{P_x}{P_y} \dfrac{M}{XY}} \right) = \frac{-\sigma P_x P_y XY}{XP_x M} + \frac{\partial R}{\partial Y} P_y \frac{Y}{X} \frac{\sigma P_y XY}{P_x M}$$

Using equations 11D.5, 11D.6, and 11D.12, we have

$$E_{yx} = -\sigma k_y + S_y \sigma k_y$$

Substituting equation 11D.23, we get

$$E_{yx} = e_x k_y - \sigma k_y \qquad [11\text{D}.50]$$

12

SUPPLY OF FACTORS AND THE FUNCTIONAL DISTRIBUTION OF INCOME

Although we used the factor labor for illustrative purposes in our discussion of factor pricing, the determinants of the supply of the different factors vary. Later we discuss briefly the other factors; in this section we deal with the determinants of the supply of labor in the short run and the long run.

One unique attribute of the labor market in most countries is that there is a market for labor services alone, not for the laborers themselves. (This can be contrasted with the factor capital where there are two markets—one for the services of capital goods and the other for the goods themselves.) Another consequence of the nonslave society is that the owner of the labor must be present when the labor service is being provided. The owner of a capital good is largely unconcerned with the milieu in which the good is operated. However, the supplier of labor is generally much concerned with the environment in which he must supply his labor.

In the short run, the population, its age/sex composition, and its education and skills level are given. The short-run supply schedule of labor relates the alternative quantities of labor units supplied to various wage rates. We demonstrate the derivation of the short-run supply curve with reference to Figure 12.1. In this diagram we show representative curves of the indifference map showing an individual's preference ranking between earnings and work. Notice that we are assuming that the maximum number of hours the individual can work is 12 hours per day. Note also that, contrary to the indifference maps of Chapter 5, the indifference curves have a positive slope and are convex to the horizontal axis and

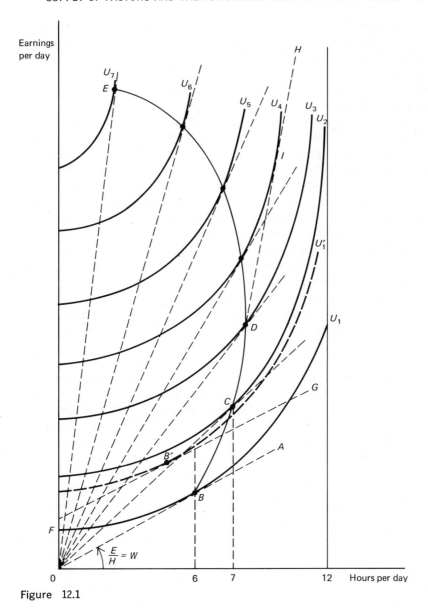

Figure 12.1

concave to the vertical axis. In terms of the utility hill of Figure 5.5, we are in quadrant II where the commodity on the horizontal axis represents a disutility. (If we had chosen to show the relationship between leisure and earnings, the indifference curves would have their usual shape.) The fact that as we move from left to right, the indifference curves become increasingly vertical, implies that as more hours of work are performed, income becomes a decreasingly good substitute for work.

The prevailing wage rate can be taken as the ratio of earnings per day to hours worked per day; or, in graphical terms, the slope of a line such as OA anchored at the origin indicates a given wage rate. We shall call this the "wage line," which when pivoted from right to left indicates ever higher wages.

In the usual manner, we generate the locus of tangency points between indifference curves and wage lines ($BCDE$). Notice that this price-offer curve (analogous to the price-consumption curve of Chapter 5) is upward sloping to point D and then bends back toward the vertical axis. This particular shape can be explained in terms of income and substitution effects. For example, suppose the individual was initially in equilibrium at point B, working six hours per day and earning \$12. Now assume that the wage rate increases from \$2 to \$2.50. If he continued to work 6 hours, his daily earnings would increase by \$3. Because his income is greater, he desires less of the disutility, work (or more of the superior good, leisure). This income effect in itself would result in a decline in the number of hours worked. However, the substitution effect is in the opposite direction; that is, since the earnings from a marginal hour worked have increased from \$2 to \$2.50, there is a tendency for the individual to work more.

In Figure 12.1, we can decompose the total effect of the wage increase (the movement from B to C) into the income and substitution effects using a Slutsky-type measure. To isolate the income effect, we construct wage line FG that is parallel to the original wage line but that intersects the vertical axis at a point \$3 higher than the original. (The \$3 represents the increase in the individual's income that would arise by working the original 6 hours at the new wage.) Such an increase in income would move the individual from B to B'; this is the income effect. Notice that B' lies to the left of B; the income effect has caused a decrease in the quantity of labor supplied. The residual movement from B' to C is the substitution effect that acts to increase work.

For the wage rate increase just described, the substitution effect outweighed the income effect. In fact, this would be the case for all wage increases up to point D. Beyond D, the reverse would be true, with the result that the total effect of a wage rate increase would be a decline in the number of hours worked.

An increase in wages to elicit an increased supply of labor is self-defeating beyond D. However, an overtime rate can be used to accomplish this purpose. Such a rate is shown by the slope of line DH that begins at point D on the price-offer curve. The wage line then becomes the angled-line ODH and the point I represents an equilibrium at a higher level of employment than at point D. It is to be noted that the overtime rate can achieve what the across-the-board wage increase cannot because the former results only in a substitution effect while with the latter there is also an offsetting income effect.

The usual supply curve can be obtained from the price-offer curve. The number of hours is read from the horizontal axis, and the corresponding wage rates are read as the slopes of the appropriate wage lines. Clearly, the supply curve derived from a backward-bending price-offer curve will be backward bending also.

To obtain the aggregate supply curve of labor, we sum the individuals' labor supply curves. It is extremely unlikely that the aggregate curve will bend backwards at a relevant wage rate due to the random distribution of psychological factors that determine the levels at which the backward bends take place.

The long-run supply curve of labor is based on neither any assumption regarding the constancy of the population nor its composition as to age, sex, education, and skills. It is instructive to view the size of the population as a function of the motive that cause families to have children. Children can be regarded in two ways: they are a potential source of satisfaction (utility) to their parents (that is, consumer goods); however, in addition they also have the characteristics of producer goods in that they are a potential source of family income and means of support for their parents in their parents' old age.

In determining the size of the family, the potential cost of having and raising children in excess of the potential returns from the children as producer goods must be weighed against the marginal utility from the children as consumer goods.[1] This model is useful in explaining much of the long-run population changes that have occurred in the United States. For example, as the United States became more urbanized, the cost of raising children increased while their value as producers' goods (which was substantial in a rural economy) declined. The result was a decline in average family size. Today, it is still true that rural family size exceeds urban family size.

In addition to the size of the population, there are economic considerations that help determine the size of the labor force[2] as well as its composition as to age, sex, education, and skills. Some of the factors determining the number of people in the labor force are average age of entry into and exit from the labor force, the supply of nonhuman substitutes for women in the home, and child-labor legislation and other legal and

---

[1] It is interesting to note that potential costs and returns are not independent, because investment in children will have an effect on their future earning capacity. One reason why parents may choose not to invest to a socially optimum degree in their children's education is that they are not assured that the investment will result in a sufficient return to them.

[2] By the size of the labor force is meant not only the people working but, in addition, the people who are actively engaged in seeking work.

institutional restrictions. The level of education within a society can be thought of as of two kinds: (1) a basic level provided mainly by society, which, in the United States at this time consists of at least a secondary education and increasingly encompasses some college training, and (2) a more advanced level, which consists of preprofessional, professional, and graduate training. The extent of the basic level is determined in part by a desire on the part of society for a minimally educated electorate and a minimally literate labor force. What is considered to be a basic level of education varies from country to country and over time. In general, the higher the levels of income and education, the greater will be the demand for further basic education.

The extent that advanced education will be pursued is largely a private decision. The individual may be thought of as weighing investment in nonhuman capital against investment in human capital. The comparison would consist of estimating the future income stream attributable to the extra education and the income stream that would result from an alternative investment and then discounting these future income streams to the present, using the current rate of interest. The individual, basing his investment decision on rates of return alone, would choose that investment that yielded the highest return.[3]

[3] A simple numerical example will make clear the meaning of discounting to the present. Suppose that the annual market rate of interest is 5 percent and an individual has $100 for investment. At the end of one year, this $100 will be worth $105.

$$\$105 = 1.05(\$100)$$
$$FV = (1 + i)(PV)$$

where

FV = the future value of the investment
i = annual market rate of interest in decimal terms
PV = the initial investment

Next assume that an offer is made to this individual to sell him an IOU that comes due one year hence and will pay $105. Because he can earn $105 for $100 investment in the market, it is clear he would be willing to pay a maximum of $100 to acquire the $105 IOU. This same result can be obtained by solving the above equation for PV

$$PV = \frac{FV}{1 + i} = \$100 = \frac{\$105}{1.05}$$

Now assume the initial investment of $100 is left in the market for 2 years. We have seen that at the end of 1 year, the $100 was worth $105; that is $100(1.05). Assuming the rate of interest remains at 5 percent, the $105 at the end of the second year would be worth $110.25, that is, $105(1.05) or

$$[\$100(1.05)](1.05) = \$100(1.05)^2$$
$$FV = (PV)(1 + i)(1 + i)$$

Once again, if the individual was offered an IOU of $110.25, payable in 2 years, he would clearly only be willing to pay $100 for it because this sum invested for 2 years

Should the individual choose to invest in advanced education even though the discounted return is less than that from some alternative investment, he must expect the education to yield some satisfaction to him other than the monetary reward. The same kind of comparison can be used by an individual in deciding among different occupations or in choosing an advanced educational track. The individual can compare both the monetary and nonmonetary returns from different fields. Some of the nonmonetary factors to be taken into account are the variability of income, life-time earnings patterns, and the risks involved (this involves the distribution of income within the occupation and the probability of achieving a given income). It should be noted that in assessing the net monetary returns, included in the costs (in addition to education) would be the foregone income during the period of training and apprenticeship, the cost of tools and equipment, and the living costs at the place of occupation.

In the long run we would expect competition to equalize wages for a specific type of labor in different occupations and different geographical areas. The fact that wage differences do exist should not be taken as evidence of a lack of competition. These differences are often "equalizing" differences; that is, they exist to equalize the net advantage from different lines of work. The net advantage includes both monetary and nonmonetary factors. Among the nonmonetary factors are danger, pleasantness of surroundings, and social esteem for the occupation.

There are rigidities, which while lessened in the long run, nonetheless exist. These are known as "nonequalizing" differences and include such factors as the inability to borrow funds for investment in advanced education, the time required to acquire necessary skills and training, government licensing, and union restrictions on entry. These nonequalizing differences result in the existence of noncompeting groups. These noncompeting groups are of more importance in the short run because in the

---

would pay this much. In other words,

$$PV = \frac{FV}{(1 + i)^2} = \$100 = \frac{\$110.25}{(1.05)^2}$$

This can be extended for n years so that

$$FV = (1 + i)^n (PV)$$

and

$$PV = \frac{FV}{(1 + i)^n}$$

Last, consider an investment that yields net returns over costs, R_i, in a series of years $(R_1, R_2, \ldots, R_n)$. The present value of this stream of future earnings can be calculated as

$$PV = \frac{R_1}{(1 + i)} + \frac{R_2}{(1 + i)^2} + \cdots + \frac{R_n}{(1 + i)^n}$$

long run there is increased mobility among occupations due to the longer period of time to acquire the education and skills needed in order to shift jobs. (Given a long enough period of time, manual laborers can become engineers.)

THE EFFECT OF GOVERNMENT REGULATION ON MONOPSONY

Minimum-wage laws are sometimes defended on the ground that they help to counter the effects of monopsony power. In Figure 12.2 we show

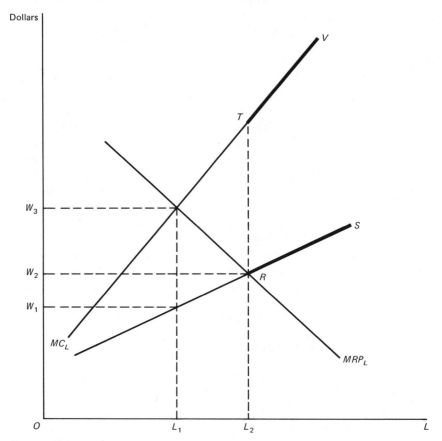

Figure 12.2

the effects of minimum-wage legislation on a monopsonist. We assume that prior to the imposition of a minimum wage, the equilibrium quantity of labor employed is L_1 and the corresponding wage rate is W_1. If a minimum wage of W_2 is imposed, the effective supply curve facing the firm becomes W_2RS, and the corresponding MC_L curve is coincident with the supply curve over the range W_2R, becomes discontinuous at R, and then becomes TV. If the firm is to maximize its profit, it will hire L_2 units of labor, since at L_2 the equilibrium conditions are being fulfilled:

$$\text{Below } L_2,\ MRP_L > MC_L$$
$$\text{Above } L_2,\ MRP_L < MC_L$$

Because the monopsonist was maximizing profit before the imposition of the minimum wage (and consequently L_1 was the optimum quantity of the factor hired), when the monopsonist hires L_2, profits decline.

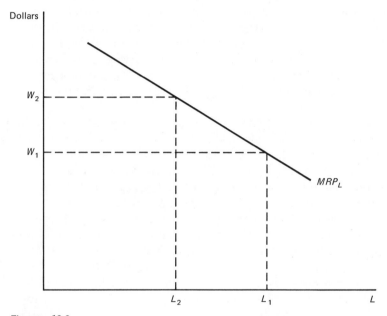

Figure 12.3

It is true that if monopsony exists and if the minimum wage can be set at the level where the supply curve cuts MRP_L, the monopsonist will be forced to pay the higher wage as well as to offer more employment. But if monopsony is not often encountered, it would be foolish to set an economy-wide minimum wage to offset it. In more competitive labor markets, the minimum wage will certainly reduce employment in industries paying less than the minimum; this is shown in Figure 12.3.

Further, even if it were true that monopsony pervaded the economy, it would be highly unlikely that an economy-wide minimum wage would be for all, or even most, monopsonists the wage that would increase factor employment. If the economy-wide minimum wage were set higher than W_3 in Figure 12.2, this would cause the monopsonist to reduce the quantity of labor hired. We must conclude, therefore, that an economy-wide minimum wage is too gross an instrument for dealing with diverse monopsony.

EFFECTS OF UNIONS

Unions can affect wage rates and total labor income in several ways, the most important of which is restricting the supply of labor and the determination of wage rates through collective bargaining.

We first investigate the effects of a union on a firm with no monopsony power. In Figure 12.3 we assume that W_1 is the competitive wage rate and that the firm hires the equilibrium quantity of labor, L_1. Now assume that, through collective bargaining, the wage rate that the firm must now pay increases to W_2. Consequently, the firm will now employ L_2 units of labor. Thus, the short-run effect of the higher wage is a decrease in employment. The new total wage bill of the firm, W_2L_2, can be greater than, less than, or equal to the old wage bill, W_1L_1, for labor, depending on the elasticity of demand.[4]

Most likely, the elasticity of demand will be greater in the long run than in the short run. This is true because the demand for the finished product will tend to be more elastic in the long run; and, because in the long run all factors are variable, the firm will be able to achieve the most economical combination of factors. Furthermore, in the long run, the supply of other factors will tend to be more elastic.

Next, let us assume that the firm in Figure 12.3 is a perfect competitor in the product market and the only one, or one of several, to be unionized. In the short run, the firm's costs will be higher because of the unionization; however, it will keep producing as long as $P \geq AVC$. In the long run, price in a perfectly competitive industry will be equal to minimum LAC; therefore, because the firm's costs will be higher than those of the other firms in the industry, it will be forced to leave the industry.

If the firm in Figure 12.3 is perfectly competitive but all other firms in the industry are also unionized, then the costs of all firms will be higher and in the long run the price of the good will also be higher. As a result of the higher costs, the long-run industry supply curve is higher, and long-run equilibrium output will be reduced. Thus, factor employment will also go down.

Perfectly competitive industries are generally difficult to unionize because of their large numbers of firms. Thus, the most effective unions are in industries where there are a small number of firms and/or industries that are geographically concentrated.

If the union deals with a firm that is an imperfect competitor in the product market, the adjustment of the firm to the higher wage rate will

[4] The determinants of the elasticity of demand for a factor were discussed in the previous chapter.

be an increase in the price of the product and a decrease in the quantity of the good sold. In fact, the reduction in employment will be less for the monopolistic firm than for the competitive one. This is illustrated in Figure 12.4, where we assume that both firms have the same marginal

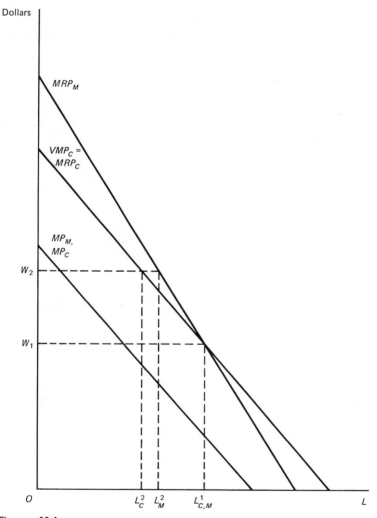

Figure 12.4

productivity schedules. Because the perfectly competitive firm faces a constant market price, the MRP ($\equiv VMP$) schedule will be parallel to the MP schedule. The monopolist, however, faces a downward-sloping demand curve; therefore, marginal revenue is also negatively sloped. We assume that for the output corresponding to the input $L'_{C,M}$, the MR

for the competitive firm is equal to that of the monopolist. Therefore, at $L'_{C,M}$, the MRP's are the same. Because the monopolist has a negatively sloped MR schedule, for inputs less than $L'_{C,M}$ (and thus for smaller outputs), MRP_M will be greater than MRP_C; and for greater inputs than $L'_{C,M}$, $MRP_M < MRP_C$.

In the absence of unionization and a wage rate of W_1, both firms will hire $L'_{C,M}$ units because, for both firms, $MRP = W_1$. Now let us assume that a union imposes a wage of W_2. The competitive firm will hire $L_C{}^2$ units of labor; the monopolist, $L_M{}^2$ units. The reason for the greater reduction in the amount of labor employed by the competitive firm is that a greater burden is thrown on output adjustment; in fact, this is the only adjustment possible for the competitive firm. On the other hand, the monopolist adjusts both price and quantity and, therefore, reduces labor employment by a smaller amount.

In the long run, the ability of the union to keep the wage above its free-market equilibrium level, in the face of resulting unemployment, will depend on the union's ability to maintain its power under these conditions. If the unionized industry is a growing one, the union will be able to accomplish this if it has control over entry into the union. Instead of creating unemployment under these conditions, employment will be prevented from growing as rapidly as it would in the absence of the union wage.

The effect of a union dealing with a monopsony is demonstrated in Figure 12.2. Before the imposition of a union wage rate, the monopsonist hires L_1 units and pays W_1 per unit. A union wage of anything greater than W_1 but less than W_3 will force the monopsonist both to increase labor hire and to pay a higher wage rate. W_2 is the wage rate that maximizes employment. If the union is interested not in the maximization of employment but in the maximization of the total wages paid by the firm, the wage rate selected will depend on the elasticity of demand for labor.

OBSERVATIONS ON THE FACTORS OF PRODUCTION OTHER THAN LABOR

Our discussion of factor pricing has been centered about the factor labor that accounts for approximately 80 percent of the United States' national income. In this section, without going into detail, we shall discuss the most important unique attributes of the other factors of production. First we consider land.

Historically, rent has been the return to land. Land was considered a unique factor of production because of its fixity of supply from the point of view of the economy as a whole.[5] The term *rent* has come to be used

[5] In reality, the supply of land is not completely fixed. For example, land can be eroded away over time and land-fill projects can reclaim swamps. In addition, if we

to mean the return to any factor of production in fixed supply and, more generally, the return to a factor in excess of its return in its most remunerative alternative occupation. This is called the opportunity cost.

Because rent is a payment of a factor that is fixed in supply, it is not a necessary payment to elicit a supply of the factor. In some cases, a factor is fixed in supply only temporarily, and this led Alfred Marshall to call the payment to this factor in the short run a "quasi-rent."

The most fixed attribute of land is its location, so that the reason it receives a rental payment is due to such factors as its distance from the central city, its proximity to means of natural transportation, and its proximity to scenic wonders. A factor of production that is specific to a given industry may receive a rent payment from the point of view of that industry. Consider a ball player, appropriately named Home Run Harry, whose only other skill is digging ditches. Assume the going wage rate for ditch diggers is $5000 a year and that Harry has signed a contract with the Spaders Club for $100,000 per year. From the point of view of any club within the baseball industry, the $100,000 represents a cost; however, to the industry as a whole, $95,000 represents a rent because this is the excess over Harry's opportunity cost outside the industry. The rent received by Harry is shown as the shaded area in Figure 12.5 and represents the excess of $100,000 over the opportunity cost of $5000.

It will be recalled that prices play two roles in the economy: (1) to bring about changes in the supply of a factor and (2) to ration the available supply of a factor. However, rent fulfills only the second of these functions. As an example, assume a lake stocked with fish that is owned by an individual who charges a fee for fishing with the use of power boats. This fee limits the use of the lake. Now assume the government acquires the lake and decides to remove the fee. This results in an increased use of the lake that directly decreases the supply of fish, and of more importance, the waste from the gasoline engines plus the increased refuse discarded by the fishermen unfavorably alters the ecology of the lake, which may irreparably reduce the ability of the lake to support a fish population. It is clear in this case that, although the payment for the use of this fixed resource (rent) does not effect the supply, it does serve the important purpose of rationing the use of a valuable natural resource.

It should also be noted that because the demand for a factor in fixed supply is a derived demand, the price for its services will reflect the level

---

are concerned not only with the physical area of land but also with land as a productive agent, then the productivity of soil can be changed by fertilization, irrigation, and so on. Furthermore, it is obvious that the mineral content of land is subject to depletion. It is true, though, that relative to other factors of production, the supply of land can change only very gradually over time.

of demand for the product that it produces. In this sense, the price per unit of the factor's service is price determined. From the point of view of the firm, these payments represent a cost, that is, an amount that must be paid to obtain this factor (because the factor has alternative uses in the other firms in the economy). However, from the point of view of the economy as a whole, the payments do not represent a factor cost because they are not necessary to obtain the supply of the factor. Thus, from this point of view, it may be said that rent is price determined rather than price determining.

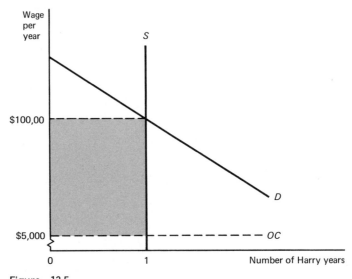

Figure 12.5

We now briefly turn to capital and interest, which is perhaps the most complex area in all of economic theory. Because of its complexity, we merely attempt to clear up some definitional problems in our discussion.

A general definition of "capital" is any asset that yields a flow of services over any appreciable period of time; furthermore, this flow is augmentable through investment. Thus, capital is a stock concept, that is, it can be measured at a given moment of time; whereas, investment is a flow concept, that is, so many units per time period. The net investment (investment over and above the capital goods that have worn out, that is, replacement purposes) during a year measures the change in the stock of capital for that year.

There are two prices associated with a capital good. The first is a price for the use of the capital and the other is the price for the capital good itself. This latter price (as we saw on p. 280) is equal to the present value of the discounted stream of future earnings. The former price is simply a payment for factor hire; in the case of labor, it is called a wage, and in the case of capital, it is called interest.

Assume a firm that has available a given sum of money, X dollars, which it can either lend out in the money market at the market rate of interest or use internally for investment in capital goods. In order to make a decision, the firm will compare the expected rate of return from these capital goods with the market rate of interest. In order to illustrate this comparison, let us assume that the investment in the capital goods is a 1-year investment. Assume that the sum of money earned from the capital goods at the end of the year, exclusive of all costs except depreciation, is R and that the cost of the capital is C. Then $R/C > 1$ if this is a profitable investment. Or $R/C = 1 + r$ where r is the internal rate of return on the investment. We can also write $C = \dfrac{R}{1 + r}$ where r can be seen to be the discount rate that equates C with R. Obviously, if the market rate of interest exceeded r, the firm would not undertake the investment, but instead put its funds in the money market.

Now let us assume the capital project is for a period of n years and that the returns are $R_1, R_2, \ldots, R_n$. Then

$$C = \frac{R_1}{(1 + r)} + \frac{R_2}{(1 + r)^2} + \cdots + \frac{R_n}{(1 + r)^n}$$

where, it should be remembered, $R_1 \cdot \cdot \cdot R_n$ and C are knowns and the firm must solve for r.

The last factor payment to be considered briefly is profit. There are various definitions of "profit." First, there is "monopoly profit," which we have already discussed. Second, there is a return to a unique factor of production that we have discussed under the heading of "rent" but that is often called "profit" when the unique factor is entrepreneurship. Finally, in the absence of a unique factor of production or monopoly power, the presence of pure economic profits in short-run competitive equilibrium can be said to be a return to the entrepreneur for bearing the unavoidable risks of the firm.

PRODUCT EXHAUSTION WITHIN THE FIRM

By the "functional distribution of income" we mean the distribution of the value of output among the cooperating factors of production. At first, we will discuss distribution within the context of the firm and then for the economy as a whole. We have already seen that a perfectly competitive firm pays each variable factor the value of its marginal product. The question that logically presents itself is, Will the payment to the factors of the value of their marginal products just exhaust, overexhaust, or underexhaust the total value of the product?

If the production function is linear homogeneous, Euler's theorem holds.[6] This theorem states that for any linear homogeneous function where output is a function of X and Y [that is, $q = q(X, Y)$], it is true that

$$q = MP_xX + MP_yY \qquad [12.1]$$

If we multiply both sides by the price of the product, P, we get

$$Pq = MP_xPX + MP_yPY \qquad [12.2]$$

This can be rewritten as

$$Pq = VMP_xX + VMP_yY \qquad [12.3]$$

In words, this means with a linear homogeneous production function, if the factors receive the value of their marginal products, then these payments just exhaust the value of the product.

As we explained in Chapter 10, competition in any industry that consists of firms with constant returns to scale will probably break down because the size of the firm is now indeterminant. The usual assumption concerning perfect competition is that the firms are subject to increasing returns to scale followed by decreasing returns to scale. The point at which decreasing returns to scale sets in, acts as the effective limit to the size of the firm. We have seen that each firm in the long run produces at the point where average cost is at its minimum. At this output, average cost is momentarily stationary, and the firm may be said to be momentarily subject to constant cost or constant returns to scale. In terms of the two-dimensional cross section of the production surface (Figure 12.6), a ray from the origin, such as OZ, is tangent to the total product curve at P. Thus, the average returns to scale, q/k, is a maximum at k_1. Every factor proportion can be represented by a different ray from the origin of the three-dimensional production surface. Where a given ray touches the three-dimensional surface gives a point such as P. Then, for a given factor proportion defined by this given ray, slicing down perpendicular to the horizontal plane gives a total product schedule such as OPq. By assuming different rays from the origin (that is, different factor proportions), a series of points such as P can be obtained that trace out a locus of maximum average product points (which, given factor prices, also is the locus of minimum average cost points) that may descriptively be called the "horizon line."

Because we know that the perfectly competitive firm produces at minimum average cost and that the point of minimum average cost lies on the horizon line, and consequently is a momentary point of constant returns to scale, then Euler's theorem holds at the long-run competitive output and there is product exhaustion.

[6] *See* Appendix 6A.

Of course, in the short run, product exhaustion does not necessarily take place. The competitive firm need not produce at minimum average cost in the short run, and the fixed factors of production need not receive any remuneration at all. In the short run, any excess revenue over payments to the factors of production is absorbed by the entrepreneur in the form of pure economic profit, whereas any deficiency of revenue compared to the sum of the values of the marginal product is absorbed by the fixed factors of production.

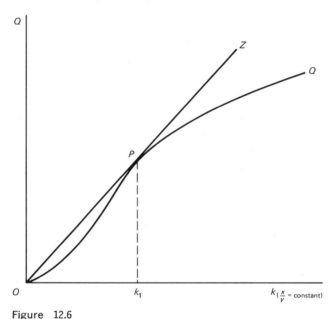

Figure 12.6

It should be noted that the long-run product exhaustion theorem necessarily holds only for perfectly competitive firms. First of all, the monopolist pays its factors their marginal revenue products rather than the value of their marginal products, and $VMP > MRP$. Second, there is no necessity for the monopolist to operate at minimum average cost; furthermore, even if he did, price would exceed average cost.

FUNCTIONAL DISTRIBUTION OF INCOME WITHIN THE FIRM

The definition of the elasticity of substitution that we have used, which is due to J. R. Hicks, is (using the subscript "H" to denote Hicks)

$$\sigma_H = \frac{d\left(\dfrac{Y}{X}\right)}{\dfrac{Y}{X}} \bigg/ \frac{dMRS_{xy}}{MRS_{xy}} \qquad [12.4]$$

The student should recall that MRS_{xy} is defined as the absolute slope of any isoquant, $-\dfrac{dY}{dX}$. Thus, equation 12.4 can be rewritten as

$$\sigma_H = \frac{d\left(\dfrac{Y}{X}\right)}{\dfrac{Y}{X}} \bigg/ \frac{d\left(-\dfrac{dY}{dX}\right)}{-\dfrac{dY}{dX}} \qquad [12.5]$$

Furthermore, the reader should recall that the MRS_{xy} is the ratio of the marginal products of the factors. Thus,

$$\sigma_H = \frac{d\left(\dfrac{Y}{X}\right)}{\dfrac{Y}{X}} \bigg/ \frac{d\left(\dfrac{MP_x}{MP_y}\right)}{\dfrac{MP_x}{MP_y}} \qquad [12.6]$$

Joan Robinson has defined the elasticity of substitution as

$$\sigma_R = -\frac{d\left(\dfrac{Y}{X}\right)}{\dfrac{Y}{X}} \bigg/ \frac{d\left(\dfrac{MP_y}{MP_x}\right)}{\dfrac{MP_y}{MP_x}} \qquad [12.7]$$

As a first step in our discussion of functional distribution, it is necessary to show that the Hicks and Robinson definitions are identical. Notice that the numerators of equations 12.6 and 12.7 are the same. Furthermore, the denominators can be shown to be equal.[7]

[7] Rewrite the denominator of equation 12.6 as

$$\frac{d\left(\dfrac{f_x}{f_y}\right)}{\dfrac{f_x}{f_y}} \qquad (1)$$

where $f_x = MP_x = \dfrac{\partial q}{\partial X}$ and $f_y = MP_y = \dfrac{\partial q}{\partial Y}$

Rewrite the denominator of equation 12.7 as

$$-d\left(\dfrac{f_y}{f_x}\right)\bigg/\dfrac{f_y}{f_x} \qquad (2)$$

Taking the differentials as indicated in equation 1, we obtain

$$\frac{f_y df_x dX - f_x df_y dY}{(f_y)^2} \cdot \frac{f_y}{f_x} = \frac{df_x dX}{f_x} - \frac{df_y dY}{f_y}$$

Likewise, for equation 2,

$$\frac{-f_x df_y dY + f_y df_x dX}{(f_x)^2} \cdot \frac{f_x}{f_y} = \frac{df_x dX}{f_x} - \frac{df_y dY}{f_y}$$

The least-cost conditions require that $MP_y/MP_x = P_y/P_x$. Thus, we can substitute in equation 12.7:

$$\sigma = -\frac{d\left(\dfrac{Y}{X}\right)}{\dfrac{Y}{X}} \Bigg/ \frac{d\left(\dfrac{P_y}{P_x}\right)}{\dfrac{P_y}{P_x}} \qquad [12.8]$$

If we further assume competitive long-run equilibrium, it will be true that payments to the factors exhaust the value of the product. As P_y/P_x

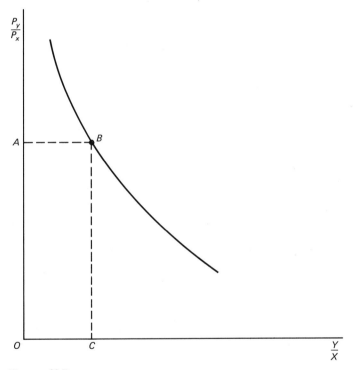

Figure 12.7

decreases, Y/X increases, reflecting the firm's substitution of the relatively cheaper factor for the relatively more expensive factor. Thus, the graph relating P_y/P_x to Y/X will have a negative slope as in Figure 12.7.

The absolute elasticity at any point on the curve is measured by

$$-\frac{d\left(\dfrac{Y}{X}\right)}{\dfrac{Y}{X}} \Bigg/ \frac{d\left(\dfrac{P_y}{P_x}\right)}{\dfrac{P_y}{P_x}}$$

and this is, of course, the elasticity of substitution. For any point on the curve, such as B, we can construct a rectangle such as $OABC$. The area of such a rectangle is equal to $\dfrac{P_y}{P_x}\dfrac{Y}{X} = \dfrac{P_yY}{P_xX} = \dfrac{\text{Payment to factor } Y}{\text{Payment to factor } X}$. This represents the ratio in which the value of the total product is divided between the two factors.

The relationship between the elasticity of substitution and the factor payment ratio area can be developed in a fashion analogous to the relationship between the elasticity of demand and total revenue. (See Chapter 3.) We start with the definition

$$\left(\frac{P_yY}{P_xX}\right)_1 = \frac{P_y}{P_x}\cdot\frac{Y}{X}$$

Now assume a change in P_y/P_x and a resulting change in Y/X.

$$\left(\frac{P_yY}{P_xX}\right)_2 = \left(\frac{P_y}{P_x} + \Delta\frac{P_y}{P_x}\right)\left(\frac{Y}{X} + \Delta\frac{Y}{X}\right)$$

Multiplying out we get

$$\left(\frac{P_yY}{P_xX}\right)_2 = \frac{P_y}{P_x}\cdot\frac{Y}{X} + \Delta\left(\frac{P_y}{P_x}\right)\Delta\left(\frac{Y}{X}\right) + \Delta\left(\frac{P_y}{P_x}\right)\frac{Y}{X} + \Delta\left(\frac{Y}{X}\right)\frac{P_y}{P_x}$$

Thus the change in P_yY/P_xX is

$$\Delta\left(\frac{P_yY}{P_xX}\right) = \left(\frac{P_yY}{P_xX}\right)_2 - \left(\frac{P_yY}{P_xX}\right)_1 = \Delta\left(\frac{P_y}{P_x}\right)\Delta\left(\frac{Y}{X}\right) + \Delta\left(\frac{P_y}{P_x}\right)\frac{Y}{X} + \Delta\left(\frac{Y}{X}\right)\frac{P_y}{P_x}$$

If we let $\Delta(P_y/P_x)$ and $\Delta(Y/X)$ approach zero, we can write

$$d\left(\frac{P_yY}{P_xX}\right) = d\left(\frac{P_y}{P_x}\right)d\left(\frac{Y}{X}\right) + d\left(\frac{P_y}{P_x}\right)\frac{Y}{X} + d\left(\frac{Y}{X}\right)\frac{P_y}{P_x}$$

Since the first term on the right is the product of two infinitesimal amounts, its value is nil and can be ignored. Thus, the previous equation can be rewritten as

$$d\left(\frac{P_yY}{P_xX}\right) = d\left(\frac{P_y}{P_x}\right)\frac{Y}{X} + d\left(\frac{Y}{X}\right)\frac{P_y}{P_x} \qquad [12.9]$$

We can rewrite equation 12.8 as

$$\sigma = -\left[d\left(\frac{Y}{X}\right)\cdot\frac{P_y}{P_x}\Big/d\left(\frac{P_y}{P_x}\right)\cdot\frac{Y}{X}\right] \qquad [12.10]$$

Note the relationship between equations 12.9 and 12.10. The numerator of equation 12.10 is the second term on the right of equation 12.9 while the denominator is the first term.

If we move from left to right along Figure 12.7, P_y/P_x decreases and $XY/$ increases. Thus $d(Y/X)$ is positive and the numerator of the expression in brackets is positive. On the other hand, $d(P_y/P_x)$ is negative, making the denominator negative. If $\sigma > 1$, the numerator of equation 12.10 is greater than the denominator and, thus, the positive component of equation 12.9, $[d(Y/X) \cdot P_y/P_x]$, exceeds the negative component and $d(P_yY/P_xX) > 0$, which means the share going to factor Y, relative to factor X, is increasing. Using analogous reasoning, if $\sigma < 1$, the relative share going to Y decreases. In summary, we can state: If

$$\sigma > 1, \quad d\left(\frac{Y}{X}\right)\frac{P_y}{P_x} > d\left(\frac{P_y}{P_x}\right)\frac{Y}{X} \quad \text{and} \quad d\left(\frac{P_yY}{P_xX}\right) > 0$$

$$\sigma = 1, \quad d\left(\frac{Y}{X}\right)\frac{P_y}{P_x} = d\left(\frac{P_y}{P_x}\right)\frac{Y}{X} \quad \text{and} \quad d\left(\frac{P_yY}{P_xX}\right) = 0$$

$$\sigma < 1, \quad d\left(\frac{Y}{X}\right)\frac{P_y}{P_x} < d\left(\frac{P_y}{P_x}\right)\frac{Y}{X} \quad \text{and} \quad d\left(\frac{P_yY}{P_xX}\right) < 0$$

Thus far we have discussed the relative shares going to the factors. We can demonstrate the absolute returns to X and Y by assuming a one product economy. In Figure 12.8 assume that initially the fixed supplies

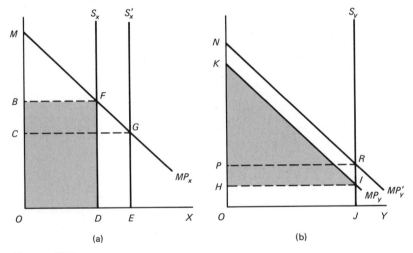

(a)   (b)

Figure 12.8

of X and Y are given by S_x and S_y and the demand curves by MP_x and MP_y. (These are the equivalent of the VMP curves discussed before, where the price of the product is assumed to be $1.) The initial P_x is OB with OD units being employed. Thus, the total product going to X is $OBFD$. Similarly, the price of factor Y is OH with OJ of the factor being used and total payment being $OHIJ$.

It will be remembered that the area under a marginal curve up to a point gives the total to that point. Further, if we assume that Figure 12.8 represents a competitive long-run equilibrium or that the product is produced with a linear homogeneous production function, there is product exhaustion. Consequently, the return to factor B can be measured as the residual area under the MP_x curve; that is, the triangle BMF. Conversely, the return to factor A can be measured as the area of the triangle HKI.

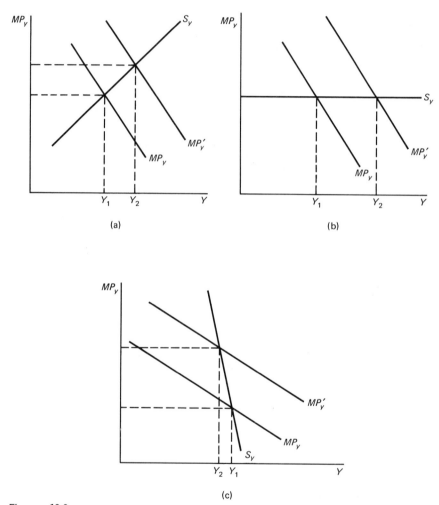

Figure   12.9

Let us assume an increase in the supply of X such that the supply curve shifts from S_x to S_x'. The price of X changes from OB to OC, the employment increases from OD to OE, and the total payment to X changes from $OBFD$ to $OCGE$. Whether the former rectangle is greater or less than the latter will clearly depend on the elasticity of demand for the factor.

The increase in X results in a shift of MP_y to MP_y'. This shift results in an increase in the price of Y from OH to OP; and because a higher price is being paid to the fixed supply, there is necessarily an increase in the total payment to Y. From our previous discussion, we know that the relative share going to A will increase only if the elasticity of substitution is greater than one.

We have seen that an increase in the relative use of X results in a change in its relative remuneration that depends on the elasticity of substitution. However, if the supply of Y is not fixed, an increase in the absolute quantity of X does not necessarily increase its relative share. This can be demonstrated with respect to Figures 12.9a and b. In Figure 12.9a, we show the case of a positively sloped supply curve, and the MP_y schedule has shifted to MP_y' due to an antecedent increase in X. As a limiting case, consider S_y in Figure 12.9b—an infinitely elastic supply curve. An increase from MP_y to MP_y' causes an increased use of Y with no change in its marginal product. However, by the assumption of linear homogeneity, in order for the marginal product of Y to remain constant, the increase in X must be in the same proportion as the increase in Y. For any positively sloped S_y, the marginal product of Y increases; again with the assumption of linear homogeneity, this means that the ratio of X to Y must have increased. Thus, with a rising supply curve of Y, it is impossible, when the quantity of X increases, for the quantity of Y to rise sufficiently to result in X/Y decreasing.

With a downward-sloping S_y (Figure 12.9c), as MP_y shifts upward, the quantity of Y decreases as its marginal product increases. Thus, an increase in X that causes the quantity of Y to decrease must cause an increase in X/Y.

In our analysis, we considered a two-factor, one-product economy. A more realistic model would be multiproduct and multifactor. In our discussion of the elasticity of derived demand, the reader will recall that two of the determinants were commodity substitution and technical substitution between factors. In a more realistic model, these two concepts could be extended by computing weighted averages of every relevant commodity and factor pair.[8]

It should be noted that the approach used in our discussion of distribution has been a partial equilibrium approach in that the demands for goods were taken as givens in deriving the demands for factors. A general equilibrium approach would simultaneously determine product and factor demands. Furthermore, our discussion has been limited to the case of constant returns to scale for the industry and to perfect competition.

[8] The actual expressions for these weighted averages are somewhat complex. The reader is referred to J. R. Hicks, *The Theory of Wages* (2d ed.; 1964) pp. 298–303.

13

GENERAL EQUILIBRIUM

The market economy is an interrelated whole, and changes in any part of it cause changes and reactions of a greater or lesser magnitude in every part of the economy. Our ability to deal with a large number of economic variables and interrelationships is limited, and so, for the purpose of simplification and to make the analysis manageable, we usually resort to partial-equilibrium analysis. That is to say, we classify our variables into (1) those directly impinging upon the phenomenon in question, (2) those less closely related but of great importance, and (3) those whose influence is much less direct and that can, for the purpose at hand, be ignored. Thus, when we write $Q_{d_x} = f\ (P_x,\ cet.\ par.)$, P_x represents the prime variable, and those assumed to be temporarily constant—income, tastes, the prices of good substitutes and complements—are in the second category of variables; other variables are ignored. In theory, a general equilibrium approach to an economic problem would take into account the interdependence of all economic variables—a change in any of these variables causes ripples of effect to spread throughout the economy. No such complete analysis is possible, given the present state of our knowledge.

The first general equilibrium equation system that demonstrated this general interdependence of economic quantities was presented by Leon Walras in 1874. Although economic analysis is still primarily carried out in a partial equilibrium context, Walras' contribution was to emphasize the interdependence of the sectors of the economy and to give us an overview of the interrelationships.

Although Walras' analysis is in completely general terms, we shall be somewhat more concrete, limiting ourselves to an economy of 2000 people and 200 firms, 100 of which produce a good X and 100 of which produce a good Y. Further, there are two factors of production, A and B, used in the production of both X and Y; these factors are held in initial endowments by the individuals.

Thus we have

2000 persons	$1 \cdots 2000$
2 goods	X, Y
2 factors	A, B
100 firms producing X	$1 \cdots 100$
100 firms producing Y	$101 \cdots 200$

We use the following symbols.

1. Consumption of the individuals (including consumption of factors):

$$X_1, X_2, \ldots, X_{2000}$$
$$Y_1, Y_2, \ldots, Y_{2000}$$
$$A_1, A_2, \ldots, A_{2000}$$
$$B_1, B_2, \ldots, B_{2000}$$

2. Production of the firms:

$$x_1, x_2, \ldots, x_{100}$$
$$y_{101}, y_{102}, \ldots, y_{200}$$

3. Initial endowments of the factors:

$$\bar{A}_1, \bar{A}_2, \ldots, \bar{A}_{2000}$$
$$\bar{B}_1, \bar{B}_2, \ldots, \bar{B}_{2000}$$

4. Supply of the factors:

$$a_1 = \bar{A}_1 - A_1, a_2 = \bar{A}_2 - A_2, \ldots, a_{2000} = \bar{A}_{2000} - A_{2000}$$
$$b_1 = \bar{B}_1 - B_1, b_2 = \bar{B}_2 - B_2, \ldots, b_{2000} = \bar{B}_{2000} - B_{2000}$$

5. Demand for the factors:

demand for $A = A_x{}^1 + A_x{}^2 + \cdots + A_x{}^{100} + A_y{}^{101} + A_y{}^{102} + \cdots + A_y{}^{200}$
demand for $B = B_x{}^1 + B_x{}^2 + \cdots + B_x{}^{100} + B_y{}^{101} + B_y{}^{102} + \cdots + B_y{}^{200}$

The following unknowns must be determined:

1. For an individual i, X_i, Y_i, A_i, B_i

There are 2000 persons, giving 8000 unknowns.

2. For a firm k, A_x^k, B_x^k, x_k

There are 100 such firms, giving 300 unknowns.

3. For a firm l, A_y^l, B_y^l, y_l

There are 100 such firms, giving 300 unknowns.

4. With X used as numeraire, so that $P_x = 1$,

P_y, P_a, P_b must also be determined.

This adds *three additional unknowns.*

We have a total of 8603 unknowns.
Given, for each consumer i,

$$U_i = U_i(X_i, Y_i, A_i, B_i) \tag{13.1}$$

There are 2000 of these utility functions.

For each individual there is also the initial endowment of factors $\bar{A}_i$, $\bar{B}_i$.

There are 2000 of these initial endowments.

Given, for each producer k, the production function

$$x_k = f_x(A_x{}^k, B_x{}^k) \tag{13.2}$$

There are 100 of these production functions.

Also,

$$y_l = f_y(A_y{}^l, B_y{}^l) \tag{13.3}$$

There are 100 of these production functions.

Consumer Sector

For each consumer, i, maximization of utility function (13.1) subject to a budget constraint will involve fulfilling the equations

$$\frac{MU_y{}^i}{MU_x{}^i} = P_y \tag{13.4}$$

$$\frac{MU_a{}^i}{MU_x{}^i} = P_a \tag{13.5}$$

$$\frac{MU_b{}^i}{MU_x{}^i} = P_b \tag{13.6}$$

This gives 6000 equations.
Subject to the constraint that the value of the initial endowments of factors must equal the amount spent on goods plus the factors retained for consumption,

$$P_a\bar{A}_i + P_b\bar{B}_i = P_xX_i + P_yY_i + P_aA_i + P_bB_i \tag{13.7}$$

This gives 2000 equations.
Once we have A_i and B_i, the demand for factors, for each consumer we then have his supply of factors $a_i = \bar{A}_i - A_i$, and so on. We may therefore rewrite equation 13.7 as

$$P_aa_i + P_bb_i = P_xX_i + P_yY_i \tag{13.7a}$$

There are alternatively 2000 of these equations—13.7a$_1$ to 13.7a$_{2000}$.

When each individual equation, such as 13.4 through 13.7, is solved for X_i and Y_i in terms of P_x and P_y, we have the individual product demands, and when we aggregate the demands over all individuals, we have the market demands for the products X and Y.

Producer Sector

The conditions for long-run equilibrium require that in each of our industries the firms maximize profits and that profits be zero in equilibrium. This amounts to maximizing equations 13.2 and 13.3 subject to the constraint that total receipts from output be equal to total expenditures upon factors—each firm is to move up the long-run expansion path until the point where payment to factors just exhausts the value of output.

For each firm,

$$\frac{MP_a{}^x}{MP_b{}^x} = \frac{P_a}{P_b} \qquad [13.8]$$

and

$$\frac{MP_a{}^y}{MP_b{}^y} = \frac{P_a}{P_b} \qquad [13.9]$$

Also,

$$P_x x = P_a A_x + P_b B_x \qquad [13.10]$$

and

$$P_y y = P_a A_y + P_b B_y \qquad [13.11]$$

The last two equations are the zero profit constraint. There are 100 of each of these equations, making 400 equations that, along with 200 production function equations, give 600 *equations in all*.

For each firm these equations, along with the production function, yield its supply function for the commodity and its demand function for factors; if we aggregate across all firms we have the total supply of goods and the total demand for each of the factors.

Finally, we have the condition that both factor and product markets must clear in equilibrium.

$$X_1 + X_2 + \cdots + X_{2000} = x_i + x_2 + \cdots + x_{100} \qquad [13.12]$$
$$Y_1 + Y_2 + \cdots + Y_{2000} = y_{101} + y_{102} + \cdots + y_{200} \qquad [13.13]$$
$$a_1 + a_2 + \cdots + a_{2000} = A_x{}^1 + A_x{}^2 + \cdots + A_x{}^{100} + A_y{}^{101} + A_y{}^{102}$$
$$+ \cdots + A_y{}^{200} \qquad [13.14]$$
$$b_1 + b_2 + \cdots + b_{2000} = B_x{}^1 + B_x{}^2 + \cdots + B_x{}^{100} + B_y{}^{101} + B_y{}^{102}$$
$$+ \cdots + B_y{}^{200} \qquad [13.15]$$

These market clearing equations *add a total of 4 equations to the system.*

Summary

Unknowns	Equations
8000 household unknowns	8000 household equations
4000 product demands	
4000 factor supplies	
600 firm unknowns	600 firm equations
400 factor demands	
200 product supplies	
3 prices	4 market clearing equations

We see that there is one excess equation and that the system is over-determined—if all the equations are independent, one of them cannot be fulfilled; it turns out, however, that one of them contributes no independent information and can be abandoned.

Proof of the Redundant Equation

We may aggregate the right and left sides of equations 13.12 through 13.15.

$$X = x \qquad [13.12']$$
$$Y = y \qquad [13.13']$$
$$a = A \qquad [13.14']$$
$$b = B \qquad [13.15']$$

$$\text{I} = 13.10 + 13.11 \qquad P_x x + P_y y = P_a(A_x + A_y) + P_b(B_x + B_y)$$
$$= P_a A + P_b B$$

$$\text{II} = 13.14' \times P_a \qquad P_a a = P_a A$$
$$\text{III} = 13.15' \times P_b \qquad P_b b = P_b B$$
$$\text{IV} = \text{II} + \text{III} \qquad P_a a + P_b b = P_a A + P_b B$$
$$\text{V} = \text{I} - \text{IV} \qquad P_x x + P_y y = P_a a + P_b b$$
$$\text{VI} = 13.12' \times P_x \qquad P_x X = P_x x$$
$$\text{VII} = 13.13' \times P_y \qquad P_y Y = P_y y$$
$$\text{VIII} = \text{VI} + \text{VII} \qquad P_x X + P_y Y = P_x x + P_y y$$
$$\text{IX} = \text{VIII} - \text{V} \qquad P_a a + P_b b = P_x X + P_y Y$$

If IX is disaggregated, it reads

$$X = P_a a_1 + P_a a_2 + \cdots + P_a a_{1999} + P_a a_{2000} + P_b b_1 + P_b b_2 + \cdots + P_b b_{1999}$$
$$+ P_b b_{2000}$$
$$= P_x X_1 + P_x X_2 + \cdots + P_x X_{1999} + P_x X_{2000} + P_y Y_1 + P_y Y_2 + \cdots$$
$$+ P_y Y_{1999} + P_y Y_{2000}$$

Now we subtract equations $13.7a_1$ to $13.7a_{1999}$ from IX.

$$\text{XI} \quad P_a a_{2000} + P_b b_{2000} = P_x X_{2000} + P_y Y_{2000}$$

This is equation $13.7a_{2000}$, a redundant equation, because its information is implied by the other equations. We have, therefore, 8603 independent equations in 8603 unknowns.

In general, if the number of equations is less than the number of unknowns, the information is insufficient to specify a solution (there are rare exceptions). The equality of the number of equations and unknowns by no means, however, guarantees a unique solution. It is possible to have inconsistency, so that there is no solution or so that there are multiple solutions. Checking the number of equations against the number of unknowns is, therefore, only a preliminary step to check that there are a sufficient number of restraints specified. A complete analysis of the conditions under which a unique (and economically meaningful) solution will exist requires somewhat high-powered mathematical analysis. It has, however, been shown that under certain reasonable assumptions concerning the shapes of the functions, such a solution does exist.[1]

The system of equations we have discussed is static. That is, it does not specify the path by which the economy approaches equilibrium nor whether the equilibrium will be stable or unstable. We can clearly see, then, that a good deal remains to be done in addition to comparing the number of equations with the number of unknowns. The rudiments of a general equilibrium system as presented here are nevertheless useful to tie together the partial equilibrium study presented in the earlier chapters.

In order to make the concept of general equilibrium more concrete, let us assume a simple economy that is initially in equilibrium and then trace through the effects of a change in demand. In our example economy, we assume:

1. There are initial factor endowments.
2. There are two factors of production, labor and capital.
3. There are two goods, food and clothing, with food being produced with a higher labor-to-capital ratio than clothing for any factor price ratio.
4. There is an increase in the demand for food. We wish to trace out the impact of this shift on the various sectors of the economy.

The immediate effect of the increased demand for food is to raise the price of food and to increase the quantity produced. Because food is labor intensive, the demand for labor will rise relative to the demand for capital and will cause an increase in the wage rate relative to the interest rate (that is, the price of the services of capital). Insofar as factor substitution is possible, firms will substitute capital for labor, and this will then act to limit the rise in the wage rate.

This change in the factor price ratio results in a change in the distribution of income, and this causes further income-induced shifts in the product demand schedules leading to another series of economy-wide

[1] For a further discussion of this proof by Abraham Wald, see George J. Stigler, *Production and Distribution Theories*, New York: (Macmillan, 1941), p. 243.

adjustments. A new equilibrium will have been achieved when all product and factor markets are once again cleared.

The previous example, although very simple, should give meaning to the system of general equilibrium equations just discussed. The student should be able to trace out some other change, such as a technological improvement that permits clothing to be produced more efficiently.

14

INTRODUCTION TO LINEAR PROGRAMMING

Up to this point this book has dealt with traditional price theory, which is concerned with the explanation of resource allocation in the economy as a whole. At the center of its analytical apparatus, price theory has marginal analysis, which is dictated by the assumption that entrepreneurs as a whole desire to maximize profits.

In price theory the usual assumptions made are (1) the firm is given its production function as a technological datum; (2) the firm can substitute factors of production for each other continuously (smoothly continuous isoquants); and (3) the firm has knowledge of the demand curve it faces. The usual problems faced by businessmen are not of the type that require a choice between a little more of one factor and a little less of another in order to produce a given output as cheaply as possible, but rather a choice among production processes each of which has fairly rigid factor proportions dictated by its technological character. Economists, interested in prescribing for individual business firms, must take into account the multifarious complexities and diversities of the firms, and in this area (sometimes called managerial economics) marginal analysis often fails them.

Although marginal analysis abstracts from the details of the decision making of individual firms, its very "simplicity" makes it useful in analyzing the allocation of resources for society as a whole. As far as the decisions of the individual firms are concerned, a generally more useful tool is mathematical programming, which deals with the problem of maximizing (or minimizing) some function (called the objective function) subject to constraints that take the form of inequalities. Marginal analysis is also concerned with maximization (or minimization) subject to constraints, but in marginal analysis the constraints are equalities.

In this chapter we shall discuss linear programming, which is the most widely used form of mathematical programming. It is not our purpose to teach the student the technique of solving linear-programming problems but rather to acquaint him with the nature of the technique and the problems the technique can best deal with. At the end of the Chapter we provide a selective bibliography listing some of the outstanding works in the field.

In linear programming we make the following assumptions: (1) Each input contributes to the fulfillment of the objective function in proportion to its utilization, and each process (to be defined later) uses up the scarce inputs in proportion to its utilization. (2) The prices at which the firm buys its factors and sells its products are assumed constant. In their economic context, these assumptions amount to assuming a linear homogeneous production function and perfect competition in both the product and factor markets. We demonstrate this in Figure 14.1.

Lines OA, OB, and OC represent three process rays—three different methods of producing a good, each one of which requires a given proportion between the factors. For example, q_2 units of output may be produced at point D on process ray OA, or point E on process ray OB, or point G on process ray OC. q_2 can also be produced by utilizing a combination of processes such as at point F.[1] When we connect points such as D,

---

[1] It is not intuitively obvious that output at F is the same as at E or G. See Robert Dorfman, "Mathematical, or 'Linear,' Programming: A Nonmathematical Exposition," *American Economic Review*, XLIII, No. 5 (December 1953), 805–806, who has proven this rigorously as follows (see accompanying figure):

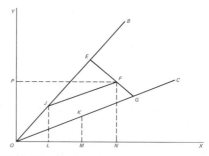

1. From F on segment EG draw a line parallel to OC that intersects OB at J. Mark off the distance OK on OC so that $JF = OK$.

2. Assume the firm uses a production plan consisting of process OB at the level OF and process OC at the level OK. Process OB at level OJ uses OL of factor X. Process OC at level OK uses OM of X. Thus, the two processes together use $OL + OM$ units of X. However, by construction, $JF = OK$ and JF is parallel to OK. Therefore, $LN = OM$, and together the processes use ON of X. And ON is the X-axis coordinate of F.

E, F, and G, we generate an isoquant. Notice that the isoquant is not the smoothly continuous one of Chapter 6, because there are only a finite number of processes the firm can use.

The reader has seen linear expansion paths along which equal proportional increases in input resulted in equal proportional increments in output, and he will identify this as a characteristic of linear homogeneous production functions.

It should be kept in mind that in the linear-programming view of production the firm no longer changes inputs and outputs directly but does so indirectly by changing the levels at which the various processes are being used. In Figure 14.1 the firm is conceived of as facing only one constraint (an expenditure constraint) and as wanting to maximize output with this level of expenditure. If the expenditure constraint is II, the

---

3. Similarly, OP represents the amount of Y used by the production plan calling for OJ of process OB and for OK of process OC.

4. Thus, F can be interpreted as the combined production plan made up of OK of process OC and of OJ of process OB, if we assume that when the two processes are used together, neither process interferes with or enhances the other.

5. Next, it is necessary to show that output at F is equal to output at E and G. Based on the linearity assumption,

$$\frac{\text{output } K}{\text{output } G} = \frac{OK}{OG}$$

and

$$\frac{\text{output } J}{\text{output } E} = \frac{OJ}{OE}$$

Because we assumed output E = output G,

$$\frac{\text{output } K}{\text{output } E} = \frac{OK}{OG}$$

Adding, we get

$$\frac{\text{output } K}{\text{output } E} + \frac{\text{output } J}{\text{output } E} = \frac{OK}{OG} + \frac{OJ}{OE}$$

But by construction, $OK = JF$. Thus,

$$\frac{OK}{OG} + \frac{OJ}{OE} = \frac{JF}{OG} + \frac{OJ}{OE}$$

Since $\triangle JEF \sim \triangle OEG$ ($\angle JEF = \angle OEG$; $\angle EOG = \angle EJF$; $\angle OGE = \angle JFE$),

$$\frac{JF}{OG} = \frac{JE}{OE}$$

We can write

$$\frac{JF}{OG} + \frac{OJ}{OE} = \frac{JE}{OE} + \frac{OJ}{OE} = \frac{OE}{OE} = 1$$

In words, if [(output K + output J)/output E] = 1, output K + output J = output E. But output F is the sum of output K and output J. Therefore, output E = output F, and E, F, and G lie on the same isoquant.

firm will accomplish its objective by producing at point E, on the highest attainable kinked isoquant. Graphically, one can see that such an equilibrium will occur at a corner or anywhere along a segment that has the same slope as the constraint line.

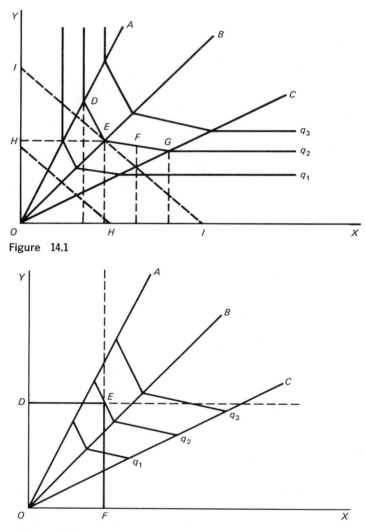

Figure 14.1

Figure 14.2

The usual situation in which the firm finds itself in the short run is the one in which it is constrained by various limited capacities that may be used in a number of alternative processes to produce a number of products. In Figure 14.2 we visualize the simplest of these cases. We assume the firm produces only one product and that OF and OD are its limited capacities in factors x and y. Thus a feasible area (the one in which the firm can produce) is $ODEF$. It should be noted that the constraint is no longer a straight line but is an area and that the boundary DEF represents the maximum combination of the factors the firm can use. With the firm trying to maximize output, it will produce at point E.

A more relevant situation is one in which the firm must decide on a product mix that will maximize its profit and can be produced within the capacity constraints. This kind of problem may be generally stated as follows:

Let

$a, b, \ldots, n$ be the products the firm can produce
$P_a, P_b, \ldots, P_n$ be the prices at which the firm can sell its products
$A, B, \ldots, N$ be the fixed amounts of the productive capacities

Let the amounts of the fixed capacities used per unit of output for each product be as follows:

$$A_a A_b \cdots A_n$$
$$B_a B_b \cdots B_n$$
$$\cdot$$
$$\cdot$$
$$\cdot$$
$$N_a N_b \cdots N_n$$

The problem then becomes one[2] of maximizing

$$TR = P_a a + P_b b + \cdots + P_n n^2 \tag{14.1}$$

subject to

$$A_a + A_b + \cdots + A_n \leq A$$
$$B_a + B_b + \cdots + B_n \leq B$$
$$\cdot$$
$$\cdot$$
$$\cdot$$
$$N_a + N_b + \cdots + N_n \leq N$$
$$A \cdots N \geq 0 \tag{14.2}$$

We now present a specific example of such a problem. We have two products, x and y.

$$P_x = \$10$$
$$P_y = \$8$$

[2] Note that in this case, miximizing total revenue is identical with maximizing profit. Linear programming is based on the assumptions of constant returns up to capacity in the short run and constant factor prices; in other words, marginal cost is constant. The costs stemming from the capacity limitations are fixed.

We have four capacities: A, B, C, and D. The following are the input requirements:

	Inputs needed in		
Input	x	y	Input capacity
A	2	2	1500
B	5	3	3000
C	3	0	1500
D	0	1	600

Maximize

$$TR = P_x x + P_y y$$
$$= 10x + 8y \qquad [14.3]$$

subject to

$$2x + 2y \leq 1500$$
$$5x + 3y \leq 3000$$
$$3x + 0y \leq 1500 \quad \text{and} \quad x \geq 0 \qquad [14.4]$$
$$0x + 1y \leq 600 \qquad\qquad\qquad y \geq 0$$

The graphical solution to this problem is shown in Figure 14.3. The A-capacity constraint is shown on the diagram as a straight line with an x-axis intercept equal to the maximum amount of x that the firm can produce if it devotes all of A to the production of x and with a y-axis intercept equal to maximum y production if A is used only to produce y. The B-capacity constraint is determined in analogous fashion. Since the C-capacity is used only in the production of x, the constraint appears as a vertical line at the maximum amount of x that can be produced with full utilization of C. Similarly, the D-capacity constraint appears as a horizontal line at the maximum quantity of y that can be produced with full utilization of D. These constraints delimit the feasible area, $PNKLM$, the area within which the constraints permit the firm to operate.

The objective function that is to be maximized $(TR = P_x x + P_y Y)$ is represented by a series of parallel lines with the slope P_x/P_y. Clearly the firm desires to be on the highest possible isorevenue line permitted by the constraints. This is at point K where the firm produces 375 units of x and 375 units of y. Thus, $TR = 375(\$10) + 375(\$8) = \$6750$. Note that two of the capacities, C and D, are not being fully utilized. The amount of C being used is 1125 (out of 1500 capacity), and $375D$ are being used (with capacity at 600).[3]

At the optimal point, there is no tangency condition being fulfilled and we cannot find this point, therefore, using ordinary calculus methods.

[3] It can be proven that at the maximization level, there will usually be as many products produced as there are facilities used to capacity. See W. J. Baumol, *Economic Theory and Operations Analysis* (Englewood Cliffs, N.J.: Prentice-Hall, 1961), pp. 73–74.

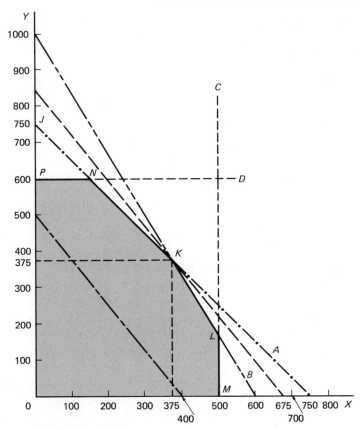

Figure 14.3

Thus, other methods must be used for finding the optimal solution;[4] these methods are iterative methods, the most commonly used being the simplex method.[5]

To every problem of this kind (called a primal problem) there is a corresponding dual problem. To illustrate the meaning of the dual problem, we present the dual form of the primal problem just solved.

[4] The optimal solution can always be at a corner. This can be demonstrated as follows: If the isorevenue line is not parallel to any of the facets of the feasible area boundary, then, clearly, the point of contact between the boundary and the highest possible isorevenue line will be at a corner. Furthermore, if the isorevenue line is parallel to one of the segments of the boundary, contact will exist along that segment. Thus, the entire segment (including the corners) will be optimal. Because the optimal solution can always be found at a corner, the simplex method involves searching consecutive corners of the boundary of the feasible region and comparing the values of the objective equation at these corners until no movement away from a particular corner can increase the value of the objective equation.

[5] The student interested in this mathematical technique is referred to the bibliography at the end of the Chapter.

Minimize imputed cost

$$IC = AI_A + BI_B + CI_C = DI_D \qquad [14.5]$$
$$IC = 1500I_A + 3000I_B + 1500I_C + 600I_D$$

subject to

$$A_x I_A + B_x I_B + C_x I_C + D_x I_D \geq P_x$$
$$A_y I_A + B_y I_B + C_y I_C + D_y I_D \geq P_y$$

or

$$2I_A + 5I_B + 3I_C + OI_D \geq \$10$$
$$2I_A + 3I_B + OI_C + 1I_D \geq \$8 \qquad [14.6]$$
$$I_A, I_B, I_C, I_D \geq 0$$

The terms I_A (imputed value of A), I_B, and so on require some explanation. Each of these represents the value to the firm of acquiring an additional unit of a presently fixed capacity (the value of the marginal product of a fixed facility). If a facility is not being used to capacity, the worth to the firm of an additional unit of it will clearly be zero, and the imputed value assigned to it by the firm will be zero. If, on the other hand, a facility is being used to capacity, its imputed value will be positive and represents the opportunity cost (in terms of the forgone outputs) to the firm of utilizing the input to produce a particular output. If the sum of the imputed costs of producing a particular commodity is greater than the price of the commodity, this means that the factors can be more profitably used in the production of some other good. (In the primal problem, the output of this product will be zero.) If the sum of the imputed costs is less than the price of the good, this means that the accounting prices (imputed values) assigned by the firm are too low because they do not allocate the total value of the unit of output. Thus, for an output being produced, the sum of the imputed values will just equal the price of the good.

In our example, facilities C and D are not being fully utilized; therefore, the imputed values of C and D will be zero. Thus the constraints become

$$2I_A + 5I_B \geq \$10 \qquad [14.7]$$
$$2I_A + 3I_B \geq \$8$$

These constraints are shown graphically in Figure 14.4. Note that the feasible area is the unbounded one lying above the boundary PQR; for all points lying within $OPQR$, either or both of the constraints are not being fulfilled.

In order to demonstrate why a firm must minimize its imputed cost if it is to maximize its total revenue (and, therefore, profits with our linearity assumptions), we present the following example.

Let us assume that we have two processes, E and F, capable of producing two products, G and H, that have the same prices. The two processes are used to capacity, and the marginal unit of each process is capable of the following additions to output:

$$\Delta Q$$

Process E $\begin{cases} 10 \text{ units of } G \\ \quad \text{or} \\ 5 \text{ units of } H \end{cases}$

Process F $\begin{cases} 5 \text{ units of } G \\ \quad \text{or} \\ 10 \text{ units of } H \end{cases}$

Now, if the marginal unit of process F is used to produce G, the imputed cost will be 10 (the 10 units of H foregone when process F is used to produce G instead of H); and if process E is used to produce H, imputed cost is 10.

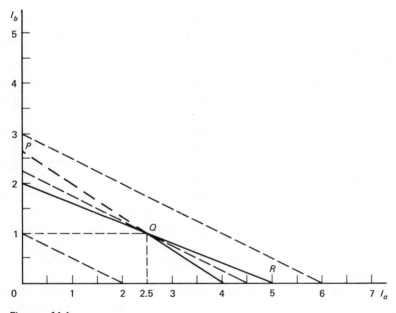

Figure 14.4

If production methods were changed so that process E were used to produce G and process F to produce H, output at capacity would increase by 5 units of G and 5 units of H (and, therefore, profits would increase) and the imputed costs would fall from 10 to 5 for both processes. It is therefore clear that, so long as it is possible to reduce imputed cost, profits are not being maximized.

Thus, in Figure 14.4 we show parallel isoimputed-cost lines with the slope equal to $\frac{1}{2}$ (this slope is determined from the objective equation

$IC = 1500I_A + 3000I_B + 1500(0) + 600(0))$. Point Q represents the optimal imputed values for A and B: $I_A = \$2.50$ and $I_B = \$1$.[6]

Note that the minimum imputed cost figure derived from the dual solution is the same as the maximum total revenue that was derived from the primal. We can substitute I_A and I_B in the objective equation:

$$IC = 1500(\$0.50) + 3000(\$1) = \$6750 \qquad [14.8]$$

Clearly, from the following conditions, it follows that the maximum total revenue must be totally imputed:

1. If the sum of the imputed values of the resources used in producing a unit of a good is greater than the price of the good, the good will not be produced.
2. The price of a good must be imputed completely to the resources utilized.

The following are some types of problems that can be handled by linear programming.

1. Determining the optimum product mix when the firm has some of its facilities at or near capacity. This is the type of problem just described. For example, suppose that a company can produce both automobiles and trucks and that there are certain capacities, some of which are used exclusively for one product and some of which are required in the production of both goods. What should the output of trucks and automobiles be?[7]
2. The blending problem, for example, minimizing the cost of a diet that fulfills certain minimal nutritional requirements; and minimizing the cost of gasoline with the constraints of minimum octane and certain other quality requirements. Ice-cream manufacturing, textile production, and metallurgy are other areas in which this kind of problem arises.
3. The transportation problem—minimizing costs of transport subject to certain constraints. For example, if a firm has several plants with fixed capacities and in different locations and has customers scattered geographically, it will want to minimize its costs of transportation subject to the demands of the consumers and the output capacities of the plants.

[6] In solving the dual problem mathematically, the zero-accounting prices for C and D would appear as part of the solution. However, from the primal problem we know that neither of these facilities would have been used to capacity, and thus, both would have zero opportunity cost. Therefore, by assuming $I_C = I_D = 0$, we were able to present the dual solution graphically using two dimensions.

[7] See Dorfman, "Mathematical, or 'Linear,' Programming."

The dual solution to the linear-programming problem that we discussed above is useful, first, because many times the dual problem is easier to solve computationally than the primal problem and, second, because the imputed values derived from the dual solution have some interesting applications. One of these is to permit a firm with several plants to use decentralized rather than centralized decision making. If there are certain scarce facilities utilized by all the plants, they can simply be allocated by a central management decision; or the plant managers can be permitted to use as much of the scarce resources as they want, but the home office will debit them the imputed value of the resources they use. The managers will be cautioned to avoid losses.

The literature on linear programming is extensive. We list below a few references that the reader may find useful.

Baumol, W. J., *Economic Theory and Operations Analysis*. Englewood Cliffs, N.J.: Prentice-Hall, 1961.

Charnes, A., W. W. Cooper, and A. Henderson. *Introduction to Linear Programming*. New York: Wiley, 1953.

Dantzig, G. B., "Maximization of a Linear Function of Variables Subject to Linear Inequalities," in T. C. Koopmans (ed.), *Activity Analysis of Production and Allocation*. New York: Wiley, 1951.

Dorfman, R., "Mathematical, or 'Linear' Programming: A Nonmathematical Exposition," *American Economic Review*, Vol. XLIII, No. 5 (December 1953).

Dorfman, R., P. A. Samuelson, and R. Solow, *Linear Programming and Economic Analysis*. New York: McGraw-Hill, 1958).

15

WELFARE ECONOMICS

In this chapter[1] we will be concerned with the welfare implications of the general equilibrium solution to the resource allocation problems of the economy. In Chapter 13 we outlined the general equilibrium character of the economic system, that is, we showed that really everything depends on everything else. We also stated that under certain reasonable assumptions the system can be shown to have a unique solution.

This chapter is concerned with the welfare implications of this solution, that is, the conditions under which the solution can be said to be optimal. There is one sense of optimality with which it is easy to agree at once. In order for the production-distribution process to be optimally efficient, it must be impossible to make someone better off without making someone else worse off, given the resource and technology base of the society. We shall see that this criterion, although it takes us a good part of the way, is not sufficient by itself to define a single unique optimum position for the economy. For this position to be defined it is necessary to specify the society's views as to the relative merits of alternative distributions of welfare among the individuals in the society. This may be expressed in a social welfare function, and we will discuss its characteristics later.

In defining the characteristics of an optimum solution to the resource allocation problems of the economy, it will be convenient to consider a society that has fixed amounts of labor and capital (L and K) that are used to produce two products X and Y. The assumption of fixed factor

[1] This chapter depends heavily on Francis M. Bator, "The Simple Analytics of Welfare Maximization," *American Economic Review* (March 1957), 22–59.

endowments and of only two products permits graphical exposition; we will remove these assumptions later in the chapter. We assume two production functions as follows:

$$X = x(L_x, K_x) \tag{15.1}$$
$$Y = y(L_y, K_y) \tag{15.2}$$

These functions are assumed to yield convex isoquants of the usual type and to exhibit constant returns to scale.

There are two individuals, A and B, each with an ordinal preference function of the form

$$U_A = \mu_A(X_A, Y_A) \tag{15.3}$$
$$U_B = \mu_B(X_B, Y_B) \tag{15.4}$$

These are assumed to yield convex indifference curves of the usual type.

We also assume a social welfare function

$$S = s(U_A, U_B) \tag{15.5}$$

which gives a unique preference ordering to the combination of indices derived from the individual preference orderings. This is the function that expresses in an ordinal index the values of the society as to the distribution of welfare between its individual members.

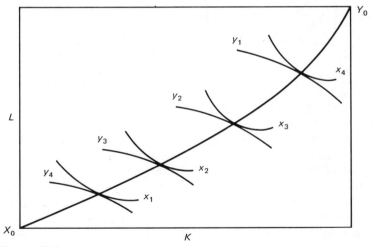

Figure   15.1

In Figure 15.1, we place the isoquants for X and Y on an Edgeworth box that has dimensions that measure the factor endowments and derive the locus of efficient outputs. When this locus is transcribed on a set of axes showing the outputs of the two commodities X and Y, we have the production transformation curve of Chapter 6 (Figure 15.2). On the efficiency locus it is impossible, given the resources and technology of the society, to increase output of one commodity without decreasing the output of the other. The transformation curve that is derived from the efficiency locus gives the outer boundary of the output possibilities of the economy and its slope, dY/dX, represents the marginal rate of transformation of Y into X as demonstrated in Chapter 6.

For each point on the transformation schedule TT such as α or β, it is possible to construct an Edgeworth box with the dimensions of the X, Y combination at the point. Thus α on TT results in the Edgeworth box

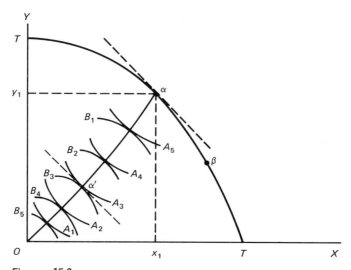

Figure 15.2

$Oy_1\alpha x_1$ with the dimensions (x_1y_1). The efficient distribution of this output combination requires that the individuals involved be on the contract curve that represents the locus of efficient distribution.[2] We may transcribe the points on the contract curve in terms of their utility indices on a pair of utility index axes, and this gives utility possibility curves for points such as α and β as shown in Figure 15.3; because there are an infinite number of such points on TT, there will be an infinite number of utility possibilities curves such as aa and bb in Figure 15.3.

We now wish to find the envelope curve of this infinite number of utility possibility curves. This utility possibility frontier will have the characteristic that it gives for each U_a that can be created by the production-exchange process the maximum U_b that can be created, and vice versa.

Each utility possibility curve will contribute one point to the utility possibility frontier. This point will be found at that point on the contract curve where the equalized slope of the indifference curves, the equalized

[2] See Chapter 5.

marginal rate of substitution, is equal to the slope of the transformation curve at the point defining the output combination for which the box is drawn. (This is discussed in detail later.) The respective envelope points on the transformation curve and contract curve are shown as α and α' in Figure 15.2 and as α' in Figure 15.3.

In order for the economy to be on the utility possibility frontier it must be impossible by the production-distribution process to make someone better off without making anyone worse off. We will show that for

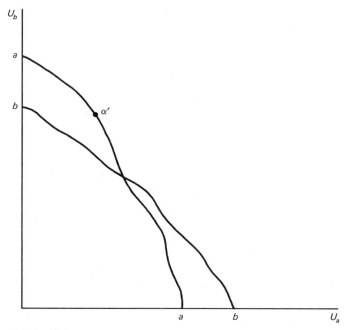

Figure   15.3

each output combination, this is only true when the marginal rate of transformation at that point is equal to the marginal rate of substitution at the distribution point along the contract locus. Let us suppose that at α the marginal rate of transformation is $\frac{1}{4}$, that is, the sacrifice of one unit of Y will release resources that permit the production of four units of X. We further assume that at the current distribution point the equalized MRS is $\frac{1}{2}$, which means that consumers will be kept as well off if they give up one Y and receive in compensation $2X$.

Now, suppose that $2Y$ is given up in production and in consequence eight more X are produced; each consumer is compensated with $2X$ for a total of $4X$, and $4X$ are left over, permitting an aggregate increase in utility for all. On the other hand, this sort of increase in satisfaction is no longer possible when the equalized MRS is equal to the MRT along the transformation schedule.

Choosing, then, the point on each contract curve that fulfills our condition of equalized slope, we generate the grand utility possibility frontier shown in Figure 15.4. This is a frontier of optimally efficient points, but it is a curve with an infinite number of points and, therefore, does not give a unique solution to our quest for a point of welfare maximum. Such a point on FF in Figure 15.4 can only be chosen through a social value

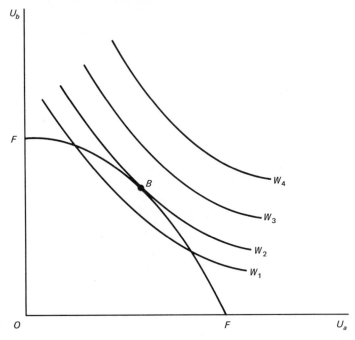

Figure 15.4

judgment concerning the desirability of the welfare states of the individuals involved. We now have recourse to our social welfare function, from which we generate the set of social indifference curves $W_1 \cdots W_n$. These indifference curves represent the contours of equal desirability expressed in the social consensus (derived through the ballot box or some other means) that we call the social welfare function.

The tangency of the grand utility possibility frontier with the highest possible social indifference curve gives the "Bliss point"—a uniquely defined welfare maximum for the society. It should be noticed at this point that the *objective* welfare criterion that welfare is increased as long as someone is made better off without making anyone worse off, is not sufficient to define this unique position. This condition of Paretian optimality is necessary but is insufficient to define the Bliss point. It leaves us with a utility frontier among the points of which a choice can only be made by referral to the *values* of the society.

The Pareto optimality conditions that we have derived for our simple economy are the following.

1. Production must take place along an efficiency locus defined by the equality of the MRS in production between the commodities produced. This gives the condition

$$MRS_{KL}{}^x = MRS_{KL}{}^y \quad \text{or} \quad \frac{\partial X}{\partial K}\bigg/\frac{\partial X}{\partial L} = \frac{\partial Y}{\partial K}\bigg/\frac{\partial Y}{\partial L} \qquad [15.6]$$

Transposed into commodity space, the efficiency locus gives the production transformation curve. The slope of the production transformation curve is derived as follows. We may write equation 15.6 as

$$\frac{\partial Y}{\partial L}\bigg/\frac{\partial X}{\partial L} = \frac{\partial Y}{\partial K}\bigg/\frac{\partial X}{\partial K} = \frac{dY}{dX} \qquad [15.7]$$

along the transformation schedule.

2. Exchange must take place along the contract curve so that the MRS between commodities in consumption are equalized among individuals. This gives

$$MRS_{xy}{}^a = MRS_{xy}{}^b \quad \text{or} \quad \frac{\partial U_a}{\partial X}\bigg/\frac{\partial U_a}{\partial Y} = \frac{\partial U_b}{\partial X}\bigg/\frac{\partial U_b}{\partial Y} \qquad [15.8]$$

3. To reach the envelope curve of the utility possibility curves, we must equate equations 15.7 and 15.8. Thus,

$$\frac{\partial Y}{\partial L}\bigg/\frac{\partial X}{\partial L} = \frac{\partial Y}{\partial K}\bigg/\frac{\partial X}{\partial K} = \frac{\partial U_a}{\partial X}\bigg/\frac{\partial U_a}{\partial Y} = \frac{\partial U_b}{\partial X}\bigg/\frac{\partial U_b}{\partial Y} \qquad [15.9]$$

The extension of the conditions for a welfare maximum for many products and many consumers presents no difficulty. Equations 15.6, 15.7, 15.8, and 15.9 must then hold between all pairs of consumers and all product pairs.

Our next task is to compare the optimum conditions just derived with those that would be achieved by a competitive solution to the resource allocation problem. We now write the conditions for product market and factor market equilibrium of the firm under competitive conditions.

$MC = P$ (of product) $\qquad\qquad\qquad VMP = P$ (of factor)

$$\frac{\partial K}{\partial X} P_K = P_x \qquad [15.10a] \qquad\qquad P_x \frac{\partial X}{\partial K} = P_K \qquad [15.10b]$$

$$\frac{\partial L}{\partial X} P_L = P_x \qquad [15.11a] \qquad\qquad P_x \frac{\partial X}{\partial L} = P_L \qquad [15.11b]$$

$$\frac{\partial K}{\partial Y} P_K = P_y \qquad [15.12a] \qquad\qquad P_y \frac{\partial Y}{\partial K} = P_K \qquad [15.12b]$$

$$\frac{\partial L}{\partial Y} P_L = P_y \qquad [15.13a] \qquad\qquad P_y \frac{\partial Y}{\partial L} = P_L \qquad [15.13b]$$

Combining equations 15.10b and 15.12b, we get

$$P_x \frac{\partial X}{\partial K} = P_y \frac{\partial Y}{\partial K} \qquad [15.14]$$

Combining equations 15.11b and 15.13b, we get

$$P_x \frac{\partial X}{\partial L} = P_y \frac{\partial Y}{\partial L} \qquad [15.15]$$

The last two equations say that the VMP of a factor must be the same in all of its uses.

Exchange optimum follows from competition because, given the price ratio P_x/P_y, fixed in the market, each individual will equate MRS_{xy} to this ratio, and consequently all the subjective MRS are equal to each other and all consumers are on the contract curve.

Thus,

$$\frac{\partial U_a}{\partial X_a} \Big/ \frac{\partial U_a}{\partial Y_a} = \frac{\partial U_b}{\partial X_b} \Big/ \frac{\partial U_b}{\partial Y_b} = \frac{dY}{dX} \qquad \text{(in consumption)} \qquad [15.16]$$

Now, divide equation 15.14 by equation 15.15, and we get

$$\frac{\partial X}{\partial K} \Big/ \frac{\partial X}{\partial L} = \frac{\partial Y}{\partial K} \Big/ \frac{\partial Y}{\partial L}$$

that is,

$$\frac{dL}{dK \text{ (in } X)} = \frac{dL}{dK \text{ (in } Y)}$$

This gives the equalized slope of the isoquants, and we see that competition places firms on the efficiency locus. Mapped into output space, we get

$$\frac{\partial Y}{\partial L} \Big/ \frac{\partial X}{\partial L} = \frac{\partial Y}{\partial K} \Big/ \frac{\partial X}{\partial K} = \frac{dY}{dX} \quad \begin{array}{l} \text{(in production) the slope of the trans-} \\ \text{formation curve.} \end{array} \qquad [15.17]$$

Divide equation 15.14 by P_y and $\partial X/\partial K$ and divide equation 15.15 by P_y and $\partial X/\partial L$ and we get

$$\frac{P_x}{P_y} = \frac{\partial Y}{\partial K} \Big/ \frac{\partial X}{\partial K} = \frac{\partial Y}{\partial L} \Big/ \frac{\partial X}{\partial L} \qquad [15.18]$$

and by equation 15.17 we may write

$$\frac{P_x}{P_y} = \frac{dY}{dX} \qquad \text{(in production)} \qquad [15.19]$$

and by equation 15.16 we may write

$$\frac{P_x}{P_y} = \frac{dY}{dX} \text{ (in production)} = \frac{dY}{dX} \qquad \text{(in consumption)} \qquad [15.20]$$

This establishes the "grand Paretian optimum." That is, we have shown that competitive equilibrium will allocate resources and distribute output so as to place the economy on the utility frontier. However, it is only by the most startling coincidence that the distribution of productive factors would be such as to result in the final welfare distribution being the one that society considers optimum. The attainment of the "Bliss point" is not, therefore, guaranteed by the competitive allocation solution. The society may adjust the position along the grand utility frontier by a tax-transfer process so as to reach the Bliss point. This may in principle be done by a lump-sum tax-and-transfer combination that will have no effect upon incentives but will serve to redistribute income so that the Bliss point may be reached. The lesson of this analysis is that socially optimum income distribution is not an automatic consequence of perfect competition, although the otherwise efficient allocation of resources and distribution of output is, given our initial assumptions.

In our chapter on the factor markets, we put great stress upon the presence or absence of equality between value of marginal product and factor price in various types of factor markets. The crucial role of this equilibrium condition for efficient resource allocation is clear from equations 15.14 and 15.15 and from what depends on them.

When each firm equates the value of the marginal product of a factor to its market price, this ensures that the value of the marginal product of the factor will be equalized for all the uses of the factor. We may show the crucial nature of this condition by assuming that it is not fulfilled.

Assume a monopolist and a competitive firm each hiring a factor of production that is supplied competitively. When the monopolist and the competitive firm are both in equilibrium, we will have

$$VMP_{fm} > MRP_{fm} = P_f = VMP_{fc}$$

It will thus be true that the value of the marginal product of the factor will be higher for the monopolist than for the competitive firm. A transfer of a unit of the factor from the competitive sector to the monopoly sector would increase the value of total economy output; that is what we mean by saying that the monopolist's output is too small, and as long as the gap between P_f and VMP_f exists, resources have not been optimally allocated in the economy—an increase in value of output is possible simply by the shifting of resources.

The conditions we have derived for maximum welfare may be summarized as requiring an equality between two equalized rates of transformation: (1) a subjective rate of transformation given by individual preference functions and (2) a technical rate of transformation derived from production functions. This equality is in turn assured under perfect competition by the equality of each of the previous transformation rates with a third (market transformation) rate given by a ratio of market prices.

If we now consider factor supplies to be variable, we can see that the efficient allocation of factors with variable supplies may be subsumed under the previous general condition. For labor, the MRS between earnings and effort must be equal for all workers of a given type, and this equalized rate must be equal to the equalized marginal rate of transformation between hours of work and output. This equality is assured under competition by the equality of each of these rates with the market transformation rate, the wage rate.[3]

The problem of the intertemporal allocation of resources—the allocation of output between present and future—can be subsumed under our conditions by regarding output at different dates as different products. Optimality, then, requires that the equalized subjective MRS between present and future consumption be equal to the technical rate of transformation of present into future output. Again, under competitive conditions, the required equality between subjective and technical rates of transformation is achieved through the equality of each in competitive equilibrium with a third market rate of transformation, in this case the market rate of interest.

In summary, then, we may say that once the question of income distribution has been settled by reference to the goals of the society, the general condition for a welfare maximum may be stated as follows:

1. Between any two goods or factors, the subjective and technical rates of transformation must be equal for all households and firms, respectively, and these subjective and technical rates must be equal to each other.

2. These are marginal or first-order conditions; the second-order conditions require convex indifference curves and concave transformation curves.

The conclusions that we have drawn, that perfect competition in all markets and appropriate income redistribution will bring the economy to the Bliss point has been arrived at on the assumption of production functions that exhibit constant returns to scale. Actually, this assumption is not very satisfactory because the size of the firm and the number of firms in the industry would be indeterminant under these circumstances. The usual assumption is that the firm faces first increasing and then decreasing returns to scale. In order that perfect competition be maintained, it must be true that minimum LAC comes for each firm at an output that

[3] Once we admit of variable factor supplies the lump-sum tax-transfer process just discussed will not be neutral in its effects because it will distort the work-leisure choice.

does not represent a significant part of industry output. It should be further noted that if the firms in an industry were subject to increasing returns to scale over the relevant range of output (that is, falling LAC), the LMC would lie everywhere below LAC. Thus, if such a firm were subject to a competitive delusion (or forced to it by public regulation) and if it attempted to produce at $P = LMC$, since $LAC > LMC$ it would produce at a point where $LAC < P$. This means that every feasible output can only be produced at a loss and that the firm would shut down. Perfectly competitive markets cannot exist in the presence of increasing returns to scale.

Alfred Marshall introduced the idea of *external* economies and diseconomies to explain the phenomenon of industry supply curves that were falling or rising in the face of firm supply curves that were rising. However, both Marshall and Pigou felt that external economies and diseconomies create situations in which market-directed allocation of resources does not result in optimum efficiency. Because individual competitive firms are guided by what they can control, it was agreed that decreasing cost industries will not produce enough output and that increasing cost industries will produce too much output. This is so because no single firm's behavior can cause a change in its cost curves, even though changes in industry output can. Marshall and Pigou advocated a tax on increasing cost industries and a subsidy to decreasing cost industries to restore efficient resource allocations.

Subsequent analysis in the literature on external economies and diseconomies has pointed up the importance of the distinction between technological external economies (and diseconomies) and pecuniary external economies (and diseconomies).[4] Technological economies (and diseconomies) occur when the expansion of an industry's output covers organizational and other improvements in efficiency that are not reflected in a change in input prices.

Pecuniary external diseconomies arise because factors are not available in completely elastic supply. The increment in factor price paid by the expanding industry will measure the marginal cost of transferring a unit of the factor to the industry or the cost of eliciting a supply of an extra unit of the factor. It is true that other users of the factor will have to pay an additional cost, a rent, on the inframarginal units of the factor. But these rental payments simply represent transfers and should not enter the calculation of optimum resource allocation, and so no tax is called for.

Pecuniary external economies present a different problem, because we must ask, What causes the price of the factor to fall as the demand for it

---

[4] The distinction is due to Professor Jacob Viner in "Cost Curves and Supply Curves" reprinted in American Economic Association (George Stigler and Kenneth Boulding, eds.), *Readings in Price Theory*, Homewood, Ill.: Richard D. Irwin, 1952.

increases? This implies a falling supply curve for the factor. If internal technological economies are ruled out, which would lead to monopoly, the only remaining source of decreasing factor price is technological external economies.

Technological externalities are not adequately accounted for by the price system. The reason for this can be seen by contrast with the pecuniary case. In the case of a pecuniary diseconomy, the increased use of the factor causes an increase in cost to this industry for the extra units it employs and to all other users; the inframarginal increase in cost is a rent and not an increase in real cost that should be taken into account. In contrast, a technological externality that makes other industries more efficient as the given industry expands represents a *real* efficiency to the economy, and the existence of this kind of externality will not be correctly accounted for by the price system.

The previous discussion of externalities in production is a special case of a broader classification of external effects or interdependencies that occurs when the preference and/or production functions of individuals and producers are not independent.

An example of such interdependence in production, first suggested by Professor Meade, exists when an apple orchard is located near a honey-producing firm. An increase in apple production and hence of apple blossoms make for an increase in honey production. A second example is of a firm that produces a waste product in the process of producing its output and disposes of it in a river; the level of its output will have a strong effect upon the fishing industry downstream. The case of producer-consumer interaction is typified by the effect of smoke from a factory on the utility of individuals in the surrounding area. An example of consumer-consumer interdependence is to be found in the pleasure an individual's neighbors derive from the sight of his well-kept garden or in the disutility they receive from his weedy lawn.

In terms of our production example we may show interdependence of this type by assuming that the output of commodity X has an effect upon the output of commodity Y. This gives the following production functions:

$$X = x(L_x, K_x) \tag{15.21}$$
$$Y = y(L_y, K_y, X(L_x, K_x)] \tag{15.22}$$

The goal of society is to maximize the value of its output: that is,

$$V = P_x X + P_y Y \tag{15.23}$$

The maximization of equation 15.23 for the economy, subject to equations 15.21 and 15.22 requires that the following conditions be met in equilibrium:[5]

$$P_x \frac{\partial X}{\partial L_x} + P_y \frac{\partial Y}{\partial X} \cdot \frac{\partial X}{\partial L_x} = w \qquad [15.24]$$

$$P_y \frac{\partial Y}{\partial L_y} = w \qquad [15.25]$$

$$P_x \frac{\partial X}{\partial K_x} + P_y \frac{\partial Y}{\partial X} \frac{\partial X}{\partial K_x} = i \qquad [15.26]$$

$$P_y \frac{\partial Y}{\partial K_y} = i \qquad [15.27]$$

The Y industry is required by equations 15.25 and 15.27 to equate the value of the marginal (private) product of its factors, which is also the value of their marginal social product to the rate of factor remuneration. This is exactly what will occur in the process of private profit maximization.

Equations 15.24 and 15.26 show, however, that only when the influence of the output of X on the output of Y is zero, does the private profit maximization condition $VMP = P_f$ result in the maximization of social output. When this external effect is not zero, private profit maximization in the X industry leads in equilibrium to

$$\frac{\partial X}{\partial L_x} = \frac{w}{P_x} \qquad [15.28]$$

Rewriting equation 15.24, we have

$$\frac{\partial X}{\partial L_x}\left[P_x + P_y \frac{\partial Y}{\partial X}\right] = w \quad \text{or} \quad \frac{\partial X}{\partial L_x} = \frac{w}{P_x + P_y \dfrac{\partial Y}{\partial X}} \qquad [15.29]$$

Paretian optimum production requires instead that 15.29 be fulfilled, whereas firm profit maximization results in equation 15.28 being fulfilled.

If $\partial Y/\partial X > 0$, we see, by comparing equations 15.28 and 15.29 that $\partial X/\partial L_{xP} > \partial X/\partial L_{xS}$ (where P denotes private and S social). This means that the marginal product of labor in the production of X will, in private profit-maximizing equilibrium be greater than would be required by maximization of the total output of the economy. In other words, the output of industry X is too small because the beneficial effect upon Y production $\left(P_y \dfrac{\partial Y}{\partial X} \cdot \dfrac{\partial X}{\partial L_x}\right)$ is not taken into account in private profit-

[5] See Appendix 15A. See also Francis M. Bator, "The Anatomy of Market Failure," *Quarterly Journal of Economics* (August 1958) and James M. Buchanan and William G. Stubblebine, "Externality," *Economica* (November 1962).

making calculations. The same thing may be shown to be true of the other factor utilized in X production.

Now assume that $\partial Y/\partial X < 0$ so that additional output of X causes a reduction in output of Y, assume $\partial X/\partial L_x$ and $\partial X/\partial K_x > 0$ so that the firm is not in the redundant area, and assume P_x and $P_y > 0$.

Now, if X adjusts his output to his own profit maximization and if there is no trade between X and Y, he will fulfill the conditions

$$P_x \frac{\partial X}{\partial L_x} = \omega \quad \text{and} \quad P_x \frac{\partial X}{\partial K_x} = i$$

but the Paretian optimum requires (from equations 15.24 and 15.26) that

$$P_x \frac{\partial X}{\partial L_x} + \alpha = \omega \quad \alpha < 0 \qquad [15.30]$$

and

$$P_x \frac{\partial X}{\partial K_x} + \beta = i \quad \beta < 0 \qquad [15.31]$$

Thus, when the effect of X upon the output of Y is ignored, the X output is too large for maximally efficient production; that is, the society will be within the production possibility curve.

We have indicated previously that several different types of externalities exist. The example just discussed, of the apple blossom–honey type, is an "ownership externality."[6] It exists because a scarce resource is not subject to effective ownership and control by its producer.

A second type of externality may be called a "technical externality." This is a consequence either of indivisibilities that require equipment and machinery to be purchased in discrete units or smoothly increasing returns to scale over an output range that is a significant proportion of industry output. As explained before, such a situation must lead to monopoly, or (if control is attempted) $MC = P$ becomes impossible if firms are to remain in the industry.

The third kind of externality is "public goods externality." For such goods, "each individual's consumption of a good leads to no subtractions from any other individual's consumption of that good." If Q is the total quantity of the good, if q_a is its consumption by individual A, and if q_b is its consumption by individual B, we have $Q = q_a = q_b$. For such goods, because an individual's enjoyment of Q depends on its total quantity and not on the amount he pays for it, it always pays for him to understate his preferences for Q relative to other goods. Samuelson[7] has shown that the appropriate condition for Pareto efficiency here is not that equalized MRT = equalized MRS but is that $MRT = \Sigma MRS$. The mar-

[6] See Bator, "The Anatomy of Market Failure," 465–471.
[7] The Pure Theory of Public Expenditure, *Review of Economics and Statistics* (November 1954), XXXVI p387.

ginal rate of transformation between the public goods and other goods should be equal to the algebraic *sum* of the marginal rates of substitution between the goods in individual preference functions. Many interconsumer externalities are of this type.

A common effect of the externalities just discussed is to create a divergence between private and social cost of a given activity. In the case where $\partial Y/\partial X < 0$, as discussed before, we may say that the private cost is less than the social cost of producing an extra unit of X. The private cost is the value of the resources used in the production of X that will be equal to the value of the marginal alternative output forgone by using resources in the production of X rather than in alternative uses. In the previous example, however, the loss in Y output when X output is expanded is a real social cost, but it does not enter into X's calculations, and a misallocation of resources will result in the over-production of X, if nothing else occurs.

The argument should not stop here, however, as is implied by the qualifying phrase at the end of the last paragraph. This may be seen by rewriting equations 15.24 and 15.26 as follows:

$$P_x \frac{\partial X}{\partial L_x} - w = -P_y \frac{\partial Y}{\partial X} \frac{\partial X}{\partial L_x} \qquad [15.24']$$

$$P_x \frac{\partial X}{\partial K_x} - i = -P_y \frac{\partial Y}{\partial X} \frac{\partial X}{\partial K_x} \qquad [15.26']$$

Consideration of equations 15.24' and 15.26' shows, however, that the left side of each equation gives the marginal profit to firm X from employing an extra unit of a factor; the right side of each equation (assuming $\partial Y/\partial X < 0$) gives the marginal loss to Y from X's actions. As long as the right side of either equation is greater than the left, Y has an incentive to "bribe" X to produce a smaller output than he would otherwise produce. When compensation payments have taken place so that equations 15.24' and 15.26' are fulfilled, the conditions for a social output maximum are fulfilled. Note that the achievement of a Paretian optimum does not imply the absence of externalities; it implies, instead, that there is no incentive for further trade among the affected parties. If the cost of producing the externality were zero (that is, $w = i = 0$), then the social optimum would require not the absence of external effects but require the exact opposition of the interests of X and Y. At the margin, an increment of X's output would just have a market value equal to the value of the decrement in Y's output caused by the affect of X on Y.

Two important conclusions follow from this analysis: First, the existence of external effects in production or consumption is not prima facie sufficient reason for government interference in the market. In a smoothly functioning market with costless transactions, market prices would bring the economy to the output optimum even with externalities. If, as is the case in most real world situations, the cost of using the market is too great because the external effects are too widespread or if the affected parties are not easily identified, government interference is necessary. Second, it is not true, however, that the appropriate policy is one that imposes taxes or fines on the producer of undesirable external effects in order to equate private and social cost. If a producer in a neighborhood sends forth a stream of smoke that blackens laundry and house exteriors in the surrounding area and if the market is functioning to allocate resources efficiently, the homeowners in the area will pay a subsidy to the firm that, at the margin, will measure the marginal disutility to them of the smoke nuisance. At the same time, to minimize the necessary payments, there will be every incentive to paint houses with smoke-resistant paint and to install electric and gas laundry dryers. If now the government imposes a tax upon the firm equal to the damage done to the neighborhood and does nothing else, resources will not be efficiently allocated because no incentive will exist for individuals to economize on *their* effects on the firm. Efficient resource allocation involves a dual tax on both the producer of the externality and those affected by it.

The previous discussion indicates that the introduction of externalities does not necessarily vitiate the optimal character of the solution to the resource allocation problem derived from the competitive model, although the Paretian optimal conditions are altered. Such interdependencies do, however, create a strong presumption that government interference will be necessary in real world markets that are not frictionless. It should be emphasized again, however, that contrary to the view that is usually held, the government must act to restrict both the causer and the receiver of the externality.

Up to this point we have assumed smoothly continuous indifference curves, isoquants, and transformation schedules of the proper curvature. These assumptions guarantee the fulfillment of second-order conditions. If the curves are not smoothly continuous, no real problem is encountered because the constraint conditions can be stated as inequalities and the first-order conditions can be derived by the linear-programming techniques that are discussed in Chapter 14. If the curvature requirements are violated, then corner solutions will result.[8] The most important cause of violation of curvature is increasing returns to scale, which we have seen is not consistent with the maintenance of perfect competition.

It should also be noted that our demonstration of the optimality of perfect competition has been of a static nature. The introduction of dynamic factors, such as growth, and our attendant questions of technological change and innovation can vitiate our conclusions. For example, assume two economies A and B, where A is perfectly competitive and B is not, so that resources are more efficiently allocated in A. It is still

[8] See Chapter 5.

possible for all individuals in B to be better off than in A because of a larger capital stock (and consequently more rapid growth rate) that was made possible by the monopoly elements in B.[9]

As we pointed out in Chapter 10, the existence of antitrust laws implies a judgment that competition is a desirable goal for the economy. This is true in choosing between perfect competition and a mixture of competition and monopoly. It does not follow, however, that moving one industry from the monopoly to the competitive sector will get the economy closer to the Paretian optimum. The formal proof of this proposition is complex[10] but a simple proof by exception should be illuminating. Assume that an economy consists of three industries: A and B are monopolists and C is competitive. The three industries use the two factors X and Y. Given this situation, the following conditions hold (where superscripts indicate industries and subscripts indicate factors):

$$\frac{P_x}{MP_x{}^A} = \frac{P_y}{MP_y{}^A} = MC^A = MR^A = P^A\left(1 + \frac{1}{E^A}\right) \qquad [15.32]$$

$$\frac{P_x}{MP_x{}^B} = \frac{P_y}{MP_y{}^B} = MC^B = MR^B = P^B\left(1 + \frac{1}{E^B}\right) \qquad [15.33]$$

$$\frac{P_x}{MP_x{}^C} = \frac{P_y}{MP_y{}^C} = MC^C = MR^C = P^C \qquad [15.34]$$

Using industry A as the base for comparison, we may define the slope of the transformation schedule between A and B and A and C:

$$\frac{dB}{dA} = \frac{MC^A}{MC^B} = \frac{P^A\left(1 + \dfrac{1}{E^A}\right)}{P^B\left(1 + \dfrac{1}{E^B}\right)} \qquad [15.35]$$

$$\frac{dC}{dA} = \frac{MC^A}{MC^C} = \frac{P^A\left(1 + \dfrac{1}{E^A}\right)}{P^C} \qquad [15.36]$$

Let us assume that the elasticities in all the industries are all the same; thus,

$$\frac{MC^A}{MC^B} = \frac{P^A}{P^B} \qquad \text{and} \qquad \frac{MC^A}{MC^C} = \frac{P^A}{P^C}\left(1 + \frac{1}{E^A}\right)$$

because consumers in order to maximize satisfaction will equate

$$\frac{MU^A}{MU^B} = \frac{P^A}{P^B}$$

[9] See Joseph Schumpter, *The Theory of Economic Development* (Cambridge, Mass.: Harvard University Press, 1951).
[10] See Richard Lipsey and Kevin Lancaster, "The General Theory of Second Best," *Review of Economic Studies*, Vol. 24 (December 1956).

It will also be true that $MC^A/MC^B = MU^A/MU^B$, so that for the two industries, the Paretian conditions hold, whereas they do not hold between A and C.

Next, assume that through antitrust legislation, industry B becomes competitive. Then,

$$\frac{dB}{dA} = \frac{MC^A}{MC^B} = \frac{P^A\left(1 + \dfrac{1}{E^A}\right)}{P^B}$$

Thus, no longer do the Paretian conditions hold between A and B.

Suppose industry C had been encouraged to monopolize. Then the following condition would hold:

$$\frac{MC^A}{MC^B} = \frac{P^A}{P^B} \quad \text{and} \quad \frac{MC^A}{MC^C} = \frac{P^A}{P^C}$$

And with utility maximization,

$$\frac{MC^A}{MC^B} = \frac{MU^A}{MU^B} \quad \text{and} \quad \frac{MC^A}{MC^C} = \frac{MU^A}{MU^C}$$

Of course, this implies

$$\frac{MC^B}{MC^C} = \frac{MU^B}{MU^C}$$

In other words, the Paretian condition is here achieved between every pair of goods.

Thus, we have shown, albeit with an extreme example, that piecemeal efforts to achieve competition need not achieve the goal of moving the economy closer to the Paretian optimum. No prima facie case can be made, and each case must be investigated on its merits.

Appendix 15A

Equilibrium Conditions with Production Interdependence

$$X = x(L_x, K_x) \qquad [15A.1]$$
$$Y = y[L_y, K_y, x(L_x, K_x)] \qquad [15A.2]$$
$$\bar{L} = L_x + L_y \qquad [15A.3]$$
$$\bar{K} = K_x + K_y \qquad [15A.4]$$
$$V = P_x X + P_y Y \qquad [15A.5]$$

Maximize equation 15A.5 subject to equations 15A.1, 15A.2, 15A.3, and 15A.4; this is equivalent to finding a maximum for the expression

$$F = P_x{}^x(L_x, K_x) + P_y{}^y[L_y, K_y, x(L_x, K_x)] + w(\bar{L} - L_x - L_y) + i(\bar{K} - K_x - K_y) \qquad [15A.6]$$

Differentiate F partially with respect to L_x, L_y, K_x, and K_y and treat P_x, P_y, w, and i as arbitrary constants.

$$\frac{\partial F}{\partial L_x} = P_x \frac{\partial X}{\partial L_x} + P_y \frac{\partial Y}{\partial X} \frac{\partial X}{\partial L_x} = w \qquad [15A.7]$$

$$\frac{\partial F}{\partial L_y} = P_y \frac{\partial Y}{\partial L_y} = w \qquad [15A.8]$$

$$\frac{\partial F}{\partial K_x} = P_x \frac{\partial X}{\partial K_x} + P_y \frac{\partial Y}{\partial X} \frac{\partial X}{\partial K_x} = i \qquad [15A.9]$$

$$\frac{\partial F}{\partial K_y} = P_y \frac{\partial Y}{\partial K_y} = i \qquad [15A.10]$$

INDEX